A Disciplined Intelligence:
Critical Inquiry and Canadian Thought in the Victorian Era

In this highly acclaimed and controversial contribution to Canadian intellectual history, A. B. McKillop examines the course of critical inquiry and its relationship to the assertion of moral authority in English-Canadian thought during the Victorian era.

Concentrating upon the thought of Canada's major scientists, philosophers, and clerics—men such as William Dawson and Daniel Wilson, John Watson and W. D. LeSueur, G. M. Grant and Salem Bland—the book begins by reconstructing the central strands of intellectual and moral orthodoxy prevalent in Anglo-Canadian colleges on the eve of the Darwinian revolution. These included the Scottish Common Sense philosophy and the natural theology of William Paley. The destructive impact of evolutionary ideas on that orthodoxy and the major exponents of the new forms of social evolution—Spencerian and Hegelian alike—are examined in detail.

By the twentieth century, the heart of Anglo-Canadian thought had been transformed by what had become a new, evolutionary orthodoxy. The legacy of this triumphant intellectual movement, that of British idealism, was immense. It helped to destroy Protestant denominationalism, to provide the philosophical core of the social gospel movement, and to constitute a major force behind the creation of the United Church of Canada. Throughout the nineteenth century and continuing into the twentieth, however, the moral imperative in Anglo-Canadian thought remained a constant presence. Several figures who today dominate the intellectual landscape of the country may be seen as inheritors of this tradition.

The Carleton Library Series edition of this now-classic work includes a new introduction by the author that describes its origins, autobiographical context, and impact. An up-to-date bibliographical note is also included.

A. B. McKillop teaches history at Carleton University.

Carleton Library Series

The Carleton Library Series, funded by Carleton University under the general editorship of the dean of Graduate Studies and Research, publishes material relating to Canadian history, politics, society, economy, geography, and related subjects. It includes important new works as well as reprints of classics in the fields. The editorial committee welcomes manuscripts and suggestions, which should be sent to the dean of Graduate Studies and Research, Carleton University.

192 *The Blacks in Canada: A History (second edition)*
    Robin Winks
193 *A Disciplined Intelligence*
    Critical Inquiry and Canadian Thought in the Victorian Era
    A. B. McKillop
194 *Land, Power, and Economics on the Frontier of Upper Canada*
    John Clarke
195 *The Children of Aataentsic*
    A History of the Huron People to 1660
    Bruce G. Trigger
196 *Silent Surrender*
    The Multinational Corporation in Canada
    Kari Levitt
197 *Monetary Policy and Central Bank Independence*
    The Bank of Canada and Responsible Government
    H. Scott Gordon
    Edited by T. K. Rymes

A Disciplined Intelligence

Critical Inquiry and Canadian Thought
in the Victorian Era

A. B. McKillop

Carleton Library Series 193
McGill-Queen's University Press
Montreal & Kingston · London · Ithaca

© McGill-Queen's University Press 1979, 2001
ISBN 0-7735-2141-0 (cloth)
ISBN 0-7735-2142-9 (paper)
Legal deposit 3rd quarter 2001
Bibliothèque Nationale du Québec

Published as part of the Carleton Library Series, 2001

Printed in Canada

This book was first published with the help of a grant from the Social Science Federation of Canada, using funds provided by the Social Sciences and Humanities Research Council of Canada.

McGill-Queen's University Press acknowledges the financial support of the Government of Canada through the Book Publishing Industry Development Program (BPIDP) for its activities. It also acknowledges the support of the Canada Council for the Arts for its publishing program.

National Library of Canada Cataloguing in Publication Data

McKillop, A. B., 1946–
A disciplined intelligence :
critical inquiry and Canadian thought in the Victorian era
(Carleton library series ; 193)
Includes bibliographical references and index.
ISBN 0-7735-2141-0 (bound).—ISBN 0-7735-2142-9 (pbk.)
1. Philosophy, Canadian (English)—19th century.
2. Canada—Intellectual life—19th century. I. Title. II. Series.
B988.M6M45 2001   191   C2001-900886-4

To ROGER GRAHAM
Scholar and Gentleman

They change their skies but not their minds
who cross the sea in ships.
Seneca

Contents

	Preface	ix
	Introduction to the Carleton Library Edition	xiii
1	**Education and Intellect**	1
	Intellectual Anarchy	5
	The Institutionalization of Concern	9
	Education as Disposition	13
	The Basis of a Liberal Education	16
2	**The Colonial Philosophers**	23
	The Scottish Legacy	24
	James George and the Web of Gossamer	32
	William Lyall: *Intellect, the Emotions, and Man's Moral Nature*	44
	The Apogee of Common Sense	52
3	**The Uses of Natural Theology**	59
	The Prevalence of Paley	62
	James Beaven and the Eye of Faith	65
	Dr. Bovell's Quadrilateral Mind	73
	Sequela	85

4 The Veils of Isis — 93

- The Veils of Isis — 95
- The Reception of Darwin in Canada — 99
- Support from the Flanks — 110
- Christian Guardians — 116
- Man's Place in Nature — 125

5 A Critical Spirit — 135

- The Spectre of Doubt — 137
- The Critical Intellect — 141
- Freedom and Concern — 146
- Science, Ethics, and Evolution — 154
- A Defence of Modern Thought — 158

6 The Secret of Hegel — 171

- The Rejection of Common Sense — 173
- John Watson and the Secret of Hegel — 181
- Science and the Idealist Alternative — 186
- Conscience and Community — 195

7 The Sadness and Joy of Knowledge — 205

- Faith through Reason — 206
- Pastoral Epistles — 212
- The Sacred, the Secular, and the Social Gospel — 216
- Religion through Sociology — 224

Epilogue — 229

Abbreviations — 233

Notes — 235

A Bibliographical Note — 275

A Bibliographical Note, 2001 — 279

Index — 283

Preface

The rise of an inquiring frame of mind, critical of different forms of orthodox thought, was one of the most important characteristics of the nineteenth century. This book examines the course of critical inquiry and its relationship to the assertion of moral authority in the thought of some of the major figures in English-speaking Canada's intellectual life for the period before the First World War. Caught historically between a British heritage, which many of them conceived to contain the best elements of Western civilization, and an American neighbour, which advanced ineluctably towards modernity in its modes of thought and action, Anglo-Canadians in the Victorian era sought to establish and to preserve in Canada a broad moral code that would constitute the core of a way of life reconciling belief and inquiry, tradition and innovation, concern and freedom. For some of them, critical inquiry was a serious threat to the social bond; others came to see in the very process of inquiry a means of preserving it in the modern age.

The central theme of this book is the interplay between critical inquiry and moral affirmation within the Anglo-Canadian mind. It is suggested that a central and continuous element of Anglo-Canadian intellectual life—so much so as to constitute a virtual imperative—has been its moral dimension. The term "moral," it should be noted, is used here in a broad sense. Edmund Burke had used the phrase "moral imagination" to suggest man's general power of ethical perception, his aspiration to establish and to maintain right order both in the commonwealth and in the soul. This notion is paralleled in Northrop Frye's use of the term "concern," by which he means "something which includes the sense of the importance of preserving the integrity of the total human community." "It is clear," he goes on to say (in his essay "The Knowledge of Good and Evil"), "that concern and morality are closely connected: morality, in fact, in the sense of the kind of obligation that enables man to preserve his relation to society, is the central expression of concern." Hence, while the moral imperative informing Anglo-Canadian thought could and did find expression through the narrow focus of Protestant morality, it was also one that was capable of transcending the tenets of religious denominationalism and addressing itself to univeral questions.

The individuals considered in the following pages were the most articulate spokesmen of several systems of ideas which together informed the Anglo-Canadian mind in the nineteenth century. These men aspired to be the leaders of English-Canadian society, and they sought to give it direction. They were public moralists who wanted to help forge the ethics and the faith of the nation. As such, they gave sustained expression to some of the most fundamental intellectual concerns in the North Atlantic community during the Victorian era and after it.

Another purpose of this book is to examine in the Canadian context the tension inherent in the relationship between, on the one hand, man's desire to use his intellect—his organizational and critical capacity—to further his knowledge and to enhance his understanding and, on the other, his concurrent wish to maintain certainty of conviction. This problem was alluded to in a phrase used by Egerton Ryerson when seeking to define the nature and scope of mental philosophy. "The philosophy of mind," he said in an 1842 address on the idea of a liberal education, "inquires into the nature of those spirits of which we have any certain knowledge, or which it concerns us to know." A number of questions arise about the implications of this statement. What constitutes "certain knowledge"? Can one have certain knowledge of spiritual things? Is this certain knowledge of spiritual things not faith? If so, what is the relationship of this faith to reason? What are the implications of the words "concerns us to know"? What knowledge *is* it our concern to acquire? Of what things is it *not* our concern to know? And what is the ultimate authority from which we can determine what are to be those concerns?

Ryerson developed the core of his program for a "liberal education" from premises with inherent problems such as these. They also served as the basis of the curricula of colleges other than Ryerson's Victoria College. He undoubtedly would have taken exception to the claim that the philosophy of mind was of paramount importance in his conception of a liberal education, and he would perhaps have answered, in rebuttal, that it was only one branch of a diverse and balanced curriculum. Yet it was, never-

Preface xi

theless, a particular conception of mind—its nature, its potential, and its perceived limitations—upon which rested the educational programs of Ryerson and his colleagues at other Canadian universities and colleges. Education then, as now, was in the end a matter of knowledge and thought—knowledge learned and unlearned, training in how to think and in how not to think. In Anglo-Canadian universities during the middle of the nineteenth century, the negative side of this process was as vital a part of the educational experience as the positive acquisition of knowledge. But could this remain the case in the age of increasing intellectual inquiry? This book seeks to provide at least a partial answer to this question, and it attempts to show how Anglo-Canadian educators, clerics, and certain men of letters adjusted to the often competing demands of affirmation and criticism.

Several institutions and individuals were of great help during the years taken to conceive, research, and write this study, and it is a pleasure to record a great measure of gratitude to them. The Canada Council provided financial support and research assistance, and the Social Science Federation of Canada, using funds provided by the Social Sciences and Humanities Research Council of Canada, subsidized publication. Mrs. Carol Adam risked neglecting her infant twins in typing the manuscript at several stages, and she performed the task quickly and efficiently. The staffs of the archives cited in the notes were helpful in making their resources easily available.

Members of the Department of History at Queen's University and at the University of Manitoba have provided stimulating environments in which to teach and write. At Queen's, Professor G. A. Rawlyk made numerous suggestions. At Manitoba, Professor J. L. Finlay pointed out several ambiguous passages and weaknesses in transition. Equally kindly, he allowed the use of his cottage on the Lake of the Woods for a lengthy period one summer, during which much was accomplished. The encouragement and incentive provided there by Thomas Harvey Donini was greatly appreciated. At a later stage in the preparation of the manuscript, comments were offered by Gordon Harland, John Kendle, Gerald Friesen, and W. H. Brooks, of the University of Manitoba; Ramsay Cook of York University; Carl Berger of the University of Toronto; Goldwin French, president of Victoria University, University of Toronto. Judy Kendle, in particular, gave the manuscript of the book a discerning, sensitive, and critical reading.

Intellectual debts are often difficult, if not impossible, to record. It will be readily apparent to those familiar with the work of Perry Miller, however, that some of the preoccupations of the pages that follow are in some measure derived from a reading and an appreciation of Miller's work. Whatever sensitivity *A Disciplined Intelligence* has to the ironic results of thought in action comes from a reading of Miller and also of Reinhold Niebuhr, in particular his *The Irony of American History*. On the Canadian side, two sources need especially to be mentioned. John Irving was a pioneer investigator of the history of philosophy in Canada, and in some ways this book merely amplifies what he outlined in a number of seminal articles during the 1950s. Finally, the author's indebtedness to the ideas of Northrop Frye will be obvious to the reader from the opening page to the concluding one.

The author's two greatest debts, however, are not intellectual ones only. His friend Graham Reynolds offered extensive criticism of the original manuscript, particularly those chapters which deal with aspects of mid-Victorian science. Mr. Reynolds has been a constant source of intellectual stimulation, and has forced the clarification of numerous ideas which might otherwise have remained vague. The author's academic mentor, Roger Graham of Queen's University, has over the years provided much encouragement, understanding, and patience. In addition, his many stylistic suggestions have greatly enhanced whatever merit this book may have in the matter of literary style, although it need hardly be said that lapses of scholarship and style are solely the author's responsibility.

Introduction to the Carleton Library Edition

> Religion tends increasingly to make its primary impact, not as a system of taught and learned belief, but as an imaginative structure which, whether "true" or not, has imaginary consistency and imaginative informing power. In other words, it makes its essential appeal as myth or possible truth, and whatever belief it attracts follows from that.
> Northrop Frye, *The Modern Century* (1967)

Works of history arise out of authorial disposition as well as opportunity and interpretive conjuncture. *A Disciplined Intelligence: Critical Inquiry and Canadian Thought in the Victorian Era* is no exception. It is the result of a particular sensibility, time, and circumstance. Readers of the Carleton Library edition of the book may wish, therefore, to learn how this particular work of intellectual history came about, its relationship to the fields of intellectual and religious history in Canada, and the historiographical impact it appears to have had.

The book originated as a doctoral dissertation for the Department of History at Queen's University in Kingston, Ontario. As such, it was as much an act of faith as of scholarship. I had arrived at Queen's in the Fall of 1970 with a background in Canadian political and American intellectual history secured at the University of Manitoba. My intention was to pursue doctoral research on some aspect of twentieth-century Western Canadian urban history, the subject of my M.A. thesis, and the graduate seminar in post-Confederation Canadian political history offered by Roger Graham seemed good preparation for such an undertaking. I had studied the intellectual history of the Progressive Era in the United States under R. A. Swanson at Manitoba; so far as I was then aware, however, Canadian intellectual history—or at least its historiography—did not exist. At Manitoba, as elsewhere in those days, Canadian history was predominantly the history of politics, pure and simple.

Scholarship can subvert even the best of intentions—certainly, it proved subversive of mine. Very early in Roger Graham's seminar, thanks to fellow student Terry Cook, I was introduced to two important works that held promise for the study of Canadian intellectual history: S. F. Wise's "Sermon Literature and Canadian Intellectual History" and Carl Berger's *The Sense of Power: Studies in the Ideas of Canadian Imperialism, 1867–1914* (1970).[1] Wise's article on Canadian intellectual history pointed to the ideological connections between religious thought and the larger political culture of Upper Canada, thereby linking the history of religion to the history of ideas. For its part, Berger's book argued powerfully that a significant intellectual dimension existed within the time-worn tradition of Canadian political history. My attention was drawn once again to intellectual history. But what *was* this history in Canada, beyond that of Wise's members of the Family Compact and Berger's imperialists? Canadian historiography held few clues.

As an undergraduate, I had written a lengthy essay on Victorians and the meaning of "Victorianism" for a course in European history and had enjoyed the discovery of such books as Florence Lennon Becker's insightful study of Lewis Carroll, *Victoria Through the Looking Glass* (New York: Simon and Schuster. 1945), and Walter E. Houghton's now classic account, *The Victorian Frame of Mind* (New Haven: Yale University Press, 1957). Was there a dimension of Victorian belief I could explore as the topic of my own dissertation on Canadian history? In Swanson's American intellectual history seminar at the University of Manitoba, I had become quite familiar with the books of Richard Hofstadter, the most influential American intellectual historian of the 1950s and 1960s. Might some of the concerns of Hofstadter's Americans also have been important to Victorian Canadians? Hofstadter's doctoral dissertation, *Social Darwinism in American Thought* (rev. ed. New York: Brazillier, 1955 [1944]), had intrigued me. Did Social Darwinism also take hold in Anglo-Canadian thought in the second half of the nineteenth century? I found myself with a tentative topic, but was there evidence to confirm it?

The library, special collections, and archives of Queen's University soon provided me with a rich body of germane material, but in unexpected ways. I discovered no Canadian equivalents to the major American Social Darwinists: no William Graham

Sumner, no Andrew Carnegie or John D. Rockefeller—no great Canadian apologists of a social evolutionism dedicated to the sanctity of the unfettered marketplace. What emerged instead from the manuscript collections, pamphlets, and periodicals was an earnest and sustained debate beginning in the 1860s among members of the Canadian religious and scientific communities, often university professors, over the social, intellectual, and religious implications of Darwinian evolution.

Given Canada's colonial circumstance and its geographical and cultural location as a fulcrum balancing British and American intellectual and cultural engagement, and the importance of evolutionary theory, this did not come as a great surprise. What was surprising was the strong and central presence of a third party in addition to the clerics and the scientists within the Canadian debate over science, religion and evolutionary change: the mental and moral philosophers within Canadian colleges and universities. Their involvement pointed in the direction of a commitment to the public good and service to it, rather than to private interest.

No history department-based historians in Canada had studied or written about any of the Canadian intellectuals who gradually emerged as my subjects. The occasional historian of philosophy, such as John Irving, had mentioned philosophers such as George Paxton Young of the University of Toronto or John Watson of Queen's, but in the context of mainstream Canadian historiography they did not exist. Nor did the intellectual context in which to situate them. When Richard Allen's path-breaking work on the Social Gospel in Canada, *The Social Passion; Religion and Social Reform in Canada 1914–1928*, appeared in 1971 it gave Canadian religious life an intellectual dimension, but it began the story at the crest of the Social Gospel movement during the Great War of 1914–1918 and traced its transformation in the 1920s. My own work seemed to be the pre-history of Allen's subject. As research progressed, I came to regret that I had been unwilling to take any course in philosophy as an undergraduate— an unwillingness in part encouraged by a philosophy department at Manitoba much taken with Ludwig Wittgenstein and A. J. Ayer, but with little patience where the metaphysics they rejected was concerned. Yet all the philosophers I encountered during the course of my research into nineteenth-century Canadian intellectual history were proud metaphysicians.

The few scholarly works on Canadian religious history published before 1970 proved of little help in fleshing out the life of the Protestant mind. Invariably, they were written from an institutional perspective and in a way that reflected the dominant political history of the day—as if the Protestant denominations and their colleges were peculiar variants of political parties and the party system. Relations of Church and State figured as the dominant *leitmotif*. Works such as D. C. Masters's *Protestant Church Colleges in Canada* (Toronto: University of Toronto Press, 1966) and John Webster Grant's *The Church in the Canadian Era* (Burlington, Ont.: Welch, 1988 [1972]), invaluable as institutional studies, touched upon theological and intellectual influences only episodically. If in 1970 the history of philosophy in Canada was *terra incognita* from the perspective of "mainstream" history, religious thought was not much better mapped. As historian Michael Gauvreau wrote two decades later, "the old national history" dominant before 1970 marginalized religious experience and failed "to recognize its creative role in shaping cultural traditions, social forms, and political ideologies."[2] In this respect, he added, the old history differed little from the new social history that superceded it in the 1970s.

Historians can often be divided into those interested in origins and those concerned with consequences. My own primary interest was in the intellectual, religious, and cultural consequences of the earlier debate over social evolution. The philosophers under my scrutiny saw themselves as essential figures mediating the concerns of the religious and scientific communities. Moreover, they believed that they were part of an intellectual revolution brought about by free intellectual inquiry, for they were opponents of dogmatism and orthodoxy of any sort. This commitment to critical inquiry became, in effect, the central thread of my work. Almost to a man—and they were invariably men—the Canadian philosophers of the late-nineteenth century were members of a transatlantic community of Anglo-American idealists, inspired by Kant, Hegel, and to a lesser extent the inspirational Oxford scholar T. H. Green. But if they were part of an intellectual revolution, as they so clearly believed, what was the orthodoxy they sought to overthrow? It became apparent that to begin my story with the advent of British idealism, the major intellectual movement of the late nineteenth century, would be like studying the Jacobins without taking into account, however briefly, the *ancien régime*. I therefore turned to the beliefs Anglo-Canadian idealists thought they had helped to overturn.

Much of the early part of *A Disciplined Intelligence* therefore necessarily became a study of the religious, moral, and scientific

Introduction to the Carleton Library Edition xvii

"orthodoxy" of pre-Darwinian belief. In Protestant colleges and universities that championed evangelical accounts of Christian revelation, this took the form of a fear of "intellect" itself, especially intellect driven by open-ended inquiry. As buttresses to conventional belief, Scottish "Common Sense Philosophy," emphasising the intimate connection between God and Mind, took pride of place in liberal arts curricula, as did a natural theology intended to reconcile providence and nature, and derived from a British "Baconian" empiricism suspicious of scientific theorizing beyond evidence acceptable to the process of induction. It was against such forms of received belief, aimed at cultivation of a pious disposition, that the idealists of the last third of the nineteenth century argued so powerfully.

The basic structure of the study came about unexpectedly and in a curious way. In the early summer of 1974, I possessed only a mass of unsorted research notes. Yet when I woke up one morning, a comprehensive map of the dissertation (down to chapter titles and subsection headings) had made itself known, and done so with the force of revelation. I simply wrote it down. The work's provisional title was "Nature, Mind, and God: Science, Philosophy, and the Anglo-Canadian Moral Imagination, 1850–1914." The projected study consisted of an introductory chapter, "Education and Intellect at Mid-Nineteenth Century, and three sections, "Nature," "Mind," and "God"—each with two chapters. These sections delineated the pre-Darwinian views of the natural order in relation to Providence, the reorientation of social thought facilitated by the idealist mental and moral philosophers, and the theological consequences of this reorientation in the twentieth century. I soon dismissed the main title as far too pretentious for the rite of passage of a dissertation, but it continued to serve as a way of maintaining a steady focus on what had become my central themes and relationships. The outline required little revision during the writing of the dissertation between 1974 and 1976.

Roger Graham was a supportive thesis advisor. The draft chapters he received did not touch at all upon his area of expertise— Canadian political history—but he consistently suggested that although the dissertation moved in uncharted directions, they were potentially fruitful ones. In the late 1920s, Perry Miller, the great historian of American Puritanism, had concluded that his doctoral supervisor's attitude toward thesis supervision had been that "a student should be given enough rope to hang himself, if this he was resolved to do."[3] Miller's words came frequently to

xviii Introduction to the Carleton Library Edition

mind as my own work progressed. Then in the summer of 1976, as the sixth chapter (concluding the "Mind" section) was about to be submitted, Roger Graham suffered a serious heart attack. George Rawlyk kindly offered to look at the new chapter and to see the dissertation to its conclusion. The work was already four hundred pages long, exclusive of bibliography—the upper limit of an acceptable doctoral dissertation at Queen's at the time. It was obvious that the thesis should be completed without delay, even if this meant it would not now conform to the original, balanced three-part structure.

The finished dissertation, submitted as "A Disciplined Intelligence: Intellectual Enquiry and the Moral Imperative in Anglo-Canadian Thought, 1850–1890," was defended in the autumn of 1976. Its external examiner was Ramsay Cook, of York University. Eager to secure tenure at the University of Manitoba, to which I had returned as lecturer in 1974, I turned to the matter of revision for publication. The thesis had ended abruptly with a three-page epilogue following a chapter on John Watson and the rise of philosophical idealism. (The third section on the social and theological implications and legacy of idealism existed only in my mind). Its final words were: "Whether at the level of the church, the city or province, the national civil service, or the cause of the empire, during the thirty years that followed 1890 the idealist variant of the Anglo-Canadian moral imperative was suffused into Canadian life. The results were as important as they sometimes were ambiguous. That story, however, must be told elsewhere."[4]

The clear consequence of philosophical idealism, as the evidence presented in the thesis showed, was that, ironically, in its determination to return to the "essentials" of Christianity by questioning such basic tenets as the Divinity of Christ, the Trinity, and the Atonement it contributed to the importation of secular notions into the very religion it sought to defend. This needed to be examined, however briefly, in any sensible transformation of "A Disciplined Intelligence" from thesis to book. At the very least, a more substantive epilogue was necessary, but it soon became apparent that even an outline of the secularization inherent in the impact of British idealism on Canadian thought required more space than any epilogue could afford and it therefore became a seventh and concluding chapter. A new epilogue suggesting the continuity of a moral intelligence in Canadian social, political, and cultural thought in the decades after World War I concluded the manuscript submitted to the

Introduction to the Carleton Library Edition xix

publisher. The book appeared under the imprint of McGill-Queen's University Press in September 1979.

Possibly because it was such an oddity in Canadian historiography, *A Disciplined Intelligence* gathered immediate attention. Invitations arrived from a number of university history departments to speak on its subject. Certain historians concluded that the book held considerable explanatory power for studies on which they were engaged, particularly with respect to understanding the transformation of Canadian thought in the late nineteenth and early twentieth centuries. Ramsay Cook wrote privately to say that it helped him at last understand the origins and nature of the secularization of Canadian thought and society. Doug Owram wrote that it provided a clear sense of the intellectual and moral origins of the strong ethic of public service that emerged in the 1920s and 1930s, and beyond. The book received honourable mention for the 1980 John A. Macdonald Prize and the 1985 Prix François Xavier Garneau of the Canadian Historical Association.

The initial influence of the book hinged, ironically, less on what it examined at length than on what it merely broached. One clear challenge posed in its final chapter consisted in what it had to say about the secularization of Canadian society and the implications of this for Canadian religious thought. Yet the published work scarcely touched the surface of these concerns. The book proved sufficiently fertile and provocative, however, to help spur those interested in Canadian religious history into moving beyond the institutional framework in which the subject had traditionally been situated, and to conclude that the study of faith-based belief from the perspective of intellectual history could be fruitful rather than contradictory or, worse, perverse.

In this respect, *A Disciplined Intelligence* helped those interested in Canadian religious history to look inward, towards the intellectual elements of belief, and outward, towards the cultural and social resonances of religious practice. Despite the absence of its projected third ("God") section, where I had intended to examine twentieth-century themes such as the Higher Criticism, theological reorientation, inductive theology, and the twin ethics of social and public service, the book served as an interpretive template, used as an authority in work already underway and built upon or rejected by those inspired or irritated by its argument.

Reviewers of *A Disciplined Intelligence* praised the book for bringing to public attention and situating historically a number of Canadian intellectuals and educators then all but unknown—among them ethnologist Daniel Wilson and geologist John William Dawson, civil servant, social critic, and historian William Dawson LeSueur, mental and moral philosophers George Paxton Young and John Watson, and clergymen and theologians George Monro Grant, Nathanael Burwash, and Samuel Dwight Chown. The reviewers often dwelt, aptly, on the central thesis of the book: that a lengthy and strong tradition of moral concern developed in Anglo-Canadian thought in the nineteenth century, instilled initially by the transmission of evangelical Protestant values and ideas across the Atlantic, and that this "moral imperative" persisted, eventually in transmuted forms, well into the twentieth century.

The views of Northrop Frye loomed large in *A Disciplined Intelligence*, and they helped inform and shape my understanding of the nature and course of the moral imperative in Canadian thought. In such works as *The Modern Century* (Toronto: Oxford University Press, 1967) and *The Critical Path: An Essay on the Social Context of Literary Criticism* (Bloomington: Indiana University Press, 1971), Frye articulated the formation and continuity of Anglo-Canadian social mythology, its "myth of concern"—a collection of beliefs so deeply held as to give shape to a culture's commonality of purpose. Yet operating within this myth of concern, he noted, has been another constellation of beliefs generally located within the emancipatory and tolerant elements of the liberal tradition, a "myth of freedom." Ingrained within the Anglo-Canadian myth of concern, then, was the inherent tension—made more pronounced than elsewhere due to Canada's geographic and cultural site which linked it to both a conservative Britain and a libertarian America—between such polarities as authority and freedom, order and progress, culture and liberty. In *A Disciplined Intelligence*, such tensions originated and remained in the competing demands of piety and intellect.

The decade of the 1980s witnessed the erosion of the political history of the nation-state and the rise of social and women's history. In Canadian historiography it also saw the recognition among historians that religion, once central in Canada, was a too-little explored area of Canadian history. The result was a distinct sense of vitality and renewal in the writing of Canadian religious history, almost always from the perspective of the intellectual historian.

The theme of the continuity of a dynamic and ever-changing "moral imperative" was of secondary importance, if it was dwelt upon at all, to scholars interested in the social history of religion and critical of what they chose to call the "secularization thesis." The secularization of Canadian society had been noted in the work of Richard Allen but was made explicit in the latter chapters of *A Disciplined Intelligence* and throughout Ramsay Cook's *The Regenerators: Social Criticism in Late Victorian English Canada* (1985). Cook's Governor General Award-winning book expanded the range of those who grappled with sacred and profane concerns to include social reformers, a beekeeper, a pre-Freudian psychiatrist, and many other (often eccentric) figures, subjecting them at times to ridicule. In doing so, Cook changed the tone of the discussion, charting a clear path in Protestant thought and practice, one of unambiguous declension, from the nineteenth-century "City of God" of the Christian pulpit to the twentieth-century "Secular City" of Mackenzie King's diary. Four years later, in his book *Two Worlds: The Protestant Culture of Nineteenth-Century Ontario* (1989), William Westfall argued that in Ontario, with material and secular forces in play, a Protestant consensus had come into existence in the mid-nineteenth century. Ontario Protestantism's great strength, Westfall argued, rested in its capacity to absorb both the sacred and secular, for example in the notion of progressive historical time and in the sacred space of Neo-Gothic church architecture. "Unfortunately," wrote one reviewer in summarizing one of the book's central arguments, "in the very process of incorporating material progress into its vision of the future, Protestantism allowed the secular to replace the sacred and thus undermined its own foundation, thereby initiating its own future failure."[5]

Historiographical contention thrives on the discovery of "schools" of interpretation to which one can take exception. One now proved readily at hand in an interpretive trajectory consisting of Allen, McKillop, Cook, and Westfall. Accordingly, historians of religion in Canada began to challenge what they saw as the Whiggish and linear "decline and fall" views of proponents of an unpalatable "secularization thesis." Important books arguing along these lines appeared, written by Marguerite Van Die, Michael Gauvreau, Phyllis D. Airhart, and Nancy Christie (with Michael Gauvreau). Taken together with the earlier work of Westfall and a decidedly "secularist" later book by David B. Marshall, they helped transform the historical study of religion in Canada.

None of these critics denied that the grounds of intellectual, religious, and social authority shifted fundamentally between the mid-nineteenth century and the 1930s, or that Canadian society became overwhelmingly preoccupied with secular concerns. Most argued, however, against the apparent belief of the "secularist" historians that increased secularity meant less religious commitment. In *An Evangelical Mind: Nathanael Burwash and the Methodist Tradition in Canada, 1839–1918* (1989), Van Die maintained that while Burwash's views at times changed, his evangelical religious commitment did not; that his struggle to reconcile faith and reason was an enduring dynamic within the Christian church, not a specific response to challenges posed by an incipient secularism. Michael Gauvreau's more broad-ranging study, *The Evangelical Century: College and Creed in English Canada from the Great Rivival to the Great Depression* (1991) went even further.

Gauvreau sought to turn the "secularist" argument on its head. The Social Gospel of the early twentieth century, he asserted, was the product of a church still rich with spiritual vitality and theological resonance. He accepted the importance of Baconian induction but minimized that of the Scottish Common Sense tradition in Canadian mental and moral philosophy. He also disputed the degree to which speculative idealism left an ironic, secular legacy. In his view, neither Darwinism nor the "higher criticism" resulted in a nineteenth-century crisis of faith; this occurred instead as a result of developments, apparent by 1905, "in biblical scholarship associated with historical relativism." Professionalisation and psychological impulses toward self-actualization, as much as anything, fractured the alliance of pulpit and lecturn. The crisis of faith in Canadian evangelical culture was, in Gauvreau's view, a twentieth-century phenomenon, and even then a robust commitment to theological understanding continued well after 1900. In this work, Gauvreau did not just marginalise such movements as idealism; he also attempted to reorient the "mainstream" of Canadian intellectual thought towards the theological churchmen who maintained the "college-pulpit" connection. As with the work of Van Die, that of Gauvreau pointed to difficulties inherent in any rigid separation of commitments to individual regeneration and social action.

The appearance of Phyllis D. Airhart's book, *Serving the Present Age: Revivalism, Progressivism, and the Methodist Tradition in Canada* (1992), enabled Gauvreau to claim in a review of the book that "Two rival historiographic schools have hotly contested the question of how Victorian evangelicalism balanced its traditions of individualist piety with the insistent demands of social reform. Were the old ways eroded and rendered irrelevant by the vast social and intellectual transformation of the industrial age? Or did the Protestant churches successfully adjust and preserve their traditions and creatively shape the forces of cultural and political change?"[6] Between 1900 and 1910, Airhart argued, tensions within the Methodist community resulted in the emergence of a "progressivist" piety that diminished the role of revivals and individual conversion in favour of a commitment to sacrificial service. Pietistic evangelical commitment continued (as did notions such as free will, experiential religion, and holiness) but it had become reoriented and reconfigured. If a crisis existed in Canadian Methodism, it was one of identity, not faith.

Among the few dissenters to the argument for a continuity of belief that had found pride of place in this new work in Canadian religious and intellectual history was David B. Marshall. In *Secularizing the Faith: Canadian Protestant Clergy and the Crisis of Belief, 1850–1940* (1992), Marshall sought to demonstrate Canadian Protestantism's accommodation to the secular, away from the "Kingdom of God." This work marked both a narrower and broader approach to the question of secularization. It was narrower in that the book concentrated largely on the thought of clergymen; it was broader in the way it included such trends in society as the growth of a pluralistic consumerism in the marketplace—the marketplace of ideas, values, and belief as well as of consumer goods. The Social Gospel, from this perspective, reflected a movement among those who opted for a future of material more than spiritual benefit. "In the end," Marshall concluded, "a defeated church, uncertain about its message, mission and future, floundered." Religious accommodation and the search for contemporary relevance resulted only in reinforcing secular engagement and in marginalizing a once-central spiritual force.

Four years later, Nancy Christie and Michael Gauvreau attacked such views. In *A Full-Orbed Christianity: The Protestant Churches and Social Welfare in Canada, 1900–1940* (1996), they insisted that Protestant values remained central to Canadian society well after the Great War. Far from having been eclipsed at the end of the Great War, the Social Gospel lived on in the core values of postwar mainstream churches and the social agencies they created and sponsored for the purpose of social service, thereby paving the way for the welfare state in Canada. "By the mid-thirties," Christie and Gauvreau concluded, "progressive clergymen had achieved their aim of converting provincial and federal governments to the principle of providing social security." Having achieved this objective, the United Church of Canada—the embodiment of the progressive—then rediscovered personal redemption and salvation in the form of the Oxford Movement, for, in the view of the authors, church leaders had promoted social evangelism because it was "the outward manifestation" of the other stream of evangelism, "inner piety."[7] A nagging question remains: Was the surrender of social and welfare services to the state and the return to personal piety a sign of the centrality of the churches or a retreat from the public sphere that resulted from the erosion of their public authority within a social environment driven by a secular and materialistic ethic?[8]

If at the end of the second millennium any consensus existed among Canadian historians committed to the study of religious history, it was two-fold. First, it accepted that a fundamental reorientation and transformation had taken place in Canadian Protestantism between the late nineteenth century and the end of the first third of the twentieth. Secondly, it held that, at the very least, the notion of secularization was by no means adequately understood, and that as a conceptual tool it might, indeed, be highly problematic. This was certainly the view of those who claimed that, however major the transformation in religious belief and practice may have been, fundamental religious yearning persisted and found new and enduring forms of expression. Historians Van Die, Gauvreau, and Airhart have argued, in effect, for the existence and continuity of a moral imperative in Anglo-Canadian thought.

The fact of secularization within the larger public culture is scarcely a matter for debate: it has become a palpable reality, and was so for much of the twentieth century. Those who argue for the continuing influence of evangelicalism well into the twentieth century accept this, arguing amongst themselves mainly on the timing of the crisis of authority. Did it occur in the 1890s? 1905? The years of the Great War? In their search for advantageous interpretive positions on which to base their scholarly authority, such studies at least had the advantage of prior work to rebut. *A Disciplined Intelligence* had had no such luxury; historiographically, it had nothing to refute except the almost total silence of scholarship on the subject. In its final, controversial chapter, it did not attempt to argue for a loss of religious belief but for the displacement of it, and for the concomitant marginalisation of a commitment to organized religion in its institutional forms.

We still scarcely understand the process by which this shift in spiritual, moral, and social authority took place, and much is to be done by scholars before we will. One can fully accept the argument that theological concerns persisted in the years after the Great War of 1914–18, however disruptive that tragic war had been in matters of faith. The ongoing work of Marguerite Van Die, Michael Gauvreau, and Nancy Christie goes a long way in demonstrating this. So does Hubert Krygsman's comprehensive study of Canadian Protestantism in the twentieth century, "Freedom and Grace: Mainline Protestant Thought in Canada, 1900–1960," a Ph.D. dissertation submitted to the Department of History, Carleton University, in 1997. We can accept, with Van Die, that figures such as Nathanael Burwash had reconciled the public use of reason and the inner life of the spirit, and remained just as religious late in life as they were when they were young. In the case of Burwash, as well as others, what we need to know in more precise detail is how this man, so central a religious figure in the late nineteenth century, became so peripheral by the end of his life in the twentieth. What, well within the span of a generation, had turned an icon of Methodism into a marginal man?

If we are to understand the relationship of the sacred and the profane in Canada, and its working-out in Canadian culture, we need to explore more fully not only the formalities of theological thought and practice but also the transference of religious sensibilities and concerns into areas of expression not normally considered within the ambit of "religion." The brief epilogue of *A Disciplined Intelligence* attempted to prod scholars in this direction. A tradition of moral concern, it claimed, is an ongoing thread in Canadian intellectual and cultural life; but inheritance of religious tradition is only one means by which such concern is absorbed and transmitted. Religion and culture exist in uneasy proximity, demarcated mainly by orientations toward the transcendent or the immanent. But they occupy the same realm, and it is the realm in which human beings negotiate meaning through the power of symbol, and the meaning of symbol through actions and words.

But which actions, which words? And in which directions? The imperatives of an increasingly integrated market economy and industrial infrastructure absorbed the attention and energy of Canadians as the twentieth century unfolded, and thoughtful people often harnessed themselves to the organizational capacity and ideological structures of the nation-state. The commitment of Christians persisted, even as the spiritual idiom of English-speaking Canadians shifted from the language of personal redemption to that of social service, and then to culture and self-fulfillment. But the voice of that commitment gradually came to be heard at the periphery of formal religious belief and practice. In an increasingly pluralistic society, the spiritual directions of people became a matter of open choice within a broad range of occupational and social spaces. By the late nineteenth and early twentieth centuries, many voluntary associations and professional occupations with no religious affiliation existed; they, too, forged social bonds offering solidarity and interest for the like-minded. Particularly for women, they also made possible new options in life.

Churches, once symbols of an overarching unity of belief, became symbols of private choice—sanctuaries often "Neo-Gothic" in style, self-consciously drawing upon the anti-modern myth of an integrated and holistic Medieval Christendom. They also drew attention to themselves as spiritual sites where commitment stood at odds with a wide variety of new social and cultural choices in the world of an interconnected and interdependent industrial and commercial economy. Increasingly, providential dispensation stood at odds with the belief in the laws of the natural order championed by the accountant and the life insurance actuary. "The skyscraper," Harold Innis later observed, 'has become the modern cathedral; long-term credit is the new basis of modern belief."[9] Secularization indeed took place, but its locus was less in any arithmetic decline in church membership or increase in "unbelief" than it was in the directions taken by those whose spiritual need to "connect" with others took them outside church walls and into the occupational structures of "secular" society itself.

The final pages of *A Disciplined Intelligence* suggested that among the vocational choices associated with the moral imagination in twentieth-century Canadian life were those linked to social and public service, the academic arts and social sciences, social criticism and cultural analysis, and the writing of poetry and fiction. Once largely confined to the Protestant pulpit and the philosopher's lecturn, the new agents of the moral imperative in Canadian life often chose instead to become social scientists and social workers, cultural critics and professors of English,

Introduction to the Carleton Library Edition xxvii

historians and journalists, and diplomats and Ottawa mandarins. Subsequent scholarship has abundantly borne this out. Doug Owram's *The Government Generation: Canadian Intellectuals and the State 1900–1945* (1986) and Barry Ferguson's *Remaking Liberalism: The Intellectual Legacy of Adam Shortt, O. D. Skelton, W. C. Clark, and W. A. Mackintosh, 1890–1925* (1994) demonstrate clearly the ways new ethical notions set forward in the late nineteenth century helped inspire a twentieth-century commitment to public service and the social good. Sara Z. Burke's prize-winning book, *Seeking the Highest Good: Social Service and Gender at the University of Toronto, 1888–1937* (1996), situated the origins of social service and social work at the University of Toronto specifically in the context of nineteenth-century British idealism and its Canadian exponents. Similarly, the title of Marlene Shore's book, *The Science of Social Redemption: McGill, the Chicago School, and the Origins of Social Research in Canada* (1987), testified to the religious origins of Canadian social analysis, practiced now in a secular intellectual and social environment. Shore's major figures, like those of Owram and Burke, sought redemption by means other than those Christianity alone could provide.

In the arena of the humanities, this continuity of moral concern remained even more forcibly intact. In *Image and Identity: Reflections on Canadian Film and Culture* (1989), film-maker and critic Bruce Elder fixed upon the influence of Canadian variants of Common Sense philosophy and Hegelian idealism to account for the idea of community that helped shape a distinctive Canadian film tradition. Similarly, literary historian Henry A. Hubert drew upon variants of the British idealist tradition, perpetuated in half-secularized form by the hold of Arnoldian humanism on university English departments, in *Harmonious Perfection: The Development of English Studies in Nineteenth-Century Anglo-Canadian Colleges* (1994).

My own work after the publication of *A Disciplined Intelligence* attempted to expand its compass and extend its argument beyond 1914. In 1980, I contracted to write an intellectual and social history of the university in Ontario for the Ontario Historical Studies Series. Parts of the first half of the book, which eventually appeared as *Matters of Mind: The University in Ontario, 1791–1951* (1994), necessarily recapitulated and refined the nineteenth-century aspects of the educational, intellectual, and religious history first dealt with in *A Disciplined Intelligence*. But much of the post-1920 intellectual, religious, and cultural history of Ontario remained unexamined by scholars. To the extent possible within the boundaries specified by the editors of the series, *Matters of Mind* extended the general argument of *A Disciplined Intelligence* into this new territory, eventually reaching the Massey Commission of 1951.

Matters of Mind can therefore properly be viewed as a thematic sequel to the earlier book on which it built. Except in institutions maintaining direct denominational connections, the overpowering influence of evangelical Christianity was diminished in the twentieth century. Gone, after the disillusionment of the Great War, was imperial fervour. Eroded, too, were the remaining ties of philosophical idealism to the Christian tradition—except in the minds of certain philosophers and theologians, now increasingly distant, and at times estranged, from the popular Protestantism of the pews.

Major twentieth-century academic figures in Ontario, men such as E. J. Urwick, R. M. MacIver, Harold Innis, Charles Norris Cochrane, Northrop Frye, and Marshall McLuhan, lived and worked in a secular environment. Yet their sensibilities and concerns were scarcely less religious than those of a generation or two earlier. Theirs were prophetic voices linked to earlier prophets of the Christian tradition. They may have been sociologists and historians, classicists and English professors, but these northern prophets drew upon a philosophical and religious inheritance, which they rearticulated through different vocabularies and a different cultural grammar—for example, that of the Arnoldian humanism which dominated the humanities until the 1960s.

Such new means of expressing age-old yearnings helped delineate their concerns as they sought ways of alleviating the crisis of spiritual authority in an age where the struggle between spiritual authority and material interest was no longer the only, or even the central, site of engagement. From the 1920s on, the contest over meaning also took place within the arena of culture itself, between the hierarchical and prescriptive conception earlier epitomized by poet and essayist Matthew Arnold and the horizontal and relativistic one of nineteenth-century anthropologist E. B. Tylor. Through the Massey Commission report, the lingering remnants of Christian spiritual authority, now displaced and marginal but given new wind, made one final attempt to counteract the mass culture industries and the appeal of the popular by an innoculation of Arnoldian idealism. Apart from the quotation from St Augustine with which the report began, direct Christian witness played little substantive role in this contest over spiritual authority and direction, but the moral imperative, its origins deep in the Canadian "evangelical century" and beyond, permeated the document and its supporting studies.

Several recent doctoral dissertations examine the cultural transformation of Canada in new ways, drawing on *A Disciplined Intelligence*'s theme of a continuity of moral concern amidst an increasingly secular Canadian society. "'What's Past Is Prologue': Canadian Intellectuals, the Tory Tradition and the Challenge of Modernity, 1939–1970," by Philip Massolin (1998), builds directly on the notion of a "moral imperative" in Anglo-Canadian intellectual life. "This work," he notes, "accepts the existence of a moral imperative: the preservation of the total human community and a moral code to allay the dangerous effects of modernization. . . . It argues that a group of prominent Canadian intellectuals brought forward the moral imperative into the mid-twentieth century. Through their social and philosophical criticism, these critics endeavoured both to understand the modern world and to provide alternatives, based in what they thought were the best Canadian and western traditions, to modernization. . . . As such, these intellectuals establish a link to their predecessors and contribute to the development of the Anglo-Canadian mind."[10]

Massolin's study concludes on a pessimistic note. The conservative prophetic vision of those he examined could and did provide "a devastating critique" of the ills of modern society, but by the 1970s modernity had triumphed. Like the evangelical creed of his Methodist father in the 1920s, Donald Creighton's historical vision had lost its hold, and at his death it held sway, if at all, only at the margins of his profession. This had not been true earlier. Donald Wright's "The Professionalization of History in English Canada to the 1950s" (1999), argues that "the question of morality and values lies at the heart of the historiographical debate on the emergence of the social sciences in English Canada." In the case of the discipline of history, until at least the middle of the twentieth century no clean break took place between "fact" and "value."[11]

A dissertation by Leonard Kuffert, similar in substance and theme to that of Philip Massolin, focuses on the inter-relationship of elite and popular culture from the Second World War onward. In "'A Secret Understanding': Critical Responses to 'Modern Life' and Mass Culture in English Canada, 1939–1963" (2000), Kuffert focuses on the difficulties Canadian cultural critics faced in attempting to maintain an "authentic" Canadian culture in the face of the mechanization of culture found in popular media and in advertising for the masses. In doing so, he argues that while humanistic culture became marginalised in a way not unlike organized religion earlier, a religious sensibility and yearning remained strong within the Canadian intellectual community. In the author's words, "the implicit need to live in both worlds—to transcend the borders between science and faith—was both an axiom and a commandment of Canadian life at mid-century."[12] His study amply demonstrates that this generalization is by no means overdrawn: the tradition of moral concern and criticism in Canada remained very much intact, and it involved, as it had for the better part of a century, a public use of reason that almost invariably sought to mediate extremes regardless of the subject at hand.

The moral imperative in Canadian thought would be maintained and reshaped by others, and in different ways. Very early in the research that resulted in *A Disciplined Intelligence*, I came across a quotation from *Idealism in National Character* (1920) a book published in the wake of the Great War by Robert Falconer, president of the University of Toronto. The words represented, for Falconer, his generation's understanding of the Anglo-Canadian sensibility, and for this reason I placed it in my penultimate paragraph. "What we are," he said, "is the long process of education of the will rather than the intellect; a few simple convictions have laid hold upon the people." A little later, he added: "A well educated community, that is one with a disciplined intelligence, will be ready to take part in the new forum without serious disturbance." At the time, those words epitomised for me the continuity of moral concern ranging from the earliest days of Canadian Protestant colleges to the final report of the Massey Commission.

Looking back at the second half of the twentieth century in Canada from the cusp of the twenty-first, these words hold no less resonance even though they continue to bring with them the burden of Sisyphus. Names abound of those who have readied themselves to participate in the "new forum" of their own day—among them, a generation ago, Graham Spry and Irene Spry, Hilda Neatby and Margaret Laurence, Walter Gordon and C. B. Macpherson, Bernard Lonergan and Marshall McLuhan, George Grant and Robertson Davies, Hugh Hood and, above all, Northrop Frye. The tradition continues today, refracted in still more ways, in such figures as John Polanyi, Bruce Elder, John Ralston Saul, Charles Taylor, and Michael Ignatieff. Linked to

Introduction to the Carleton Library Edition xxxi

them should be Canadian historians such as those already noted, concerned as they are with the interconnection of the spiritual, intellectual, and political dimensions of their country. If, in whatever ways, *A Disciplined Intelligence* has helped them on their journeys, it will have served its purpose well.

A. B. McKillop
Ottawa, February 2001

Notes
1. S. F. Wise, "Sermon Literature and Canadian Intellectual History," *The Bulletin* of the United Church of Canada Archives 18 (1965), in S. F. Wise, *God's Peculiar Peoples: Essays on Political Culture in Nineteenth Century Canada*. Eds. A.B. McKillop and Paul Romney, 3-17 (Ottawa: Carleton University Press, 1993); Carl Berger, *The Sense of Power: Studies in the Ideas of Canadian Imperialism, 1867–1914* (Toronto: University of Toronto Press, 1970)
2. Michael Gauvreau, "Beyond the Half-Way House: Evangelicalism and the Shaping of English Canadian Culture," *Acadiensis* 20 (Spring 1990), 158–77
3. Perry Miller, "Preface to the Second Edition," in Miller, *Orthodoxy in Massachusetts 1630–1650* (New York: Harper & Row, 1970 [1933]), xxxi
4. Alexander Brian McKillop, "A Disciplined Intelligence: Intellectual Inquiry and the Moral Imperative in Anglo-Canadian Thought, 1850–1890" (Ph.D. dissertation, Queen's University, 1976), 414
5. Henry Hubert, *Canadian Literature* 128 (Spring 1991), 184
6. Michael Gauvreau, *American Historical Review* 98 (June 1993), 1981
7. Nancy Christie and Michael Gauvreau, *A Full-Orbed Christianity: The Protestant Churches and Social Welfare in Canada, 1900–1940* (Montreal and Kingston: McGill-Queen's University Press, 1996), 248–9
8. Ibid. Christie and Gauvreau argue that "the flood-tide of American popular culture" occurred "for the first time" only "in the late 1940s." This assertion minimizes the extent of American influence earlier. See Mary Vipond, "Best Sellers in English Canada, 1899–1918: An Overview," *Journal of Canadian Fiction* 24 (1979), 96–119; A. B. McKillop, "Science, Values, and the American Empire," in McKillop, *Contours of Canadian Thought* (Toronto: University of Toronto Press, 1987), 11–28; Allan Smith, *Canada, An American Nation? Essays on Continentalism, Identity, and the Canadian Frame of Mind* (Montreal and Kingston: McGill-Queen's University Press, 1994) and Smith, "Doing the Continental: Conceptualizations of the Canadian-American Relationship in the Long Twentieth

Century," *Canadian-American Public Policy* 44 (December 2000), 1–70; Daniel J. Robinson, *The Measure of Democracy: Polling, Market Research, and Public Life 1930–1945* (Toronto: University of Toronto Press, 1999).
9. Harold Innis, "The Penetrative Powers of the Price System" quoted in Robert E. Babe, *Canadian Communication Thought: Ten Foundational Writers* (Toronto: Toronto University Press, 2000), 335n129
10. Phillip Massolin, "'What's Past Is Prologue': Canadian Intellectuals, the Tory Tradition and the Challenge of Modernity, 1939–1970" (Ph.D. dissertation, University of Alberta, 1998), 1–2
11. Donald Wright to A. B. McKillop, 15 January 2001
12. Leonard Kuffert, "'A Secret Understanding': Critical Responses to 'Modern Life' and Mass Culture in English Canada, 1939–1963" (Ph.D. dissertation, McMaster University, 2000), 169

A Disciplined Intelligence

They change their skies but not their minds
who cross the sea in ships.
Seneca

1
Education and Intellect

Religion has not confined itself to enriching the human intellect, formed beforehand, with a certain number of ideas; it has contributed to forming the intellect itself.
    Emile Durkheim, *Elementary Forms of the Religious Life* (1926)

Maxim 429. Knowledge. An eager desire of Knowledge ought to be Govern'd and restrained (being as Dangerous and Sinful) as any oth^r inordinate appetite. . . . Happ^{ss} is promised—not to the Learned, by to ye Good.
    Bishop Thomas Wilson,
    Maxims of Piety and Christianity (1781)

In 1853 Matthew Arnold wrote a troubled letter to his close friend Arthur Hugh Clough. "You certainly do not seem to me sufficiently to desire and earnestly strive towards—assured knowledge—activity—happiness. You are content to *fluctuate*—to be ever learning, never coming to the knowledge of the truth. This is why, with you, I feel it necessary to stiffen myself—and hold fast my rudder."[1] One of Arnold's biographers, Lionel Trilling, has adduced from this statement and similar ones by Arnold that what he feared, not only in Clough but in himself and others, was "the driving restless movement of the critical intellect trying to solve the problems of the 19th century." An acute observer of human sensibilities, Arnold reacted to this aspect of Clough's thought, especially as it was revealed in his poetry, with considerable alarm. Clough's poetry seemed to Arnold to be that of the head, and, for Arnold, true poetry must appeal not only to the head but to the whole of man's being.

Arnold's problem, as Trilling states so well, was not his alone.

Its roots lay in the conflict between the creative imagination and the critical intellect that in Trilling's view went to "the very heart of the romantic philosophy."[2] Nor was the fear of the critical intellect restricted to the lofty circles in which the poet travelled. In a remote corner of Canada West, a decade after Arnold had unburdened his mind to Clough, a settler named Mrs. Holiwell sent a piece entitled "The Poetry of Every-Day Life" to the *British American Magazine*. "This is a sceptical age," she wrote, "in mundane things as in heavenly, nothing is taken for granted, or received without inquiry. . . . There is no superstition so sanctified by antiquity; no prejudice so hallowed by time-honoured adherence, no custom so venerable by long observance, whose just claims to respect, the analytical, curious, doubting mind of the nineteenth century does not test and examine."[3]

Like Arnold, Mrs. Holiwell was by no means a reactionary, simply digging in her heels against any and all social change. She found it in fact delightful when the critical spirit of the age helped to alleviate specific religious, social, or political grievances. The problem was that modern criticism did not stop there. In the domain of the intellect there was apparently little room for the world of poetry. Mrs. Holiwell found herself living in an age in which "we are taught to believe nothing but what we can understand, pursue only the practical, cultivate only the useful." The muse of poetry, on the other hand, admitted no such boundaries. She "does not confine herself to so limited a sphere. She is democratic, universal, enlarging and improving minds of fair development and generous culture, and even elevating the thoughts and humanising the sentiments of the ignorant and rude."[4]

As far apart as Matthew Arnold and Mrs. Holiwell may have been in intellectual acumen or social class, both were united in their concern for the implications of the seemingly self-sustained intellect of the nineteenth century. Nor was Mrs. Holiwell alone with her fears in British North America. "Need I remind you, that we live in most portentous times," a Presbyterian minister, Alexander Mathieson, warned from a Montreal pulpit in 1836. He was not referring to Chartist agitation or Jacksonian democracy. "That fearful excitement,—that restless mental energy, which distinguishes the age" was what concerned him. Here was something to be feared much more than movements of social unrest, for how could one combat "the reckless affection of mental independence which has infected so many" and which made people "spurn both the counsels of experience, and inspiration"? The problem was not political or ideological, not "democracy" or "republicanism." It went deeper:

> It cannot be denied, that the spirit of the age, is anything but a Christian spirit. It is a spirit of intellectual might and energy, but of religious indifference. There is a rage for novelty and innovation,—a fondness for speculation and theory,—an extreme aversion to be guided by the revealed Word of the Living God. . . . We have much reason to fear, amidst the prevailing excitement, that we may be so carried away with the specious but ill founded speculations of visionary theorists, as to join in an attack on those institutions which time hath rendered venerable, and which the blessings they have conferred on mankind ought to have made sacred.[5]

Here, with regard to the critical intellect, can be noticed a difference between the experience of Matthew Arnold and that of many Anglo-Canadians of the nineteenth century. Arnold's mind was witness to a conflict between the claims of the critical intellect and the moral imagination. The words of both Mrs. Holiwell and the Reverend Alexander Mathieson indicate that, for them, unrestricted "intellectual" inquiry above all threatened the continuity of an inherited cultural experience. Mrs. Holiwell conceived the poetic function in moral and cultural—not purely aesthetic or imaginative—terms. The Reverend Mathieson feared an undue attack by "visionary theorists" upon the inherited institutions that were the basis of the social fabric. Theirs was a moral imagination, their concern for preserving cultural tradition a moral imperative that has long been central to the Anglo-Canadian frame of mind.

These and other such statements represent particular manifestations of what the Canadian literary critic and theorist Northrop Frye would call the Anglo-Canadian "myth of concern," an element of immense significance in the formation and continuity of the social mythology of English-speaking Canada in the nineteenth century. Frye notes that "as a culture develops, its mythology tends to become encyclopaedic, expanding into a total myth covering a society's view of its past, present and future, its relation to its gods and its neighbours, its traditions, its social and religious duties, and its ultimate destiny."[6] The function of the myth of concern is to establish within a society the commonality of purpose that alone can give that society unity; as such, it is what Frye calls a "closed myth," intolerant of dissent and anxious for continuity:

> The myth of concern exists to hold society together, so far as words can help to do this. For it, truth and reality are not directly connected with reasoning or evidence, but are socially established. What is true, for concern, is what society does and believes in response to authority, and a belief, so far as a belief is verbalized, is a statement of willingness to participate in a myth of concern. The typical language of concern therefore tends to become the language of belief. In origin a myth of concern is largely undifferentiated: it has its roots in religion, but religion has also at that stage the function of *religio*, the binding together of the community in common acts and assumptions.[7]

The particular myth of concern of the Anglo-Canadian was an extension of a larger European cultural context, a product partly of racial heritage but mostly of the Judaeo-Christian tradition. The physical separation of the Anglo-Canadian from Great Britain by the vast expanse of the North Atlantic was largely negated, at least for some, by the greater cultural context of which they knew they were a part. This obliteration of space by time, this transcendence of geography by the sense and the burden of heritage, is captured perfectly in a poem by Susanna Moodie written at mid-century:

> The spirit of past ages never dies—
> It lives, and walks abroad, and cries aloud—
> E'en from the silent dwellings of the dead;
> The vanished dust of generations gone,
> It utters forth a voice—and tells to man,
> The wisdom, power, and eloquence that dwelt
> In human forms, and sway'd this goodly earth—
> Truth, wisdom, virtue, the eternal three,
> Great moral agents of the universe—
> Shall yet reform and beautify the world,
> And render it fit residence for Him,
> In whom these glorious attributes combined
> To render perfect manhood, one with God.[8]

As much as material circumstances governed everyday life, at least to literate Anglo-Canadians, these conditions were clearly subordinate to the larger life of the mind. For such people, life at the edge of the forest was as close to the heart of European thought and culture as the nearest reading lamp. "What matters the rudeness of the roof that shelters us, the pine table on which we lean, the mean light that reveals the charmed page," Mrs. Holiwell asked rhetorically. "We are in spirit dwelling in palaces, beside thrones, holding high converse with power, and feeling in our exaltation, superior to the paltry distinctions of a petty world."[9]

Intellectual Anarchy

It is significant that Mrs. Moodie's poem appeared as an epigraph to her article entitled "Education the True Wealth of the World," for throughout Canadian history the Anglo-Canadian moral imperative has found its most continuous expression in the field of education. In education, too, the Anglo-Canadian quest for cultural unity has been most pervasive through the articulation of its own myth of concern. It should not be surprising, therefore, to find that the conflict in the nineteenth century between the critical intellect and the moral sensibility of Anglo-Canadians was also most evident within the educational institutions of the British North American colonies, for, above all, the free-wheeling intellect of the nineteenth century challenged the unity of ideas and assumptions that lay at the basis of that myth of concern. The education Mrs. Moodie extolled was fundamentally one of moral unity—one in which "moral improvement . . . must go hand in hand with increasing literary and scientific knowledge."[10] Elsewhere in her essay she noted that the power to improve one's self is the product of "moral and intellectual culture"; that the true wealth of a nation must be measured, not in pecuniary terms, but in terms of whether or not an enlightened system of education can produce "a people . . . held together by the strong bands of moral and intellectual fellowship." It was, after all, she added, not the navy or the gold of England that had made it a great nation. It was, rather, "the learning, the wisdom, the moral power of her educated classes." If this was the case for England, so should it be for Canada:

> Think Canadians, of what importance it is to your rising country, to bestow this inestimable gift upon your children. Put your sons in a situation to acquire solid and useful information, from masters who will not merely teach them to repeat lessons like parrots, by rote; but who will teach them to think—to know the meaning of what they learn—and to

be enabled by the right use of those reflective faculties, to communicate the knowledge thus acquired to others. . . . While the vigor of young life is yet yours, and you have before you the experience of all other nations, . . . it becomes an act of duty, of true *patriotism*, to give to your children the best education which lies in your power. In so doing, you bestow upon them a heritage which no misfortune can deprive them of again, which will survive the dissolution of the body, and the destruction of the world.[11]

What most Anglo-Canadians feared in the critical spirit of their age was not that this spirit inhibited creativity in education. Mrs. Moodie's plea indicates that there was very little that was creative, little extension of the boundaries of human knowledge, in education as they conceived it. They were troubled instead by the suspicion that freely critical intellectual inquiry might lead students away from the central purpose of education. The pursuit of knowledge, they insisted, must also be a pursuit guided by the prior recognition and acceptance of universal moral principles. Only in such a fashion could a community of purpose in British North America be established and maintained. The critical intellect was the major threat to that unity.

The leading spirit of the age, warned President Eliot of Harvard University in 1853, was one of "intellectual anarchy." The principal of Victoria College, S. S. Nelles, agreed fully, and quoted his Harvard colleague. Nelles also pointed out, for the benefit of his students, some of the symptoms of the dreaded disease. They included "the want of fixed and well-defined views; or a certain sickly irresolution, the result of a conscious blindness; or perhaps a rampant and headlong dogmatism; or a certain impatience of investigation or incapacity for it; or perhaps a feverish spirit of search without any sure method or any discernible progress." The antidote to this intellectual anarchy was, for Nelles, clear and independent thinking; and such thinking was above all to be guided by principles derived from religious inspiration. Nelles's message to his students boiled down to the following homily: "Study without prayer is arrogance, prayer without study is fanaticism; and neither arrogance nor fanaticism will find true wisdom."[12]

Throughout the middle decades of the nineteenth century, professors at Anglo-Canadian colleges attempted to combat the intellectualization of university life, later characterized by the Methodist leader Nathanael Burwash as one of "a subtle and dangerous character." The problem, he claimed, lay in "the rationalizing, or rather the reduction to an intellectual process or programme of the Spirit in the inner religious life." Eighteenth-century rationalism had overtly attacked basic Christian doctrines; but the intellectualizing tendency of the nineteenth century, which presumed to offer "what the student so much desires—a rational explanation of facts embodied in the Christian experience," was the more insidious precisely because it was so much less obvious. This process was essentially parasitic and destructive, for it attempted, said Burwash, to substitute "the confidence secured by an intellectual process . . . for the deep and regenerative convictions and revealing light of the Holy Spirit."[13] Once it came about that students were given the impression that all mental processes—even the inner resources nurturing the pious disposition—must be subjected to the scrutiny and given the sanction of the intellectual faculty, the result would be to call into question the very basis of the religious experience.

One of the most important factors contributing to this sense of intellectual anarchy was the explosion of knowledge, of new ideas and new ways of making them known, that characterized the nineteenth century. Improvements in communications, the refinement of the technology of print, the resultant growth of monthly and weekly periodical literature—not to mention the daily newspaper—made the critical thought of the day the intellectual fodder of Everyman. The anarchy noticed by President Eliot and Principal Nelles was not, therefore, a result only of an increasing tendency of men to criticize subjects not hitherto subject to criticism; it was also the result of the fact that the critical thought of others was now readily and quickly available to a mass reading-public. "During the last fifty years," declared a speaker at a well-attended public meeting in Kingston's City Hall one blustery winter evening in 1860, "such wondrous facts have been elicited from the fields of nature and science, that with respect to their influence on our physical and social condition, it may in some sense be said that a new era has dawned on our existence; and of these facts such a number that we are astonished by their quantity no less than by their quality."[14] For the next two and one-half hours the audience listened attentively as Mr. A. J. O'Loughlin, a local cabinet-maker and secretary of the school board, held forth earnestly on the lofty subject of "Man, a Material, Mental and Spiritual Being." Almost a decade earlier, an Anglo-Canadian railroad entrepreneur had confided to a friend: "I find myself falling behind the age and cannot keep pace with the

'March of Intellect.'"[15] Mr. O'Loughlin and his Kingston audience were trying their best to keep abreast of the latest results of that "March," but were finding the task a difficult one indeed:

> Such is the rapidity with which, in the present day, the results of investigation are presented to our view, that just as we have fully enquired into the nature of its relation to ourselves, another succeeding, presents itself to our attention, claiming for itself enrolment in those annals wherein are recorded the triumphs of the human intellect, the achievements of the human mind. . . . Knowledge seems desirous of hiding herself no longer from the masses.[16]

Later the same year, the principal of Queen's College, William Leitch, echoed the same sentiments:

> The public mind, on both sides of the Atlantic, is fermenting with grave religious questions. The speculative tendency was never more decided, and theological controversy is no longer confined to dry and bulky volumes from which the masses shrink with aversion. The newspaper, the magazine, the novel, teem with theological speculation, put in the most attractive forms. Even works on special theological questions are now written with such literary taste and ability, and the appetite for religious speculation is so strong, that they are read by vast multitudes. The number and the successive editions of such works amply attest to the enquiring but unsettled state of the public mind. One cannot mingle much in society without finding that a large proportion of the well educated classes are conversant with the questions which arise from the apparent conflict of faith and reason, and the difficulties started by the progress of science. The public are receiving a theological education through the press, such as at no former time they enjoyed.[17]

As Primarius Professor of Theology, Principal Leitch believed that the major way he could help to combat the dangers inherent in such unbridled speculation was to keep his theology students aware not only of "the various forms . . . of theological speculation and controversy," but also of the basic, practical art of preaching.[18] Yet if Canadians were to maintain a proper appreciation of the moral and spiritual priorities necessary for cultural development in the face of the speculative tendencies and intellectual anarchy of the age, the arena of battle would not be in the schools of theology alone. Most of the nation's future leaders, those in whose hands was to be entrusted the extension into Canada of the best elements of Western civilization, were to be found in the newly developing universities and colleges of British North America. It was in the lecture halls and laboratories of the faculties of arts and science that the standards of civilized life in Canada would be set; it was there, too, that the battle for the Canadian mind would be lost or won.

The Institutionalization of Concern
The primary agencies held responsible for maintaining, on the one hand, the unity of concern seen to be the basis of cultural life in British North America and, on the other, the sense of proportion and balance in thought necessary to keep in check the freewheeling intellect of the nineteenth century were the various Christian churches. Yet for a century after the British Conquest, no aspect of British North American life, not even politics, provoked more bitterness and division than did religion. The intensely subjective nature of the judgements by which "correct" religious principles were determined only widened these rifts.

The most obvious source of division was the presence of competing religious institutions. In Church-State relations the first half of the nineteenth century witnessed unremitting attempts by the non-Anglican denominations to undermine the validity of the Anglican assumption that the established Church in England was also to be the state church of the British colonies in America. Doctrinal divisions, both between and within the various churches, while not as obvious (because not as politically inflammable) as the denominational rivalries for external support, nevertheless existed and added the force of religious conviction to disagreements over polity. Presbyterians naturally fought strenuously against the Arminianism of Methodists, and were equally opposed to the extreme emotionalism of both Methodists and Baptists. Methodists complained of widespread antinomianism and predestinarianism. Anglicans decried the extreme Calvinism which they believed not only characterized Presbyterians, but also reached out and infected Methodists, Baptists, and even some of their own clergy of an evangelical persuasion. Within the churches, quarrels continued—at synod meetings, in church newspapers, and in numerous pamphlets. Anglicans in the colonies divided, with the rise of the Tractarian movement in England, between High and Low churchmen. Presbyterians split during the 1840s into Kirk and Free Kirk adherents. A rift developed between the British Wesleyan Methodists and the more democratic American branch. Baptists divided on the questions of exclusivism, the nature of the communion, and on free will. Two other factors heightened divisiveness even more. The first was a strong regional variation in the different denominations; the second was a tension between an ecclesiasticism derived from Britain (which tended to coincide with the perception of diplomatic or military threats from the United States) and the growth of sects spawned in part by a revolt against this ecclesiastical tendency.[19]

The divisive questions of Church and State, sect and church, doctrine and polity, parent and colonial church, were carried into the British North American Protestant church colleges established in the years before Confederation. By 1867 the Protestant churches in Canada had established a dozen such institutions, but few of these had escaped either sectarian or doctrinal discord. The first colleges were predominantly Anglican. King's College was established at Windsor, Nova Scotia, largely through the efforts of Bishop Charles Inglis, and was granted its charter in 1802. In New Brunswick, Loyalists set up Fredericton Academy in 1787, but the institution did not reach college status, as the College of New Brunswick, until 1800. This was due mainly to the fear of Bishop Inglis that the college would compete with King's, Nova Scotia. The institution was finally chartered as King's College, New Brunswick, in 1828, and only then assumed the function of a university. Both King's Nova Scotia and King's New Brunswick were highly exclusive in admissions and "narrowly Anglican" in personnel and aims.[20]

To a large degree so was McGill College, at least in its early years. Thanks to the urging of John Strachan, the strong-willed Presbyterian clergyman turned Anglican priest, James McGill had left upon his death in 1813 a legacy for a nondenominational college to be established in Montreal; but litigation by the McGill family and quarrels between the board of governors of the Royal Institute (to which the original bequest had been made) and the governors of McGill College delayed its opening until 1843. No religious tests were to be given to students of McGill, but such was the degree of bitterness between Anglican and Church of Scotland adherents over the college's Faculty of Divinity that the faculty was eliminated and was reconstituted only after nearly a century had passed. Bishop G. J. Mountain subsequently set up Bishop's College at Lennoxville, Quebec. Chartered in 1843 and operating by 1845, Bishop's filled the gap in training for Anglican clergymen created by the suspension of McGill's theological faculty.[21]

The main Anglican institution for higher education in Upper Canada was King's College, York. Having its origins in John Graves Simcoe's provision for clergy reserves to be used for this purpose, King's charter would have established Anglican control of the institution, and Strachan would have been its first president. Reform opposition to the seeming exclusivism of these measures was so strong that its charter was suspended, and the college did not open until 1843, with Strachan as president. The Reform antipathy to King's was still vehement, however, and in 1849 the University Act completely secularized King's, its name now changed to the University of Toronto. Not to be thwarted, Strachan was able within four years to obtain both financial support and a charter for another church college, named Trinity. This, however, merely provoked more division. Benjamin Cronyn, Anglican bishop of Huron, protested in 1860 against the High Church teachings of the provost of Trinity, and by 1863 Cronyn, a strong evangelical, had succeeded in setting up Huron College at London, Ontario.[22]

Colleges sponsored by Methodists, Baptists, and Presbyterians were also established before Confederation. The centre for Methodist higher education was Victoria College at Cobourg, Ontario. An outgrowth of the Upper Canada Academy at Cobourg, Victoria was given its charter as an institution where teaching was to be nondenominational in 1841. Instruction began there in the next year. One of the major reasons for the establishment of Victoria was fear of an Anglican proselytization, which, it was thought, might proceed unchecked unless an attempt was made to ensure that the Methodist church provide an institution in which to train its clergy. The predominantly Presbyterian nature of Dalhousie College in Halifax, though by charter (1818) a nonsectarian institution, brought charges of discrimination in hiring against it in 1838 (the first year in which teaching at the college level began) by a prominent Baptist minister and scholar, E. A. Crawley, who had hoped to obtain an appointment there. Crawley and a number of Baptist supporters then founded Queen's College in Wolfville, where Horton Academy—of which Crawley had been principal—was in operation. In 1841 its name was changed from Queen's to Acadia College, and by 1844 boasted not only a Faculty of Arts but a Baptist theological seminary as well.

Queen's College in Kingston, Ontario, founded in 1839, became the main hope for training the Presbyterian clergy in Canada. No religious tests were asked of the students, but all staff members were required to subscribe to the Westminster Confession. Activity at Queen's had scarcely commenced, however, when the secession of dissidents from the Kirk in 1843 spread to Canada from Scotland. As a result, Queen's was deprived of supporters and students precisely when the young institution most needed them, and Knox College at Toronto was created as part of the Free Kirk in Canada. Knox, which met for over a decade in houses and basements, received its charter in 1858.[23]

Various divisive factors played a large part in shaping the development of religious and educational institutions in British North America and they should by no means be underestimated; but not so obvious at the time was the fact that a broad and fundamental agreement on the basic principles and aims of education existed. The divisions between churches were largely due to the problems of institutionalization in what was still a frontier environment. Many squabbles arose out of the difficulties of finding sources of public or private financial support, establishing organizational and academic control, and maintaining both, while extending as much as possible the size and influence of the institution. But as real and divisive as these factors were, they tend to obscure the extent to which the Protestant churches and church colleges shared similar broad educational ideals. This unity of concern is especially evident in the ideas of their leaders.

Virtually all English-speaking educators in British North America at mid-nineteenth century agreed that the prime function of education was to instil into their students sound principles of morality. Once this was done, the obligations of that morality would fall logically and naturally into place. John Strachan and his supporters held that a university should, above all, strive to "impart religious and moral learning" (in the words of Lieutenant-Governor Simcoe), and to make certain that all secular instruction was "subordinate to a clearly defined Christian end" (in the words of Arnold of Rugby).[24] The Methodist clergyman and educator Egerton Ryerson and his supporters may have disagreed with the establishmentarianism of Strachan, but they, too, believed in the providential nature of God's work in British North America. They rejected Strachan's design for King's at York, feeling that it was an example of the very sectarianism to which Strachan was so vehemently opposed, but they were one with

Strachan in his insistence that the separation of instruction for the moral and spiritual aspects of mind from that of the intellectual would be the very negation of education. "A university," stated the special committee of the Upper Canadian Assembly, appointed to review the petitions against Strachan's plans for King's, ". . . should be the source of intellectual and moral light and animation, from which the glorious irradiations of literature and science may descend upon all with equal lustre and power."[25]

Strachan may well have disagreed with Ryerson's statement in 1831 that the Upper Canada Academy would not teach any "peculiar system of theological opinions," but he would not have disagreed with Ryerson's insistence that the school must make certain that "those principles and precepts of morality will be carefully inculcated and enforced which will guard the pupil from the contagion of vicious practice and example and will lead him to the love and practice of virtue."[26] And for both, the way towards the practice of virtue was through reverence for God. Despite Strachan's reputation for a crotchety exclusivism in religion, he would probably have agreed with that portion of Ryerson's Special Report for 1847 which stated that even though the different denominations had their own facilities for the instruction of youth, there yet existed "a wide common ground of principles and morals, held equally sacred, and equally taught to all, and the spirit which ought to pervade the whole system of Public Instruction, and which comprehend the essential requisites of social happiness and good citizenship."[27] Perhaps Susanna Moodie's husband, Dunbar, captured the prevailing disposition of the Anglo-Canadian moral imagination at mid-century in an article that lamented the divisive influence of sectarian disputes. "We hold . . . that almost any religion is better than no religion, and the sooner the ideas of moral restraint are impressed on the mind the better." The inculcation of the basic principles of religion through a sound education was, for Moodie, the only way social harmony could be brought about. "The harmony we contend for," he concluded, "is the result of the vigorous exercise of reason and of christian charity. It is the agreement in essentials . . . enlightened by education."[28]

Education as Disposition

Knowledge, said Francis Bacon, is power. Those whose duty it was to conduct the affairs of the various English-language British North American colleges at mid-nineteenth century were well aware of the implications of this dictum. The social function of these colleges—beyond the training of clergymen—was to provide the cultural leaders of the colonies,[29] whether in religion, politics, education, or commerce; and upon the question of the success or failure of these institutions in providing a sound education was seen to rest the fate of a British form of civilization on the North American continent. Anglo-Canadian educators were therefore burdened with their common recognition that as founders, as administrators, as teachers, and as spiritual counsellors, theirs was the awesome responsibility of making certain that the citizens who emerged from the lecture halls and chapels of academe were imbued with the correct principles. The education their students were to receive was above all to be a religious and moral one, and the responsibility for imparting that education fell heavily upon their shoulders.[30]

The problem and burden of education was not simply a matter of imparting information. Knowledge, professors and students alike agreed, was an important aspect of the educational experience; but it was not all, nor even the most important part. After graduation the theorems of Euclid and the classifications of Linnaeus would slowly fade away, and a certain amount of knowledge would thereby be lost forever. "While however we cannot make our minds full storehouses," wrote a student in his college's newspaper, "we can acquire the materials for doing so in the future. In us all there exist the germs of those powers and faculties upon the mere development of which the possibility of our becoming great men depends."[31] The benefits of education were not, therefore, lost with the gradual evaporation of facts from students' memories, for the principals and professors in the British North American colleges at mid-nineteenth century—and for decades after—were not so much interested in imparting knowledge, as such, as they were in cultivating a disposition of mind.

This disposition was overwhelmingly God-centred, and all aspects of education—whether in theology or literature, in philosophy or geology, whether the object was to study the constitution of nature or the constitution of the human mind—were clearly directed towards making the student aware of the extent to which his life and his thought must be governed by a proper relationship between himself and his God. The addresses of university presidents make this abundantly clear. As his 1863 University Lecture drew to a conclusion, Principal John William Dawson of McGill said:

> But lastly I would direct your attention to the duties of the educated man in his relation to his God, and to the example that he sets before his fellow-man. The religious life of a people is its only true life. If this is wanting, or if it is vitiated by infidelity, by superstition, or by any of the idolatries which are set up between man and his Maker, nothing will avail to give prosperity and happiness.[32]

The religious influence must pervade the "whole course of study," said John Mockett Cramp in 1851 in his inaugural address as president of Acadia. It must sanctify all the activities of the university. "This college is open to all denominations, no religious tests being imposed either on students or Professors," he went on. Nevertheless, "we must claim the right of aiming to imbue literature with the spirit of religion, and of inculcating, from time to time, those principles of our common Christianity, and those moral lessons which are admitted by all who wish to shun the approach of infidelity."[33] Six years later, in 1857, the principal of Bishop's College, addressing a group of prospective employers on the subject of the end and object of education, asked rhetorically: "Where else will you find the man you require, but among those whose powers of mind have been carefully nurtured under a system which took pains with the formation of character, which stamped that character with a firm and lasting outline, by giving to it an abiding sense of the fear of God and desire of His favour."[34]

That education brought power was very evident to Canadian college presidents and teachers; but this meant little unless the power thus gained was used to carry out the will of God. "Seek the power education confers," Principal Leitch enjoined the students of Queen's in 1860, in order "that you may be fellow-workers with God for the promotion of His glory and the best interest of man. God needs your services for the accomplishment of His purpose with man, and the dignity of education lies in this, that it fits you for working with and under God." And this was to be the case not only for theologues but for the general student in the arts and sciences as well. "Forget not that, though you never enter the sacred profession of the ministry, you are bound to be priests of God, and to serve Him in the various secular callings to which you may devote yourselves in life. Your education here is designed to dignify and sanctify those callings, so that they may be subservient to God's glory."[35] Part of a similar address by President Cramp of Acadia made clear, in three sentences, the desired social consequences of an education infused with an evangelical piety that transcended sectarian lines:

> Habitual recognition of God should distinguish every seat of learning, so that while the din of controversy is never heard, and party contentions are unknown, all may be taught that "the fear of the Lord is the beginning of wisdom." It has been well observed, that "it is our educated young men who will give the tone to society, and control the destiny of the generation in which they live." How desirable, nay even necessary, it is that the education they receive, while truly liberal in its plans and provisions, should be connected with that moral conservatism, without which, the advantages of knowledge itself may prove comparatively valueless.[36]

The process of education, to these Anglo-Canadian educators, was therefore something other than the simple pursuit of knowledge for its own sake; it was instead the regulated pursuit of those examples of human knowledge which were in accordance with the religious and moral truths they deemed necessary to cultivate a pious frame of mind. Education should be "truly liberal"; but it should bring about a "moral conservatism." The university should be a place of learning; but it must also be a place away from "the din of controversy." In fact, the unrestricted pursuit of knowledge simply for the sake of the pursuit constituted the greatest threat to a proper education, for it meant the development of one part of a student's mind—the intellectual faculty—at the expense of his moral and spiritual faculties. Christianity, Egerton Ryerson once said, must be the soul of intellectual growth.[37]

In other words, the intellect must not be allowed to become its own motive force; it must be given its inspiration and direction from the other, equally important, parts of the human mind. For all Anglo-Canadian educators, a truly "liberal" education meant the cultivation of all the faculties, the whole being. This meant, however, that the intellect of the educated man was one disciplined by the will. To understand this, it is necessary to consider in more detail the liberal education upon which so much faith was placed.

The Basis of a Liberal Education

Probably the most important statement of the nature and object of a "liberal education" made in Canada during the nineteenth century was Egerton Ryerson's inaugural address as principal of Victoria College. Delivered in 1842, at the beginnings of Canadian university life, this declaration set forth certain assumptions which governed the structure and development of Anglo-Canadian arts and science curricula for many years. Victoria College, it is true, was Methodist in its general atmosphere and staff. Yet the curriculum Ryerson suggested as one that could best achieve a truly liberal education was also one that he believed incorporated the best elements of the mathematics and classics-weighted curriculum of King's (York) or Acadia and the philosophy and theology-oriented program of Queen's at Kingston. An elaboration of Ryerson's general design, allowing for these differences in emphasis, can therefore be viewed as a general outline of the structure of the arts and science programs at the other Anglo-Canadian universities.

The act that had established Victoria College in 1841 made no provision for ensuring the orthodoxy of its staff members. It simply stated that "literature and science must be taught on Christian principles."[38] This broad appeal to a common Christianity was the basis of Ryerson's design for a liberal education. "Man," he said,

> is made for physical, mental and moral action; and the grand object of education is to develope [sic], improve, and perfect, as far as possible, his physical, mental, and moral faculties. ... In the formation of those faculties, God has furnished the richest display of wisdom and goodness; and to develope, expand, and mature them, is the noblest work of man or angel. ... To promote this object, in the most comprehensive sense, is the design of this institution—embracing as it does ... the several branches of a Classical and Scientific Education.[39]

Ryerson's design for a liberal education entailed the construction of two academic programs: first, a preparatory level, "requisite for the ordinary duties of life," intended for those who did not plan to go to college; second, a collegiate level for those who were to engage in "professional pursuits," such as the ministry, law, politics, and business. When speaking of the preparatory level, Ryerson placed no little emphasis upon the study of the English language and literature, in the hope that students would be inspired to emulate British philosophers and historians, orators and poets, as much as they already did Plato and Aristotle through their study of the classics. Behind this wish, and essential for the proper education of those who were soon to take up the "ordinary duties of life," was Ryerson's hope that by gaining an appreciation of their linguistic and literary heritage, these students would become "inspired with veneration and attachment for the Institutions and Laws" which had nurtured and protected the development of British *belles-lettres*. Other subjects to be taught at the preparatory level were to include mathematics and natural science (the latter comprising natural philosophy, chemistry, physiology, geology and astronomy), the outlines of mental and moral philosophy, evidences of Christianity, geography, and general history.

The collegiate level of Victoria was to be divided into five departments: classics, mathematics and the physical sciences, moral science, rhetoric and *belles-lettres*, and theology. The role and importance of the classics were reduced in comparison with colleges such as King's or Acadia. (Ryerson did not wish to minimize the classics; simply to place more emphasis upon other subjects.) English language and literature were to receive the same emphasis as at the preparatory level and for the same important reasons. Ryerson also placed more emphasis upon the study of the physical sciences than was customary at the other Canadian universities.[40]

As important to Ryerson as classics, the physical sciences, and modern literature were as part of the general enrichment of the human mind, it is clear that at the collegiate level the subjects at the heart of his program for a liberal education were moral science and theology. Yet here he was distinctly ambivalent. Absolutely certain of their extreme importance as part of a liberal education, he was nevertheless by no means sure that in the end moral science did not make a claim to knowledge that was in conflict with the requirements of theology. But that they *were* vitally interrelated there was no doubt in his mind, for the whole purpose of moral science was to bring about the mental disposition necessary for the study of theology.

"Moral Science," he believed, was "a most important and extensive department of a liberal education"; and no less than the study of theology was it to be God-centred in purpose and orientation. All its branches—mental philosophy, natural theology, moral philosophy, and logic—were to reflect this:

> The philosophy of mind inquires into the nature of those spirits of which we have any certain knowledge, or which it

concerns us to know—the Deity and the soul of man. The former branch of the inquiry is termed Natural Theology; the latter has sometimes been termed Psychology, or the philosophy of the human mind. The latter prepares the way for the former. From the knowledge of ourselves and our Creator arise our duty to both. This is the province of *Moral Philosophy*,—to explain our obligations and duties to ourselves, to our fellow-men, and to our Maker—to elucidate and apply the cardinal principles of the Scriptures to the various relations and circumstances of human life. . . . To Know our Maker and ourselves—to understand and discharge our duties towards both—to employ our intellectual and moral powers according to the principles of reason and truth, is the great end of our existence. It should, therefore, constitute a leading feature in every system of sound education.[41]

Moral science was clearly fundamental to the idea of a liberal education as Ryerson conceived it, for above all it stressed the idea of duty, man's obligation to his Creator, to his fellowman, and to himself.

This sense of obligation, the prime requisite for a pious disposition, was to be brought about by disciplining one part of the student's mind through adherence to the dictates of another. Both the moral faculty and the intellectual faculty were involved in this process, but the former was to keep the latter on a tight rein. Only that knowledge was to be sought "which it concerns us to know." The "right principles of *acquiring* knowledge" were to be determined according to "the right principles of *employing* it." And this knowledge was to be sought and employed only if it illustrated "*moral* interests and relations" derived, in the end, from the basically intuitive processes of the moral faculty.[42]

Here, once again, we are confronted with the potential challenge of the critical intellect, for man's mental processes required a necessary involvement with the intellectual aspect of mind. And here Ryerson's moral sensibility took firm control. The cultivation of the intellectual powers, he insisted, must also involve the actions of the moral sense. But which is supreme? Which ultimately exercises control? Which serves as the basis of judgement on critical issues? Clearly, for Ryerson, it was the moral faculty, for the very nature of that faculty made it fundamentally independent of intellectual processes, and no coldly rationalistic mode of thought should be allowed to disturb the influence of the moral faculty on other aspects of thought. "Let it not for one moment be supposed from these observations," he declared emphatically, "that I would make the House of God a philosophical Lecture-Room, or the Christian Minister a literary teacher or metaphysical disputant, or divert his chief meditations from the great truths of the Sacred Scriptures."[43] He could not express his own views on this all-important point better than by means of quoting the "eminent divine" Richard Watson:

> The purposes for which we go into the philosophical lecture-room, and into the House of God, are so distinct and call forth exercises of mind so different, that they cannot be brought together in a sermon without disturbing or neutralizing each other.... Science creeps, while religion expands the wing and soars. One passing pious thought, in a devotional moment, on the structure of a pebble, shall produce deeper piety of feeling than if, in scientific adoration, we bowed before the sticks and stones of geological theories.[44]

This passage is more than simply a statement of the purpose for which students and professors alike were to enter the "philosophical lecture-room." It is in fact a commentary on the purposes of lecture rooms in general, and its selection by Ryerson indicates something of his ambivalence as to the relationship between the intellectual and moral faculties, between scientific inquiry and the "piety of feeling" which for him constituted the essence of the educational experience.

The truly liberal education was above all to be pervaded by the study of theology, "the most extensive and important science in the world." All other subjects in the curriculum—classics, history, geography, astronomy, mathematics, and so forth—were to lead up to this. The ultimate purpose of each was to help one discern the will of God. Accordingly, the whole college program at Ryerson's Victoria was to be theological in the broadest sense of that word. "The fundamental principles of the Christian faith and of Christian morality belong, indeed, to all who are educated in a Christian land," he noted. "The Bible is the common inheritance of Christendom; and its principles—unconnected with the dogmas or bias of sectarianism—should form a part of the education of all christians."[45] Ryerson's counterparts at the other Anglo-Canadian universities and colleges might well have taken exception to the claim that the principles of Christendom should be taught independently of sectarian "dogmas or bias," but apart from this traditional disagreement between Methodists and other denominations, they shared his views as to the aims and structure of a truly liberal education. They also shared his apprehension as to the place and possible consequences of intellectual inquiry within the sphere of education.

2
The Colonial Philosophers

It is reasonable to think that as the mind is a nobler work, and of a higher order than the body, even more of the wisdom and skill of the Divine Architect hath been employed in its structure.
   Thomas Reid, *An Inquiry into the Human Mind* (1764)

Every being who is conscious of the distinction between right and wrong carries about with him a law which he is bound to observe, notwithstanding he may be in total ignorance of a future state.
   Dugald Stewart, *The Philosophy of the Active Powers and Moral Powers of Man* (1828)

In the middle decades of the nineteenth century, the primary function of Anglo-Canadian educators was to show their students and readers that a properly conducted inquiry into the world of nature, whether physical or human, would reveal the wondrous handiwork of God. One group was of cardinal importance in this endeavour: the men hired by college and university officials to set forth the principles of mental and moral philosophy. Like their religious and scientific colleagues, these colonial philosophers were also given the responsibility of defending Christian orthodoxy and protecting religious values against the erosion that resulted from heterodox intellectual speculation. Theirs was the world of the human mind, theirs the task of outlining for students and the literate Canadian public its structure and functions, its capabilities and limitations.

The basic problem faced by Anglo-Canadian educators during these years was that of establishing the essential relationship between intellectual and moral activity. It fell upon a handful of teachers of philosophy in Canada to turn the minds of Canadian students from the physical world and the world of Scripture to that of their own consciousness in order to establish the relationship between intellect and moral conviction. An understanding of the human mind was an essential link between the study of nature and the vision of God.

Fortunately for those educators, the British Isles had produced a philosophical tradition that suited their needs perfectly. In the creation of academic curricula as well as in other walks of life, Canadians drew heavily upon the Scottish element in their heritage. The country that had given them the thought of Calvin and Knox, Adam Smith and the Mills, had also bequeathed them the legacy of the Scottish "Common Sense" school of philosophy. Offering a philosophical rather than a theological perspective, the school of Thomas Reid, Dugald Stewart, and Sir William Hamilton became a central part of the framework of ideas that dominated Anglo-Canadian thought in the middle of the nineteenth century. The Common Sense philosophy, adapted for use in Canada, sought to establish clearly the natural connection between God and Mind. It, too, aimed at preserving the pious spirit.

The Scottish Legacy

The contribution of Scotland to nineteenth-century Canadian life was immense. A glance through W. J. Rattray's four-volume compendium, *The Scot in British North America* (1880–94), indicates just how pervasive this legacy was.[1] By the 1880s Scotland provided the dominant element in the Canadian business elite. Its influence on higher education was even more profound.[2]

The intellectual aspects of this influence on higher education were of three sorts. First, the Scot brought with him to Canada a general appreciation of the necessity for popular education. To a large extent this was part of his Presbyterian inheritance. Yet it must not, insists an historian of Scottish higher education, be seen as a manifestation of an "exclusive fanatical sectarianism." It was, instead, "a complex of social aspirations, secular as well as religious, which . . . combined metaphysical intellectualism of an anti-empirical sort with a certain measure of democratic sympathies." Moreover, the "democratic intellect" of the Scot, aimed at education, was one which reflected a broad cultural outlook. In the century after the union of Scotland and England in 1707, there developed among many Scots the desire for cultural survival, which, it has been argued, gave the early nineteenth-century Scottish mind much of its dynamism, "an almost religious attachment to [its] inherited ideal of a culture in which the general should take precedence over the particular and the whole over the parts."[3]

The second intellectual influence of Scotland upon Canada derived from the cultural aims of Scottish educationists. A distinguishing characteristic of Scottish education was that in contrast with that of England it was broadly humanistic and highly philosophical. Francis Jeffrey, Lord Rector of Glasgow University and editor of the *Edinburgh Review*, addressed a royal commission in 1826 and defended orthodox Scottish education on the ground that its philosophical nature (accused by the English of being superficial) gave it a cultural value absent in England. "Young men in the Humanity class," he said, "will insist on discussing all the debatable points in history, politics, physics, metaphysics and everything." Furthermore, the Scottish pedagogical tradition, which combined the lecture, catechetical questioning, examinations, and tutorials, furthered both classroom discussion and the metaphysical spirit.[4] These teaching methods, too, were used, along with Scottish textbooks, in Anglo-Canadian classrooms.

The study of philosophy dominated Scottish education. No subject escaped its embrace. It encompassed logic, rhetoric, the physical sciences, mathematics, and the classical subjects. The *classe de philosophie*, as it often was called, had by 1826 become a time-honoured tradition in Scotland, and its preservation in the years that followed against "specialization" and "Anglicization" became a matter of national concern. A broad and humanistic philosophic education was the pride of "metaphysical Scotland." The third aspect of the Scottish influence was therefore a distrust of scholarly specialization that was to continue into the twentieth century.

Yet in the nineteenth century this educational ethos was marked by a double irony. First, it became a significant influence upon Anglo-Canadian university curricula at a time when it was under severe attack in England. Second, mental and moral philosophy were in Scotland a decidedly liberalizing force. In Canada they came to be used to enforce the arguments for Christian orthodoxy. In this respect, Canadian professors used the Scottish philosophy in a manner very similar to that of their colleagues in the United States.

The specific form of philosophy dominant in Scotland in the early nineteenth century was that of Common Sense, a product of the country's own philosophers. It was an exportable commodity. The Anglo-American philosophical community was dominated for the first three-quarters of the century by the Common Sense doctrines first articulated by Thomas Reid (1710–96), the successor to Adam Smith in the chair of moral philosophy at the University of Glasgow; Dugald Stewart (1753–1828), who occupied a similar post at the University of Edinburgh; and Sir William Hamilton (1788–1856), editor of the works of both Reid and Stewart and professor of logic and metaphysics at Edinburgh from 1836 until his death in 1856.

By the 1820s Common Sense had invaded the United States, bringing with it, in the words of one historian of American philosophy, "a significant revolution in the very idea of what constitutes philosophy, as well as instruction."[5] It was, notes another, an "amazingly diverse philosophical conquest."[6] The weapons of conquest were primarily the ideas and assumptions contained in Thomas Reid's *Inquiry into the Human Mind on the Principles of Common Sense* (1764), his *Essays on the Intellectual Powers* (1785) and *Essays on the Active Powers* (1788), as well as Dugald Stewart's treatise *The Philosophy of the Active Powers and Moral Powers of Man* (1828). Using these works for both ideas and inspiration, American philosophers wrote scores of textbooks on moral philosophy during the nineteenth century.[7]

What was the substance of this Scottish philosophy? Why did it appeal to Anglo-American educators for over half a century? The first question may be dealt with by examining briefly the main ideas of Thomas Reid, accurately described by S. E. Ahlstrom as "the archetypical Scottish Philosopher."[8]

Reid wrote his *Inquiry into the Human Mind* as an attempt to combat the philosophical scepticism of David Hume. Building upon Francis Hutcheson's earlier appeal to man's "moral sense," a faculty independent of God or revelation, Reid attempted to refute the theory of ideas set forth first by Locke and carried to its extreme formulation by the inexorable logic of Hume. In place of the Lockean notion of ideas as representative substitutes for an external reality, Reid turned to what might be termed an "empiricism of the mind." His, he claimed, was a "realistic" theory of perception, which appealed directly to the data of consciousness. The great truths of mankind and the little truths of everyday experience, he insisted, were matters of common sense: they rest within "the reach of common understanding." This is why ordinary men's judgements on many matters are of equal weight with those of the trained philosopher. As he expressed this claim in *Intellectual Powers* (essay VI, chap. 4): in "a matter of common sense, every man is no less a competent judge than a mathematician is in a mathematical demonstration."[9]

This internalization of the British empirical tradition, apart from its philosophical subtleties, rested upon an assumption and a process. The assumption, derived from Hutcheson, was that an assessment of the nature of the human mind would show it to be divided into many "senses" or "faculties"—and that these faculties were not simply analytic constructs, but were in fact more or less accurate descriptions of the actual physiology of the mind. As referred to by British and American philosophers influenced by Common Sense, these faculties often varied in name. Always among the faculties of the mind, however, was man's "moral sense" or "moral nature," an innate capacity to arrive at moral truth. Reid divided the faculties into "speculative" and "active" powers, or "understanding" and "will." Sir William Hamilton divided mental phenomena into "knowledge" (cognition), "feeling" (pleasure, pain), and "will" (or desire).[10]

The assumption was that such faculties existed. The process consisted of an appeal to introspection, the observation of the data of one's consciousness, in order to discuss their attributes. Together they constituted perhaps the most significant contribution of the Scottish philosophers to the history of philosophy, for they led philosophy towards psychology.[11] Yet the reason for the influence of Common Sense was not simply the fact that it marked a significant departure in philosophy. Common Sense also served some eminently practical purposes both in Scotland and in North America.

By the time he published his studies of the "intellectual" and "active" powers in the 1780s, Thomas Reid had moved beyond the refutation of Hume's scepticism; by then he was actively engaged in combating materialism, ethical relativism, and other such "errors." In Scotland, Common Sense provided a means of preserving the British empirical tradition (in a transmuted form) without undermining metaphysics. The virtues of Baconian empiricism (then dominant in science) could be extolled, yet the intuitive judgements of the "moral faculty" could at the same time be allowed to prevail. Reason could be trusted as a legitimate power of the mind but it "could not be used to question truths that are self-evident, for which no proof can be demonstrated, truths which should be accepted intuitively."[12] In short, whereas Common Sense began in Scotland as a liberalizing, heterodox movement which potentially could undermine both Grace and revelation, it could also be used as an apologetic philosophy *par excellence*.

Common Sense came to be used in America in just such a way. American educators in the early nineteenth century feared the influence of French "infidelity" and of "experimentation" in the sciences. The Scottish philosophy was safe and sane, and so constituted "an ideal pattern for preventing youth from indulging in speculative extremes." Evangelical churches used the exponents of Common Sense as authorities on the scientific grounds of orthodox morality. "For them," writes Herbert Schneider, "educators like McCosh, who would expound as a reasoned metaphysics the 'first and fundamental truths' of orthodox theology and at the same time showed some sympathy for science, even for evolution, and who would try to meet positivism and agnosticism on their own ground, were a 'revelation' and filled a desperate need."[13] Common Sense "came to exist in America," adds Ahlstrom, ". . . as a vast subterranean influence, a sort of watertable nourishing dogmatics in an age of increasing doubt."[14]

A further characteristic of the school of Common Sense remains to be considered: its dualistic nature. The Scottish philosophy, writes its leading modern expert, "maintained that the principles of common sense, imposed upon us by the constitution of the human mind, are principles by which our cognition is conformed to its objects, to things as they really are in themselves."[15] Aside from indicating again the rejection of Locke's conception of ideas, this statement also points towards the fact that the Scottish philosophers insisted upon a clear and inviolable distinction between subject and object. Such a strong dualism posed certain problems for the articulation of a logically consistent philosophy in the face of certain developments in science in the later nineteenth century; but in the decades preceding the Darwinian epoch, it afforded certain specific benefits.

Reid's theory of knowledge had set the world of consciousness against that which men perceived. This dualism met several socially and intellectually desirable ends. S. E. Ahlstrom sets these forward clearly and forcefully:

> On the mind-matter problem dualism facilitated an all-out attack on both materialism and idealism, as well as the pantheism that either type of monistic analysis could lead to. Furthermore, by a firm separation of the Creator and His creation, the Scottish thinkers preserved the orthodox notion of God's transcendance [*sic*], and made Revelation necessary.

Dualism also made possible a synchronous affirmation of science on one hand, and an identification of the human intellect and the Divine Mind on the other. Scottish philosophers could thus be monotonously consistent in their invocations of Bacon or Newton and at the same time certify those rational processes of man which lead toward natural theology and contemplative piety and away from relativism and romantic excesses.

The Scottish Philosophy, in short, was a winning combination.[16]

In Canada the natural theology taught by Professor James Beaven and Dr. James Bovell in Toronto, the geological science of Principal William Dawson of McGill, and the ethnology and literary criticism of Professor Daniel Wilson at University College, Toronto, shared this dualism of mind and matter, reason and revelation. In each case, the epistemological foundations for that dualism were provided by their acceptance of the major tenets of the Common Sense philosophers. The subject-object dualism, faculty psychology, and the appeal to introspection—three basic elements constituting the basis of the Common Sense philosophy—were meanwhile made a basic part of the Canadian student's elementary assumptions by the teachings of philosophers who, in the mid-nineteenth century, were usually newly arrived in the British North American colonies.

Canadian education was shaped by men who were trained at Scottish universities. Their ideas on education greatly influenced the hiring of professors for Anglo-Canadian colleges, the specific subjects which were taught there, and the content and aims of those subjects. While the many claims for an immense Scottish influence made in the nineteenth century may often have been exercises in filial piety, they were nevertheless fully justified by facts. "There is not a college or university in Canada," Peter Ross wrote in *The Scot in America* (1896), "where at least one 'son of the heather' is not to be found in some capacity, and the entire educational system of the country, from the primary school to the university is more indebted to the Scottish section of the community than to any other."[17]

The university curricula, as developed under the influence of such Scots as Bishop John Strachan of Trinity College, Thomas McCulloch of Pictou Academy, Daniel Wilson of University College, and Thomas Liddell of Queen's, uniformly showed their Scottish orientation by the preeminence afforded to the mental and moral philosophy of the Scottish Common Sense school.[18] Just as William Paley's natural theology was almost universally in use at Anglo-Canadian universities between 1840 and 1870 because it made the crucial connection between a providential design in nature and an "orthodox" science, so Common Sense, without challenging the Paleyite argument, provided the equally important link between the design of the mind and a conservative social ethic. Like late nineteenth-century pragmatism, Common Sense was not so much a technical philosophy as it was a mode of thought. As such, it served the needs of Anglo-Canadian educators for several decades, and its central assumptions maintained a grip on the educated Canadian mind long after it ceased to be taught.

Indeed, by the 1880s it could be claimed that Common Sense was one of the defining characteristics of the Scottish mind in Canada. The Scots' major attribute, said the Presbyterian minister Robert Campbell, was a general "mental hospitality" which made them "citizens of the world." The Scot may appear to others, Campbell admitted, as a person with an "air of rugged independence," with an "assertive self-respect"—characteristics which, in a certain light, might make him appear to be "a narrow bigot, full of conceited prejudices, who is unwilling to be taught." Yet an intimate acquaintance with the Scot would show this "bigotry" to be an intense "inwardness," a capacity which courts truth wherever he might find it. Why is it that he is more open to intellectual currents than others? The answer, Campbell insisted, lay in the influence of Common Sense upon the Scot's way of thinking. A Presbyterian heritage may have aided in making him an inward-looking person, but the Scottish philosophy allowed him to proceed in his thinking at once both objectively and subjectively. "It does rest on facts, but then these facts are gathered to consciousness—are to be discovered by inquiring after the internal operations of the mind itself,—rather than by forming conclusions from its external products."[19]

It is easy to see how, viewed by others, a Scot with such a mental training could be seen as insufferably narrow-minded and full of "conceited prejudices." He could claim that his conclusions accorded with the best empirical science of his day. Did he not gather his "data" from the experiences of everyday life, from the observation of nature, both external and human? Furthermore, if he followed the dictates of his philosophical school, he would set forth his own convictions only after they had been tested by the most demanding, yet most basic, standard of all—by an appeal to his own inner nature which held the capacity to intuit right and wrong. Nathanael Burwash captured this process perfectly in his description of the nature of the liberal arts program at Victoria College in the middle of the nineteenth century. "The course," he said, "was not one to make a specialist, but to gain a broad outlook over the varied fields of human thought, and to give a sound mental training in the use of language, in exact reasoning, in the observation of nature, in the development of the intuitive convictions, especially in morals, and in the deduction of general truth from observed facts in the physical world and in history."[20]

Any examination of nineteenth-century moral philosophy and its influences cannot limit its inquiry solely to "doctrine," for it will fundamentally miss the point of the entire enterprise—which was to instil a general philosophical outlook that could be used in the everyday experience of living. Plato once expressed the central concern of virtually all forms of moral philosophy when he said, "It is no light matter to discuss the course we must follow if we are to live our lives to the best advantage."[21] Hence, this very broad concern must be kept in view when the thought of any philosopher or the doctrine of any specific philosophic school of a hundred years ago or more is assessed in a cultural perspective. The twentieth-century "academic" conception of philosophy as only one discipline among many must be swept from mind, and its place taken by the recognition that before the proliferation of such disciplines, "moral philosophy" took almost all departments of human thought as its compass.

One example will suffice to show the universality of moral philosophy's claims. On 5 May 1853 young Geordie Grant, then eighteen, attended his first moral philosophy class at the University of Glasgow. His professor was William Fleming, given the name "Moral Will" by his earnest, yet occasionally irreverent, students. Some of Grant's first day's notes read as follows:

> Before entering directly upon the subject of Moral Philosophy, it may be advantageous to give you a sort of bird's eye view of the whole, so that you may perceive the extent of the field and the number of subjects which it includes. Let us first attend to the signification of the term philosophy. In Germany and in some parts of France it is used synonymously with our word Metaphysics. This acceptation of the term is finding its way into England and some of the Seminaries of the United States. In the notes it is employed similarly with science, so that Moral Philosophy and Moral Science

are the same. . . . You might here be on your guard against mistaking the term Moral Philosophy. It does not only include what is strictly called morals,—the difference between and origin of Virtue and Vice. Moral comes from *mor* (which has a very wide simplification—manners—the whole of man's life—his experience).

From this basic assumption—that moral philosophy was the equivalent of nothing less than the nature and course of civilized life—"Moral Will" led young Grant and his fellow students through the provinces of knowledge that were the concerns of the moral philosopher. Because it viewed man as an "active being," the course dealt with the source of mental "action." This led to the "exceedingly knotty, abstruse, and also very interesting question" of freedom of the will. Since man, it was assumed, is also a *moral* being, it was necessary to ask "in what morality consists." Consideration of that, said Fleming, "will lead us to the principle that the standard of virtue is the will of the Creator." The question of "the existence of the Deity and the immortality of the Soul" was a logical concomitant of this problem. By the end of the course, attention was to be paid to the consideration of man as a social being (which Grant, significantly, had seen fit to underline twice in his notes), as a member of society. Finally, consideration was to be given to "the steps by which [man] emerged into civilization," through nomadic and agricultural stages, to a point at which he is "resolved to stand, loyally and gratefully one with the mother that gave [him] birth; and what God has joined together let no man nor nation, by wicked ways or words or acts, attempt to put asunder."[22] This concluded "Moral Will"'s introductory lecture on moral philosophy.

James George and the Web of Gossamer

In the autumn of 1853, when George M. Grant was about to enter his second year of training in moral philosophy at the University of Glasgow, Canada's first professor of mental and moral philosophy assumed his academic duties. Earlier Canadian educators, such as Thomas McCulloch, John Strachan, and Egerton Ryerson, had taught the subject at the institutions which they had founded, but the Reverend James George was the first university teacher to hold a specific chair in it. George's various writings, along with those of the Reverend William Lyall (another Presbyterian clergyman), who occupied a chair in philosophy at Dalhousie University a decade later, afford a glimpse into the philosophic enterprise in its formative stages in Canada. In their thought the Common Sense school can be seen in operation as part of what was meant to be the official ethic of mid-Victorian British North America. One can also perceive their belief that "philosophy"—as a discipline in its own right—was an enterprise which potentially could come into conflict with the Christian piety it was meant to nurture.

That ironic possibility of conflict is more apparent to the historian than it was to the nineteenth-century clergyman-philosopher. College courses in moral philosophy all over North America had precisely the opposite purpose. They were intended to accommodate new discoveries to old truths, to relate the life of the mind to the world of business and commerce, and above all to co-ordinate all branches of knowledge. In short, they were "to draw the higher learning together, providing students with what one historian has called a 'unified interpretation of life.'"[23] Accordingly, transcending the denominational differences, intrigues, and squabbles which otherwise so characterized the history of higher education in colonial British North America was the web of moral authority provided by mental and moral philosophy in its Scottish Common Sense form.

The course in theology given at Queen's College in the mid-1840s included, for example, "Lectures on the connection between Moral Philosophy and Christian Theology and particularly on the principles of moral obligation."[24] The arts curriculum at Queen's, as will be seen, was heavily dominated by Common Sense assumptions during the tenure of James George. George's successor, John Clark Murray, came to be critical of the Common Sense tradition, but his students, nevertheless, were well schooled in its tenets. In 1872 Murray moved from Queen's to McGill, and pass students there in second year studied from volume one of Dugald Stewart's *Outlines*. The next year they mastered the second volume. In fourth year they studied Murray's *Outline of Sir William Hamilton's Philosophy*. Texts used by Honours students in their graduating year at McGill included Hamilton's *Discussions* and his *Notes to Reid*, as well as John Stuart Mill's *Examination of Sir William Hamilton's Philosophy*. These were used in the metaphysics course, lectures of which were described in the McGill calendar as dealing with "The Philosophies of Kant and Hamilton." The moral philosophy course included Stewart's *Philosophy of the Active Powers and Moral Powers in Man*.[25]

E. A. Crawley at Acadia College had depended during the 1840s upon the widely used textbook *Elements of Moral Science* (1835) by Francis Wayland.[26] At Victoria College, in Cobourg, philosophic studies were strongly emphasized from the outset. The tradition began under Egerton Ryerson, and continued when the college was under the direction of S. S. Nelles and Nathanael Burwash. There, too, Common Sense held sway in the middle of the nineteenth century. As early as 1844 at Victoria, an observer could write that he had been struck at "the degree to which the students seemed at home in the analysis of Dugald Stewart's 'justly celebrated work.'"[27] Two decades later, Victoria's calendars still contained those long-familiar names and abbreviated titles: "Stewart's Active and Moral Powers"; "Hamilton's Metaphysics." The stated purpose of the curriculum there, built around mental and moral philosophy (required of all students in the second and fourth years), spoke for all curricula in the arts at other Anglo-Canadian colleges. "The Curriculum," noted the calendar, "is constructed on the principle of encouraging a well-balanced and varied culture, and not with the view of stimulating extraordinary proficiency in particular departments."[28]

One could lengthen the list of universities and professors influenced by the Common Sense school, but perhaps sufficient examples have been given. Those teachers of philosophy who had been trained as philosophers tended invariably to work from within the framework of Common Sense; those who had received their academic training in theology, such as James Beaven at the University of Toronto, tended to gravitate towards it.[29] Yet even as they stressed the importance of philosophic reflection in their classrooms, and emphasized the nature and force of moral obligation in their lectures and examinations, they helped unwittingly to give rise to the ironic possibility implicit in the nature of their muse. Philosophic contemplation was a coin the other side of which was the "intellectual anarchy," the critical inquiry, they so dreaded. It would take a disciplined intelligence indeed to maintain the crucial equation of Christian piety and philosophic study while avoiding at the same time an anarchic inquiry into all matters. The network of assumption provided philosophically by Common Sense was unquestionably one that left few North American colleges untouched; but if all-embracing, it was also a deceptively fragile web, gossamer-thin and held together by strands of thought which each day were subjected to the increasing weight of hostile forms of modern inquiry.

Take, for example, the thought of James George, a Christian clergyman engaged in the teaching of philosophy because he had been called upon to do so by the needs of his particular denomination. An emigrant in 1829 from Scotland, where he had attended St. Andrew's and Glasgow universities, George held pastoral charges in Philadelphia and Fort Covington, New York, before moving to British North America in 1834. During the 1830s and 1840s he held charges in Belleville and Scarborough, Upper Canada (later Canada West). Of republican sympathies in his youth, George had been highly critical of the British "governing classes." But by the time of his move to Upper Canada, he (in the words of one of his former students) had "exchanged his early Utopian principles, which he found it necessary from further reading, thought and experience to abandon as impracticable, for a sturdy conservatism and admiration of the British constitution."[30] So much, indeed, had he repudiated his earlier views that during the Upper Canadian rebellion of 1837, it was he who led the "Men of Scarboro" in their march to York to defend Queen and country.

George remained at Scarborough, except for a brief pastoral charge in Belleville, until called in 1853 by the Synod of the Church of Scotland in Canada to assume the chairs of mental and moral philosophy and logic at Queen's College. By that time he already occupied a prominent place both in the church and in the college, having been elected moderator of the synod in 1841 and having been appointed interim professor of systematic theology and divinity at Queen's after Dr. Liddell had resigned from the principalship and professorship of divinity in 1846. Upon moving permanently to Kingston in 1853, George also assumed the vice-principalship of the college. Two years later, at the suggestion of the Scottish divine Norman Macleod, whom George had met in Scotland, he was awarded an honourary Doctorate in Divinity from his alma mater, the University of Glasgow. From 1846, when he first began to lecture in divinity at Queen's (he continued to do so during his tenure there), to 1862, when he resigned to return to pastoral work, virtually every Presbyterian minister trained at Queen's came under his tutelage. Between 1853 and 1862 this was also the case with the students in arts and science.

George was seen as "one of the ablest and most successful" teachers of his day. An admirer of Dr. Thomas Arnold, he, too, left his mark upon those whom he taught. "No student ... ever passed out of his class," wrote the Reverend Robert Campbell, "who did not feel himself more of a man than when he entered. He conducted his pupils into the intricate apartments of their own minds; introducing them to a new region of thought he taught them the response of the Greek oracle, 'know thyself,' so that entering his class was an epoch in their mental history." His approach, Campbell wrote, was not so much to impart theories and facts to his students as to "whet the intellectual powers" and to so qualify them that they could "obtain and assess the significance of information later in their lives." In George's view, giving students "a learned knowledge of other men's notions, which would be of no practical value in life,"[31] was clearly a case of mistaken priorities.

In his classes George imbued his students with the basic tenets of the Common Sense school. Inclining personally towards the views of Thomas Brown, who had gained Dugald Stewart's chair in moral philosophy at Edinburgh with the death of Stewart in 1828, George probably used Brown's *Physiology of the Human Mind* and *Lectures on the Philosophy of the Human Mind* as textbooks. The latter was immensely popular, reaching nineteen editions by the time George had begun to teach philosophy. Even so, George remained wary of close adherence to any specific philosophical system. He distrusted metaphysics and concentrated instead upon psychology. "Intensely earnest in the search after truth," wrote one of his students, "the tracing out of the workings of the Divine Mind in the phenomena of the human one, was to him a most interesting study." The Reverend Robert Campbell, another of George's students, agreed: "The perfection of the Divine nature, and the will proceeding therefrom, was the basis of his system of *Moral Philosophy*."[32]

For this reason one searches in vain for direct references to the Common Sense school in the writings of James George. He was quite simply not concerned with philosophical quibblings. His aim was, rather, to combine the premises of Common Sense with the fundamentals of Christian doctrine to achieve in his students' minds a balance between the pious disposition and intellectual inquiry, and to show that the mental constitution was such that, without the guidance of the former, both mental and social anarchy could result. In George's view, philosophy could not be divorced from Christianity without becoming a useless—and perhaps dangerous—set of sterile propositions.

At first glance it would appear a difficult task to determine just how James George used the Common Sense school to advantage outside the classroom. We know that he drilled his students in its tenets, yet none of his writings refer to Reid, Stewart, or Hamilton, or for that matter make any sort of technical reference to the school. None of his lecture notes exist and he wrote nothing of an academic nature. His thought is mainly embodied in a collection of his sermons, *Thoughts on High Themes* (1874), published after his death in 1870; a book entitled *Sabbath School of the Fireside* (1859); and about a dozen miscellaneous sermons and addresses given for the most part to students of Queen's College between 1853 and 1862. The titles of several of them reflect the fact that George was a clergyman first and foremost: *Christ Crucified* (1837); *On Baptism* (1841); *The Value of Earnestness* (1854); *Moral Courage* (1856); *The Field and the Men For It* (1860). Yet others are of more general interest, for they cross the border from a concern for personal Christian morality to a Christian's social ethics, a shift in focus from religion to culture. On Thanksgiving Sunday in 1838 George preached to his Scarborough congregation a sermon entitled *The Duties of Subjects to Their Rulers*. And in 1859 he aided the Queen's College bursary fund by giving a public lecture entitled *What Is Civilization?* in the Kingston City Hall.

In one of the only studies of the development of philosophy in nineteenth-century Ontario, John Irving examined the thought of James George and drew the attention of the reader to these two excursions by George into the broad area of social and cultural values. As one might expect of the leader of the "Men of Scarboro," one learns from Irving's essay that in 1838 George revered the British constitution, thought it to be the cradle of genuine liberty, and urged his parishioners to "Be on your guard against those new and untried theories, which are now so often put forth, and never put forth . . . without some portion of censure levelled at Great Britain and her institutions." Irving paraphrases George's list, in his 1859 address, of the destructive and constructive tendencies in modern civilization. George saw civilization in the nineteenth century decaying because of "insubordination to law and government; dishonest dealings in the ordinary transactions of life; the growing practice . . . of assassination; and the prevalence of atheism." At the same time, however, four progressive forces outweighed the century's factors of decay: "the triumphs of physical science; the development of world-wide communications; the opening up to Western influences of China, Japan, and other hitherto isolated regions of the world; and the extension of Christianity through the unparalleled missionary efforts of the nineteenth century."[33]

These are adequate descriptions of George's articulation of a conservative social ethic, and similar examples could be found elsewhere in his writings. But they say little, if anything, about the philosophical foundations of that ethic. Only at one point does Irving provide the reader with a glimpse of the web of assumption and conviction that lay beneath George's social attitudes. He quotes from *What Is Civilization?* to put forward George's conception of its essence: "the conscience and intellect of a people thoroughly cultivated, and the intellect in all cases acting under the direction of an enlightened conscience."[34]

Here we have the first signs that certain philosophical assumptions informed George's social vision. Civilization, he said, embodies a particular relationship between conscience and intellect. This would be a simple statement that civilized life consists largely of duty and reasoning power were it not for the fact that the terms "conscience" and "intellect" here have a far broader contextual significance. Placed against the background of the Common Sense school, their use indicates that George had in fact described an association between two faculties of the mind. Man, went the assumptions of faculty psychology in its popular form, was a mental, moral, and spiritual being. Conscience was an operation associated with the moral faculty, as intellect was with the mental and piety with the spiritual. Truly rational, sound, thought was the product of these three faculties functioning in harmony. So it was with whole civilizations.

It was possible for George to bring his understanding of individual psychology to bear on nations and civilizations because he conceived of "a people" and "a civilization" in individualistic terms. "When I speak of the conscience of a people," he wrote, "I mean that of the individual man, for before you can have a public conscience you must have individual responsibility to righteous principles."[35] One's conscience, the instrumentality of the moral faculty, must, of course, be regulated by the will of God. Once men recognized this, they would have no difficulty knowing their proper duties to God, to society, and to themselves:

> Plainly, he who is thoroughly under this heavenly guidance, never can be false in his moral sentiments, or fail in his relative duties. A good moral condition of mind, then, is *the first*, and I will add, the *indispensable* element in the civilization of the individual man. Without this you could no more civilize a man than you could civilize a brute, or a devil. Civilization, then, must begin within or there can be no fruits of it without. A God regulated conscience is that which can alone regulate the passions and appetites, and of course the outward conduct of man.

> I do not say that this is all that is necessary to give that harmony to the mental powers ... which produces and extends civilization. But I do aver that a good conscience is not only first in order to this, but first in importance.[36]

Four brief observations may be made about this passage. First, George insists on the "harmony of the mental powers" as a prerequisite for civilization; second, amongst those powers, that of the moral faculty is primary; third, the conscience must be in harmony with the spiritual faculty and directed by a pious disposition; finally, so guided, a man cannot be deceived by false moral sentiments. George's writings are pervaded with these and related propositions. Together they helped him, in sermons, at convocations, and doubtless in the classroom, give expression and authority to the important tenet of the Common Sense school that man was by his very nature a moral being and could therefore correctly intuit moral laws.

Of particular importance in this regard was the belief that certain laws operated for the moral world much as natural laws did for the physical. Ideas of "moral law" and its extension into the realm of polity, "moral government," were widely prevalent in North America in the middle of the nineteenth century, and were found useful by academic moralists to provide a rational justification for traditional moral standards—for by then the social and theological frameworks of those standards were threatened as never before.[37] The idea of moral law was conceived and expressed in various ways—"a divinely prescribed set of rules ... : a principle of order within man, or nature, or both; or a law of sequence and necessary connection like cause and effect"—but each variation nevertheless offered a unified moral cosmology. "Moral obligation—the argument went—is a natural fact that is evident in our consciousness and implies a moral universe. The universe is moral because it contains moral men and is engineered to serve a moral purpose. Man is moral because he is so created by God. God is moral because he has created and continues to sustain a moral universe."[38]

Throughout the sermons in *Thoughts on High Themes* occur phrases that indicate the wedding in George's thought of Common Sense assumptions and the moral government tradition in Anglo-American theology. He speaks of "the moral conscience with which man is endowed." Man, the sinner, is seen as proof that he can "be a subject of moral government." The reader is told that "the moral law implies far more than mechanical and bodily performance of outward rites" and that the moral law involves "all the duties which, as moral creatures, we owe to God and to our fellow men."[39] In his first address to the students of Queen's, George stated that "man is so emphatically a moral creature, that his happiness, in all his social and civil relationships, is at last found to hinge on his moral and spiritual condition." The moral law and moral government tradition, and the Common Sense view that man could perceive the essential direction of his moral obligations by simple introspection, were twin buttresses propping up the structure of George's social ethic. The recognition of God's moral government also helped him define human rationality. "The rational soul," he noted in an 1853 address to Queen's students, "not only feels the force of moral government and discerns its equity and its benefits, but can see the whole flowing from the Divine mind." He continued:

> This is the peculiar excellence of rational creatures, and in this lie their responsibilities. . . . Hence, to deny the necessity of the moral reign of God is at once to dishonour Him and to sink man down to a creature of mere instincts and physical influences. Thus it is that atheists, while they strip man of his moral responsibilities, always deny him every hope of a future existence. Whatever, therefore weakens our notions of the moral reign of God is to the last degree pernicious.[40]

One element in the mind constituted such a pernicious threat: the intellect.

Intellect divorced from a true Christian piety, like reason divorced from the gift of Divine revelation, was at best only a half-blind wanderer in search of truth. At worst, it could become a positive evil:

> [For] . . . if the intellect be severed from God, and the heart in opposition to Him, the mind can give forth nothing but mere coruscations of light, which rather bewilder than guide, and are sure to land us at last in some disastrous folly. Unsanctified genius lives on the edge of madness, and may drive the world mad. For what, in truth, is the highest intellectual power without piety, but a Satanic light, leading in the end to the darkness of the pit. Real piety, we repeat, is the believing knowledge of the true God.[41]

The fact that this stern admonition was part of a long address that opened a session of Queen's College indicates the high degree of importance George gave to the subject. In that 1855 address, entitled *The Relation Between Piety and Intellectual Labor*, George sought to make students absolutely aware of the relationship between those two forms of mental activity. "My object," went his opening words, ". . . is to point out the connection betwixt a healthy piety and the cultivation of the intellect," and to remind students that in their "blind enthusiasm for learning" they risked "overlooking the relation which God has established betwixt body and mind."[42]

Here the gossamer web was at its thinnest. The very fact that George felt it necessary to give his address was an indication of that. The framework of the Common Sense school was based upon a rigid dualism between the material and the spiritual, and the psychology of the school depended upon the inviolability of that dualism. Yet while the dualism seemed to imply that the physical and moral (or spiritual) worlds were coequal, the insistence that the universe was fundamentally moral seemed also to imply that the moral law must prevail. Even in a small Loyalist town like Kingston in the middle of the nineteenth century, however, signs could be seen that the inheritors of this frame of mind, which consisted at once of an epistemological dualism and moral monism, had assumed a defensive posture.

Even then, and even in Kingston, Canada West, the "relation which God [had] established between body and mind" was not as clear as it once had been. George's first address to the academic community at Queen's had been given against this background. The fact that man is not born with perfect mental powers and must aspire to excellence is a sign, he had insisted in 1853, "that he . . . is placed under moral, rather than physical laws."[43] And since most of the students at Queen's looked forward to "the task of instructing . . . the minds of their fellow men" in one walk of life or another, whether as clergymen, politicians, or lawyers, it was imperative that they remember that this must above all be a moral instruction. While this, the scholar's noblest employment, could never be an easy task, the responsibility was particularly difficult to bear in the modern age:

> To him who studies the spirit of the times—and no man can serve his day and generation who does not—it must be apparent that this is every hour becoming a more difficult and more responsible task. . . . For under the influence of *active*

thought, all things are now moving with new and amazing velocity, while a feverish and most unhealthy state of the passions pervades every fibre of society.[44]

It was on one hand a time of hope and wonder, for progress in the physical sciences and the "amazing triumphs of mind in detecting and applying the laws of nature" had brought wonderful benefits to the commonest of people. Yet man, he reminded his students, is overwhelmingly a moral and spiritual creature. The great risk of the age, therefore, was that the multitudinous benefits derived from science might seduce one into elevating the intellectual labour needed by science above the moral and spiritual ends of all thought and action:

> The truth is, if man be not taught the relation in which he stands to his God, and what, as an accountable creature, he owes to Him, and what he owes of relative duties to his fellow-creatures, . . . his attainments in physical science, with all that he may have extracted from material nature by its aid, will utterly fail to make him happy. The intense activity which these discoveries have infused into every department in society *renders a very high order of moral guidance especially needful*. But you are now preparing to be intellectual and spiritual guides in a world in which all things are moving with a velocity which awakens astonishment not unmingled with fear. . . . For, very plainly, without the morale, all that we may amass of *the materiale* will prove a curse and not a blessing.
>
> What could it avail a country to have scientific chemists, engineers, and ingenious artists, if the common schoolroom, the bar, the bench, and the pulpit were occupied by selfish, vain, and unprincipled men? Even the wealth of a people is doomed to perish, if not under the safeguard of a healthy morality. The world cannot learn too soon, what it should have learnt from the first, that if men disown the moral government of GOD, the laws of his physical universe will not obey them for good, but war against them for evil, until they are destroyed by the instruments they have unpiously wrought with, and the benefits which they have ungratefully abused. Let there be a true faith in GOD, *and then faith in nature* cannot be misplaced. But the error, or rather the atheism of our times is to look to nature, or the successful

triumphs of physical science over nature, for all that man needs to make him happy. You will require to study this well to be able to see the relation in which man must stand to GOD in order to be in harmony with the laws of nature, so that modern inventions shall minister to his good.[45]

Such a study involved not only a recognition of the "false achievements of reason," but also an understanding of the drastic changes in social institutions and values—an erosion of the spirit—that characterized the age.

Recognition of the ability "to distinguish betwixt the precious and the vile," to know "what to preserve as of lasting worth," as George put it, was a capacity that, however important, would be developed necessarily and only after students were thoroughly grounded in the structure and functions of the mind and its faculties, and imbued with the correct form of reasoning that would result from that study. That was the ultimate responsibility of the mental and moral philosopher, as far as James George was concerned. "Intellectual labor" was both desirable and necessary, but it must not be allowed to lead to forms of speculation which questioned or denied "all first principles in morals and politics." To do so was to undermine the "unquestioning faith" in the moral government of the Author of those principles, to question the tripartite harmony of the faculties of the mind, and to abandon fixed moral principles for a life of "temporary expediency."[46] The very existence of society depended upon men whose "high intellectual powers" were properly guided by the pious disposition. George had long made this proposition central to his pulpit sermons. "Nothing is farther from my mind than to cast any disparagement on such labours," he had told his congregation in 1837 when referring to intellectual activity. "When sanctified— when viewed as the means to an end, and that end the knowledge of Christ, in his office and person, they become eminently beneficial."[47]

Eighteen years later, when George spoke to the students of Queen's College in his address *The Relation Between Piety and Intellectual Labor*, he was therefore giving them a lecture on what he considered to be the key to their mental lives. Meanwhile, another colonial philosopher, a thousand miles to the east, also attempted to teach his students the proper relationship between Christian piety and intellectual activity. For William Lyall, too, this was the most crucial consideration of the day.

William Lyall: *Intellect, the Emotions, and Man's Moral Nature*
In 1863, a year after James George retired from teaching, Dalhousie University in Halifax opened its doors, which had been shut for twenty years. Its new principal was the Reverend James Ross, a graduate of Thomas McCulloch's academy at Pictou. Ross, the founder of West River Theological Seminary (later to become Pine Hill Divinity School), was a disciple of the Common Sense school of philosophy. Under him, Dalhousie University became the centre in the Maritimes from which the influence of Common Sense radiated. Texts used by Dalhousie undergraduates during Ross's tenure as principal included those by Reid, Stewart, Hamilton, and the French philosopher and historian Victor Cousin. But in 1863 Dalhousie could boast that its students also used a text in moral philosophy written by one of its own professors. The book was *Intellect, the Emotions, and Man's Moral Nature*, written in 1855 by the Reverend William Lyall.

The thought of William Lyall shows much in common with that of James George. Philosophy, for both, was of significance only insofar as it was infused with the spirit of the Christian Revelation; philosophical principles were true only inasmuch as they pointed towards the unquestionable reality of that Revelation. Yet in other ways Lyall and George mark different stages in the history of the philosophic endeavour in Canada. George was a clergyman who had been called upon to teach philosophy; Lyall was a philosopher who happened to have been ordained. Lyall's was a more specialized and professional approach to the study of philosophy, and his writings contain references to specific philosophers and schools of thought.

By the time he joined the staff at Dalhousie, William Lyall was already an experienced teacher of philosophy. Born in 1811 at Paisley, Scotland, Lyall had studied theology and philosophy at Glasgow University and Edinburgh University. An emigrant from Scotland in 1848, he joined the staff of Knox College as a tutor, and two years later he moved to Halifax to occupy the chair of classics and mental philosophy in the Free Church College. There he remained for the next ten years. In 1860, when the Free Church and the United Presbyterian church combined to form a collegiate in Truro, Lyall was transferred. Three years later, upon the reorganization and opening of Dalhousie, he was asked by Principal Ross to assume the chair of logic and psychology. It was a position held until his death, twenty-seven years later, in 1890.[48]

An obituary of Dr. Lyall (he was given an honourary Doctorate of Laws from McGill University in 1864), which appeared in the *Dalhousie Gazette*, suggested that he, like George, viewed "philosophy" in the broadest possible sense:

> In philosophy, Dr. Lyall inclined to the Scottish school: never left the firm ground of experience to accompany in their wanderings, the Metaphysicians who, with airy tread pursue the *Ding-ansich* [sic]. Accordingly his Philosophy was not *Vocabular* Philosophy: but an intelligible view of man in his relation to the Universe—and this, even if you didn't agree with his postulates. If he may have had somewhat of prejudice against some modern types of Philosophy (Spencer and Darwin) probably this was a "failing that leaned to virtue's side." Hundreds of his old students will be ready to confess the philosophical impulse which his lectures gave them, and the caution and moderation with which he taught them to form and express their opinions; for he taught as if Philosophy were the one thing needful for the life that now is and for that which is to come.[49]

Of Lyall's opposition to certain "modern types of Philosophy" more will be said later; for the moment it is necessary to consider the nature of his commitment to the tenets of the Common Sense school. The writer of the obituary was certainly correct in stressing Lyall's adherence to the tradition of Reid, but he might have said more on the matter. Lyall was a strong intuitionist, and he opposed developments in the Scottish philosophy that pointed it towards the analytical psychology later represented in the work of Alexander Bain and John Stuart Mill. A key figure in this transition had been Thomas Brown, whose *Inquiry into the Relation of Cause and Effect* (1818) attempted to reconcile the writings of David Hume with Christian teachings and who, while remaining an intuitionist, nevertheless refused to accept the view that the mind consisted of separate "faculties."[50] Lyall's earliest philosophical work, written in 1842 while he was a preacher in Uphall, Linlithgow, was a long attack on Brown and Hume.[51]

Lyall's essay dealt with Brown's conception of the idea of "power," the cause-effect relationship. Brown, following Hume, had argued that power had to be conceived solely in terms of a sequential relationship or succession in time; nothing more could be implied. No metaphysical characteristics were inherent in the cause-effect relationship. As Brown had stated: "There are not substances, therefore, and also powers or qualities, but substances alone."[52] This seemed to some Christian observers to call into question the whole of Christian teleology. How could there have been a Divine Purpose at work in the universe when the ideas of "cause" and "effect" were denied purposive direction? For Lyall, the idea of power was meaningful only when connected with the argument for the existence of the Divine Creator. Furthermore,

> Such a doctrine as that of sequence must cloud and darken every subject with which it is connected, introduce hesitation, and almost scepticism into the mind, where a more rational belief would have afforded secure ground for the farther persuasions or convictions of the understanding. We have seen no reason to renounce the belief of Power.... It is rash, we again repeat, unphilosophical, and fraught with peril, to call into question any of our fundamental notions or convictions. It is the way to prepare the mind for all "sceptical doubts"; and we see in Hume, the impugner of power, the example of one, who either was, or professed to be, dissatisfied with any information the mind gave us of the most fundamental and necessary beliefs.[53]

Once the purposive power of God was denied, Lyall went on, it was but a short step to the denial that there was a God at all. There could then be no "Providence," no "future state"; they would be seen simply as figments of the imagination.

Lyall had a simple refutation of the argument of Hume and Brown, and it was based upon the two fundaments of the Common Sense school: an appeal to introspection, to the data of one's consciousness (based on a belief in the validity of the intuitive process as a means of knowing); and belief in a faculty psychology. Certain ideas, went the appeal to introspection, arose naturally within the mind. "Power" was one of these, and it was not necessary to observe external circumstances in order to comprehend it. "It has long been received as sufficient in philosophy for our belief in the external world, that we have that belief," Lyall wrote. "Our ultimate convictions or feelings are what we have to retire upon in all the fundamental and important points of belief and conduct."[54] Brown himself had claimed that the belief in the relation of sequence was intuitive. Why, then, deny that the idea of "power" itself could be conceived by the same introspective process?

Here was one of the great advantages of the Common Sense

school as a means of preventing the questioning of eternal principles. In the name of rational inquiry, it could justify a cessation of the quest for rationalistic understanding. "The idea of power," Lyall wrote, "is not so much an idea, as a belief; or, like all our simple and elementary ideas, it is one not to be explained." Earlier in the essay he had said: "It is not necessary, then, we contend, to tell what power is, distinct from the substance; our knowledge of it is the idea we have of it, suggested by the contemplation of nature's changes; and to conceive of it farther is not required." It was necessary only to rely on the ability of the mind to comprehend the essential truth of such a basic idea as power by use of the faculties of the mind working in harmony. Only then could the observer note of power what had escaped the attention of Hume and Brown: that power involved the will of God working in the material world and that matter "was a thing which God could not do without, for the purposes of creation, and therefore he created it." "It is not so absurd," Lyall went on, "to suppose ... that the will of Deity is every thing, and that matter produces its effects, not from any possessed or inherent powers or efficiencies, but by the will of God interposing ... at all times, and in every spot, pervading the vast mechanism, and working out the stupendous, the minutest results."[55]

Thirteen years separated the publication of Lyall's *Strictures on the Idea of Power* and his treatise *Intellect, the Emotions, and Man's Moral Nature* (1855), a ponderous tome of 627 pages. In that interval, certain of Brown's ideas had taken strong hold upon Lyall's mind, particularly Brown's dismissal of faculty psychology. Here was another point at which the gossamer web was wearing thin. Travelling phrenologists continued as late as the 1860s to fascinate large audiences in British North America with often sensational visual presentations which assumed the reality of the faculties,[56] but the philosophical basis of faculty psychology was by then being eroded. Thomas Brown played no small part in that process, and Lyall's *Intellect, the Emotions, and Man's Moral Nature* is a good example of the confusion that could result.

The rhetoric of belief in the reality of the faculties had been present in Lyall's 1842 *Strictures* on Brown. He had spoken there of "our faculties of inquiry," "our faculties of observation," and "the reasoning or judging faculty."[57] The very division of man's mental capacities into separate intellectual, emotional, and moral realms in his book is further evidence that he believed in some way in the idea of faculties. Yet by the mid-nineteenth century exponents of faculty psychology had created a veritable bureaucracy of the mind: as well as the traditional tripartite division indicated by the title of Lyall's book, there were now what seemed like myriads of subordinate "faculties." In the realm of the intellect alone, this philosophical division of labour had produced faculties responsible for memory, conception, imagination, abstraction, judgement, and reasoning. Moreover, each philosopher had his own set of labels. By 1855 Lyall had become convinced that the unity sought by philosophy was in fact hindered by this compartmentalization. "The laws of mind underlie all philosophy," he wrote in the introduction to his book, "and it is its formative processes that put its laws even upon matter. A few original ideas are the roots of all science."[58] Although a glance at the detailed table of contents for his book might suggest at first that few books could conceivably have broken down the structure and functions of the mind into more compartments or assign to them more labels, in fact Lyall was attempting to show the way certain "original ideas" threaded themselves throughout the parts of the mind. He was not entirely successful.

Lyall's intuitionism helped him explain how ideas are arrived at. Yet he was also actively engaged in a search for the laws of the mind which would unify the whole range of mental activity. Hence, following Brown, he discounted the "supposed faculties" of the mind. "Our ideas, and their various modifications, then—and these capable of following, or inevitably following, each other in a certain order of connexion—give us the whole of the mental phenomena; *the laws or principles by which the ideas are at first obtained, and are afterwards modified, and follow in trains*, being supposed. We can thus account for all the faculties." The villain was not now Brown, but Dugald Stewart, for it had largely been he who conjured up the many "faculties," thereby needlessly complicating conceptions of the mental process. "It is the supposition of faculties which has occasioned those minute distinctions which have been drawn between one faculty and another, or in order to keep the province of one faculty separate from that of another. Discard the notion of faculties, and what have we but ideas passing through the mind, or the mind existing in states, called ideas, according to certain laws or characteristics of mind?"[59]

Yet the very structure of Lyall's treatise, divided into separate sections on the philosophies of the intellect, emotions, and moral nature, indicates that he had not entirely discarded this compartmentalization of the mind. Intellectually, he recognized that much of Brown's argument was well taken. The title of Brown's book, *The Physiology of the Human Mind*, had pointed in one direction in which philosophers might go in order to explain the "laws" of mind without recourse to faculties, and physiologists such as Karl Vogt were advancing the frontiers of physiological psychology in the 1840s and 1850s. But Lyall proved incapable of making such a transition. A critic of the multiplicity of faculties he may have been, but his thought remained rooted in the Common Sense tradition. His treatise began with a commitment to the inviolable dualism of mind and matter, the spiritual and the material:

> We call attention to this distinction as a fundamental one in philosophy, 1st, as marking its two grand provinces . . . and 2dly, as furnishing the characteristic of two separate tendencies, according to which more or less of the phenomena which we ascribe to mind is assigned to matter, or matter is excluded, and all is assigned to mind—the only true system in philosophy, being one which allows a real existence to both provinces or departments, assigning to matter all that appertains to it, and to mind all that appertains to it.[60]

So long as Lyall held such a view, it would have been impossible for him to look to physiologists for the key to the laws of mind. This dualism dictated, too, that he could not wholly jettison the idea of faculties.

In the end he did not. "Our faculties have all an absolute character," he wrote in *Intellect, the Emotions, and Man's Moral Nature*, "created in the image of God, and their grand design was, besides being an end in themselves, that God's glory may be reflected in them."[61] Lyall had discarded functional faculties (imagination, abstraction, judgement, etc.), but he remained firmly committed to a mechanistic, structural conception of mind. Mind was by nature a tripartite entity, and the intellect, the emotions, and the moral nature of man, when acting in harmony, reflected God's glory because they embodied rational intelligence infused with moral law.

If the idea of moral law were accepted, this all made sense; if not, the result was a welter of contradiction. Lyall's book was used at Dalhousie until 1890, and for some years also at other colleges. One can only wonder how many puzzled brows and scratched crowns of the head there might have been in university residences when passages such as the following were read—and probably re-read:

> What is so admirable in our spiritual being or constitution, is the mutual dependence of the different parts, or the mutual action between these parts, the influence which the one has upon the other—the sensational upon the intellectual—the intellectual again upon the sensational—giving its forms to it, the intellectual upon the emotional, the moral, and the spiritual, and these again upon the intellectual, and upon one another. But as distinct as the boundary is between the sensational and the intellectual, it is scarcely more so than that between the intellectual and the emotional part of our being, while there is an entirely distinct element again in the moral, and still an additional element in the spiritual, though this and the moral element are very nearly allied, if they are not altogether. That the moral is also emotional, there can be no question, and we know how much of this latter element enters into our spiritual nature; but there is a department purely emotional, in which there is nothing that is either moral, or in the sense spiritual.[62]

How many dormitory arguments began over the meaning of passages such as this? How often was it asked whether faculties existed or not? For that matter, how often was the silent but nagging question posed as to whether such passages as this should be considered gospel or gibberish?

Dalhousie's undergraduates, however, could not have failed to grasp certain lessons in mental priority. They were identical with those learned at the same time by James George's students at Queen's. Man was not only an intellectual being. "Pure intellect," Lyall warned, "unconnected with feeling, would be a very curious object of contemplation." Much attention had been paid in his book to qualities of the intellectual nature, so to guard against an undue elevation of the role of intellect he began his discussion of the philosophy of the emotions with the following caveat: "The spiritual constitution of man is composed of more than a merely intellectual provision or apparatus; the intellectual is but a part of his compound being, and not the most important part.... The intellectual part of our nature is a surpassing mystery... but marvellous as this is there are mysteries of our nature far greater than these, and the intellectual part may be said to be the least wonderful [aspect] of our compound being." It is not known whether *Intellect, the Emotions, and Man's Moral Nature* was ever seen by James George. Yet passages from it such as the following would clearly have met with his entire approval:

> There is a danger of the intellectual acquirements displacing the due cultivation of the heart, of the feelings. . . . It is by his emotions that the intellectual being becomes the being of action, and of dignified, and amiable, and lively feeling, that we find him. Otherwise, he would be incapable of forming into society; or, at all events, that were a strange congregation . . . which the world would present, when intellect was all, and feeling was entirely absent,—no loves, no hatreds, no sympathy, no wonder, no fear, but the cold ray of mind enlightening, guiding, directing, actuating. Man is not so constituted. He is not all intellect merely. . . . There is an atmosphere in the mind as well as a light.[63]

Fear of the intellect was a very important common element in the thought of James George, the clergyman as philosopher, and William Lyall, the philosopher as clergyman.

There were other beliefs held in common. One was their piety and, as important, the role ascribed to it in the realm of the mind. George's 1855 address, *The Relation Between Piety and Intellectual Labor*, and Lyall's book of the same year cannot fully be understood apart from their common theological commitment. Man was, after all, a fallen creature, and sin the simple reason why his faculties—which reflect his corporeal needs and his moral nature—so often work inharmoniously. It had not been so before the Fall. "God arranged our compound nature," George told his students, "and when he beheld it at first, all was very good. But the whole nature of man is now deranged: all has gone into frightful confusion." He continued:

> Sin hath made the derangement. Had the mind of man remained in harmony with God, all his powers would have wrought harmoniously together, while he himself would have continued in harmony with all the Divine dispensations. . . . It is not to be questioned, that when man came from the hand of God, his mind apprehended truth readily; his memory retained it accurately; his reason saw its nice relation; while the passions were moved by right motives, and the appetites were under the guidance of reason in administering to the body. There was then perfect harmony among all the powers. But sin hath deranged all.[64]

Intellect, the Emotions, and Man's Moral Nature made the same point in the discussion of the emotional life[65] as did *The Philos-*

ophy of Thought, a lecture Lyall delivered at the opening session of the Free Church College in 1853. "It may be fairly made a question," he said, "... whether, if the world had continued in its state of primitive innocence; had there been no apostasy; if man had not wandered from his God; there would have been problems of human intellect to solve." He continued:

> For, what are these problems, or what is all philosophy, but the gropings of the human mind after truths which would have been the common attainment, or familiar possession, of a state of innocence? Room, no doubt, would have been left for the excursions of intellect, and the wanderings of fancy. ... But instead of beginning where human intellect now commences, the mind would have been in the possession of all those truths of a moral and spiritual kind at least, which philosophy vainly struggled to attain, which may be discerned by the intellect, but before it could discern or perceive which, it would seem, the light of revelation was necessary to purge the intellectual vision.[66]

What a powerful imperative this was to add to the Scottish philosophy! The search for harmony between the faculties of the human mind, both George and Lyall proclaimed, could not be separated from the Christian's search for union with the mind of God. "Now piety," said George, "by bringing the soul into union with God, brings it at once under the influence of motives, which will rightly affect your minds in all the circumstances in which you can be placed." This, he insisted, was the highest form of reasoning; through it, one could not fail to arrive at moral certainty.[67] Lyall, meanwhile, reminded his students that philosophy involved a study of the works and laws of God, just as in the sciences. When studying the workings of the human mind, he said, "we are seeing the mind of God. We see the system of his operation. *We see the laws of all mind*. ... We enter into the spiritual arcana. ... Intellectual law and moral law, unfold themselves."[68]

The Apogee of Common Sense

The decades of the 1850s and 1860s marked the peak of the influence of the Scottish Common Sense philosophy upon the Anglo-Canadian mind. Virtually all professors of philosophy at English-speaking universities had been educated within the Common Sense tradition. Textbooks based upon the Scottish philosophy continued to be used. University examinations on the thought of the founders of the school continued to be given, at one institution as late as 1890.[69] The school of Reid and Stewart, by the 1870s, had become the philosophical pentateuch from which an Anglo-Canadian public ethic, based upon the balanced union of moral conviction and intellectual acumen, was to be built. "Civilization has ever sprung from morality," James George had written, "and . . . a people becomes great and civilized just in proportion as they are intellectually moral and morally intellectual. It is in the combination of these two forces, morality and reason, that the inner power of civilization resides."[70]

It was not, at least in potential, a narrow vision. It was not meant to create citizens of a nation, but defenders of a conception of civilization. The expanding power of British imperial might, the emergence of British North America from colonial to national status within the empire, and the expansive zeal of Christian missionary enterprise in the second half of the nineteenth century lent substantive meaning to this variant of the moral imperative in Anglo-Canadian thought. For men such as Lyall and George, Common Sense, in one form or another, served as a viable philosophy of life. It was their duty to share it with others, to make it the basis of a public ethic.

It was one thing to hold a philosophy of life from the wellsprings of conviction, as did the colonial philosophers; it was quite another to hold that one *ought* to believe in the truth of a philosophical system because it fostered piety, combated intellectual infidelity, and upheld the standards of civilization—in short, because it was the proper thing to do. Nevertheless, to an extent Common Sense became such an ethic—even though its importance may have been proclaimed by a lay public motivated as much by the recognition that it ought to believe in that ethic as by belief itself. By the 1860s it had reached beyond the confines of English-Canadian universities and penetrated somewhat into the public imagination. By then, heterodox thought in numerous forms was ascendant, and the Scottish philosophical tradition was often invoked by religious authorities to check the rise of Darwinian evolutionism, rationalistic infidelity, and materialistic science. It had, by then, become as much an authority to be invoked for the cause of orthodoxy as it was a philosophy to be understood in order to reshape the human condition.

Two nineteenth-century Scottish philosophers were sacrosanct in this regard. One was James McCosh, who immigrated in 1868 to Princeton, New Jersey, in order to accept the presidency of Princeton College and to uphold the Common Sense tradition in

North America. In him, the Scottish school reached something of a culmination, for his thought, an historian of philosophy in America once wrote, represented "perhaps the most articulate summary of American academic philosophy in the first three-quarters of the century."[71] McCosh became the philosophical patron saint of the *Christian Guardian*, Canadian Methodism's official journal, during the 1860s and 1870s. His books were praised; his speeches were noted at length; his warnings (for example, about free thought) were heeded; his defence of order in creation was reprinted, as was his declaration of the limitations of rational understanding in the comprehension of truth. The *Guardian* urged that his study *The Intuitions of the Mind* should find a place at Canadian universities. His thought was invoked as an antidote to the various heresies of mid-nineteenth-century science.[72]

The second philosophical figure invoked to give authority to the dictates of Common Sense was Sir William Hamilton, the major intellectual heir of Stewart and Reid, editor of their writings, and commonly regarded as the most widely read man in nineteenth-century Great Britain. "In the Universities and Churches of this country [Canada], the name of no modern teacher of mental science is more familiar than that of Sir William Hamilton" began an 1880 article on the Scottish philosopher.[73] Hamilton's writings, too, were used by the Christian press in Canada to defend basic religious tenets and to combat materialistic science. Hamilton's philosophy reaffirmed the reality and importance of a world of conscious intelligence in which man exerted a "moral power" because he was the creation of the "Moral Governor of the Universe." He insisted that "the universe is governed not merely by physical but by moral laws." Man, he declared, can transcend "the chain of physical necessity" because he is conscious of the reality of "prescriptive principles of action, absolute and universal, in the Law of Duty." It was this "rule of duty," Hamilton stated, which defined the character of man as a free moral agent.[74]

In this way, through the Scottish Common Sense tradition, the Anglo-Canadian mind was first introduced to Kant's "categorical imperative." Hamilton had been the first of the Scottish philosophers to give detailed consideration to the Kantian tradition, and while many Anglo-Canadians looked askance at German philosophy in the second half of the nineteenth century, the idea of a law of duty was something they could understand as complementary to their own philosophic and cultural tradition. It was a

German idea to which they could warm, and did, in the age of Rhodes and Kipling.

Other aspects of Sir William's thought were drawn upon by Anglo-Canadians to suit their needs. In one of her "Holiday Musings of a Worker," Mrs. Holiwell sought to justify the integrity of the poetic frame of mind against the criticisms of a utilitarian and analytic age. To do so, she invoked a simplistic version of Hamilton's "philosophy of the unconditioned," which asserted, in John Passmore's words, "that although we are directly conscious of independently existing qualities of mind and matter, we have no direct acquaintance with mind-in-itself or matter-in-itself; we know things only as they are related to our experience of them." Since the mysteries of science, the areas open for analysis, said Mrs. Holiwell, were so vast, the greatest scientist could experience the feeling of scientific mastery no more than could the rudest mechanic when he wondered "if the end and aim of human life is to work iron or spin cotton." She added:

> Sir William Hamilton says, finely, on this subject: The highest reach of human science is the scientific recognition of human ignorance. . . . This learned ignorance is the rational conviction by the human mind of its inability to transcend certain limits; it is the knowledge of ourselves—disproportion between what is to be known, and our faculties of knowing—the disproportion, to wit, between the infinite and the finite. In fact, the recognition of human ignorance, is not only the one highest, but the one true, knowledge; and its first fruit is humility.

Having thus limited the reaches of the cognitive aspect of mind, Mrs. Holiwell then stressed the infinite capacity of poetic fancy. The poetic dreamer, she concluded, found "no ambition beyond his ken; no fortitude or love exceeding his belief."[75]

Hamilton's conclusions on epistemology could therefore be used to reinforce the tendency of the Common Sense tradition to subordinate intellectual inquiry to the dictates of piety. It gave authority to a passive conception of mind and to the view that since the mind had definite weaknesses and limitations critical inquiry must necessarily be limited. Hamilton's writings on logic were used in a not unrelated way. In 1870 the Reverend S. S. Nelles, professor of logic and principal at Victoria College, published an edition of Hamilton's lectures on logic, and was thanked by the *Christian Guardian* for his contribution to the "progress of truth" in so doing. The book, added the *Guardian*, would doubtless be of great advantage to "young ministers" as well as formal students of logic. The closing words of Nelles's preface were quoted to prove the reviewer's contention:

> We live in times remarkable for the awakening and emancipation of thought. This is [a] matter of rejoicing; but freedom of thought brings corresponding dangers and responsibilities, and we cannot do too much to aid the inquiring multitudes in the proper use of that right of private judgment of which we are so justly proud. Works like the one here presented may serve to show that all intellectual activity has its laws, the violation of which brings invariable and heavy penalties; may teach us to beware of the immoralities of the intellect; may put those who are trying to think, in the way of thinking soundly, by furnishing them with the best rules and cautions known to the world's great thinkers; and may help us forward to that "good time coming," when in moral, political, and religious affairs, men shall proceed with something like the steadiness, precision, and certainty, which have already begun to mark the pursuit of mathematical and physical science.[76]

By 1870 Common Sense in Canada neared both the peak of its influence and the height of its vulnerability. William Lyall continued to instil in his students the assumptions of the school, and would continue to do so until his death in 1890. James George, who died in 1870, had been replaced eight years earlier by a leading student of Sir William Hamilton. For a decade that student, Clark Murray, taught mental and moral philosophy at Queen's College, and when he was asked by Principal William Dawson of McGill to teach there, it was expected that he would uphold the traditions of both Common Sense and orthodox Christianity. Little did Dawson then realize how much difficulty he would have in keeping Murray in line on these and other matters. In Toronto, another philosopher with impeccable Scottish credentials as an upholder of Christian orthodoxy was beginning by the 1870s to make his influence felt. George Paxton Young had been professor of divinity at Knox College from 1853 to 1863; for the next four years he was the provincial inspector of grammar schools, shortly after which he accepted the professorship of metaphysics and ethics at University College, Toronto. But Young, like Murray, was not to escape the intellectual and spiritual transitions of his age. In 1864, beset with spiritual problems, he resigned from the Presbyterian ministry as well as from his post at Knox. When he returned to the lectern in a different capacity in the 1870s, he taught a brand of philosophy significantly different from that of the Common Sense tradition in which he had been reared.

By the 1870s Common Sense had become a fragile creed for the defence of orthodoxy in thought and faith. James McCosh was quoted often and at length in the *Christian Guardian*, but as he himself observed in his 1875 preface to *The Scottish Philosophy*, "The English-speaking public, British and American, has of late been listening to diverse forms of philosophy—to Coleridge, to Kant, to Cousin, to Hegel, to Comte, to Berkeley,—and is now inclined to a materialistic psychology. Not finding permanent satisfaction in any of these, it is surely possible that it may grant a hearing to the sober philosophy of Scotland."[77] By 1875 McCosh's philosophical stance was a defensive one, as he searched for ways in which to make his creed consistent with evolutionary theory without undermining Revelation. By sheer weight of reputation Sir William Hamilton continued to be cited by students for authority and profundity of thought,[78] but at least one observant Anglo-Canadian could state as early as 1873 that the metaphysical system erected by Hamilton "on the ruins of that of Brown" had "been shattered by the merciless artillery of Mr. Mill" in his *Examination of Sir William Hamilton* (1865).[79]

The ultimate judgement placed upon the Scottish Common Sense philosophy in Canada was perhaps given in 1895 when Professor F. Tracy published an article, "The Scottish Philosophy," in the *University of Toronto Quarterly*. Summing up the capacity of the school to withstand the barrage of questions posed by the age of Darwin and Huxley, Tracy wrote that "however sincere their purpose, and however great their ability, they have not succeeded in . . . solving the epistemological enigma which has puzzled all modern philosophy. The question: How does mind know its object? and, what is the relation in which mind stands to the material world? are left almost where they were before."[80]

That, however, was the judgement of a later age. In 1870 Common Sense was the philosophical orthodoxy in British North America, and it was by no means certain that it would not prove sufficient to meet the challenges of evolutionary science. Regardless of weaknesses in Scottish philosophers' arguments, despite the contradiction between the idea of mental faculties and the implications for "mind" of the discovery of a central nervous system of which the brain was part, the moral philosophers in the mid-nineteenth century still held one trump card. Canadian academic moralists, like their American counterparts, were ultimately not deeply concerned with the intricacies of moral philosophy considered as a system. Some, like James George, believed that such systems could solve no fundamental human problem.[81] "Their real concern," an American historian, D. H. Meyer, states, "was to re-establish the connection between man and God's law. And this connection need not be a strictly logical one—for the law of God is directed at man as a totality, and not only at his reason."[82] The impulse to piety was still a powerful imperative.

The moral philosophers addressed themselves in Canada to cultivating this frame of mind by illustrating for their students the different mental laws. But in the 1850s and 1860s, when James George, William Lyall, and others in Canada emphasized the importance of knowing the laws of mental life, the attention of the literate English-speaking public in the North Atlantic community was rapidly turning to the many discoveries of the world of science. Accordingly, a second network of ideas—often used in conjunction with those of Common Sense—gained ascendance in English-Canadian colleges. British North America's moral philosophers were aided in the task of fending off potential infidelity by a group of colleagues whose responsibility was to show the workings of God's laws in the world of external nature. These were the teachers of natural theology, the second major buttress of religious and social orthodoxy at the level of ideas in mid-nineteenth-century Canada. The natural theology of Archdeacon William Paley, like the Common Sense doctrines of Professor Thomas Reid, provided Anglo-Canadian educators with a key weapon to protect the pious disposition against heterodox intellectual speculation.

3
The Uses of Natural Theology

> For all that may be known of God by men lies plain before their eyes; indeed God himself has disclosed it to them.
> Rom. 1:19–20

> The expansion of mind which rises in us at the sight of the starry heavens, the cloudcapt mountain, the boundless ocean, seems intended to direct our thoughts by an indefinite, but most impressive feeling, to the infinite Author of all.
> William Paley,
> *Natural Theology* (1802)

Nowhere was the connection between nature, mind, and God more in evidence in the middle of the nineteenth century than in the thought of those Britishers who found themselves at British North American colleges and universities teaching the lessons that could be learned through the study of nature herself. What makes their thought of great interest and importance is the fact that most of the colleges at which these men held positions had come into existence as functioning institutions precisely at a time when "science," in its modern sense, was beginning to challenge, to an unprecedented degree and on a larger scale than ever before, traditional religious, philosophical, and scientific thought. Since the heart of a proper liberal education at mid-century in British North America was an overwhelmingly religious one, it is perhaps to be expected that the study of nature began for the student with the necessary religious orientation. Such religious bearings were provided by a thorough grounding in natural theology.

In Great Britain the study of external nature, particularly in the areas of what are today called "biology" and "geology," was a pursuit that was overwhelmingly providential before the publication of Darwin's *Origin of Species*. As much contemplative as analytic, it was at the time still essentially a branch of philosophy in its steadfast refusal to exclude from its scope the higher meanings which its students derived from their observances of the Divine Presence in nature. In England by the 1840s, however, the term "natural philosophy" was beginning to give way to the simple word "science," an indication, notes one historian of science, "in a rough sort of way, [of a] decline of interest in elucidating providential implications from nature."[1]

Most of those who taught scientific subjects in Canada during this period were educated in Great Britain,[2] and they were greatly influenced by this providential tradition. For the most part, they had completed their English or Scottish educations at a time when that tradition was still strong—or at least was still the basis of what they themselves were taught. These educators were therefore little, if at all, willing to concede that the study of external nature could properly be conducted, or nature's lessons fully understood, by a conception of the scientific endeavour that insisted that the evidence of secondary causes operating in nature could alone provide a legitimate explanation and understanding of natural phenomena.

This attitude was in perfect accordance with the ideas then dominant in Canada as to the proper functions of the university. Even the most ardent opponent of the Anglo-Catholic Dr. Pusey in British North America (and there were many) would scarcely have challenged him seriously when he claimed, in 1852, that "the problem and special work of an university is, not how to advance science, not how to make discoveries, not to form new schools of mental philosophy, nor to invent new modes of analysis ... but to form minds religiously, morally, intellectually which shall discharge aright whatever duties, God, in His Providence, shall appoint to them."[3] That this was the case, and that all branches of university studies were seen to exist in order to reveal the presence of the Divine fiat in all human affairs, are evidenced in the following excerpt from an address by President J. H. Nicholls of Bishop's College in 1860:

> For it is the business of an University to gather unto itself all the branches of learning, to adopt and interweave with the old and well-tried, what is new and modern; to assist in its measure, and according to its capability in the work of scientific discovery, but far more to sanctify scientific discovery.

> When man searches and investigates, argues and proves, pronounces at his study-table that this or that field of rock, produces or does not produce a certain precious metal, or indicates by calculations the existence of some hitherto undiscovered heavenly body, and points out the very spot it occupies at the moment; when the human mind thus strides onwards, let it be the University's privilege to demonstrate that the excellence of all this, is not of man, but of God; that while man discovers, he discovers what God has made, what *God gives* him to understand. Universities let us remember are Christian institutions.[4]

In British North America, as in Great Britain and in the United States during the first half of the nineteenth century, convictions as to the nature of the scientific endeavour were marked not as much by any overt antagonism between science on one hand and religion on the other, as by the continuing presence of religious assumptions within the domain of science itself.[5]

Such a conception of scientific inquiry was highly dependent upon the extent to which one was willing to subordinate pure intellectual effort to the religious conscience. James George, vice-principal of Queen's College, proclaimed in 1855—when discussing the relationship that should exist between a "true piety" and "intellectual labor"—that scientists such as Humphrey Davy had accomplished what they had only because their intellects were guided by the pious disposition. "The enthusiasm which enabled them to accomplish so much in unfolding the laws of nature," he noted, "was but the form that their piety took in doing homage to the God of nature.... Their piety furnished them with a kind of compass, telescope, and microscope, which enabled their intellect to go farther and to see farther and deeper into nature than it otherwise could have done." The commonly held functional relationship between piety and intellect, the workhorses of the spiritual and mental faculties, also extended into the study of nature. The union of a pious disposition and the scientific endeavour was a strong one in the mid-nineteenth century because it was considered to be utterly essential. George stated this clearly:

> The lovers of science, whether their fields be chemistry, geology, astronomy, or some department of natural history, will aim chiefly at ascertaining the great laws of nature, in the innumerable beautiful connections which God has established between causes and effects.... The note of impiety in

the mind's eye, in many ways, unfits it for making grand discoveries in nature. Infidels should rather ponder this than sneer at it, for whether they believe it or not, it is nevertheless true, that *the high priests* whom God admits within the veil of nature to see its hidden laws, are those who approach the Holy of Holies with clean hands and a pure heart.[6]

In an age which some chose to describe as one of intellectual anarchy, it was above all necessary that educators choose their subject matter for the classroom as they would their sabres for war: from swordsmiths whose allegiance was unquestionable and whose products, used in battle by previous generations, had successfully stood the test of time. Canadian university leaders at mid-nineteenth century thought they had found such a swordsmith in William Paley. Their chosen weapon was natural theology.

The Prevalence of Paley
In his 1842 inaugural address at the opening of Victoria College, Egerton Ryerson had urged the importance of combating "infidelity," a phenomenon that "endeavoured to press into its service almost every department of natural and mental science." "How important is it," he went on, "that the appointed defenders of the citadel of truth should be able ... to wrest from the adversary his own chosen weapons, restore them to the christian armory, and employ them with unerring precision and deadly effect against the goliath of scepticism and infidelity! The God of grace is also the God of nature; how delightful to trace his footsteps in the works and laws of the material universe, as well as in the pages of Revelation!" The revealed word of God, as found in the Bible, spoke for itself. But how much more powerful would that message be if complemented by a revelation of God's power, grandeur, and love in the natural world, if only nature could be so revealed! Such an endeavour could not "fail to excite, in the mind of the diligent and devout student, feelings of veneration, gratitude and praise."[7] The surname of three candidates was put forward by Ryerson as knights-errant in this providentially guided mission: Campbell, Butler, and Paley.[8]

There can be little doubt that when Ryerson spoke of defending the "citadel of truth" by wresting from the adversary "his own chosen weapons," he had primarily in mind the natural theology of William Paley, for Paley had done precisely that within Ryerson's own lifetime. An empiricist and utilitarian, while also a religious divine, Paley was able—in *The Principles of Moral and Political Philosophy* (1785), *A View of the Evidences of Christianity* (1794), and especially in *Natural Theology; or, Evidences of the Existence and Attributes of the Deity, Collected from the Appearances of Nature* (1802)—to fashion the arguments and assumptions of both empiricism and utilitarianism into a Christian apologetic that was at the time eminently satisfying, if not brilliantly original.[9] The essence of his argument, as found in *Natural Theology*, was that everywhere in nature there is evidence of design, and that there cannot be design without a designer. Paley's thought in this regard was based therefore upon the notion of planned expediency or contrivance in nature.[10]

Once having inferred the existence of the Deity as designer from the nature and extent of His attributes as found throughout creation, Paley was free to assess man's duties and obligations to society and to God. As the major exponent of this providential, Christian teleology at the beginning of the nineteenth century, Paley noted that the most important of man's duties to God was the observance of "that silent piety, which consists in a habit of tracing out the creator's wisdom and goodness, in the objects about us, or in the history of his dispensations."[11]

It was Paley's fate, as C. C. Gillispie has noted, to become after his death, like Euclid or Cicero, a subject rather than a man.[12] This was certainly the case at Anglo-Canadian universities, for during much of the nineteenth century a Paleyite natural theology served as a staple in the academic diet. At Victoria College in 1842 Ryerson himself gave the course in Christian evidences, and a year later a contributor to the *Christian Guardian* described his class as having "excited the admiration of all present, from the completeness of information, and strength and vigour of intellect, displayed by the young gentlemen who composed it." It remained a basic unit of the curriculum at Victoria well into the 1870s.[13]

At the University of Toronto after 1854 the only subjects which the student was required to study in each of his four years were metaphysics and ethics; and (perhaps not by coincidence) from the year of the publication of Darwin's *Origin*, natural theology and evidences of Christianity were substituted for a part of the metaphysics course. After 1864, when a degree of specialization was allowed within the Honours program at Toronto, natural theology and evidences remained the sole mandatory courses, regardless of a student's specialty. This remained the case until 1877.[14]

The Huron College calendar for 1871–2 featured two works by Paley as required texts for second-year theology students: *Horae*

Paulinae and *Evidences*. In third year, students continued their studies of Christian evidences from Paley's work, and this was supplemented by Joseph Butler's *The Analogy of Religion* and Charles P. McIlvain's *Evidences*.[15] Similarly, professors of either church history or philosophy, or both, taught the lessons of Paley and Butler at King's (York), Trinity, Bishop's, and Knox colleges between the years 1843 and 1863. Queen's College also used Paley's works in arts and theology courses during these years. In fact, the analogical form of logic, which was the basis of the theistic arguments of Paley and Butler, was given additional emphasis by the offer, in 1867, of the Montreal Prize (of forty dollars) for the best essay entitled "Reasoning by Analogy, with Illustrations."[16]

The University of Manitoba, patterned after the University of Toronto's college system, consistently gave specific examinations on Paley within the Department of Mental and Moral Philosophy from the year of the university's founding (1877) to the 1890s. Seldom in these examinations was a question ever posed that called for a critical response that would have seriously challenged Paley's argument or assumptions. In 1882, for example, the examiners asked: "Shew how, according to Paley (a) the unity (b) the goodness of God are evidenced by the works of nature." A question in 1890 stated: "Illustrate the argument for design by a reference to what Paley calls 'peculiar organizations.'" Two years later students were required to respond to the following: "Show how 'comparative anatomy' supports the Theistic argument from design."[17] These questions were entirely typical of those asked by University of Manitoba examiners in natural theology during the late nineteenth century.

University calendars and examination papers cannot, however, show in any detail precisely how natural theology was adapted for the use of Canadian students. Fortunately, two university instructors of the mid-nineteenth century have left evidence to help answer this question. One was James Beaven, professor of metaphysics and ethics, first at King's College, Toronto, and later (after 1851) at the University of Toronto. The other was James Bovell, M.D., at various times professor of physiology, physiology and chemistry, and natural theology at Trinity College, Toronto. In 1850 Dr. Beaven, then professor of divinity at King's College, published what was probably the first university textbook written in Canada: *Elements of Natural Theology*. Nine years later, on the eve of the Darwinian revolution, Dr. Bovell wrote *Outlines of Natural Theology, for the Use of the Canadian Student*.

Since both books reflect many of the assumptions, interconnections, and nuances of the thought of their day, they will be considered separately and at some length. Moreover, the work of Beaven and Bovell on natural theology illustrates—for the Canadian context—the intricacy of the relationship of the study of external nature, their particular conceptions of human reason and of the role of the mind in general, and the relationship of both to God. One can also see the extent to which they attempted to integrate the assumptions of the Common Sense school into their natural theology. The writings of Beaven and Bovell are historically important precisely because they lacked originality. Neither claimed to be making any great stride in the name of science or theology. They were, to use Ryerson's phrase, "defenders of the citadel of truth" and not at all concerned with risking forays beyond the boundaries of the garrison.[18]

James Beaven and the Eye of Faith

James Beaven had been a resident of Canada for seven years when his *Elements of Natural Theology* was published in 1850. Ordained by the Church of England and High Church in his religious commitment, he learned in 1842, while the vicar of Welford in Northamptonshire, that he was Bishop Strachan's choice as professor of the religious principles upon which a university should be constructed. Among the subjects the new professor of divinity, then in his early forties, was required to teach was natural theology—with which he was undoubtedly well familiar from his years of training in arts (B.A. 1824, M.A. 1827) and divinity (B.D. and D.D. 1842) at Oxford.[19] *Elements of Natural Theology* was the product of his lectures to his students during the 1840s.

Probably the most significant section of Beaven's book was its introductory chapter, appropriately entitled "On the Utility of the Study of Natural Theology." There he put forward his reasons why the Canadian student should make a careful study of the subject. *Elements of Natural Theology* began by making the important distinction between theology and religion. "Theology," the author began, is the "doctrine or science concerning God." Religion is the practical end of theology, "the recognition and practical application of the truths which Theology teaches; the believing and acting out of those truths in our character and conduct."[20] Having made this point, he then turned to the part played by the mind as mediator between Divine truths and the practical application of those truths in everyday life. From the outset Beaven also made clear to his students that his primary concern was with the means by which certainty in religious belief could be established.

The basis of the faith upon which theological truth—hence, religion—is founded is twofold. Religious belief must be based upon the twin truths contained in Hebrews 11:6, that "he that cometh to God must believe that He is, and that He is a rewarder of them that diligently seek Him." Since part of the very purpose of natural theology was, in Paley's view, to provide proof from nature of the existence of the Deity, Beaven's textbook had therefore accepted without question the major premise of the subject purportedly under investigation. The essence of religious belief, for Beaven, was rooted in the nature of the pious disposition and was centred in the relationship between man and his Creator. As James George told the students of Queen's College in 1855: ". . . true piety brings the soul into an intelligible and loving union with the Divine mind . . . it is only the eye of faith that can see Him in His moral glories and in His infinite loveliness."[21]

It is highly significant that James George should have characterized a true piety as being in part an "intelligible" union with the Divine mind, for contained within such a statement is the question of the nature of intelligibility, of rationality, itself. It was precisely this question that Beaven found himself facing as he sought to discuss the primary elements of natural theology. Revealed truth, he claimed, as found in the Holy Scriptures, takes natural religion and its truths for granted; the Scriptures comment upon the existence and attributes of the Creator, but do not attempt to undertake *proof* of His existence or the fact of His attributes.[22] Man was endowed with natural powers of reasoning for this purpose.

But this raised a problem that had been the concern of Christian philosophers throughout the centuries: to what extent man could rely upon "unaided" human reason to perceive religious truths. Beaven's answer was essentially an attempt to strike an intellectual compromise between the view of the eighteenth-century Deists, who had claimed that by reason alone (that is, without the aid of revelation) man could establish "the whole system of necessary truth, both theological and moral," and of those who had replied to the Deists only by overreacting to the extent that they claimed, in Beaven's words, "that no part of our knowledge of Divine things is derived by man from reason or the observation of nature." He called particular attention to Romans 1:19–20, wherein, he explained, "St. Paul teaches that natural reason *might* lead men to the knowledge of God, and that they were inexcusable if it did not so lead them." Man, Beaven stated, can only come to infer the existence of God through the evidences and workings of His attributes.[23] The door was thus opened for the study of a natural theology that could serve as a means of preserving certainty in religious conviction.

Although Beaven's primary concern was to establish the means by which religious certainty could be achieved, throughout his adult life Beaven himself perceived influences at work challenging in different ways both the credal and logical bases of this certainty. Before coming to Canada, he had written a long defence of the doctrine of religious celibacy as developed by early church leaders. He had done so, not because of some conviction that the doctrine should be revived within the Anglican communion, but rather because he was worried about the increasing tendency to question the dogmatic basis of his faith. "There are times," he stated, "in which reflecting men have felt that the whole current of the feelings and habits of society has [been] mischievously set in one direction ... the whole range of the doctrine and discipline, and moral and religious habits, and tone of mind of the primitive depositories of the faith, have been to a certain extent examined." Critics of the church had sought to undermine the correctness of early doctrines such as religious celibacy, but had done so, not by appealing to original sources, but by building, he believed, upon "the particular prejudices of this age." Beaven concluded that the main lesson to be learned from his study of celibacy was "the great value of *primitive unbroken tradition.*" Any discrepancies between such doctrines and Scripture were, in his view, an indication, not of mistakes on the part of early church fathers, but of errors of thought that had come about as the result of "the supposed improvements of a later age."[24]

Similarly, in a sermon preached before the Synod of the Diocese of Toronto in 1859, Beaven warned of the dangers that unchecked critical thought could mean to certitude—and, hence, unity—in religious affairs. "The evil of division does prevail all around ourselves," he warned on the eve of the long quarrel between Bishops Strachan and Cronyn. Phrases such as "independence of mind" and "individuality and self-reliance" were, he admitted, part of the national character. But, he stressed, it must also be remembered that such attributes were only a few aspects of a many-sided character. Let this "independence of mind" run wild and the virtue becomes a signal fault.[25]

In his *Elements of Natural Theology*, Beaven attempted to

show his students that they had within their mental reaches a double-edged sword with which to fend off the scepticism and infidelity he noticed so much in evidence. The revealed word of God was of course the primary source of religious truth, hence, certainty. But another was even antecedent to relevation: the evidences of religion in nature. And these could be perceived through simple observation and reflection. It is true, he admitted, "that only those favoured with Divine revelation have been able to appreciate *duly* the phenomena of nature and providence, and to reason *correctly* from them." Yet even those not so favoured by revelation could—by simple observation of the natural world and due reflection upon it—perceive, however imperfectly, evidences of the existence of the moral power who is the Author of the present state of things and who governs the world. All this, Beaven noted, could be perceived by those who have *not* the benefit of revelation. How much more powerful and accurate would this human perception of Divine truth then be if guided by God's word itself! He went on:

> In the case of those who do actually receive Divine revelation, man's intellectual vision has been so cleared, and his judgment and reason so strengthened, that, wherever the arguments of believers have reached, Atheism has been constrained to shrink and retire, or assume some other form. It is therefore important that the minds of the young should be instructed in the evidences and doctrines of Natural Theology, that they may not be at a loss for suitable arguments to repel and silence gainsayers.[26]

By furnishing this double means of ascertaining religious truth, Beaven hoped to gain the attention of the young Christian "whose mind is of an active and speculative turn, [and who] will be apt at times to look back and search into the principles and hidden sources of things."[27] Here was where firm pedagogical direction was absolutely essential, for in the unguided speculations Beaven so feared was also to be found the basis of the similar fears of James George. Here was "the intellect . . . severed from God," where human genius could be found actively seeking truth, but without the sanctifying guidance of the human soul resolutely in search of God's grace. The result of such a misguided use of human reason, for George, was a way of thinking that could lead only to the "darkness of the pit."[28] Beaven was similarly convinced that this direction of thought could lead the student only "into depths in which painful doubt and fear may agitate his soul, as to the grounds and foundations of all religious truth."[29]

Beaven's purpose in writing *Elements of Natural Theology* was to prevent the student from reaching such a state of mind. He proposed to turn his students' minds from "speculation" to "reflection" by furnishing them "with the arguments and conclusions which have been the refuge and safeguard of others." He also wanted to present the basic evidences of natural theology in order that they might understand better, by means "such as enlightened reason furnishes," the various providential truths brought out by the study of theology in nature.[30]

The main body of the text of *Elements of Natural Theology* was divided equally between the traditional Paleyite proofs of the existence and attributes of God as seen in the evidences of design throughout creation and another aspect of natural theology that in Beaven's view Paley had largely neglected. Beaven was influenced by the ideas of moral government then prevalent in North America no less than those, like James George, who taught moral philosophy. Hence, he stressed the duties and obligations of men as derived from the evidences of God as moral governor of the world. Any complete system of natural theology also had to consider "the evidence for a future state, and rewards and punishments in that state, as well as for the immortality of the soul." Making no claim to originality, Beaven sought rather to use Paley's arguments when discussing design in the natural world, and to update Paley with the more recent findings of the authors of the Bridgewater Treatises,[31] a series of studies published between 1833 and 1836 which attempted to examine scientific subjects within Paley's schema. When discussing the question of God as moral governor and the evidence for the existence of a future state (with its attendant questions), he was content to rely heavily upon the close attention paid to this specific subject in Bishop Butler's celebrated *Analogy of Religion*. "My business," he stated plainly, "will simply be to render the proof more complete than it has yet appeared in any single treatise with which I am acquainted."[32]

Beaven found that Paley and the Bridgewater Treatises provided evidence sufficient to refute certain theories then deemed radical. Buckland's *Geology and Mineralogy*, Prout's *Chemistry, Meteorology, and the Function of Digestion*, and Whewell's *Astronomy and General Physics, considered with reference to Natural Theology* were all cited at length to combat what Beaven believed to be "the most serious of the objections to the argument from design," that of the "modern atheist." Such a man, he said, "points to the fact that generation is constantly going on in animal and vegetable nature, without any apparent purpose or design on the part of any being whatever." Against the Lamarckian theory of descent, which claimed that "all creatures whatever may have been evolved, gradually and spontaneously from one extremely simple type,"[33] he put forward what was then an orthodox and respectable refutation. There were too many material gaps in the chain of evolution to speak of "continuous descent." Was there not evidence of disruptions in the earth's crust, causing extinction of certain species while leaving others unaffected? And did evidence not exist of certain throwbacks or regressions in animal forms that made nonsense of the idea of "progressive development"? Surely any correct study of the facts could draw only one conclusion: "that the present state of existing things has been brought about by supernatural intelligence, giving laws to matter, and superintending the operation of those laws."[34]

Beaven's selection from the works of previous writers on natural theology was, however, somewhat eclectic. It therefore ran the risk of inconsistency. As a convinced empiricist, Paley had accepted the Lockean conception of ideas, which asserted that no special faculty was required in order to have moral knowledge. There was, then, no need of a "moral sense" or any intuitive perception of right and wrong. In accepting such an epistemological position, Paley took direct issue with the Scottish Common Sense school of moral philosophy—Thomas Reid in particular—which had repudiated the Lockean theory of ideas both on moral and on theological grounds.[35] Beaven could not have been unaware of this epistemological conflict between the Common Sense school and Paley's natural theology. Later, as professor of metaphysics and ethics at the University of Toronto, he sought to enlighten his students with the truths and principles of the Common Sense tradition.[36] The basic Common Sense notion that there existed, as part of man's being, a "moral sense" that allowed him to make correct decisions could only have appealed to him. Yet, far from pointing this conflict out to his students, Beaven incorporated certain Common Sense phrases and assumptions into his natural theology.

When he insisted that the proof of God's existence and attributes be based, as with Paley, upon observation, Beaven was relatively safe from the problems of inconsistency or contradiction (although even here his insistence that the study of natural theology be undertaken only after a commitment by faith to the truth of Hebrews 11:6 showed that his was not so much an attempt to *prove* the existence of God as to *affirm* it). He ran into more difficulties, however, in the section of his book that attempted in a similarly empirical fashion to discuss such elusive matters as the moral government of God and the correct relationship of man to that God. Here the influence of the Scottish Common Sense philosophy shows through Beaven's rather thin empirical cloak. He uses such phrases as "our moral being"; he is found speaking of "the moral nature that the Creator has given us"; he speaks again of "man's moral faculties." And in his conclusion he seems expressly to acknowledge his debt to the school of Reid and Stewart: he speaks there of "that intuitive perception of right and wrong of which we are all sensible."[37] Beaven wished to have what he considered to be the best of both schools: he wished to maintain an empirical means of deriving Divine truth from nature, yet he appears not to have been willing to give up the Common Sense notion that moral truths can in fact be perceived intuitively through the "moral sense." Such an appeal to man's moral nature, he realized, could help nicely to provide an additional means, antecedent to recourse to His Word, of discerning God's providential being in nature.

The second major section of Beaven's manual of natural theology, comprising about a hundred pages, dealt with God as moral governor of a moral world. Beaven now turned from the *obvious* laws of nature, with which he had up until now been dealing, to the laws—no less natural for being speculative—of the moral world. He wished, in short, to discuss within the scheme of his natural theology the laws that govern the relationship between God and man. His analysis was essentially as follows. If God is a moral governor, that is, "He is a rewarder of them that diligently seek Him" (Hebrews 11:6), it follows that He must reward and punish men according to whether or not they live up to the moral code He has laid down. This being the case, man's moral and intellectual progress must derive from God and be determined by the way men fulfil their duties and obligations. Man is thus a Moral Being. But how is it that men can find out what these duties and obligations are without a necessary recourse to revelation? The answer is that just as God in his grand design for physical nature has provided for our physical needs, for the continuation of the species, and for the adequacy of our bodily frame, He has also provided us with our emotional faculties: kindness, resentment, desire of esteem and honour, and so forth. Furthermore, God has placed these and other emotions in a definite relationship to each other (amounting to a kind of psychological equivalent to the genetic code):

> When we consider man in his *relations* to his fellowmen, then comes in the idea of duty. We are all sensible that others owe something to us, in consequence of those relations; and we must, consequently, own that we owe something to others. . . . And we are continually led (without any previous intuition of our own, and by an involuntary and unavoidable process of our minds) to form judgments concerning the actions of others, and concerning our own actions as right and wrong; or what we ought or ought not to do or feel in regard to others. . . . And when we apply that judgment to ourselves, to our own actions or emotions, we call it conscience.[38]

Beaven had thus established for his students the connection between natural theology and moral philosophy, for the notions of duty and conscience—central to the study of moral philosophy at the time—were simply part of the Moral Providence by which man is an accountable being. To Beaven the logic of this was plain, for the same Providence which had so wonderfully adapted structure to function in the world of nature had also provided for the structural basis of man's duties with respect to himself, his fellowmen, and his Creator.[39]

This potential unity of concern between natural theology and moral philosophy—the melding of design and obligation—had important ramifications in the sphere of civil relations, and Beaven undoubtedly took no little time in his classroom to point them out to his students. The Creator has established all relationships, including our social ones. He has placed us in human society, and the consequence of this is immense, for "whatever, therefore, tends to preserve society is agreeable to his will; whatever tends to break it up is opposed to his will. In order, then, that society may be maintained, it becomes necessary that men should control themselves; and, as all will not do so, some must be controlled by others."[40]

But Beaven's final words to his students turned from the areas of social relations and obligations back to the role of reason in correctly discerning the Divine will. He had attempted to provide the means by which they could come to establish certainty in their religious convictions, and he had done this by showing how —by "natural reason" alone, independent of revelation—the unbeliever, distrustful of the "revealed word," could be approached on his own ground and have his false position "driven step by step from every refuge of lies." But the final way of ascertaining religious truth, he warned, rested in the end with revelation. God has revealed His will to men in writing, and this revelation is in fact "anterior to evidence." The conclusions of natural reason must therefore always be subject to possible correction by the preevidential truths of revelation. Hence, any good student must be prepared "to examine carefully into such Divine revelation, for the express purpose of correcting and enlarging those ideas as to the will of God, which we derive from natural reason."[41] Whether his students, good or bad, did so was entirely another question.

Dr. Bovell's Quadrilateral Mind

The second textbook on natural theology published in Canada was given to the Canadian public in the same year that Charles Darwin's *Origin of Species* was released to the world. *Outlines of Natural Theology, for the Use of the Canadian Student* appeared in print in 1859. Its author was Dr. James Bovell, one of Canada's leading medical figures.

Sixteen years younger than James Beaven, Bovell had immigrated to Canada from Barbados in 1848. The staunchly Anglican son of a wealthy West Indies banker, he had by then studied medicine, with particular interests in physiology and microscopy, for more than a decade under several prominent physicians in London, Dublin, Edinburgh, and Glasgow. After setting up practice in Toronto, he soon took a leading part in the organization of the Trinity University Medical Faculty. He was its first dean.[42] A year later, in 1851, he founded and was editing the *Upper Canada Journal of Medical, Surgical, and Physical Science*. When the Trinity Medical Faculty ceased operations (if the expression may be permitted) in 1856, owing to a disagreement over expenditures between the board of governors of the Medical Faculty and Bishop Strachan, Bovell was appointed lecturer in physiology and pathology with the Toronto School of Medicine. Later he taught physiology at the Upper Canadian Veterinary School, which had been established in 1862. From 1857 to 1870 (when he left Canada for the West Indies), he also lectured to the students of the Faculty of Arts and Science at Trinity University. The title of his lectureship indicates his major concern: "Physiology in its Relation to Natural Theology."[43]

This title also suggests why it is important to give detailed attention to Bovell's *Outlines of Natural Theology*, for unlike

Professor Beaven, whose textbook on the subject made few excursions into the writings of nineteenth-century scientists (other than to attempt to update Paley by incorporating into his schema the conclusions and evidence of the authors of the Bridgewater Treatises), Dr. Bovell attempted to move beyond Paley and to incorporate the latest findings of both modern philosophy and modern science into his own thought and work. Indeed, the works cited in his *Outlines* must have constituted much of the reading required for any earnest man of science in the mid-Victorian period.

Dr. Bovell shared with James Beaven many assumptions regarding the uses to which natural theology could be put as part of the Canadian undergraduate's course of studies. Yet there were important differences. Beaven was an Anglican priest first and foremost, forced into the use of scientific evidence because of his concern both for his own faith and for that of his students. Bovell was neither priest nor scientist—and that was his main problem. His was a mind agonizingly divided. Natural theology was his means of bridging the widening gap between theology and science. Because of this, some understanding of the workings of his mind is necessary to provide an adequate background to the thought of those in British North America who took upon themselves the task of engaging in a purely "scientific" study of nature.

The title of Bovell's lectureship also implies the fact that his intellectual concerns were ones which combined the study of nature with the worship of God. Yet despite the unquestionably central unity of science and Christianity within his thought, he was quite capable of dividing his mind, when necessary, into two compartments, as it were, where scientific inquiry and devotional concerns could be conveniently separated. As one who prided himself on keeping abreast of the results and implications of the latest scientific research, he could write a number of papers that reveal a willingness simply to describe physical phenomena and uncover uniformities of behaviour that on the basis of predictability could be described as laws. Such a conception of causation did not require necessary recourse to any teleology derived from a divinity in order to be considered an adequate basis for understanding. Nor did Bovell draw any religious or moral conclusions in these papers. The titles of several of his scientific articles are accurate indications of their contents: "Apparatus for the exhibition of vapour"; "Clinical remarks on two cases of tumour of the uterus complicating parturition"; "Note on the preservation of some infusoria with a view to the display of their cilia"; "Observations on the climate of Barbadoes [sic] and its influence on disease..."; "On the white globules of the blood in disease."[44]

Notwithstanding this professional commitment to the methods and aims of the scientist, Bovell was at the same time a profoundly devout man, as evidenced by his works *Preparation for the Christian Sacrifice, or Holy Communion* (1859); *Passing Thoughts on Man's Relation to God and on God's Relation to Man* (1862); *The World at the Advent of the Lord Jesus* (1868). What is more, Bovell was not always willing to separate fully the truths perceived through the lens of the microscope or in the dissecting room from those glimpsed through the eye of faith. For him, science was in the end the manifestation in nature of a Christian God; and where his scientific articles nowhere invoke the Divinity, his textbook on natural theology makes abundantly clear that a science without the presence of God may still be known, but is bereft of meaning.

Sir William Osler, Bovell's most famous student, who was profoundly influenced by him, once recalled of Bovell:

> Only men of a certain mettle rise superior to their surroundings, and while Dr. Bovell had that all important combination of boundless ambition with energy and industry, he had the fatal fault of diffuseness in which even genius is strangled. With a quadrilateral mind, which he kept spinning like a teetotum, one side was never kept uppermost for long at a time. Caught in a storm, which shook the scientific world with the publication of the *Origin of Species*, instead of sailing before the wind, even were it with bare poles, he put about and sought a harbour of refuge in writing a work on natural theology which you will find on the shelves of second-hand bookshops in company at least made respectable by Paley. He was an omnivorous reader and transmuter. He could talk pleasantly, at times transcendently, upon anything of the science of the day; from protoplasm to evolution. But he lacked concentration and that scientific accuracy which only comes with a long training (sometimes, indeed, never comes) and which is the ballast of the boat.... The bent of his mind was devotional.[45]

As interesting as this assessment is in its description of Bovell's failure to develop into a great scientist, it nevertheless does not do justice to the nature of his thought. Osler gives the impression that Bovell's mind was constantly in a tizzy. There may be an element of truth in this, but if so, it was probably the result, not of a lack of concentration, but rather of a divided mind.

Bovell's inability to apply himself in a singleminded fashion to the pursuit of scientific truth was the result of his incessant effort, not less worthy for being "diffuse," to reconcile the pathways to understanding of the scientist and the theologian. His task was made more difficult because he was never fully certain just which of these he was. His scientific writings testify to his strong belief in the fact that the pursuit of natural laws through observation and experiment and the determination of man's place in the natural scheme of things represented two entirely different endeavours. Yet his natural theology indicates that he was equally convinced that these two endeavours were ones which must somehow be considered together for Christians to understand fully their relationship with physical nature. His major interest was to understand man's place within the context of the totality of nature; and his devotional, pious inclination of mind—which was always more deeply rooted than his declared professional interests—dictated that the deeper level of meaning lay in the extension of a Christian teleology into the realm of natural science. Hence his concern in education was, not to provide a specialized knowledge of physiological theory, but to establish for his students the correct relationship between physiology (and the other aspects of science) and natural theology.

Sir William Osler's claim that Bovell sought a "harbour of refuge" from the Darwinian challenge is inaccurate and misleading: it must be remembered that Bovell's *Outlines* was published on the eve of the Darwinian revolution, not in the aftermath of it. When Bovell referred to "Darwin" in his book, he was speaking of Erasmus, not Charles. By no means did he believe himself to be fleeing from a battle; he was, rather, retiring to what he regarded as the strongest line of defence. It has been noted that the heirs of William Paley in the nineteenth century "displayed divine Providence in every nook and cranny of the physical system of things."[46] James Bovell, like Professor Beaven, provided no exception to this claim, and he was not about to decline to do battle with an enemy which challenged the very assumptions upon which both his science and his religion were built.

Let us, then, spin the teetotum, remembering, as the quadrilateral mind whirls, that if it should come to rest revealing Bovell's thought before the publication of his *Outlines of Natural Theology*, we may expect to see Bovell the scientist reflected in his writings. Most of his purely scientific articles were published between 1849 and 1856 (only one of the titles quoted previously was published after 1856). But should the teetotum, when it stops, show Bovell's thought as reflected in his writings after the publication of his *Outlines*, we may equally expect to see the devotional side of that mind uppermost. Virtually all of Bovell's devotional writings were published after his *Outlines*. There was, in other words, a clear progression, if not in Bovell's intellectual development, at least in the direction of his personal commitment—one that saw an inductive, Baconian form of science gradually subordinated to his particular strain of piety. *Outlines of Natural Theology, for the Use of the Canadian Student* marked the mid-point in this transition, a point at which there *seemed* to exist a virtual balance between the attention he gave to the two competing compartments of his mind. The teetotum will be made to stop, therefore, at Bovell's thought as it stood in 1859.

As with the nearly decade-old textbook of his colleague James Beaven, Bovell's *Outlines* was forced into print by its author's sense of alarm. "In mixing with our fellow creatures," he began, "the startling conclusion comes upon us, that numbers are living in a state of practical infidelity, and seem to be careless whether their opinions are erroneous, or just and true according to the standard of revealed truth." The fact that "the standard of revealed truth" was no longer the basis of the judgements of some students of science was of paramount concern to the devotional side of Bovell; as he had noted on his first page, his principal aim in writing *Outlines of Natural Theology* was "to prove not only that the creation of the world had been the work of a Mighty Creator, but that the revelation which has been made to us, by inspired writers, of the method and order of that creation, need not be considered as false, and that the proofs rather tend to support and confirm the Mosaic History."[47]

Only by this double exposition of the evidences for God's active presence throughout creation and the defence of the literal interpretation of the origins of that creation, as put forward in Genesis, could the Canadian student engaged in the study of natural science "contemplate the works of creation" in such a way as to "deduc[e] therefrom principles calculated to improve the mind, and to furnish the moral nature with such food for reflection as may tend to elevate and adorn, rather than degrade and corrupt it."[48] (Again we note the legacy of the Common Sense school, for the term "moral nature" had a specific meaning in the middle of the nineteenth century.) But how could such students, especially those at the edge of infidelity, be made to contemplate such matters without also incurring the risk that this "contemplation" might result in unbridled—hence, dangerous—"speculation"? How could the Canadian student be made to inquire, with the natural theologian, into the evidences of design in nature without, in the spirit of modern philosophical scepticism, also questioning the validity of that evidence? How could such "inquiry" be conducted without risking the dangerous intrusion of the critical intellect? "Man . . . is freely permitted and incited to make enquiry into the origin of things," Bovell admitted, "so that men shall speak of his marvellous acts who made them." He went on:

> To enquire, therefore, is not only a privilege, it is a duty; but in entering on such a momentous enquiry, surely it becomes us reverently and thankfully to undertake so wholesome and pleasurable a task, not with a predetermination to doubt, and at length disbelieve what we cannot instantly prove, but rather with a distrust of our own finite capabilities, and the recollection that too often the splendid fictions of philosophers, which have seduced thousands into error, disappear one by one, and leave sceptic and believer alike astonished and confounded.[49]

Indeed, it was largely these "splendid fictions of philosophers," said Bovell, that were causing religion to be replaced by a "cold morality." The doctrines of Spinoza, Leibniz, Locke, and "an emasculated Platonism" had served only to divide men, not unite them. "We look in vain," he noted, "for the impress of a system which assuming the revelation of God to man to be true, examines the grounds and proofs of that revelation, and on such a foundation proceeds to raise a superstructure."[50]

But if the acceptance of no philosophical system in its entirety could be risked lest it supplant religion, then how could a student establish the proper means of determining the "grounds and proofs" of revelation? How could the problem of the critical intellect be solved? Bovell's solution, however inadequate it may appear to the modern observer, was to use the findings of certain moral philosophers, but to be rigidly selective both in his choice of philosophers and in the parts of their systems. Apart from recourse to Revelation itself, the Canadian student could determine the presence and providence of God in nature in either, or both, of two ways: he could search for the manifestations of Him in the physical world or look for His presence within his own consciousness. In neither case was a truly critical intellectual inquiry necessary, for knowledge of Him was given, Bovell claimed, in the former case by generalization and in the latter by intuition.[51] It is to Bovell's appeal to "intuition" that we must now turn.

Despite Dr. Bovell's fear of a total commitment to any particular philosophical system, he looked with no small degree of approval upon Common Sense. The presence of certain basic Common Sense notions in James Beaven's natural theology has already been noted; but with Beaven they operated mainly at the level of his assumptions and in his use of certain phrases. Bovell's *Outlines*, on the other hand, made no attempt to exclude mental and moral philosophy from the scope of natural theology. Indeed, the book's first, all-important section, "The Origin of Creation," began, not with a defence of the truth of Revelation from the evidence of contrivance in external nature, but with a consideration of the various contrivances of the *mind* as put forward in the psychological theories of Victor Cousin, a French philosopher and historian whose thought was heavily indebted to the school of Thomas Reid.

The Scottish school, it appeared to Cousin, had managed to reconcile an empiricism amenable to science with a spiritualism necessary to religion by admitting knowledge drawn from sensation, even while insisting upon the existence and importance of an innate "moral sense."[52] Following Reid, Cousin maintained that in addition to having a merely "passive will," which receives and responds to sensations, man also possesses an "active will" or "power" by which he is capable of determining permanent moral principles through the *a priori* categories of substance and causality. At one point in his *Outlines*, Bovell quoted Reid to this effect. "It is evident," he wrote,

> that our notion of active power is derived from our own energies as understanding and willing beings. Hence it follows that the only intelligible and distinct conception that we can form of power, is, as Dr. Reid has observed, "that it is the attribute of a being who can do certain things if he wills, and that it can exist only in beings that are endowed with understanding and capable of volition."[53]

Working from the same premise, Cousin had proceeded to conceive of the mind as a triad of faculties which may be described as "sensibility," "reason," and "heart." All human thought is a combination of all three. To "think" is therefore not a mere act of cognition; it is a complex interaction of qualities aesthetic, epistemological, and ethical in nature. Bovell depended heavily upon Cousin's faculty psychology. "In man we find an organism fitted for the performance of the highest functions—," he wrote, in a passage which might well have been drawn from Cousin's *Du Vrai, du beau et du bien* (1853),

> the material substratum adapted to the manifestations of faculties which transcend those of all creatures co-temporaneous with him, and in the possession of the gift of Reason, leading him up to association with being which, in the same orderly differentiation, stands as it were between him and the Supreme. The organism is subordinate to, or is the instrument of, the ME; for the beautiful, the true, and the right are in the Reason itself, and instead of copying them from nature and experience, it judges both nature and experience by them.[54]

If Bovell's students had dwelt at all upon this passage, and had reflected—as their professor desired—upon the implications of this psychological theory for the future development of their own thought, they would necessarily have concluded (unless they rejected the tenets of the Common Sense school out of hand) that the essence of their rationality transcended by far any mere equation of "rationality" with "intellectuality." The process of reasoning, they had been taught, was not a simple matter of "intellectual" analysis. Lest the less observant of his pupils should miss this key point, Bovell drew out its lessons himself:

> Man has, beside the sentient animal life, the far higher endowment of a rational existence. The peculiarities of his rational being are in the following distinctive elements: he can originate for himself what to him are the perfect ideal patterns or archetypes of that which is the beautiful, the true, and the good, and use them to measure, criticize, and estimate all that experience may offer. Not what is taken from experience, but what his own genius creates for him, is his criterion for testing what he shall approve and what disapprove. He has his own principles or standards of judgment within himself, and with which the material and sentient world has nothing to do. He has also that self-knowledge which determines the intrinsic excellency of this his rational being, and what is due to himself and worthy of himself in

all his actions. He can thus feel the claims of self-respect and responsibility to his own conscience, and know the retributions of self-approbation or self-reproach according as his deeds sustain or violate the law which his own rational being imposes upon himself. *Here are peculiar self-relations and self-conditions, all subsisting within the rational, and having no dependence upon his animal being.*[55]

This last sentence sums up the functions Common Sense fulfilled for Bovell: if taken to heart, it invalidated the equation of reason and intellect by enlarging thought to include moral and aesthetic qualities; it liberated men from a purely sensationalist psychology; above all, it directed thought towards the religious conscience and the "moral nature" for the ultimate recognition and sanction of permanent moral principles.

Having thus given his students some indication of the nature and grounds of their own rationality, and hence of the boundaries of "rational" thought, Bovell was free to use the mental philosophy of Reid and Cousin for the purposes of natural theology. There was little use, after all, in coming to an understanding of the mechanisms of one's own thought without turning such self-insight towards lofty purpose. "'All labour is useless,'" he stressed, quoting Laurens P. Hickock's *Rational Cosmology*, "'unless we turn to the use of the reason solely to discover the absolute reason, the faculty for direct and immediate insight.'" Accordingly, Bovell turned his students' minds towards such discovery. Since man *is* a reasoning being, he argued, he may use his faculty of "reason"—which he, alone of all creatures, possesses—to "attain to a knowledge of the existence of immortal life and of a Supreme Being." He may do this either by turning this special faculty to a dissection of "the myriad forms of matter by an analysis of matter itself" or, even more, by relying upon the "existence of a moral law and craving for truth" by which "he becomes conscious of the existence of a self-determining power which is capable of leading to higher results, anon the necessary existence of a self-existing Supreme Power, at once the fountain and origin of all that is manifest."[56] Again Bovell looked to the thought of Victor Cousin for a source of authoritative information and practical guidance for his students:

Whether we turn our attention, says Cousin, to the forces and the laws that animate and govern matter without belonging to it, or as the order of our labour calls us to do, reflect upon the universal and necessary truths which our mind discovers, but does not constitute, the least systematic use of reason makes us naturally conclude from the forces and laws of the universe that there is a first intelligent mover, and from necessary truths that there is a necessary being who alone is their substance. We do not perceive God, but we can conceive him, upon the faith of this admirable world exposed to our view, and upon that of this other world, more admirable still, which we bear in ourselves. By this double road we succeed in going to God. This natural course is that of all men: it must be sufficient for a sound philosophy.[57]

But what of the students, naive or presumptuous, who were content to rest their conclusions—and their convictions—upon "sense experience" alone? What of those who did not look beyond a mere "phenomenon" to search for its "cause"? Acting as if he had never heard of David Hume (the name scarcely appears in Bovell's *Outlines*), Bovell asked his students to look again to the nature of their reason for the answer: "Reason has been given us for the very purpose of going, and without any circuit of reasoning, from the visible to the invisible—from the finite to the infinite—from the imperfect to the perfect, and also from necessary and universal truths, which surround us on every side, to their eternal and necessary principles. Such is the legitimate and natural bearing of reason. It possesses an evidence of which it renders no account." To stray beyond the boundaries of reason so conceived, Bovell warned, is to be punished at either extreme; for the "revolt against reason" which admits only sensory perceptions as a legitimate source of knowledge could result only in a fruitless mysticism, while that revolt which aspired "to enter into immediate communication with him, as with sensible objects and the objects of consciousness," could lead only to an equally futile pantheism.[58]

Although there existed an apparent balance in Bovell's thought at the time of the publication of *Outlines of Natural Theology*, that balance was more apparent than real. By 1859 Bovell had fully subordinated science to devotion in his search for a Truth that would admit no relativity. Since that truth was a religious one, it is appropriate to look briefly at the devotional side of his quadrilateral mind in the period after 1859.

> As the result of the examination into the plan of creation, and as unfolded to us by the nature of the works themselves,

we cannot resist the conviction that we are the occupants and the objects of a grand and imposing world, whose aim is the glory of a Being whose goodness is over all His works, and by whom alone they are and were created. . . . We may not create a God after our own image, nor fashion Him by our own language. . . . We dare not, like those of old, make a God and worship it. We can worship Him who has made Himself known to us as the Creator, Sanctifier, and Saviour of His people. We can give the Lord the honour due unto His name, and worship Him with holy worship.[59]

With those words, Bovell drew his *Outlines of Natural Theology* to a close. Whatever the study of natural theology may have been on the eve of the publication of Darwin's *Origin*, it was still very much theological, with its sole object the worship and adoration of the Christian's God. From the outset of the Darwinian controversy, Bovell tenaciously kept this object uppermost in his mind. He published only one scientific article after 1859. While the assumptions of the natural theologian remained in his writings, gone was the lengthy and detailed marshalling of scientific evidence. Three of his books appeared between 1859 and the year of his emigration from Canada. Each was overwhelmingly devotional in tone and content.

The first in chronological sequence, *Preparation for the Christian Sacrifice, or Holy Communion* (1859), was a book of prayers, lessons, and scriptural passages meant for daily use by the Christian who wished to prepare for Communion. The third, *The World at the Advent of the Lord Jesus* (1868), was a study intended for use by Sunday School teachers and by families for readings at home. Its purpose, in the words of the author, was "to portray the condition of the world at the Advent of the blessed Saviour, and the benefits flowing to man from this wonderful event in the history of the human race." Significantly, its contents and purpose were derived from the "more systematic teaching of [his] College course." Here, once again, the influence of Victor Cousin made itself felt, for "the idea pervading these papers," Bovell noted, was "that, as in the kingdom of Nature, so in the kingdom of Grace, the footprints of the great I AM are everywhere manifest, preparing and perfecting a world for future years."[60]

But Bovell's popularization of natural theology is best revealed in the second of his three devotional books. Published in 1862, *Passing Thoughts on Man's Relation to God and on God's Rela-*

tion to Man was natural theology extended into the realm of social ethics. It was a book calculated to cultivate a pious disposition within the minds of Bovell's readers. Its immediate purpose, however, was to combat "the denial of a personal omnipresent God . . . , the result of that lamentable want of humility which caused an apostle to warn men of his time, 'not to be wise in their own conceits.'" Also to be fought was the sceptic who, clothing his "wretched pantheism" with "the cloak of reverence, seeks to destroy traditional forms of religion," while at the same time, with fake humility, "expresses his regret that the old should not have so firm a basis of truth to rest on as the new." The solution to such challenges, said Bovell (as, indeed, he also had said in *Outlines of Natural Theology*), was to produce arguments that support the omnipotence, omnipresence, and mercy of God and to show evidence of His "creative interference" in Creation.[61]

The book then followed a pattern of presentation and argument familiar to all students of natural theology, certainly familiar to those of Beaven or Bovell. Had any Trinity College student of the 1860s been given a copy of *Passing Thoughts* as a Christmas or graduation present, he need scarcely have read it, for he could have constructed a fairly accurate summary of the book's contents with only a glance at the table of contents and recourse to his notes in natural theology and divinity. Absent from the pages of *Passing Thoughts* were the fold-out geological charts, the illustrations of biological and zoological creatures, the circular diagrams of the life cycle of "all organic nature," the illustrations of prehistoric and other animals ranging from Ichthyosaurus to *Elephas primogenius*, and the phrenological charts and illustrations that had graced the pages of *Outlines of Natural Theology*. Gone, too, were the long extracts from scientific works which had accounted for much of its length. *Passing Thoughts* gave little space to the specific conclusions of modern science, but beneath the devotional surface of the book there remained in the logic of its chapters the unmistakable imprint of Butler, Paley, and their nineteenth-century followers.

The universe, it was stated at the outset, is one of law and order. Part of that order, and subject to its laws, is man, with a God-given spiritual nature that allows him to entertain the possibility of an eternal life. Such a life is possible because, as part of the scheme of things, man has a moral nature. This makes him supreme among earthly creatures because he alone is capable of perceiving the moral truths which are necessary to man, yet which exist independently of him. Man, however, is a fallen creature, and therefore yearns to determine the moral principles that have been established by the Divine law-giver. Revelation and His manifestation in nature allow man to perceive these truths, thereby helping him to attain Divine absolution. To aid man on this quest for the essence of his very humanity, God has provided proofs of His continuing presence in Creation by various acts of "divine interference in the progress of the world." Present in nature, therefore, is proof of a thinking mind at work: the Christian miracles are signs of God's wish that we might perceive this. But man is, by the nature of his reason, unable to worship God solely through his own unaided power. Hence, recourse is necessary to the Gospel and to its scheme of Redemption through Christ. This alone can reclaim man's nature; and to remain in this redeemed state a life of holiness, repentance, and service is required. Finally, his life in Christ is justified by a recognition of the meaning of, and participation in, the Holy Sacraments. *Passing Thoughts on Man's Relation to God and on God's Relation to Man* began, it might be said, in the spirit of William Paley on natural theology and ended in the spirit of "Pearson on the Creed."[62]

Sequela

Upon the completion of the 1869–70 university term, Dr. James Bovell retired from university life in order to spend his remaining years in the place of his birth, the British West Indies. Within a year James Beaven was also absent from the classroom; he retired from the chair of metaphysics and ethics at University College, University of Toronto, in 1871. The authors of the two most extensive Canadian treatises on natural theology were thus gone. Their own significance will be assessed in due course, but what must now be considered is the significance of their common denominational affiliation.

It is possible to argue that natural theology in Canada was primarily an Anglican preoccupation. That the church of Bishops Strachan, Inglis, and Mountain should have found natural theology congenial to its needs is scarcely surprising. One need only recall the responses of those same Anglo-Canadian clerics to the French Revolution and to the War of 1812. "Subordination in the Moral World is manifest and this appearance of nature indicates the intention of its Author," John Strachan declared in a sermon given several times during the 1820s and 1830s. Hence members of the "established" church in British North America found a combination of providentialism and Burkean conservatism with a philosophico-religious argument for design in nature of considerable value for the inculcation of social values of a decidedly traditional nature.⁶³ Such a utilization of the argument from design remained a common rhetorical device long after Bishop Strachan had died, and it was by no means reserved solely for the use of Anglicans.⁶⁴

But the Anglican hierarchy in Canada did not confine its use of natural theology to the preservation of desired social values. As the contents and aim of Bovell's *Passing Thoughts* fully indicate, Canadian Anglicans (perhaps more than any other denomination in Canada) sought to use natural theology as a support for the credal basis of their faith. George Whitaker, the provost of Trinity College from the 1850s to the 1880s, lectured for many years on Divinity. In that part of the course which covered the Catechism, Whitaker provided his students with a catechism of his own—of 744 questions and answers:

> 105. Q—Prove from Scripture the existence of God, as seen from his works.
> A—"Because that which may be known of God is manifested in them; for God hath shewn it unto them. For the invisible things of him from the creation of the world are clearly seen being understood by the things that are made even his eternal power and Godhead." Rom. 1 19–20. also Acts xvii 26–27
> 106. Q—What other proofs of his existence has God given to men?
> A—By his supernatural shewing of himself by prophecies and Miracles.
> (Pearson mentions power of Conscience).⁶⁵

These lectures were based upon, and accompanied by, a detailed examination of William Paley's natural theology. The irony of using the utilitarian "Pigeon Paley" as the basis of furthering the cause of High Church Anglicanism is significant; but if the irony was noticed by the Anglican community in British North America in the nineteenth century, it meant little, for Paley was serving the cause of God however he might be adapted. In the end that was all that mattered.

This affiliation of the Anglican church in Canada with natural theology is testimony to the extent to which the history of ideas in Canada is linked to the history of ideas in Great Britain, for it was but part of an intellectual bond that existed in England between the established church and the natural sciences in general. That the Church of England and Ireland could have created such an alliance at all serves as a reminder, one historian notes, of "how different the English Enlightenment was from the French. Sheltered under Newton's great name, science and religion had developed a firm alliance in England, embodied in that very British person, the scientific parson of the Anglican Church."[66] (William Paley was, after all, an Anglican archdeacon.) Working from the traditional Christian assumption that Truth was absolute and indivisible, early Victorians in general tended to extend the findings of natural science by analogy into the domain of Christian apologetics. In the half century that preceded the publication of *The Origin of Species*, natural sciences increasingly provided religion with the norm of truth. And this was the case even for those who were suspicious of the implications of science for religion. Cardinal Newman, for example, concluded the first discourse of *The Idea of a University* as follows: "Religious Doctrine is knowledge, in as full a sense as Newton's doctrine is knowledge. University teaching without Theology is simply unphilosophical. Theology has at least as good a right to claim a place there as Astronomy."[67]

In England, as a consequence of this, the standard elucidation of natural theology was one that was essentially independent of such traditional *a priori* proofs for the existence of God as the gift of Revelation or the argument from "Being."[68] The proof of God's existence rested, for an orthodox Paleyite, ultimately upon probability: the more contrivances—evidences of design, of conscious will—in nature the natural theologian could muster, the more probable it was that a designer, a Divine will, existed (or, perhaps put more appropriately, the less probable it was that a designer could not exist).[69]

Within the Canadian context, however, as the thought of both Beaven and Bovell attests, natural theology proceeded only in part from such assumptions. Its value in British North America, as in England and the United States at mid-nineteenth century, lay in the fact that it seemed to have combined successfully the inductive method of Baconian science with the then still widely accepted Newtonian conception of the cause-effect relationship, thereby adjoining the two most eminent figures in British science to the cause of religion. But to this mechanistic and empirical science, Beaven and Bovell added the Scottish philosophy of Common Sense. Regardless of the existence of an epistemological conflict between the school of Paley and that of Reid at the level of philosophical analysis, the Common Sense notion of an indwelling "moral sense" that was part of man's nature provided the means by which the two Anglo-Canadian natural theologians could insist that their ultimate aim was moral and spiritual, not merely utilitarian, even while they made use of Paley's arguments from utility elsewhere in their tomes.

The significance of the thought of James Beaven and James Bovell lies, therefore, not in their actual reputations as teachers,[70] for neither was remembered as an outstanding teacher, or even in the degree of excellence achieved in their textbooks. It lies instead in the extent to which their writings revealed the premises from which they worked and the assumptions to which they took exception; in the sources to which they went for their evidence and, as well, in the sources available to them which they chose to ignore; in the conclusions they drew and those which, following logically from their arguments, nevertheless remained undrawn.[71] There can be no doubt that the use of natural theology by Beaven and Bovell for the purpose of giving the authority of science to their creed—especially with regard to the Sacraments and the adoration of saints—was criticized by members of other denominations as being perversions of Paley's natural theology. Indeed, each found powerful and vocal critics even within his own communion.[72] Yet neither the use of that natural theology for the purpose of forging a Christian apologetic underpinned by the authority of science nor the strain of piety which made that natural theology at once so complex and so eclectic in the Anglo-Canadian context was theirs alone.

If James Bovell's *Passing Thoughts on Man's Relation to God and on God's Relation to Man* resolved, in its final chapters, into a kind of Paleyite complement to John Pearson's *Exposition of the Creed*, it was nevertheless paralleled in its other concerns with the peroration of a sermon entitled "God's Plan in Nature" given to the Mechanics' Institute of Baltimore, Canada West, by the young Methodist preacher Nathanael Burwash in the late 1850s:

> But Nature is supplemented by another & still more striking revelation of the Glory of God. There was a time when such additional revelation was unnecessary. Man's heart was

pure & his intellect unclouded. He enjoyed the communion of his elder brethren from the skies & from them would learn the story of the wonders done before his day & in the distant parts of the universe. Sun broke off that communion weakened his powers & left him in darkness. Then came a still richer display of divine glory in a divine law—an Incarnate Deity an Atonement & the promise of a day when the justice of God shall be vindicated & those who are found worthy shall like the angels of old behold again the display of almighty power when this universe shall again be wrapt in flame & the heavens & earth pass away with a great noise & old chaps return whence God shall call forth a new heavens & a new earth inconceivably more beautiful & wonderful than these.

This universe then is but one vast display of the glory of God. And we too are forced to promote the same great object by the study of that revelation. Here is the connection of Science & religion. This it is which makes the researches of laboratory the examinations of the microscope the ranging of the telescope all hallowed employment. There are some who seem to think that the study of Nature can ennoble & cultivate the mind apart from its connection with its great Author. But take a God out of Nature & science is dead her beauty is gone & the soul cramped & confined in every effort at an upward flight.[73]

The form of Christian piety at the heart of such a natural theology as this transcended denominational barriers, and few clerics of any denomination in British North America in the middle decades of the nineteenth century resisted its dictates, for it reached to the very nature of the Christian's faith. The call to Christian office, stressed Provost Whitaker in an 1852 sermon, may come in two ways: in an outward form in which the theologue asks himself "Do you think?" or in an inward form, where the question posed is "Do you trust?" The true call, the correct question to ask and to answer, is that from within: "For respecting the outward call the case is widely different—we have not here to deal with any objective truth—we have to search our own hearts, to examine ourselves. Here, then, we can but trust."[74]

As taught in the various colleges and universities in British North America in the years before 1859, natural theology was the primary means by which the Truth of Christian theology in its two basic forms—revealed and natural—was placed into a harmonious relationship.[75] Yet it was an uneasy, artificial harmony at best, for there were many problems to be faced by the natural theologian by the middle of the nineteenth century. Both David Hume, in *Dialogues Concerning Natural Religion* (1779), and Immanuel Kant, in his *Critique of Pure Reason* (1781), had seriously questioned—even before Paley had formulated his argument—both the conception of causation and the use of analogy upon which the Paleyite version of natural theology was based. And as Darwin prepared at last to send his work to the press, Henry Mansel, in his Brampton Lectures at Oxford, questioned whether the Paleyite use of analogy could validly either deny *or* affirm the existence of God from evidences in nature.[76] Nor were these the only problems with natural theology that were noticed by observers. Decades before the pivotal year, 1859, the "developmental hypothesis" was in the air, and many individuals—scientists, clerics, and lay members of the public alike—were beginning to have their doubts about the scientific correctness of the traditional argument from design in nature. Were the static conception of design and the evidences of change in specific forms reconcilable? And if nature, as Paley would have it, was one of beneficence and harmony, how could the many examples of obvious cruelty and harshness in the natural world be explained? Was Tennyson right when he spoke, in *In Memoriam*, of a "Nature, red in tooth and claw"? And did the defenders of Paley have a solution to the problem of Job?

Nevertheless, on the eve of the publication of Darwin's *Origin*, there did remain a semblance of balance and harmony in the study of natural theology in British North America. Its exponents —indeed those of the natural sciences in general—retained for the most part the traditional Christian conception of a Truth indivisible and absolute, whether taken from evidence found in external nature, human nature, or Revelation. Natural theology was but part of an orthodoxy of ideas which was to be ingrained into the minds of the Canadian clerisy of the higher learning then attending college, an orthodoxy based upon a conception of Christianity and its foundations that was in fact already suffering a serious decline in appeal and becoming increasingly difficult to justify credibly.

But if the idea of the unity of all truth was challenged by manifestations of the modern critical spirit, there existed all the more reason why it should be met sternly and with as much weight of argument as the Anglo-Canadian educator could muster; for in that unity of ideas and concern lay, it was believed, the basis of the cultural experience. After Darwin, "truth" would be fragmented and relative, and in British North America such a serious challenge was to be met with considerable resistance. The first group to meet it comprised those men to whom the interested observer of "modern thought" would first turn for guidance and authoritative judgements: the scientific community.

4
The Veils of Isis

> Christianity indeed lifts for us the veil of Isis, tells of the Righter of all the wrongs of ages.... Science cannot supersede the work of the great Consoler; but in searching into those lesser truths with which alone it has to deal, it may grope and peer hopefully, if still darkly, gladdened by the faith which rests on "the evidence of things not seen."
> Daniel Wilson, *Prehistoric Man* (1863)

> Ah, Science, teach us that the finite thing
> But veils the Infinite!
> Charles Morse, "To Science," *Trinity University Review* (1902)

In September 1859 Albert, Prince Consort, delivered a speech to a distinguished body of British gentlemen in Aberdeen, Scotland. Itself, this was scarcely a remarkable event. Albert gave many speeches during his lifetime, and many Victorian gentlemen listened patiently to such addresses. Yet this occasion was somewhat singular. The gathering to which Albert spoke comprised the elite of the British scientific community, the British Association for the Advancement of Science. Albert was its president for that year. A friend of British science throughout his life in England, and one of the architects of the Great Exhibition of 1851, he began his address with a general discussion of the nature of science—a review which has been described as one "that summarized prevailing philosophical views and did not break new ground."[1] It was, all in all, a concise reflection of the prevailing consensus about the nature of mid-Victorian science.

Early the next year, the Prince Consort's presidential address found its way into the *Canadian Journal*, the main publication of the Central Canadian scientific community. Those who read Albert's remarks were treated first to some grand generalizations.

"To me," they read, "Science, in its most general and comprehensive acceptation, means the knowledge of what I know, the consciousness of human knowledge. Hence, to know, is the object of all Science; and all special knowledge, if brought to our consciousness in its separate distinctiveness from, and yet in its recognised relation to the totality of our knowledge, is scientific knowledge." The primary activities of the scientist, Albert continued, are those of analysis and synthesis, the reconstruction of "a unity in our consciousness," a new understanding of that aspect of the natural world under observation. "The labours of the man of Science are therefore at once the most humble and the loftiest which man can undertake," for the process of organized and purposive observation of phenomena which relates the observed object to "the general universe of knowledge"—through arrangement and classification—has as its end nothing less than the discovery of "the internal connexion which the Almighty has implanted" in previously incongruous elements of nature.[2]

Hence, the central concern of the different sciences is to establish the essential unity of all nature. But this, Albert warned, is an onerous task because it is also an endless one: "for God's world is infinite." Onerous or not, he added, it is the duty of the scientist to remain conscious of the "unity which must pervade the whole of science," and the major way this can be done is "in the combination of men of science representing all the specialities, and working together for the common object of preserving that unity and presiding over that general direction." The true science, the best science, he concluded, must "proceed . . . by the inductive process, taking nothing on trust, nothing for granted, but reasoning upwards from the meanest fact established, and making every step sure before going one beyond it. . . . This road has been shown to us by the great Bacon, and who can contemplate the prospects which it opens, without almost falling into a trance similar to that in which he allowed his imagination to wander over future ages of discovery!"[3]

Given this encomium of Bacon, it is important to note briefly the major tenets of "Baconian" science, for Albert's declaration points to the important fact that on the eve of the Darwinian revolution, in English-speaking countries the scientific enterprise was still conducted along lines laid down by Bacon.[4] This was certainly the case in British North America, where "Bacon," like "Reid" and "Paley," was a surname that bore the stamp of final authority. Baconian science completed the triumvirate of intellectual orthodoxy that dominated many educated Anglo-Canadian minds for the first three-quarters of the nineteenth century.

Bacon had used his ideas as a kind of battering ram against scholasticism, insisting that only by observing nature empirically could man come to know reality. Compared with the vague inquiries after Truth offered by the scholastics, Bacon's new definition of science—as an instrument of inquiry rather than as a repository of information—seemed to allow human bias and error to be overcome for the first time in history. His creed was simply that "the whole of philosophy is founded upon experience, and is nothing more than a classification of the facts and phenomena presented in nature."[5]

The Baconian method was rationalistic and empirical, deduction after observation, but it did not exclude the Almighty. "And all depends," he had written in the introduction to *The Great Instauration*, his blueprint for the new science, "... on keeping the eye steadily fixed upon the facts of nature and so receiving their images simply as they are. For God forbid that we should give out a dream of our own imagination for a pattern of the world; rather may it be graciously granted to us to write an apocalypse or true vision of the footsteps of the Creator imprinted on his creatures."[6] Albert's recapitulation of the commonplaces of mid-Victorian British Baconian science had not overtly equated the cause of science with that of religion, except, perhaps, for its almost gratuitous mention of the Almighty. But there were many individuals, both in Albert's learned audience and among his later readers, for whom the Prince Consort's articulation of the assumptions of that science was little less than royal approval of just such an equation.

The Veils of Isis

Not a few such readers were to be found at the time among those who practised science in British North America. While James Beaven, James Bovell, and other men of religion in Canada sought to lay the appropriate religious foundations for the study of nature through the teaching of their own adaptations of natural theology, some of the leading scientists in the colony sought, in their lectures and writings, to build, upon the edifice so carefully constructed by their colleagues, a science in accordance with the orthodox Christianity of their day. "Let us remember this at least," concluded the president of the Canadian Institute, Daniel Wilson, early in January of 1860, "that that great ocean of truth does lie before us, and even those pebbles which our puerile labours gather on its shore, may include here and there a gem of purest ray; and meanwhile the search for truth ... will bring to each one of us his own exceeding great reward."[7]

Wilson's peroration closely paraphrased a famous example of Sir Isaac Newton's sense of humility in the face of the seeming boundlessness of nature and the unity of its laws. But as put forward by the president of the Canadian Institute, that truth and unity were given their essential meaning by the fact that they were, and could only be, a Christian truth and a Christian unity. "The experience of the past shows how frequently men have contended for their own blundering interpretations," Wilson concluded, "while all the while believing themselves the champions and the martyrs of truth." Such self-delusion would not occur if one was careful to remember the religious nature of truth, for "all truth is of God, alike in relation to the natural and the moral law, and of the former, as truly as of the latter may we say: 'if this counsel or this work be of men, it will come to nought; but if it be of God, ye cannot overthrow it; lest haply ye be found even to fight against God.'"[8] A year later, Professor Wilson, still president of the Canadian Institute, reiterated the same theme. The aim of the institute, he said, should be to investigate the laws of nature and to uncover "new truths in every department of human knowledge." As humble labourers in the great phalanx of the world scientific community, members of the Toronto-based organization would therefore share

> in that glorious advancement of knowledge by which God, who has revealed himself in his world, is making ever new revelations of himself in his works; and having made known to us Him who is the wisdom and the power of God, through whom we have the assurance of life and immortality in the gospel of his grace, is anew, in the great volume of nature, adding evidence of man's immortality, by revelations of the inexhaustible wonders of that creation, which, I doubt not, is to employ the purified and enlarged faculties of man in its study through all the ages of that future life to which it is his attribute [sic] to aspire. May we, while seeking here the pure and elevating enjoyments which spring from the discovery of nature's truths, find in knowledge of the humblest works of God an incitement to the adoration and love of Him, whom to know is life eternal.[9]

A sonnet from a volume of Daniel Wilson's poems published in the mid-1870s strikes to the heart of this theme:

> I stood upon the world's thronged thoroughfare,
> And saw her crowds pass by in eager chase
> Of bubbles glistening in the morning rays;
> While overhead, methought God's angels were
> With golden crowns of which all unaware
> They heedless crowded on in folly's race.
> But yet methought a few were given grace,
> With heavenward gaze, to aspire for treasures there,
> All trustfully as an expectant heir;
> Through whome [sic] the soul shone, as the body were
> But a veil, wherein it did abide,
> Waiting till God's own hand shall it uncover.
> O God! that such a prize in vain should hover
> O'er souls in nature to Thyself allied! [10]

At one level Wilson's sonnet expresses the common Christian desire to transcend his finiteness through the pursuit of the eternal; at another it is a gesture of thanks for the existence of a scientific elect, those "few [who] were given grace,/With heavenward gaze, to aspire for treasures there,/All trustfully as an expectant heir." Science thus could serve as a means of grace for the select few to whom were given both the ability and the duty to lift the veil with which God had obscured the presence of His hand in nature. This view also finds close parallels in Wilson's scientific work. To the individual, Wilson wrote in *Prehistoric Man* (1863), "'The drift of the Maker is dark, an Isis hid by the veil!'"; but with the aid of the inspiration and guidance of religion, such darkness is dispelled, for "Christianity . . . lifts for us the veil of Isis, tells of the Righter of all the wrongs of ages."[11]

The dictates of piety were not, then, confined only to the pew on Sundays, not just to the notebooks of philosophy students, nor to lectures on natural theology. They also found their place in the field trips taken by professors of science, and they took their hold as well upon the minds of anyone, academic or layman alike, who looked to science as a source of religious inspiration and affirmation. The inductive, Baconian science extolled by Prince Albert required no abstract "hypotheses" unprovable by simple observation and induction, no ingenious theories. James Bovell, in fact, had warned his students of the dangers of such unwarranted extensions of the scientific imagination. "While false systems of philosophy may tantalize and fret the mind," he said, "the calm and reflecting reasoner on revealed truth is content to curb his imagination, and to accept the creator as He has thought fit to shew himself."[12] The main requirement was simply a "child-like heart" and the humility that must necessarily accompany the thought of any Christian who, aware of the limitations of his own reason, nevertheless yearns for a measure of unity with the Divine.

Those of such a mind who read Prince Albert's address to the British Association for the Advancement of Science might well have placed such an interpretation on his remark that the man of science "only does what every little child does from its first awakening into life, and must do every moment of its existence; and yet he aims at the gradual approximation to divine truth itself." He might well have concluded that by the simple inductive process of observation in the Baconian tradition, "we thus gain a roadway, a ladder by which even a child may almost without knowing it, ascend to the summit of truth."[13] Such lessons were not lost on Canadian students only a few years removed from childhood. Writing in the first volume of the *Dalhousie Gazette*, the first Canadian university newspaper, one anonymous student declared that "the great object of science is the ascertainment of causes—the search after the ultimate,—the making of generalizations—the resolution of plurality into unity." Its "indirect (although equally great) object," he concluded, "is the cultivation of all those qualities which dignify and adorn the moral nature of man." Science, too, could come to the aid of the nineteenth-century moral philosopher and his insistence on the reality of the "moral nature." It should therefore come as no surprise to find editorials in Canadian student newspapers such as the one that wondered: "What can have a greater influence in purifying and elevating the mind of man than the study of the beautiful and yet wonderful works of Nature around him! What could raise our thoughts more towards the Supreme Being than the contemplation of Nature, and a knowledge of its wonderful laws."[14]

But such a conception of the methods and aims of science was possible only as long as the essentially static, mechanistic universe of Newton's physics and Paley's physico-theology remained intact. From the late eighteenth century on, however, the idea of the immutability of nature's design had been constantly undermined: by Kant, Buffon, Laplace, Herschel, Cuvier, Lyell, and others. Work in astronomy, geology, and paleontology, in particular, pointed to the fact that nature itself was mutable, changing. By 1859 the *fact* of organic change was well known; there was lacking only a theory of the *mechanism* by which such change took place. "In this development," John C. Greene has observed, "Darwin played a last-minute but decisive role."[15] It was Darwin, more than anyone else in the nineteenth century, who helped to lift the corner of the veil of Isis. And as with Bluebeard's last wife, impelled to unlock the last door in the castle, many were aghast at their first glimpse of what hitherto had been shrouded in darkness.

The Reception of Darwin in Canada

The task of reviewing Charles Darwin's long-awaited book in British North America fell to two men who, along with George M. Grant, were to exert a very strong personal influence upon higher education in Canada. In 1859 William Dawson and Daniel Wilson were both approaching the full vigour of their physical and intellectual maturity. Dawson was thirty-nine years of age when *The Origin of Species* reached his hands; Wilson, forty-three. Both had strong Scottish ties. Wilson was a native of Edinburgh and had attended its university; Dawson was born in Pictou County, Nova Scotia, had obtained a Master of Arts degree at the University of Edinburgh in 1842, and had married into one of the city's better-known and respected families.[16]

Each man was also beginning to acquire a respectable international reputation in the field of science. Wilson had come to science after first considering careers in art (he studied for a time with William Turner and had considerable talent as an artist) and in popular literature (he had written reviews and essays for magazines such as *Chambers' Journal*, and had published anonymously a *History of Oliver Cromwell* and a *History of the Puritans* with the firm of his lifelong friend Thomas Nelson).[17] By the early 1840s, however, his mind had turned to antiquarian and ethnological concerns. In 1847, while secretary of the Scottish Antiquarian Society, he published the massive *Memorials of Edinburgh in the Olden Time*, with illustrations executed by himself. Four years later appeared *The Archaeology and Prehistoric Annals of Scotland*, which earned for its author an honourary Doctorate of Laws from St. Andrew's University and gave to the world the word "prehistory." The impressively researched volumes which made up this latter work also marked a substantial attempt by the author to effect, in the words of the preface to the first edition, "the transition from profitless dilettantism to the intelligent spirit of scientific investigation."[18] In 1853 Wilson immigrated to Canada with his wife to accept a position at the University of Toronto as professor of history and English literature. By 1859 he had established himself in the newly built University College, was an active member of the Canadian Institute, and had become editor of the *Canadian Journal*.

William Dawson had led a life that was equally varied and active. By 1859 he had studied natural history under Robert Jameson at Edinburgh; had met, worked with, and gained the respect of geologists Charles Lyell and William Logan; and had published in the prestigious *Edinburgh New Philosophical Journal*.[19] Two series of lectures in natural history at Dalhousie College in 1849 had resulted in his appointment, at the age of thirty, as superintendent of education in Nova Scotia. The outstanding work in public education that followed led in 1855 to the principal's office at McGill College. When asked by the editor of the *Canadian Naturalist and Geologist* to review Darwin's *Origin*, he had already published what probably was his prime contribution to nineteenth-century science, *Acadian Geology* (1855), and he was on the verge of seeing the release of *Archaia* (1860), his first book-length study of the relationship between modern scientific research and scriptural cosmogony.

When the reviews of Darwin's *Origin* by Dawson and Wilson appeared in print, many of the major contributions of both men to science, education, and the cultural life of Canada still lay in the future. They must be viewed, therefore, in their capacity as men whose reputations in these fields were on the increase, men to whom students, colleagues, and the literate Canadian public might have turned for authoritative judgements on the major scientific question of the day.

Their initial reactions to Darwin's theory of the origin of species were similar, especially on two of the basic issues raised in the *Origin*: first, that there is in nature no absolute distinction between species and varieties because all organic creation is descended from a common primordial stock; second, that the survival or extinction of species rests primarily upon a process, which Darwin chose to call "natural selection," that led to the "survival of the fittest" (a term which Darwin borrowed from Thomas Malthus and lived to regret).[20] The two reviewers shared a commitment to an inductive, Baconian science based upon observation. They rejected as a consequence the notion of a science which set forth "hypotheses" unproven by such observation and resting mainly upon an evidential basis of statistical probability extrapolated from a mass of evidence.[21]

Dawson and Wilson had in common another characteristic: their scientific judgements were largely shaped by their essentially moral outlooks. Although in quite different ways, both were as much men of religion as they were of science. Dawson was an orthodox Presbyterian, and Wilson, a broad church Anglican; and the scientific works of both were profoundly affected by the demands of their religious consciences. In the mixture of religious and scientific assumptions can once again be seen the problem of determining the ultimate sources of conviction. The nature of that authority shall be examined further as we look at the initial reactions to Darwin of William Dawson and Daniel Wilson, both of whom were drawn to science precisely because for them it held the means by which they hoped to penetrate the veils behind which was what Augustine had called the "great and hidden good."

Their basic objection to Darwin was simply that Darwin had put forward conclusions not supported (though not contradicted) by his evidence, substantial though that may have been. Furthermore, they believed that these conclusions went beyond the scope of legitimate scientific inquiry. "Nothing is more humbling to the scientific enquirer," Dawson began, "than to find that he has arrived in the progress of his investigations at a point beyond which inductive science fails to carry him." Science, he went on, was an endeavour that rested upon an insoluble contradiction. "True science is always humble, for it knows itself to be surrounded by mysteries—mysteries which only widen as the sphere of its knowledge extends. Yet it is the ambition of science to solve mysteries, to add one domain after another to its conquests, though certain to find new and greater difficulties beyond."[22] Paradoxical as it may have been, Dawson's science satisfied, rather than frustrated, him. On the one hand, an inductive Baconian science helped to establish authoritatively the "truths" of the natural world; yet, on the other, the very boundlessness and seamlessness of the web of nature meant the perpetual revelation of more mysteries of life. Since these, like the mysteries of life itself, were those of God, the endless search for their solution became, for Dawson, a kind of scientific counterpart of the Christian's quest—even in the knowledge that his fallen nature makes the mission impossible except through salvation—for unity with the mind of God, for an insight, however limited and inadequate, into the Divine will. It was for him the ultimate form of piety.

From this point of view, the benefit of Baconian empiricism was that since it was based upon a finite number of observations, limiting itself to observations of "secondary causes" operating in nature, and insisting that no conclusions be drawn beyond the evidence provided by such observations, speculations of a cosmological sort were beyond its scope. This conception of science therefore dictated a separation of scientific conclusions from metaphysical speculation. Such a science could come in handy to those, like Dawson, who owed much to the "twin theologies" tradition. In violating the canons of Baconian method by engaging in unwarranted speculation, Darwin (Dawson and Wilson alike believed) had not only transcended the bounds of proper science, but had obliterated the distinction between science and cosmology. As shown later in the chapter, however, both Dawson and Wilson themselves violated the requirements of that Baconian tradition in order to engage in their own cosmological speculations.

The general worth of Darwin's book, Dawson stated, rested on his use of evidence and inference. The author had elaborately investigated the question of variation within species, and had illustrated the laws of specific variation "in a very full and satisfactory manner." But then he had gone beyond the scope of science by attempting "to apply the laws of variation to an entirely different series of phenomena, those of specific diversity," and by seeking by analogy "to break down all specific distinction with respect to origin, and to reduce all species to mere varieties of ancient and perhaps perished prototypes." Darwin's *Origin* divided into two dissimilar parts Dawson claimed: one which consisted of "the careful induction of facts bearing on the nature and laws of variation" and a second (which in Dawson's view vitiated the admirable qualities of the first) in which the "wild and fanciful application" of the results of the inductions as to varieties was made into "another class of phenomena [that is, species]."[23] This not only violated the canons of Baconian science, but contradicted the Mosaic account of Creation to which Dawson rigorously adhered. A limited degree of variation within species he admitted, but species themselves were the special creation of God and as such were inviolable and absolute. He had put this belief in the fixity of species into print as early as 1847, and the conviction remained with him until his death in 1899.[24]

Dawson was no less unequivocal in his rejection of the theory of natural selection, which for Darwin was the mechanism that explained the transmutation of species. As with the species question, he was convinced that there "is here a huge hiatus in the reasoning of our author." In his discussion of specific variation in pigeons, Darwin had taken great pains to show that all varieties descended from the common rock pigeon and that, by domestic breeding, pigeons could be made to acquire certain desirable characteristics. Dawson readily admitted the large degree of variation within species, but he adamantly refused to accept Darwin's conclusion that in nature there was a process of "selection" at work. Above all, he rejected the Malthusian assumptions that lay at the basis of the theory of natural selection: that in nature, population will invariably increase at a greater rate than food supply and that as a consequence—to use Dawson's description of Darwin's conclusion—there is a "'struggle for existence,' a ... warfare in nature, in which the race is always to the swift and the battle to the strong, and in which the struggle makes the strong stronger." Such warfare, Dawson replied, was in fact "fanciful," for "this Malthusian doctrine, though good for a single species by itself, is false for the whole in the aggregate."[25]

A recent study of the thought of William Dawson provides abundant evidence to support without qualification the view that almost every word he uttered in print on science and religion was pervaded by the influence of the Paleyite tradition of natural theology.[26] With respect to natural selection, two basic assumptions of that tradition shaped Dawson's answer to Darwin. The first was that Creation was the result of a beneficent Creator, and the second—following from the first—was that Creation was characterized above all (as befitted a benevolent God's handiwork) by balance, order, and harmony. But if such was the case, how could one accept the Malthusian view of life as warfare and struggle? Quite simply, one could not. Failing to recognize the cardinal fact that for Darwin and his followers the idea of natural selection placed the so-called struggle for existence *within* the realm of law and order, Dawson countered what he regarded as Darwin's pessimistic Malthusianism with the more optimistic view that

> the beautiful harmony of nature provides that the feeders shall multiply more slowly than the food, and that the food shall be kept under by the feeders. When any form does locally multiply too far, the checks appear, usually in the form of a diminished reproduction or in the more rapid removal of

the infirm, the sickly, and the aged. When through the slow operation of physical causes or the introduction of new species, certain forms of life can no longer find the means of subsistence, all the facts we know indicate their disappearance, not their change into new forms. . . . In short, the struggle for existence is a myth, and its employment as a means of improvement still more mythical.[27]

Once again, Dawson concluded, Darwin had extended his conclusions by deduction and hypothesis beyond the valid inferential basis of his evidence. He had appropriated the various "effects of external conditions of existence to these supposed causes of change."[28]

Dawson's major objections to the *Origin* had now been voiced. To support his contentions that there was an inviolable distinction between species and varieties and that variation occurred only within certain fixed limits, he then turned to his major area of expertise: geology. The geological evidence of the day—and he was largely correct in this—provided no verification of Darwin's "finely graduated organic chain," one which would solidly connect man with the marsupial.[29] Dawson also noted that geology condemned the selection theory by the very imperfections of its record. "Moreover," he added, "in those parts of the geological scale which are the most perfect and unbroken, there is no graduated transition of forms." The Silurian limestones in America, and especially the post-Pliocene clays and sands of Canada, provided abundant evidence of the apparent fixity of certain species and the sudden disappearance of others. Similarly, despite the long lapse of time which might allow for variation, the example of fossilized Arctic plants whose living descendants remain unchanged also provided, in Dawson's view, both positive and "conclusive" evidence of the fixed reality of specific forms.[30]

Daniel Wilson's 1860 presidential address to the Canadian Institute, published in the *Canadian Journal* early that year, was largely a review of Darwin's *Origin*. For Wilson, as for Dawson, science was largely Baconian in method. But as we turn from Dawson to Wilson, we come upon the hazy frontier which links the religious to the poetic sensibility. The science of Dawson clearly bore the Hebraic legacy of his Calvinism (as may be observed by reading Dawson on biblical cosmology); that of Wilson was equally informed and shaped by Wilson the artist and poet. "In some respects, and perhaps with truth," G. Mercer Adam observed near the end of Wilson's life, "it may be said that Dr.

Wilson would have done more justice to himself if he had made a choice in his life's work between literature and science rather than, as he has done, given the prose side of his mind to archaeological studies and reserved its poetical side for literature."[31] As with Sir William Osler's description of James Bovell's "quadrilateral mind," there is a significant measure of truth in this statement. But like Osler's observation, it is too artificial and clear-cut. Just as Bovell's mind never had an absolutely rigid "scientific" or "religious" side, nor two equal commitments to the different sources of authority implied by these words, there was likewise not, in the mind of Daniel Wilson, any clearly defined "prose" or "poetic" side.

In fact Wilson's poetic sensibility was always a present and determining factor in his thought, including his science. One of his students at University College in the early 1870s took down the following lecture notes:

> Poetry precedes prose.... As *Rhetoric* has its own forms etc. distinct from Logic, so poetry has *its* own.... So like pulpit-preaching or pleading—*Poetry aims at giving pleasure by exciting and influencing the Emotions*—and the *license* allowed is only limited by the object the poet has in view.... Poetry addresses the *taste* or aesthetic faculty.

Or again:

> Rhetoric is the art of speaking (and writing) well and persuasively the language of Emotion.... It employs an elaborateness of structure inadmissible in Logic.... In Rhetoric—There must be *continuous emotion*, springing from the subject itself, and *true feeling*.[32]

The aesthetic bent of Wilson's mind must constantly be recalled when considering his scientific as well as his literary work; so should the function of rhetoric, thus defined, when assessing the scientific writings of Wilson (and others) in the nineteenth century.

When Wilson spoke of rhetoric, it is obvious that he did not exclude writing upon scientific subjects from its scope. Scientific writing of the Victorian period was very much an art of persuasion. Parts of Wilson's review of Darwin's *Origin* could have served as blackboard examples of that art. Canadian science, he admitted, had necessarily to be in large measure a practical one.

Yet any science of true worth must also transcend purely utilitarian concerns. "In the Canadian Institute," he therefore concluded, "it may be presumed that we pursue science for the discovery of its secret truths; that we climb the steps of knowledge, as the traveller ascends the mountain's unexplored cliffs, gladdened at every pause in his ascent with new grandeur and beauty in the widening horizon which opens on his delighted gaze."[33] Here is the rhetoric of romantic aesthetics under the guise of the aims of science. The paradox that gave Dawson's science its religious function finds a parallel here in Wilson's conception of science as of value insofar as it excites the aesthetic faculty. If Dawson's response to the *Origin of Species* owed much to the legacy of Paley's *Natural Theology*, Wilson's owed as much to the tradition of which Edmund Burke's essay *The Sublime and the Beautiful* was an integral part. The secret of the veils of Isis, as with all veils, lay in the mystery maintained, not in the actual object hidden.

Like Dawson, Daniel Wilson was clearly disturbed by the events that were then shaking modern science. The problem with Darwin's challenge to the supremacy of Baconian induction by his use of an hypothetico-deductive method (which has since served as the methodological basis of modern evolutionary biology) was that it threatened the very sense of mystery that provided the science of Dawson and Wilson with its religious and aesthetic dynamics. Not content to describe nature as it appeared after the uncovering of each successive veil, Darwin had dared to assess the natural world as if no veils existed. His discovery of natural selection, an astute observer of the Darwinian method has noted, "was, above all else, a triumph of reason. If banishing intuition from our conception of the process of discovery deprives us of a sense of mystery, it nonetheless permits us to analyze that process in a far more satisfying manner than did the mythological accounts."[34] Such a method may have been satisfying for the Darwinian, or may still be for the modern biologist, but not for Dawson or Wilson. The Darwinian hypothesis, said Wilson, appears to have had as its immediate result "the removal of many old land-marks of scientific faith, whereby we witness some of the conditions of ruin, which mark all transitional eras,—whether of thought or action. The old has been shaken, or thrown down, the new is still to build."[35]

"In this light," Wilson's review of Darwin's *Origin* began, "... we must look upon that comprehensive question which now challenges revision ... *What is Species?*" Comprehensive and important because it "forces us back to first principles," and has equal effect upon paleontology, zoology, and the relations of science and theology, the species question, as resolved by Darwin, stood as a challenge above all because of its bearings upon Wilson's own major interest, ethnology. It involved not only the question "In what forms has creative power been manifested in the succession of organic life?" but also another, more central to Wilson's particular scientific concern: "Under what conditions has man been introduced into the most diverse and widely separated provinces of the animal world?" It is clear that to Wilson, the ethnologist, the former question was in fact subsumed within the latter:

> It is to the comprehensive bearings of the latter indeed, that the former owes its origin; for what is the use of entertaining the question, prematurely forced upon us: Are all men of one and the same species? While authorities in science are still so much at variance as to what species really is; and writers who turn with incredulous contempt from the idea that all men are descended from Adam, can nevertheless look with complacency on their probable descent from apes! [36]

Much of Wilson's review of Darwin's *Origin* paralleled that of Dawson. Like the Montreal geologist and educator, Wilson perceived the fundamental challenge posed by Darwin. He was also able to summarize the essence of that challenge with admirable brevity:

> He has arrived at the conclusion that there is in reality no essential distinction between individual differences, varieties, and species. The well-marked variety is an incipient species; and by the operation of various simple physical causes, and comparatively slight organic changes, producing a tendency towards increase in one direction of variation, and arrestment, and ultimate extinction in another, the law of *natural selection*, as Darwin terms it, results, which leads to his "preservation of favoured races in the struggle for life." [37]

When he rejected the "transmutation" theory of evolution through "the tendency of species to an infinite multiplication of intermediate links," Wilson also rejected the notion of natural selection. He noted that the evidence of paleontology afforded no positive evidence to affirm the idea of transmutation. "We look in vain," he said, "among organic fossils for any such gradations of form as even to suggest a process of transmutation. Above all, in relation to man, no fossil form adds a single link to fill up the wide interval between him and the most anthropoid of inferior animals." This, he contended, is true even if one limited oneself to the purely physical characteristics by which the paleontologist is bound. But once one considered mental characteristics, as the ethnologist must, the challenge to Darwin's theory was even stronger, for

> if the difference between man and the inferior animals, not only in mere physical organization, but still more in all the higher attributes of animal life, be not relative but absolute, then no multiplication of intermediate links can lessen the obstacles to transmutation. One true antidote therefore to such a doctrine, and to the consequent denial of primary distinctions of species, seems to offer itself in such broad and unmistakeable lines of demarkation [sic] as Professor Owen indicates, between the cerebral structure of man and that of the most highly developed of anthropoid or other animals.[38]

Here was the genesis of Wilson's argument a dozen or so years later that Shakespeare's Caliban could be viewed as the "missing link." But unlike the "missing links" so long sought by later anthropologists, Wilson's did not serve the purpose of establishing once and for all time the strength of the chain of evolution. It was, instead, a means of establishing a kind of buffer between animal and man in creation.

Although Wilson rejected Darwin's theory, he treated the views of the British naturalist with the respect due to any who seriously proposed a significant advance in scientific truth. "His 'Origin of Species,' is no product of a rash theorist, but the result of the patient observation and laborious experiments of a highly gifted naturalist." There could be little doubt that Darwin's work would create as many problems as it solved. It would, Wilson noted, "tend to . . . give courage to other assailants of those views of the permanency of species, which have seemed so indispensable alike to all our preconceived ideas in natural science, and to our interpretations of revealed cosmogony." Here Wilson differed significantly from Dawson, who was convinced that Darwin's errors could only have pernicious effects upon the pursuit of Truth. In the end, Wilson said, no serious harm could come of Darwin's work: if it was incorrect, scientists would prove it so; if correct, new areas of knowledge would be opened. In either case the cause of Truth, through the practice of science, would be served: "our attitude ought clearly to be that of candid and impartial jurors. We must examine for ourselves, not reject, the evidence thus honestly given. . . . All truth is of God, alike in relation to the natural and the moral law, and of the former, as truly as of the latter may we say: 'if this counsel or this work be of men, it will come to nought; but if it be of God, ye cannot overthrow it; lest haply ye be found even to fight against God.'"[39]

Unlike that of William Dawson, Daniel Wilson's science was not tied to a dogmatic commitment to the Mosaic cosmogony; yet in its own way it was no less tied to the notion of a providential design and harmony in nature. Dawson marshalled his scientific knowledge to repudiate the Darwinian position because his own selection of the conclusions of the science of his day accorded better with the biblical views which for him gave meaning to nature and its laws. In a startling passage near the end of his review of Darwin, Dawson all but admitted that, in fact, truth or falsity, as determined by the canons of science, was not really the central issue in the acceptance or rejection of Darwin. Referring to the Darwinian analogical inference that (in Darwin's words) "probably all the organic beings which have ever lived on this earth have descended from one primordial form, into which life was first breathed," Dawson remarked:

> We may well ask what is gained by such a result even if established. The origin of species, as we now have them, it is true, is mysterious, but what is gained by reducing them all to one primitive form? . . . On the contrary, if we are content to take species as direct products of a creative power, without troubling ourselves with supposed secondary causes, we may examine, free of any trammelling hypothesis, the law of their succession in time, the guards placed upon their intermixture, the limits set to their variation in each case, the remarkable arrangements for diminishing variations by the natural crossing of varieties, the laws of geographical distribution from centres of origins, and the physical causes of variation, of degeneration, of extinction.[40]

For a man of science to ask what is to be gained by a scientific theory even if that theory is established to be "true" is strange indeed. Yet this apparent abandonment of the essence of scientific inquiry may also be found in Wilson's thought. On the one hand, Wilson applauded the work of the comparative anatomist Richard Owen (who embraced evolution but rejected natural selection) for his "grand generalizations, based not [as with Darwin] on theory, but on laborious and exhaustive induction, [thereby revealing] to us the plan of the Creator."[41] Yet on the other, he admitted that science—even that which is based upon the solid Baconian observation of laws operating in nature—becomes inadequate. "Science has achieved wondrous triumphs," he observed in his 1861 presidential address to the Canadian Institute, "but life is a thing it can neither create nor account for, by mere physics. Nor can we assume even that the whole law of life can be embraced within the process of induction, as carried out by an observer so limited as man is.... Darwin, indeed, builds largely upon hypotheses constructed to supply the gaps in the geological records; but whilst welcoming every new truth which enlarges our conception of the cosmic unity, all nature still says as plainly to us ...: 'Canst thou by searching find out the Almighty to perfection?'"[42] The reasons for Wilson's fascination with the natural world, protected by the veils of Isis, ultimately lay in the satisfaction he derived from the certainty that, behind each raised veil, was fortunately another which yet preserved the mysteries of life.

Support from the Flanks

The pronouncements of William Dawson and Daniel Wilson on Darwin's book were those of the two most eminent authorities on science in British North America, but the fact remains that they appeared in two rather obscure journals which doubtless were read only by a handful of Canadians. Their importance for the intellectual history of Canada rests, then, not in the extent of their influence in shaping the thought of Canadians on the subject of evolution, but in the fact that their thoughts reflected to a very high degree the nature of the reception of the evolutionary theory in Canada, the arguments set forward against it, and the fears which nagged articulate and thinking Canadians for more than a quarter of a century after the beginning of the Darwinian epoch.

The dozen years from 1860 to 1872 witnessed the publication of a number of books and articles by various academicians in British North America which paralleled or lent weight to the views expressed by Professors Dawson and Wilson. Much of James Bovell's *Outlines of Natural Theology*, while written just before the publication of Darwin's *Origin*, provided the Canadian student with detailed arguments, from the works of "sound" British and American scientists, with which Darwin's speculations could be refuted. Content with relying upon the Bridgewater Treatises of Knox and Owen, Bovell had concluded that the reintroduction of fixed species both in animal and in vegetable life was quite natural. "From man to the whale, all is alike," he wrote; "one theory explains all; one idea or plan pervades all." But the theory was not that of natural selection. The belief that extinct forms could be reintroduced kept the idea of species distinct from that of variations and away from the hands of Darwinians. It was "cogent proof that the same Divine Mind has ever engaged in the works of Nature." Similarly, Bovell's *Outlines* provided lengthy extracts and "proofs" from traditional scientific authorities that the Mosaic record was acceptable to the best of scientists, that abundant evidence existed of special creations, and that there was nothing wrong with the idea of evolution, so long as that idea was conceived in terms of the ultimate purpose for which the world was created and towards which it was unfolding. "It is not until we turn our thoughts from this crash of matter and wreck of worlds," Bovell wrote, "and scan the renovated earth, as it exists in the present age, that the hitherto incomprehensible becomes open to comprehension; and man, the last born of earth, crowns his Maker's work, and . . . declares a new creation indeed to have been accomplished, a moral and religious universe to have been fashioned."[43]

Similarly, a few years later William Leitch, principal of Queen's College, published a book entitled *God's Glory in the Heavens* (1862), the purpose of which was to interpret the discoveries of the astronomer in terms of the concerns of the theologian. Once again the influence of William Paley made itself powerfully evident. "The solar system," wrote Leitch, "may be viewed as a machine, manifesting intelligent design. The mechanism of the sun, planets, and satellites suggests, just as a watch, the idea of a Contriver. One of the most remarkable evidences of design, in the celestial machine, is the provision made for its stability."[44] The immensity of the universe, its apparent infinitude, makes man aware of his finiteness, and leaves him grateful for the fact that the redemptive power of Christ gives him a significance not warranted by his tiny place in the cosmos. A simple glance into the abyss of space forces a man to recognize that his true significance rests, not in his material life, but in that of his soul.

Other prominent members of the Canadian scientific community lent their weight to the views of Dawson and Wilson in writings published during the 1860s. Book reviews and articles by E. J. Chapman, professor of mineralogy and geology, and William Hincks, professor of natural history, both at University College, Toronto, appeared in the *Canadian Journal*. In 1857 Chapman reviewed a recently published popularization of natural theology, *The Testimony of the Rocks*, by the well-known Scottish writer Hugh Miller. He liked Miller's insistence that the argument for the "high antiquity of the globe" was not inconsistent with a Christian interpretation of Creation, and he found in the Scottish writer's *Testimony* a series of well-reasoned arguments that reflected "the broad views of enlightened science as distinguished from bigoted empiricism on the one hand, and from skepticism on the other."[45] Three years later, in the immediate aftermath of the publication of Darwin's *Origin*, Chapman published an assessment of J. W. Dawson's *Archaia, or Studies of Cosmogony and Natural History of Hebrew Scriptures* (1860). "We may fairly welcome it," he wrote, "and urge its perusal upon those who still blindly look upon geology, and upon natural science generally, as antagonistic in some undefined manner to the spirit of Revelation."[46]

Much of this review consisted of a long extract from Dawson's book concerning the fixity of species and the structural adaptation and contrivance of vertebrate forms as reflections of the general design of the Divine Architect. In concluding, Chapman, who generally exhibited a detachment greater than that of most of his Canadian contemporaries, noted that he did not entirely share Dawson's views. Yet he insisted that the book would be invaluable to the student of theology "who, shaking off the trammels of a too narrow school, is willing to allow a place in his philosophy to the teachings of the great cosmic harmony which circles around him, and which proclaims through all its changes, I, too, am of God."[47]

By 1863 Charles Lyell, the most eminent geologist of the age, had come to accept Darwin's theory. He did so in his book *The Geological Evidences of the Antiquity of Man* (1863). Chapman was called upon to review it. Clearly, both Lyell's reputation and his arguments challenged the Canadian scientist's religious commitments. The many facts marshalled by Lyell in support of Darwin's theory of development, Chapman admitted, "constitute grave difficulties when we strive to explain them in connexion with the usually received or 'special creation' view." But on the other hand there were equally strong difficulties in accepting the Darwinian theory: the apparent absence in existing nature and in the fossil record of any transitional forms linking various types (a fact noted both by Dawson and by Wilson in their reviews of Darwin); a strong sexual antagonism "between all but the most closely allied forms"; and the immensity of the break in the fossil record when one attempts to compare various types, even within the confines of a single class. A significant structural relationship may seem to exist between man and the higher apes, Chapman noted, but the gulf between the two is surely too great for one to accept the Darwinian hypothesis: there still existed "a dumb and stationary brute-intellect on the one side—speech, reason, and progress, on the other."[48] This was not a very satisfactory rebuttal to Darwin's claims. It rejected a theory unsupported by sufficient evidence, but did so with neither counter evidence nor any hypothetical alternative. The gulf between brute and man, however, was something which those interested in the place of man within some form of evolutionary process had to face.

Immediately following E. J. Chapman's 1863 review of Lyell's book in the *Canadian Journal* was one on T. H. Huxley's popularization of Darwin's theory, *On the Origin of Species, or the Causes of the Phenomena of Organic Nature: A Course of Lectures to Working Men* (1863). The reviewer was the Reverend William Hincks, professor of natural history at University College, Toronto. Hincks had won his university appointment in the 1850s, when his brother, Sir Francis, was at the peak of his political influence. His competitors for the position had included two young British scientists: John Tyndall and T. H. Huxley. Now, nearly a decade later, Mr. Huxley was the *bête noire* of the British scientific and religious world, and in the next decade Tyndall would come to share the same fate. But in the third quarter of the nineteenth century the authorities who had hired William Hincks had many occasions to remind themselves that they had made a wise choice. Given the criteria by which academicians were chosen for their posts, there could be no doubt after the debate between Darwin's defender, T. H. Huxley, and Bishop Wilberforce in 1860 that Mr. Huxley was not an exponent of what in their view constituted an "enlightened science." On the other hand, the writings of William Hincks gave every indication that he was "enlightened" in exactly the fashion the hiring authorities had expected him to be.

Two themes ran through Hincks's essay-length review of Huxley's book, and both had been central to the critiques of Darwin by Dawson and Wilson. First, Huxley had violated the methodology of sound, inductive science by indulging in unwarranted speculation. Second, he had not provided a case evidentially strong enough to prove that species were not "fixed." Hincks regretted at the outset that Huxley had chosen to offer instruction to England's workingmen that went beyond "the established principles and interesting facts of natural science." He had chosen, instead, to offer "speculative views on the most recondite question his science offered." Later in his essay Hincks reminded his readers of the methodological heresy Huxley (along with his inspiration, Darwin) had committed: "it is not the business of the philosophical enquirer to form some theory respecting the origin of the various species of organised beings."[49] But Hincks could make this claim only as long as he could support his major scientific premise: that variation occurred in species only within fixed limits. If he could convince his readers that Huxley and Darwin erred on this essential point, there was, in his view, no need to inquire into the origin of species at all. The "special creations" theory, which could be reconciled with the Mosaic account of Creation, would thus remain intact.

Hincks was unequivocal in his own position on the species question. "The truest notion of a species may perhaps be that of a group of developmental tendencies, fixed in the nature of things and only liable to modification by external causes within certain limits."[50] This was the extent to which he was willing to go in accommodating himself to the development theory. Once the decision was made that species are inviolate, that they vary only within fixed limits, then the very structural similarities which for the Darwinian were proof of the gradual chain of variation became, instead, examples of the validity of William Paley's natural theology. They shifted from being proofs of Huxley's theory of "variability" and became "certain determinate inherent tendencies of development, descending from the first created organisms and constituting the great plan of creation." Once the inviolability of species was accepted, the species debate was, for Hincks, necessarily at an end:

> It seems to us most unreasonable to expect that the believer in the immutability of species should want a theory as to their origin. He sees throughout nature the abundant evidence of the operation of an intelligent designing mind, the great first cause of all things. He sees every species adapted to its condition and enabled to supply its wants, and the conception of a creative act, as the expression of an almighty volition, is sufficient to account to him for the existing order

of things—objects may have been created simultaneously or successively; all in one place on the earth's surface, or in various localities; but as long as they are acknowledged to be essentially distinct objects, and to have no natural tendency to intermix and modify each other, they admit of no inquiry into the nature of modifying causes, and consequently of no theory of the formation of species.[51]

Hincks believed that the problem of variation in forms constituted one of the "most important enquiries in which a naturalist [could] be engaged." To his credit, he spent most of his intellectual energy (if that energy is reflected in his writings) in grappling with it. He had necessarily to do so, because his scientific specialty was taxonomy, the science of classification, an important aspect of Baconian science. Darwin's obliteration of the idea of species as fixed entities challenged traditional systems of taxonomy. The triumph of Darwinian ideas would mean the triumph of the idea that systems of classification were simply a "human contrivance," that there could be many such systems of classification. Not so, Hincks insisted: "a true natural classification is the interpretation of the great plan of the Creator."[52] Most of Hincks's scientific writings were derived from his search for the "natural" system of classification which would accurately reflect the purpose and design of the Creator of all things.

It cannot be said that he was successful. He had earlier agreed with Louis Agassiz that "in every really good classification, man is only the interpreter of nature."[53] But he believed Agassiz's scheme to be too rigid. He was more favourable to William Dawson's "Elementary Views of the Classification of Animals," which appeared in the August 1864 issue of the *Canadian Naturalist*. "I find in his paper," Hincks wrote with obvious satisfaction, "a remarkable agreement on what are, certainly, the most important points, with the principles I have maintained and taught for a good many years." Dawson's well-known views on the idea of species, repeated in his *Canadian Naturalist* article, were, in Hincks's view, "of fundamental importance, deserving ... and well fitted to counteract some prevalent errors." Hincks disagreed with Dawson (as he did with Agassiz) on the criteria by which genera were grouped into orders, but agreed with him on essentials: that an elucidation of the natural system of taxonomy would help men realize how marvellous and thoroughgoing was God's plan.[54]

It was, ironically, his primary commitment to the existence of such a Divine plan that caused Hincks—like Dawson and Wilson before him—to abandon the sure ground of Baconian science for the less certain footing of the very "speculation" he, like his contemporaries, distrusted in certain of the followers of Isis. In his most extensive treatment of classification in nature, Hincks declared his commitment to the "sensationalist" philosophy that was the basis of empirical observation. He insisted that classification was simply the process of "systematic generalization" based upon such observation. But then came a betrayal of his own scientific tradition. A natural system of classification consisted for Hincks not only of an assessment of structural similarities, but also of a search for their ultimate *purpose* in the scheme of Creation. Thus was introduced, as an integral part of this "natural" taxonomy, a commitment to Christian teleology. Until the true meaning of structural similarities and differences was determined, "we could not possess any means for forming a natural classification which should be the expression of the real plan of nature, the actual relations of all beings to each other and to the system of the universe."[55]

Phrases such as "the real plan of nature" or "actual relations of all beings" are pregnant with meaning in this context, for by the use of words such as "real" or "actual" Hincks meant, not an empirical reality, but a confirmation of the truth of the Divine scheme of things. "A good classification is a convenient summary of our knowledge," concluded his essay on classification, ". . . and much more than all this is the expression of the real plan of the great author of nature, enabling us to feel its beauty, and to understand the harmony which binds together the infinitely varied forms of organized beings."[56] If the spirits of Bacon and Paley can be seen in this declaration, it cannot be doubted that both were used for the purpose of elucidating the will of God in the thought of the long-forgotten brother of Francis Hincks.

Christian Guardians

Throughout the 1860s and 1870s, science was viewed by those Canadians who commented upon it as inextricably related to the fortunes of Christianity. The scientific endeavour, properly conducted, was generally seen as confirming the Christian Revelation. In the hands of the irresponsible, however, it could result in erroneous and malicious challenges to Christian doctrine through the introduction of false modes of thought. Nowhere was this more apparent than in the pages of the most widely circulated and influential religious newsmagazine in Canada during the nineteenth century, the Methodist *Christian Guardian*. While academic defenders of the faith pointed to the weaknesses of Darwin's theory and to the affirmation of religion which a properly conducted science would achieve, the contributors to the *Christian Guardian* week after week and literally for decades subjected the findings of modern science and the pronouncements of its leading exponents to careful scrutiny and criticism. What went through the minds of those British North Americans—not all of them Methodists—who read the *Christian Guardian* during the 1860s will never be known. But one can determine what subjects met their eyes, and surmise that in more than a few instances the *Guardian*'s articles were read aloud and discussed in mid-Victorian Canadian parlours as part of a weekly family activity. Such families would have had a great deal of opportunity to learn about the problems posed by science for their religious tradition. At this level of Canadian intellectual life, that of informed opinion midway between the more systematic thought of the academicians and the purely popular opinion reflected in secular newspapers, there was little "culture-lag" in the reception of ideas from the eastern shores of the Atlantic.

In the dozen years from 1860 to 1872, literally scores of items on the relationship between science and "the higher life" appeared in the pages of the *Christian Guardian*. Sometimes these took the form of original (and often lengthy) articles, signed and unsigned; sometimes they were lead editorials. Excerpts from other journals were often drawn to the attention of the Canadian reader. Recent books were reviewed, always for an unabashedly didactic purpose. The title of the journal in which they appeared must, after all, constantly be kept in mind.

One conclusion clearly emerges from a review of the many items carried by the *Guardian* during the 1860s on the subject of modern science: Darwinism in itself was not considered the major threat to orthodox religion. Not even the subject of review in the *Guardian*, Darwin's *Origin* was merely symptomatic of the general threat posed by speculative thought to eternal Christian verities. In no instance was this intrusion more in evidence than when *Essays and Reviews*, the scholarly British collection which subjected the biblical truth to the scrutiny of the Higher Criticism, was published in 1860. The furore it created within the Anglican church was picked up immediately in the *Guardian*, and a debate over the implications of this sort of scholarly activity continued in its pages for the next two years. Modern infidelity, wrote one reader, had at last been brought into the open. "Things are now called by their right names at Oxford."[57]

Indeed, so they were in the *Christian Guardian* from that point on. *Essays and Reviews*, wrote the *Guardian*'s editor, "has taken the religious public quite by surprise for the book is decidedly infidel, to an extent that must be entirely satisfactory to the most extreme class of unbelievers." In the long essay which followed, he went on to criticize the authors of the offending collection for their "fanciful philosophical analogies," their sceptical rationalism and vague pantheism, and their implicit denial of the supernatural by their insistence that "the only criterion of religious truth is the judgement, or conscience, or *verifying faculty* within us." The editor noted with obvious enjoyment that the author of that essay (Frederick Temple, headmaster of Rugby School) did not say precisely what this last power was. Yet that did not stop Temple from denying the reality of "everything that cannot be accounted for by the exercise and development of our natural powers."[58] And if this were not dangerous enough, the attack upon the foundations of religion was being conducted, as a later *Guardian* editorial pointed out, by those stationed within the citadel of faith, those who professed that their aims were, not to defend, but to reconstruct the Christian religion.[59]

By December 1864 the *Guardian* was able to claim "a clear perception of the direction in which modern thought is tending." It was not a very cheerful Christmas message for earnest Canadian Christians, for their religion was seen to be threatened by equally earnest rationalistic Christians who sought to do nothing less than replace the God of Revelation with the God of Nature and to forge a new Christianity based upon the principle of free intellectual inquiry. These new infidels were not like the atheistic rationalists of old. Their rationalism, instead, was "many-sided and subtle, intellectual and pious." Led on by free inquiry, these modern thinkers, the *Guardian* claimed, had taken scepticism to a crossroads, to "a point at which it must branch off from one side or the other in the direction of positive belief. It cannot stand still, and it cannot go on disbelieving." Of the ultimate result there could be no doubt. "The human conscience . . . reaches out on all sides for something tangible between itself and God. 'Free inquiry,' as modern enquirers employ it, will not help the soul of man here. It carries him from one speculation to another, but it confirms nothing to him." It could, that is, only dissect, and had no way of saying confidently and firmly, "This is the truth." It could afford no certainty that what is "true" today will be "true" tomorrow. Science could not help the modern inquirer "beyond a certain point":

> It is powerless to solve the problems, moral and psychological, which meet man at every step. Wherever he turns he is met by bewildering facts in human nature and history, and of very helplessness he is fain to call upon something higher to lift the cloud that makes his duties dubious and his destiny dark. It can hardly be too much to hope that, in striking wildly out for something to cling to, modern thought, as we have been considering it may grasp again the anchor which it has too recklessly let go, and find sure hold for faith and hope, and full satisfaction for all mental cravings, in that Revelation which is the Divine mind, and in that universal church which expounds the witnesses of Christendom in the interpretation of it.
>
> If it be not so there lies but a poor prospect before human nature.[60]

For the remainder of the decade, items in the *Christian Guardian* dwelt upon the prospects modern thought raised for the Christian conception of human nature. Such articles tended to be of two basic sorts: those which provided further evidence of the growing rationalism and anarchic free inquiry within the Christian community and which sought, in a variety of ways, to counter such tendencies by emphasizing the reality and significance of the spiritual and miraculous in Christian life; and those which attempted to illustrate how a properly conducted science was in fact necessarily a handmaiden to traditional Christian theology.

In the decades after Darwin, it was not difficult to provide evidence of growing rationalist infidelity. The Reverend J. F. Hurst's *History of Rationalism*, which pointed towards the magnitude of the problem posed by the "modern form of infidelity," met with a very long and favourable *Guardian* review in 1866.[61] Much of this infidelity emanated from the universities of Germany, and the danger of this Germanic influence was also pointed out. Its scepticism was of a very "rank nature," in thousands of cases consisting of nothing less than a "bald atheism" which exulted in scorning religion and worship. It profaned the holy rites, glorified the grossest materialism, and made great use of the words "liberty" and "democracy," even while being fundamentally illiberal.⁶² In making this last point, the *Guardian*'s editor noted that in their mockery of Christian rites, German infidels repeated some of the excesses of the French Revolution. This equation was used more than once to discredit the new "liberal" theology emanating from the European continent. The liberality of the rationalists was a spurious one: they professed to be friends of liberty, yet did away with all authority and customs. They would destroy all conscience, moral distinctions, ideas of right and wrong. It was this kind of liberality that had produced the French Reign of Terror.⁶³ It was this kind of moral confusion that had led many modern youths to reject the solid theological grounds of Clarke, Paley, and Butler for any of a host of obscure and paradox-ridden creeds.⁶⁴

A second way of discrediting modern rationalism and rationalistic science was to show that it quite simply was not "rational." The followers of Comte and Darwin, the *Guardian* noted, declared that a Divine Being cannot be seen. Therefore, they erroneously concluded, He does not exist. Their fundamental error lay in their mode of thought, which was false, mechanical, external, and superficial. They exalted the senses, denied the reality of the spiritual world—and "terrible is the bondage to which they thus doom the spirit of man."⁶⁵ Is this, asked the *Guardian*, a true "freedom" of thought? Does "reason" confine itself solely to the world of nature and the senses, to the exclusion of that of revelation and spiritual life? Such a narrow conception of reason was sufficiently preposterous that it scarcely merited comment. An essay by the American apostle of rationalism, R. G. Ingersoll, appeared in the *Guardian* in 1871. Entitled "Reason and Faith" it condemned any religion that required a sacrifice of rationalist principles and insisted that true faith must be based upon reason.⁶⁶ The fallacies in Ingersoll's reasoning were sufficiently self-evident that the article could be reprinted without editorial criticism. David Friedrich Strauss's, *Life of Jesus*, and the anonymous *Ecce Homo*, guilty of the same heresies, were, however, subject to lengthy criticism.⁶⁷

There *was* a war, insisted the editor of the *Christian Guardian* in 1867, between religion and infidelity; but it was not a war in which one had to choose between the opposing camps of reason or revelation. That was the rationalist's error, a mistake based upon his presumption that the world of reason was coextensive with that of empirical observation. Yet part of the rational process, the editor insisted, was the discovery of facts that came from revelation. "Religion is . . . a subject for revelation, and mere investigation of physical principles, or observation of social facts, cannot *unveil* a world which may be as superior to this, and as much unlike this, as a man is to a cabbage.... It is therefore reasonable to depend on revelation for our religious knowledge, and the facts of revelation will always be consistent with reason, will enlighten reason and give it employment." The "reason" of the new infidels was not acceptable to the editor of the *Guardian*. "We adhere," he proclaimed, "... to the truths we are bound to believe, all the essential truths of revelation and of sound philosophy, may be *proved*, may be established by honest *reasoning*, by legitimate *logic*." What were the examples of proof by such reasoning and logic? "We adhere to the old-fashioned logic of the Evidences." William Paley's star still burned brightly in Canada in the year of Confederation. "Paley's arguments," continued the *Guardian*, "remain unanswered, and almost unchallenged, by the cant and rant of modern self-styled rationalism."[68]

In the end, rationalism, having rejected the sound logic of Paley, proved "unreasonable" to the *Christian Guardian* for three basic reasons. First, it "misrepresented the office of reason" by assuming that mind either creates or discovers religious truth, thereby eliminating the need for revelation. Second, it lived upon other ideas and theories: materialism, pantheism, sometimes even mysticism. "The rationalistic spirit is an eclectic imagination, set free from fact and logic." Third, it was irrational because it "opposes evidence and argument with mere hypothesis and conjecture." Here was the violation of sound scientific reasoning. Here, too, was the ultimate danger of rationalism. It was one particular form of intellectual anarchy, "the pleasing, luxurious dream," as the editor of the *Christian Guardian* put it, "of spontaneous thought set 'free' from the guidance and restraint of sound reason."[69]

At the heart of the orthodox Christian's opposition to rationalism—the dominant form of heterodox thought—was the fact that it was characterized by the venal sin of pride: intellectual pride. The *Guardian* often stressed this in its editorials, especially during the early 1870s. "The pride of knowledge and intellectual power is one of the most marked dangers of the age," wrote the editor in April 1872. "Nothing is to be assumed or taken for granted," he had written a week earlier. "This is eminently a testing age. Men will no longer accept authority in place of demonstration.... Only the 'gold and silver and precious stones' of truth shall safely endure ... in these times of enquiry, of criticism."[70] Even the pride of money was not as insidious as intellectual pride, for the latter involved "the idolatry of mental power" at the expense of "the spirit or principle by which it is wielded and controlled." Intellectual pride was its worst form because it involved a violent disruption of the personal relationship of man and God. "This pride of intellect," the *Guardian* warned, "is at variance with that recognition of our dependence upon God for all things, which lies at the foundation of all true religion. Those who are lifted up with pride, in their intellectual achievements, are not likely to be willing to receive with meekness the engrafted Word which alone is able to save their souls."[71] In a world which was beginning to equate rationality with the operations of the intellectual faculty there could be no true piety. Nor could there be a true science, and it was the example of certain scientists, "insolent" and "contemptuous" of the spiritual world, which was used to illustrate the evils of intellectual pride in an editorial of that title.

Yet despite the many attempts made by clergymen writing for the *Guardian* to deal with the scepticism emanating from scientific quarters,[72] those who sought a philosophically consistent approach to science from the point of view of the Christian could only have been confused in the 1860s and 1870s. On one hand, a Victorian Canadian family reading the pages of the *Guardian* would have learned that there were levels of truth. There was the truth of the scientist, who observes the operation of steam and the growth of seeds, and the higher truth of eternal things—the truths of the Word of God. The two worlds, it appeared, were separate and inviolable.[73] On the other hand, they would have learned less than a year later that there could be no division between science and religion. "A man cannot believe contrary to what he knows." There could therefore be no opposition between a reasonable faith and ascertainable truth.[74] In another instance, they would have read a *Guardian* editorial entitled "The Bible's Historical Accuracy." But a few years later an article by no less eminent an authority than Henry Ward Beecher would insist that "when scientific men tell me that the great historic facts of the Bible are not to be relied upon, I tell them that the Bible does not consist of historic facts."[75]

Despite the risk of publishing contradictory statements such as these, the *Guardian* did make a significant attempt to examine the claims of mid-nineteenth-century scientists. The overwhelming intention of the authors of the many articles on the relationship between science and religion was to show that there should be no conflict between them. A properly conducted science would prove to be the handmaiden of Christian theology, and the present dispute had been created by a handful of men who had violated the canons of true science. They were exponents, in the words of St. Paul, of "science falsely so-called." To be sure, the initial reaction to the geological basis of evolutionary theory and to *Essays and Reviews* was a highly disputatious one within the pages of the *Christian Guardian;* but in both cases the controversy arose over conflicting interpretations of the offending tracts as set forth by *Guardian* correspondents. One particularly acrimonious and quibblesome dispute took place even though both correspondents believed that in Genesis and in geology the order of creation was the same.[76] Such letters to the *Guardian* simply proved to one observer that the semi-infidel views of geologists had now infiltrated the Methodist church,[77] and prompted another to suggest that while there might be much in geology which justified the idea of a lengthened antiquity, there was much also to "check the world of our fancies." "Mr. Theorist," he concluded, "the old coats are in better condition than the new."[78]

Geology was near the centre of the *Guardian*'s dispute with scientific infidels. Beginning with the anonymous *Vestiges of Creation* in the 1840s, continuing with the works of Darwin and Lyell, and now being used for equally heterodox purposes by contributors to the *Christian Guardian*, geology was the science which led the onslaught upon Mosaic cosmogony. It was an essay on that subject in *Essays and Reviews* which most raised the ire of the *Guardian* and created another controversy within its pages.[79] Especially was it necessary to correct infidelity in the science of geology as practised in Canada because it was taught in the colleges of British North America. In the hands of the infidel, geology would give to students only "a dreamy sort of knowledge which merely puffs them up with vain ideas and shadowy theories." Finally: "There is no doubt that the science of Geology if properly conducted and built solely upon known facts, might be made subservient to the purposes of science; but when it only calls forth a school of dreamers who are continually dreaming of some new discovery extending far into the fathomless depths of the unknown world, and of the infinite wisdom of the Almighty Creator, they are raising up a class of modern infidels who defile the purity of science by setting up their boasted wisdom in opposition to the Revelation of God's Word."[80]

There, in one long sentence, was a false science's heresy and a true science's purpose. The danger inherent in the arrogant intellectual presumption of a false science, contrasted with the valid commitment of true science to an inductive, Baconian method that shunned "speculation," was a lesson which the author of the essay did not wish to be lost on his readers. A sequel to this warning reemphasized science's true method and its desired results, and was addressed specifically to the nation's educators:

> Lord Bacon's theory of experimental philosophy will always be found the safest guide to true philosophy. We trust, therefore, that those who are entrusted with the education of our youth, will cease to instruct them in the certainty and actual demonstration of the theory of Geology, while it is at present built on little else than theory and conjecture, being assured that all such instruction will only lead to fallacy and disappointment. . . . [The present generation of geologists] only regard the power and wisdom of God as Creator, and the peculiarities of its creation as objects of philosophic investigation, regarding matter rather than mind, because their minds are not spiritual but carnal. Hence their teachings are dangerous, however plausible and ingenious they may appear; and of course, unsuitable to the education of youth. For whatever has a tendency to awaken doubt in the teachings of scripture, or shake the confidence of the young in its truths, is of far more consequence than all the ignorance which would result from the want of information on the subject.[81]

This correspondent's fears might have been more warranted had T. H. Huxley and John Tyndall, rather than Daniel Wilson and William Hincks, been hired at University College in the 1850s. But they had not been, precisely because university authorities shared such fears. In 1870 Hincks gave his presidential address to the Canadian Institute. "There are too many examples continually occurring," he noted, "of ingenious speculation unsupported by sufficient evidence, for it to rank as a presumption of truth. A restless grasping after novelty is a serious fault." All, however, was not lost. Although the German, influenced by his "transcendentalist philosophy," had totally adopted Darwinism, not so John Bull. "In the sober English mind it cannot be said that the Darwinians gain a rapid or easy victory."[82] But the next year Darwin himself renewed the debate over "Darwinism" with the publication of his book *The Descent of Man.*

Man's Place in Nature

The appearance of Darwin's long-awaited sequel to *The Origin of Species* inaugurated a new wave of anti-Darwinian sentiment in Canada. By the end of the 1860s, little effective accommodation had been reached in Canada between the defenders of Christianity and the scientific findings of the decade. Articles recounting scientific infidelities continued to find a welcome place in the *Christian Guardian*.[83] Few Canadians writing for the *Guardian* were willing to accept Darwin's theory of evolution, and virtually none gave countenance to the idea of natural selection. "That time has been when religion and science were thought to be conflicting and irreconcilable," wrote W. H. W. (probably William H. Withrow) in 1867. Yet his own assessment was symptomatic of the fact that the battle had been resolved by many only by making science into an exercise in Christian apologetics. "The profoundest and most thoughtful of modern *Savan*[t]s, with few exceptions, bow in lowly reverence at the shrine of truth as revealed in the Scriptures.... True science is always meek and never dogmatic.... Science is the handmaid not the rival of religion. She sits lowly at nature's feet and learns patiently the secrets she reveals."[84] A number of those more enlightened "Savants" were excerpted, quoted, and paraphrased in the *Guardian* to prove the case for a Christian science. These included Sir Charles Lyell, Lord Shaftesbury, Louis Agassiz, Dr. Norman Macleod, Mark Hopkins, Dr. Edward Carpenter, and Michael Faraday, the "Christian Philosopher."[85]

But with the publication of *The Descent of Man*, Canadian critics of modern science were drawn into a renewed struggle with the latest phase of the Darwinian heresy. Just after the publication of Darwin's new book, but before its contents were known in Canada, a long article entitled "Darwinism and Christianity" appeared in the *Christian Guardian*. It was well reasoned and moderate in tone, stating all the major objections of the decade to the theory of evolution and concluding that "all observation and research extending over the period of human and animal life testify to the permanence of species."[86] It was the last of such articles to speak with moderation of Darwin, for, within months, copies of *The Descent of Man*, stowed in the holds of steam packets plying the North Atlantic, reached Canadian shores. Not a few Canadians may later have wished that the ships carrying the offending cargo had met with a watery fate on the shoals of the St. Lawrence.

It was a book that focused the full force of evolutionary theory upon the question of the origins of man, a subject not mentioned by Darwin in *The Origin of Species*. Human beings, Darwin now argued, probably descended from some form of primate. He further enraged the Victorian sensibility by stressing the significance of "sexual selection," the choice of a reproductive partner, in the process of evolution. Finally, he argued—and here he challenged conventional mental and moral philosophy—that the intellectual and social faculties of man were adaptive and that his survival or extinction rested upon such changes.

The phrase which best describes the *Guardian*'s general reaction to *The Descent of Man* is "righteous indignation." "The appearance of the book has allayed, rather than increased, the interest felt in the subject," it wrote. *The Origin of Species* had been marred by Darwin's speculations and his hypothesis of natural selection. How seriously, then, could one consider a book which was even more "speculative and imaginary, and unattested by actual facts" and which stressed the idea of sexual selection as fundamental to its central argument?[87] The publication of T. H. Huxley's popularization of Darwin's theories, *Lay Sermons*, a year earlier did little to moderate the reaction in Canada to the latest Darwinian heresy. *Lay Sermons* was, said the *Guardian*, simply "the latest deliverance of the anti-Christian Scientific School," the product of a man "thoroughly anti-Christian and atheistic in his views."[88]

The combination of Darwin and Huxley was too much for the *Guardian*. By mid-1871 it had become defensive and intransigent. "There is a possibility," it warned in July, "that in our efforts to be liberal towards the theories and speculations of scientists, we may surrender too much."[89] The new attack on "modern infidelity" had by that time already begun in the pages of the *Guardian*. "Darwin and his friends having made brutes of themselves," C. M. D. had written two weeks earlier, "leave us in the terrible gloom of utter mental darkness; and we only get relief when we hear the voice of God as Abraham did, 'I am the Almighty God; walk before me and be thou perfect.'"[90] By September the *Guardian* had ceased to argue about natural selection or the antiquity of the earth. It had retreated to defend more important ground, and quoted at length Sir William Thompson's defence before the British Association of the argument for design as put forward in William Paley's *Natural Theology*.[91]

If an accommodation was to be made in Canada to evolutionary theory, it was clear by 1872 that it would not be initiated within the pages of the *Christian Guardian*. Would it come from the pens of the leading Canadian scientists? While the *Guardian* recalled the wisdom of Paley, William Dawson and Daniel Wilson paid careful attention to Darwin's new book and set their thoughts once again to paper.

Dawson's response to *The Descent of Man* was his own *Story of the Earth and Man*, published in 1873. By 1886 it had reached its ninth edition, and before publication in book form much of it had appeared as a series of articles in the popular British magazine *Leisure Hour*.[92] With the exception of the works of Darwin and Huxley, Dawson's book may well have been one of the most well-read popular scientific works in the late nineteenth century.

Dawson was clearly worried by 1873 over the scientific events of the past decade. He had stated why in his presidential address to the Natural History Society of Montreal, given the previous year:

> There can be no doubt that the theory of evolution, more especially that phase of it which is advocated by Darwin, has greatly extended its influence, especially among young English and American naturalists, within the few past [sic] years. We now constantly see reference made to these theories, as if they were established principles, applicable without question to the explanation of observed facts, while classifications notoriously based on these views, and in themselves untrue to nature, have gained currency in popular articles and even in text-books. In this way young people are being trained to be evolutionists without being aware of it, and will come to regard nature wholly through this medium. So strong is this tendency, more especially in England, that there is reason to fear that natural history will be prostituted to the services of a shallow philosophy, and that our old Baconian mode of viewing nature will be quite reversed, so that instead of studying facts in order to arrive at general principles, we shall return to the mediaeval plan of setting up dogmas based on authority only, or on metaphysical considerations of the most flimsy character, and forcibly twisting nature into conformity with their requirements. Thus "advanced" views in science lend themselves to the destruction of science, and to a return to semi-barbarism.[93]

In *The Story of the Earth and Man*, Dawson sought to curb the descent of science into such "semi-barbarism." Canada must be a country, he had said at McGill's Annual University Lecture for 1870, "educated not merely in general learning and literature, but in that science which is power because it wields the might of those forces which are the material expressions of the power of the Almighty Worker."[94] Dawson's reply to Darwin in 1873, in *Earth and Man*, was a powerful example of "that science."

Only the last fifty pages of *Earth and Man* dealt with man, but in them Dawson spelled out his scientific and religious reasons for refusing to accept the radical implications of Darwin's views on the descent of man. His last two chapters can in fact be viewed as the summation of a dozen years of resistance to Darwin's theory in the English-speaking world. "Principal Dawson is one of the few eminent men of science who at the same time are avowedly and distinctly Christian in their sentiments and beliefs" began the very laudatory review of his book in the *Canadian Monthly and National Review*; "[his] position is ... the only one left to those who think that the spiritual philosophy is founded on eternal facts, and who do not find themselves able to swallow the 'new decalogue' so urgently pressed upon them by the 'advanced' thinkers."[95]

The last section of *Earth and Man* refuted the scientific evidence upon which evolutionism was based (along lines set forward in Dawson's 1860 review of *Origin*); ridiculed the notion that man could be descended from (as Darwin put it) "a hairy quadruped, furnished with a tail and pointed ears, probably arboreal in its habits"; countered Huxley's criticisms of the Paleyite argument for the existence of a Creator by defending at length the validity of Paley's central metaphor of the watch; and finally vindicated the theistic conception of Creation. "The theory of creation and design," he insisted, "is infinitely more rational and scientific than that of evolution in any of its forms."[96]

Darwin's new book involved not only the study of nature but of human nature. *The Descent of Man* raised questions of fundamental importance in the areas of psychology and philosophy, as well as geology and anthropology. *The Origin of Species* had led men into the new world of geological time; *The Descent of Man* took them on a journey into the interior of the mind. Most of Dawson's book dealt only with the geological and paleontological areas of its author's expertise. But whenever he dealt with the origin of man, he found himself engaged in that journey into the interior. Man differed from brute creation by his mental constitution. For Dawson, the gap between "the nature of the animal and the self-conscious, reasoning, moral nature of man" was proof simple of the inviolability of species. Man was from the beginning separated from animal creation. "In him," Dawson wrote, "we find not merely that brain and nerve force which is common to him and lower animals . . . but we have the higher force of will and intellect, enabling him to read the secrets of nature, to seize and combine and utilize its laws like a god, and like a god to attain to the higher discernment of good and evil." Furthermore, man's mental constitution, his intellectual, moral, and spiritual faculties, was fixed from the time of his creation. He was, from the first, both a rational and a moral being.[97]

Darwin claimed, on the other hand, that "the reasoning self-conscious mind" and the "moral sentiments" (Dawson's phrases, not Darwin's) were also the result of the evolutionary process. Here, in Dawson's view, "he [leaves] the court of natural sciences, properly so called, and summons us to appear before the judgement-seat of philosophy."[98] The Canadian scientist did not further stray into the realm of the philosopher; he returned to the evidences of geology to prove his case. But there can be little doubt that the philosophical and psychological implications of the new Darwinian heresy troubled him. It is probably no coincidence that just after *The Descent of Man* appeared, Dawson greatly bolstered the strength of his philosophy department by enticing from Queen's University, Kingston, Clark Murray, the leading student of the most eminent Scottish philosopher of the years between 1830 and 1870.

In the dozen years between 1859 and 1871, Daniel Wilson, in Toronto, had followed the debate over Darwinism and had continued his ethnological researches and writing. As professor of English literature as well as history, however, he had also taught the works of Shakespeare. *Caliban: The Missing Link* (1873), Wilson's response to *The Descent of Man*, was thus a mixture of ethnology and literary criticism. It also contained not a little sheer fancy. In 1887 G. Mercer Adam wrote an article for *The Week* on Wilson. In it he described Wilson's book perfectly. "*Caliban*," he said, "is an interesting Shakespearean study, combining great imaginative power with a strong critical faculty, and giving the reader much curious information, with not a little fanciful disquisition, on the Evolution theory."[99]

It was, however else one might judge it, an extraordinary book. All the more remarkable was the fact that although the book was based upon Wilson's experience teaching Shakespeare's play *The Tempest* to students of University College, his students doubtless came away from their classes knowing at least as much about

Darwin, evolution, and the descent of man as they did about Prospero, drama, and the stuff of dreams. "The leading purpose of the following pages," Wilson wrote in his preface, was ". . . to shew that [Shakespeare's] genius had already created for us the ideal of that imaginary intermediate being, between the true brute and man, which, if the new theory of descent from crudest animal organisms be true, was our predecessor and precursor in the inheritance of the world of humanity. . . . A comparison between this Caliban of Shakespeare's creation, and the so-called 'brute-progenitor of man' of our latest school of science, has proved replete with interest and instruction to the writer's own mind; and the results are embodied in the following pages."[100]

Like William Dawson, Daniel Wilson—aided by his poetic imagination—had left the more certain domain of his scientific expertise to consider the philosophical and psychological implications made necessary by *The Descent of Man*. If one assumed that matter existed eternally, then it was difficult to accept the coming into being (and, hence, existence) of a Divine Creator. Was it not "more scientific," Wilson suggested, "to start with the pre-occupation of the mighty void with the Eternal Mind"? But if (the Divine) mind existed before matter, how could this be reconciled with the findings of evolutionary science, which implied that mind was created through "the development of the intellectual, moral, and spiritual elements of man, through the same natural selection by which his physical evolution is traced, step by step, from the very lowest organic forms"?[101]

The scientific imagination had signally failed to resolve this dilemma; nor had scientists found any fossil evidence that could help. Yet what science had failed to do, "the creative fancy of the true poet, working within its own legitimate sphere, has accomplished to better purpose." The "seductive hypotheses" and the "severer inductions" of science, Wilson believed, inhibited a solution to the problem of the descent of man. Fortunately, where Baconian inductions had proved inadequate, the poet had succeeded. Shakespeare himself had, in *The Tempest*, "presented . . . the vivid conception of 'that amphibious piece between corporeal and spiritual essence' [the quotation is from Sir Thomas Browne's *Religio Medici*], by which, according to modern hypothesis, the human mind is conjoined in nature and origin with the very lowest forms of vital organism. The greatest of poets . . . has thus left for us materials not without their value in discussing . . . the imaginary perfectibility of the irrational brute; the imaginable degradation of rational man."[102]

Those last dozen words contain the key to Wilson's interpretation of Caliban as the "missing link" between animal and man, as well as the reason why he felt obliged to rely upon the poetic imagination in order to bolster his own arguments against evolutionary science. It was the mind of both animal and man which was under consideration, and it was poetic insight, rather than scientific thought, that alone could provide the light necessary for the journey into the interior. "History tells of the acts, literature tells of the mind," read the literature notes of one of Wilson's students in the class of 1874.[103] Furthermore, lacking what Wilson had earlier called the "well-regulated fancy" of the poet, the scientist's vision was limited: he could conceive as scientifically "imaginable" the degradation of the rational man, but could only see as "imaginary" the possibility that the "irrational brute" might develop—that is, might evolve within certain specific limits—to the height of his potential and yet not become man.

For Wilson, Shakespeare's "hag-born whelp" was just such a creature: "the highest development of 'the beast that wants recourse of reason.' He has attained to all the maturity his nature admits of, and so is perfect as the study of a living creature distinct from, yet next in order below the level of humanity."[104] Wilson's book sought in a variety of ways to make the case for the inviolability and sanctity of the gap between Caliban, the poet's imaginative conception of the "natural brute mind" developed to its fullest capacity, and even the most degraded of rational human beings.

It was necessary first to dispose of the view that since scientific evidence indisputably showed that man was structurally far more similar to the higher apes than apes were to the lesser quadrumana, he was evolved from the ape. The parallel, Wilson argued, was a false one. Man and the apes are both animals; hence, they are physically similar. Yet it does not necessarily follow that the former evolved from the latter. Darwin had made this mistake in logic, and the result was of immense import for Wilson's thought. It made the journey into the interior both possible and necessary. "To all appearance," he wrote of *The Descent of Man*, "the further process in the assumed descent ... of man from the purely animal to the rational and intellectual stage, is but a question of brain development; and this cerebral growth is the assigned source of the manward progress: not the result of any functional harmonising of mind and brain.... It is difficult to dissociate from such an idea the further conclusion, that reason and mind are no more than the action of the enlarged mind; yet this is not necessarily implied.... The brain is certainly the organ of reasoning, the vital instrument through which the mind acts; but it need not therefore be assumed that brain and mind are one." Caliban, for Wilson, marked the symbolic midpoint between the brain of animals and the mind of man, the narrow gulf between irrational ape and rational man: "No being of all ... Shakespeare[an] drama more thoroughly suggests the idea of a pure creation of the poetic fancy than Caliban. He has a nature of his own essentially distinct from the human beings with whom he is brought into contact. He seems indeed the half-human link between the brute and man; and realises, as no degraded Bushman or Australian savage can do, a conceivable intermediate stage of the anthropomorphous existence, as far above the most highly organized ape as it falls short of rational humanity."[105]

Wilson was not content to rest after writing about "The Monster Caliban." His next chapter was entitled "Caliban, the Metaphysician." Here he attempted to rebut the evolutionist's claim that all the attributes of humanity—man's "intellect, his conscience, and his religious beliefs"—were simply part of the evolutionary process. As with Dawson, this was Wilson's central source of concern over the question of man's descent. "The growing difficulty, indeed," he wrote when considering the possibility of the evolution of these attributes, "is not so much to find man's place in nature, as to find any place left for mind." Nor was this the only problem. "If conscience, religion, the apprehension of truth, the belief in God and immortality, are all no more than developed or transformed animal sensations; and intellect is only the latest elaboration of the perceptions: it need not surprise us that inquiry has already been extended in search of relations between the inorganic and the organic. On this new hypothesis of evolution 'what a piece of work is man!' and as for God, it is hard to see what is left for Him to do in the universe."[106]

It is not surprising, therefore, that Wilson rejected the interpretation of Caliban rendered by Robert Browning in his poem "Caliban upon Setebos." The thoughts of Browning's Caliban suggested to Wilson that poor Caliban, after all "only a poor half-witted brute,—[had got] terribly out of his depth." Shakespeare's Caliban, and Wilson's, had been a poetic rendering of the "intermediate, half-brute, missing link." Browning's was that of the Darwinians: "the human savage, grovelling before the Manitou of his own conception."[107]

The essential points have now been made. Both Dawson and Wilson responded strenuously and at some length to the challenges posed by evolutionary science to their scientific and religious beliefs. Each replied to Darwin from the perspective of his own scientific expertise, but in the course of the dozen years between the publication of *The Origin of Species* and *The Descent of Man* two things happened. First, each man abandoned the premises of science in important ways in order to defend the religious heritage he saw under attack. Dawson retreated to a traditional religious defence of theism, and Wilson returned to the poetic fancy with which he had always been enamoured. Many Canadians, whether university students, clergymen, or Victorian families, who were perplexed by what they read in the *Christian Guardian* or other newspapers on the subject of evolution, may well have found the writings of Dawson and Wilson to be the proper response for Christians to make to such heresies; but it is questionable whether to the more reflective among them these writings assuaged the nagging uncertainties that were in the air by the decade of the seventies.

The second observation to be made about Dawson and Wilson is that whenever they considered the place of man within the framework of the evolutionary hypothesis, they were forced to deal with questions of immense philosophical import. Darwin's new book called fundamentally into question the various dualisms—spiritual and material, revelation and nature, mind and brain—which were basic to the science and the religion of William Dawson, Daniel Wilson, and all those who have been considered in this chapter. It marked the bankruptcy of the Baconian scientific method, which actively avoided hypothetical assertions about the existence of natural laws. Furthermore, it called into question the mechanistic faculty psychology on which their conceptions of the human constitution in its mental aspects were based. "The nineteenth century . . . has . . . failed as yet to arrive at a satisfactory conclusion as to man's place in nature," wrote another Canadian scientist in 1872. "We think," he later stated,

> . . . that any naturalist is justified, as a scientific man, in maintaining that all classifications of man by his anatomical characters alone, are *artificial*, and as such are indefensible. Such classifications do not embrace the totality of man's organization, and can not, therefore, be natural. . . . man's zoological definition must be made to include something more than his mere physical and anatomical structure. *That* something is man's mental and moral constitution; and we repeat our belief that any naturalist is justified, without dis-

paragement to either his knowledge or his ability, in maintaining that man's psychical peculiarities are as much an integral factor of his zoological definition as his physical structure, or perhaps more so.[108]

Such concerns for the legitimacy of the "mental and moral constitution" and for man's "psychical peculiarities" may well have been within the scientist's area of inquiry, but they were also laden with philosophical implications which transcended the limits of natural science. The high-water mark of the public influence of the earth sciences had been reached by the 1870s. Thereafter, in an ever-increasing degree, the educated public would look to social philosophers attuned to the new physiological and psychological sciences for solutions to the problems posed by modern thought. And by the 1870s, discussions of the nature of the human condition could also take place in forums other than the cloistered confines of Canadian educational institutions and the pages of religious newspapers. The ranks of orthodoxy had been breached, not only by new ideas but also by the fact that members of the lay public could now put forward their considered views in new magazines of informed opinion given their start by strange winds that gusted in the new Canadian nation.

5
A Critical Spirit

What is matter? Never mind. What is mind? No matter.
What is the soul? It is immaterial.
  Punch (1874)

If any one thing is more characteristic of this age than another, it is the restless mental activity which questions all things formerly received.
  Fidelis, "The Seen and the Unseen" (1876)

Everybody, wrote Sara Jeannette Duncan in 1887, talked about "the age." Moreover, they did so almost as if it had an existence independent of the actual lives of men. This, she argued, indicated an attitude as curious and interesting as anything men in fact said of their age. "Forgetting, apparently that we are part and parcel of it, and individually responsible for its having done those things which it ought not to do, and left undone those things which it ought to have done, we elect ourselves a grand jury to indict and try the age."[1] Miss Duncan was writing for a Canadian periodical, *The Week*. While her accusation was by no means applicable only to her own readers, by the time she put her remarks to paper she could have provided numerous examples of comments by Canadians on the age in which they lived.

One of those individuals would undoubtedly have been William Dawson LeSueur, who by the 1880s had become well known in Canadian intellectual circles. His name mentioned at the dinner table was perhaps sufficient to meet with cold silence and icy stares in a good number of Canadian households. W. D. LeSueur was an unabashed exponent of the new evolutionary science, and he searched during the 1870s and 1880s for a way of forging a new social ethic suitable to meet the challenges imposed by modern thought. Neither preacher nor professor, he nevertheless shared much of the concern of both for the maintenance of spiritual authority and social stability. Unlike many of them, however, his was a social philosophy with a decidedly modern ring. His was an ethic of freedom as well as concern.

Darwin, as Northrop Frye and many others have noted, "finally shattered the old teleological conception of nature as reflecting an intelligent purpose"; hence, "from then on design in nature has been increasingly interpreted by science as a product of a self-developing nature."[2] Frye puts this observation into the context of the larger transition in social mythologies within which the Darwinian revolution was a stage; a transition from the "closed mythology" that had characterized the Judaeo-Christian tradition to the "open mythology" of the modern century. Those in the second half of the nineteenth century who began to articulate this latter mythology were seldom revolutionaries; seldom did they reject the entire substance and thrust of the closed Christian myth. They, too, possessed a "myth of concern." But theirs was now a more complex reality.

Central to the modern myth of concern is another informed by a specific configuration of beliefs which have arisen over the past several hundred years. This configuration Frye calls the "myth of freedom," characterized by certain dominant mental attitudes, such as "objectivity, suspension of judgment, tolerance, and respect for the individual." The attributes that constitute the myth of freedom are part of the modern myth of concern; yet the myth of freedom

> is a part that stresses the importance of the non-mythical elements in culture, of the truths and realities that are studied rather than created, provided by nature rather than by a social vision. It thus extends to the safeguarding of certain social values not directly connected with the myth of concern, such as the tolerance of opinion which dissents from it. ... The myth of freedom ... constitutes the "liberal" element in society, as the myth of concern constitutes the conservative one, and those who hold it are unlikely to form a much larger group than a critical, and usually an educated, minority. To form the community as a whole is not the function of the myth of freedom: it has to find its place in, and come to terms with, the society of which it forms part.[3]

William Dawson LeSueur, more than any other native-born Canadian, gave systematic expression to this new open mythology. His was a preoccupation with both concern *and* freedom.

Like many of the greater intellectual figures of the nineteenth century—Hegel, Comte, Mill, Arnold—LeSueur sought to reconcile the basic forces of freedom and authority, progress and order, liberty and culture, and he attempted to do so on the basis of an open mythology founded upon a progressive view of man and society. In his thought, one can see the moral imperative in Anglo-Canadian thought at a kind of watershed. A social ethic comprised solely of intellectual and social constraint was no longer possible in the world of Darwin's *Origin* and Disraeli's "leap in the dark."

The Spectre of Doubt
The age observed and characterized in the 1870s and 1880s was one in which the claims of science and religion were set forward and debated by the literate middle classes, including those in Canada. From the early 1870s Canadians were able to publish their views on important matters in at least one forum that purported to be a national one, the *Canadian Monthly and National Review*.[4] They did, and a sizeable number of them sought to describe—as Sara Duncan's incisive pen later chided—the problems created by "the age." "Whatever sins of omission or commission may be fairly laid to the charge of our age and generation, indifference to the momentous problems of human life and destiny is not one of them," wrote W. J. Rattray in 1878. "Men are far too seriously-minded in their search after truth . . . to treat the solemn questions which persistently obtrude themselves for solution on every age, with levity, scorn or a flippant superficiality."[5] The opening sentences of many articles published in Canadian literary periodicals during these decades clearly illustrate the extent to which Rattray's claim was true. "If any one thing is more characteristic of this age than another," Kingston's Agnes Maule Machar wrote, "it is the restless mental activity which questions all things formerly received; a general 'shaking' and revising of opinions, which, however much temporary pain and disorganization it may produce, must at least end in the result 'that the things which cannot be shaken should remain.'"[6]

Agnes Machar was one of the most articulate and intelligent Canadian lay defenders of Christian orthodoxy during one of the most difficult periods in the history of the Christian religion. Well-read and judicious, yet deeply committed to her Presbyterian heritage, she never doubted the fundamental truths of her religion. But not everyone in Canada at the time was able to enjoy such certitude. Goldwin Smith opened one article in the *Canadi-*

an Monthly with the words: "The intellectual world is at present the scene of a great revolution, one of the most dangerous features of which is that the clergy, an order of men specially set apart as Ministers of Truth, are rendered incapable of performing the intellectual part of their functions properly by the pressure of creeds." The consequences of this "intellectual revolution" for Smith were both profound and painful, for while the claims of modern science convinced him of the weakness of many traditional articles of the Christian faith, they provided no adequate substitute for the certainty that was lost. "Doubt," he wrote, "is no longer locked in the bosom or only whispered in the ear."[7]

The spectre of Doubt was abroad. "The visible encroaches on the invisible," contended an American Anglican divine, James DeKoven, in 1878. "Between us and God appear to come laws and forces, and powers, the duration and extent of which we can grasp and measure.... What, then, if these laws begin to take... the place of God?"[8] By the 1870s and 1880s the progress of science seemed to be making its mark everywhere, especially in the area of technology. Few attacks were made upon it on that account by English-speaking North Americans. It was the extension of science into the realm of cosmogony, ethics, and man's spiritual life that turned many who accepted the desirability of the material progress brought about by science into its strongest accusers and rendered others unable to believe in either a science seemingly validated by progress or a religion that stood only on faith. The claim by one Canadian university student of the 1870s that "there can be little doubt that of late years the argument for the existence of a God from the proofs of design in Nature, has not met with so general an acceptance as formerly" was understandable in a decade when traditional Christian teleology was in the process of dissolution.[9]

This particular student's conclusions illustrate clearly the dilemma in which many of his fellow students probably found themselves. First, he accepted the validity of the findings of modern science, which "steps in and dispels such fancies" as the evidences in nature of "a great and invisible Design and Lawgiver." Indeed, science proclaimed physical nature to be solely under the dominion of natural laws. Yet the consequences of that acceptance were immense, for the student found that the tendency of modern science was "to remove God more and more into the background." Even worse, "some of its professors in their wisdom even think that they can dispense with him altogether." While the student thus accepted the reality of a world governed by physical laws, and while he noted that "everywhere around us, if we will but open our eyes, are the signs of a great and terrible struggle for existence," such "explanations" nevertheless did not further his own understanding.[10]

The Darwinian world provided abundant evidence of the "agency of evil," he said, but no *reason* for it. In the end the student was left to fall back upon the rhetoric, now largely without adequate substance, of an earlier natural theology. Science had seemingly invalidated the premises of the argument from design, but the student had been given nothing to take its place. For this student, traditional Christian teleology had been shattered by the findings of modern science, yet the traditional Christian conception of rationality, the correspondence of human reason with the perception of design and purpose in nature, remained very much with him. Because of this he could not trust the evidence of a reason guided solely by intellect. "Starting indeed with the knowledge of its great Architect, we can trace his handiwork in pillar and cornice, ceiling and floor: but with our own unguided reason we could never regard it as in all its parts a fitting monument of Omnipotence and Wisdom divine." Paley, then, no longer came to his mental aid; neither did Bacon. He noted that the modern student could not now trust the empirical evidence of his own observations of nature as the measure of Truth, for "Nature furnishes us with no solution of the enigmas of life: Revelation [alone] reveals the essential truths of existence to every humble enquirer."[11]

The problem of reconciling the Christian revelation with the findings of modern science was one which preyed upon the minds of many young men and women at Anglo-Canadian universities during the 1870s and 1880s. The American "cosmic evolutionist," John Fiske, and others may have effected, as Carl Berger has claimed, a reconciliation of evolution and religion during the 1870s.[12] But their efforts were perhaps most satisfactory to their own psychological needs. One sees little evidence of solace derived from such sources in the pages of Victoria College's newspaper, *Acta Victoriana*, Queen's University's *Queen's Journal*, or Dalhousie University's *Dalhousie Gazette* in those years. To be sure, there is a note of optimism in students' opinions that the problems of reconciliation between revelation and science will ultimately be worked out once "the book of nature" is "rightly understood" and a "true science" developed. But it is a superficial optimism at best. The day was fast approaching, concluded one such student, "when all mysteries shall be unfolded before our rejoicing intellects."[13] Another waited for the day when "the rays shot into the darkness by intellect" would reveal that perhaps the Darwinian theory of descent and the traditional Christian conception of design were consistent with one another.[14] In the meantime, however, student essays, always utterly serious in tone, spoke far more of the generally optimistic enthusiasm of youth than of any true reconciliation of the twin systems of scientific and religious belief. "We have but launched our bark on the Ocean of Life," said one student in a paper entitled "The Age and Its Tendencies," "and though we see a current in one direction, and a counter-current in another, we have yet scarcely found out in what direction the whole mass is drifting; yet we know the course is ever onward."[15]

While Anglo-Canadian university students wrote articles such as these for their college newspapers, men and women of their parents' generation put into print their own views on the question of science. In a host of articles in the *Canadian Methodist Magazine,* Canadian clergymen felt compelled to draw upon whatever sources they could in order to plead for the necessary oneness of the Author of Revelation and the Author of Nature. Evolution itself, they argued, was part of the on-going design of God. Similar articles abounded in the *Christian Guardian.*[16] Yet, like that of their sons and daughters, theirs was at best a defensive argument. Evolution could offer no certitude, only the possibility of new directions in which to follow an evolving truth—whatever that now was. A poem entitled "One Faith in Many Forms," reprinted in *Rose-Belford's Canadian Monthly* from the London *Spectator* in 1881, expressed the dilemma well:

                                        Him,—
What is His Name? What name will all express
    The mighty whole, of whom we are but part—
So that all differing tongues may join a worship
    Echoing in every heart?

Then answers one—"God is an endless sequence,
    Incapable of either break or flaw,
Which we discern but dimly and in fragments!
    God is unchanging Law."

"Nay," said another, "Law is but His method;
 Look back, behind the sequence to his source!
Behind all phases and all changes seek Him!
 God is the primal Force!"

The poet denied in subsequent stanzas that God was either "unchanging Law" or "primal Force." Nor was He solely manifested through a Love for an equally vague Humanity. God incorporates all—"Love, beauty, Wisdom and force": "God includes them, as some great cathedral includes each separate shrine."[17] The effect on the poem's readers was probably to further the desire for such an all-embracing God; yet the basic problem remained unresolved —for the shrines remained separate.

The Critical Intellect

The first major attempt by a Canadian to come to grips with the enigma of the separate shrines began in April 1871 when an article on Charles Augustin Sainte-Beuve, the French poet and critic, appeared in the *Westminster Review*. It was for the most part highly appreciative of Sainte-Beuve's lifelong commitment to "the critical spirit." In 1830 Sainte-Beuve had written: "It is the nature of the critical spirit to be quick, suggestive, versatile, and comprehensive. The critical spirit is like a large, clear stream, which winds and spreads out around the works and monuments of poetry." Quoting this passage in the original French, the author of the *Westminster Review* article added that "no words could more happily or accurately describe what criticism was, in his hands throughout the whole of his long career." Moreover, the writer claimed, Sainte-Beuve was important not simply because he was critical but also because he was systematic about it. "The first thing that strikes us when we look into [Sainte-Beuve's] works is, that criticism with him is not a mere thing of rules and precedents, but, so to speak, a living science." Sainte-Beuve had been averse to all rigid systems of thought, and therefore was suspicious when criticism was subordinated to any preconceived idea or preestablished authority. Nevertheless, his criticism was not without its own controlling idea: it should consist of systematic intellectual inquiry. "One consequence of the effort which Ste.-Beuve made to pursue criticism in a scientific spirit, is that of all critics he is the least dogmatic." Indeed, concluded the anonymous reviewer, he is "less a judge than an enquirer who tells us of his discoveries, and invites us to verify them for ourselves."[18]

The author of that article had also been an inquirer more than a judge. Exactly a year earlier he had appeared before the Literary and Scientific Society of Ottawa to deliver a shorter version of the *Westminster Review* article. Then entitled "The Greatest Critic of the Age," this critical appreciation of the French poet-critic (who had died only a few months earlier) was given by a young federal civil servant named William Dawson LeSueur.[19] Born in 1840, W. D. LeSueur had begun to work for the Post Office in Ottawa by 1871 and was to remain there until his retirement in 1902. His formal education had taken him from the Montreal High School to the Ontario Law School and the University of Toronto. There, he studied moral philosophy under James Beaven, literature and history under Daniel Wilson, and classics under John McCaul. He graduated as silver medallist in the latter subject in 1863. Most of LeSueur's long life was dedicated to an intellectual inquiry which each of his professors had taken pains to prevent, but the mark of their teachings never left him.[20]

LeSueur was thirty when he revealed to his Ottawa audience an acceptance of the necessity for—and the dictates of—the critical spirit. A long and distinguished career in Canadian letters had begun. For the next forty years and more, he put before Canadian and international audiences alike a constructive criticism of various aspects of the life and thought of his day. This career was to see him engaged constantly in debate with various orthodoxies that in his view hampered the activity of the critical intellect. Whether attacking an orthodoxy that was religious or scientific, political or historical, LeSueur insisted throughout his life that the essence of civilization lay in an individual's ability to exercise, in a responsible fashion, a critical inquiry that asked nothing more than honesty and sincerity and sought nothing less than truth. His was a moral, as well as an intellectual, vision.

The primary concern which informed all LeSueur's writings was with the nature of the intellectual life and the necessity for critical intellectual inquiry. His publishing career began on this note, and amongst his last published words were those which insisted that "the essential nature of history... is not affirmation but enquiry."[21] Having established in a series of essays the premises from which he worked, LeSueur turned in the 1870s and 1880s to one of the major intellectual questions of his day: the relationship between science and religion, as well as the various claims of both.

The years between 1855 and 1872, in which LeSueur gradually arrived at his commitment to critical intellectual inquiry, were important ones for the history of critical expression. The year 1855 marked the abolition of the newspaper tax in England, and the intervening years saw the publication of a number of critical works. Between the publication of Darwin's *Origin* and his *Descent of Man* appeared John Stuart Mill's *On Liberty* (1859), the *Essays and Reviews* (1860, by a number of authors), Bishop Colenso's *The Pentateuch . . . Critically Examined* (1862), Matthew Arnold's *Essays in Criticism* (1865) and *Culture and Anarchy* (1867–8), T. H. Huxley's *Lay Sermons* (1870), and many other controversial tomes. Any young man or woman with a reflective or speculative bent, and with access to any of the major Anglo-American periodicals or even to a well-stocked library of a Mechanics' Institute, would have had little difficulty in finding a variety of "heterodox" views that challenged preconceived notions and intoxicated the intellect.[22]

During the 1870s and 1880s W. D. LeSueur put several articles that showed abundant evidence of just such a liberated intellect before the Anglo-Canadian reading public. By the time the first of these, "The Intellectual Life" (1875), was published, he had already established something of a reputation as a Canadian critic of significance. By that time had appeared his *Westminster Review* article on Sainte-Beuve and studies of Matthew Arnold and Bernardin de Saint-Pierre in the *Canadian Monthly and National Review*. He had also turned to political and social criticism in a severe indictment of party politics, published under the pseudonym "A Radical" in 1872, and had reviewed the general state of political culture and intellectual life in Canada in a perceptive essay, "Old and New in Canada," which opened the January 1875 issue of the *Canadian Monthly*.[23] Yet LeSueur's articles on the critical intellect remain more important than these for any consideration of the premises from which he worked. Together they provide his philosophical credo, a declaration of faith in the critical path which he was to follow for the rest of his life.

The essays which together make up this philosophical testament were, by necessity, a defence of intellect and its role in human thought. Yet it is significant that LeSueur's argument was not a defensive one. He was concerned with dispelling certain criticisms levelled against the intellectual life: that it is dominated by a narrow rationalism; that the training of the intellect (given such a conception of reason) may subvert one's primary duty to consider moral and ethical questions; and that such a life leads inevitably towards scepticism, materialism, and other forms of heterodoxy. LeSueur attempted to rebut these charges not only by searching for chinks in the enemy's armour, but also by asserting what he hoped was a consistent and superior philosophy of life.

One of the fundamental tenets of this philosophy was the insistence that the intellectual life consists of a unity of "mental act" and "moral colouring." The intellectual life is above all a moral life; hence, intellectual concern is also moral concern. It therefore followed for LeSueur that such a life was not, as many of his contemporaries in Canada believed, something to be feared. He denied that it undermined the cultivation of love, disinterestedness, admiration, or enthusiasm for the true and the beautiful. Indeed, it enhanced one's esteem for such values—for the person who followed the intellectual life was also one whose life must be guided by moral purpose. This claim nears the heart of LeSueur's credo and therefore deserves to be emphasized:

> The life that such live is pre-eminently a life of thought, animated and kindled by strong moral feeling. If we call it "The intellectual life," we shall not, perhaps, use the words very inappropriately, or assign to them more meaning than they are adapted to bear. For is there not in the word "intellect" itself, something noble and imposing, and should we care to dignify with the name *intellectual activity* thought devoted to idle or selfish purposes? In such a life as I refer to, there is a pervading unity of tone and purpose. The man who thinks a noble thought does not distinguish between the mental act and its moral colouring; to him it is simply one moment of his life in which high thoughts and high aims are thus harmoniously and indissolubly blended. I know of none more suitable than the word "intellectual."[24]

The implications of this basic insistence upon uniting intellectual inquiry and moral purpose may be examined through a consideration of the concepts which pervade LeSueur's credo. The keys to his philosophy of life lie in the meanings he ascribed to the words "reason," "truth," "liberty," "culture," and "criticism."

"The Intellectual Life" and "Idealism in Life" both open with the assertion that man is distinguished from brute creation by the fact that he is self-conscious. "To man alone," he states, "is it given to regulate his own inward life, and so govern his thought that, instead of being dependent on momentary sense-impressions, they shall follow a path, and proceed in an order, of his own determining."[25] Man, like other animals, is subject to the operation of the laws of the natural world; but his ability to reflect upon their operation and upon his own relationship with physical nature affords him a form of liberation from physical laws. "The moment . . . that self-consciousness enters upon the scene, everything is altered. Law is not abolished, and yet in a very real sense liberty is established,—liberty within the bounds of law. . . . The self-conscious being knows what he wants, and within certain limits can gratify his own desires. He does not escape from the control of mechanical or chemical laws; but he can, to a large extent, modify the incidence of those laws."[26] And it is the intellect, along with the powers for rationality that go with it, that is the main agency by which man asserts this capacity, the basis of his humanity.

If LeSueur saw the intellect as man's vehicle for expressing his self-consciousness, he also saw reason as its workhorse. What is reason? LeSueur denied vigorously that it can be conceived of in any narrow sense. It is not, he insisted, "a narrow kind of calculating faculty";[27] nor is it "wholly independent of the moral nature," as some had claimed. It is, instead, the only means by which man can arrive at truth, and is vitally connected with moral concern because it is in fact "the moral or emotional nature that gives a direction to the operations of reason. . . . Reason only occupies itself with what the perceptive faculties furnish to it; and the perceptive faculties only see what they are told to see, in other words, what the mind has an interest in."[28] One must have faith in reason as a means of pursuing truth; yet to commit one's self to the *supremacy* of reason is to divorce it from the moral imperative that must provide its direction. Man must, therefore, not "make an idol of his own individual reason," for to do so would be to negate the search for unity that is the basis of the intellectual life.

Hence, just as the pious Christian, aware of his alienation from the mind of God, searches for a means of reestablishing that unity, so the man with faith in reason also seeks a functionally similar unity.[29] Just as piety demands a submission to authority, so does reason. "No one knows better than he who believes in reason," LeSueur wrote, "how to submit to authority, for no one is more impressed than he with the advantage that knowledge has over ignorance, or with the inexorable character of all natural laws. . . . In the intellectual life there is no spirit of revolt, but rather a desire to be brought into harmony with whatever may be recognized as the decrees of Providence or the laws of Nature, in a word, with whatever is permanent and essential in the general constitution of things."[30] We observe here, not a repudiation, but a transmutation of the dictates of piety.

Freedom and Concern
It was precisely LeSueur's conception of what was "permanent and essential" in life that forced him to differ philosophically from those whose moral concerns did not vary greatly from his own. This difference was an immensely important one, for it derived from conceptions of what constituted "truth" that were fundamentally at variance. The most dogmatic of the anti-Darwinians would have agreed with LeSueur's assertion that every man should "devote himself with singleness of purpose to the discovery and diffusion of truth."[31] However, they certainly would have disagreed with his conception of what constituted truth itself.

This conception of truth was based on the progressive view of man and society that LeSueur shared with several prominent British intellectuals. For all their differences, John Stuart Mill and Matthew Arnold were each "progressivists," that is, they agreed fundamentally, in Maurice Mandelbaum's words, on "the possibility of regarding man as a progressive being, capable of transforming himself through the cultivation of his capacities for higher forms of sensibility."[32] This observation applies equally to LeSueur, as do the words which open a study of Arnold and Mill: "In their attempts to reconcile the ancient and the modern, literature and science, above all culture and democracy, Arnold and Mill were also trying to synthesize the partial and diverse elements of their age into a unified whole which would survive into the next."[33]

As a progressivist, LeSueur saw the course of thought as "a progressive reduction of facts to a rational or thinkable order."[34] Yet he also insisted that "facts . . . are not in themselves truths; they are only the material out of which truth can be distilled."[35] Truth does not consist of external data whether from the natural world or from revelation. Nor, in one sense, can any conclusion be true for all time. The most that can be said is that one's considered conclusions harmonize with existing knowledge. "Whether it will harmonize with the knowledge of some future age," he admitted, "it would be rash in us to attempt to predict."[36] LeSueur rejected the notion of an eternal truth conceived as an external body of facts. In that sense he was a relativist. Yet in another way he did conceive truth to be eternal. The man who is imbued with the spirit of intellectual liberty, he said, "is prepared to welcome truth from any quarter, and the universe seems to him full of truth." Such a man knows that "though he were proved wrong on every point, there is a *right* elsewhere." What was important to him was the cultivation of a disposition of mind—a critical spirit —in which men could freely pursue certain ends while remaining open to the possibility—indeed, the inevitability—of error. This is what he meant by the phrase "there is a *right* elsewhere," for he continued the sentence by adding ". . . that in fact, only in the light of higher truth could he be rationally convinced of his own errors." LeSueur's was an open mythology: he advocated, not a rigid creed, but a set of mental coordinates.[37]

At the level of epistemology, LeSueur's progressive view of mind allowed him, without being a Hegelian, to follow Hegel's conception of truth, as put forward in *The Phenomenology of Mind*.[38] "The truth is the whole," Hegel had said. "The whole, however, is merely the essential nature reaching its completeness through the process of its own development."[39] At the social level, LeSueur's progressivism caused him to see a close alliance between man's faith in reason and his faith in progress. He was more concerned, however, with the means by which progress comes about than with its manifestations. "For in what does progress consist," he asked, "if not in the gradual assimilation, so to speak, by the social organism, of successive discoveries of truth?" The progress of society will be checked only if "the conquests of the human mind" cease.[40]

But in what direction should the critical mind turn for these conquests? What are the ideals to which it should aspire? What should be the basis of its moral concern? Again one turns to LeSueur's conception of the progressive course of thought and to the universalistic nature of the truth which will inevitably result from inquiry—for from them is derived his conceptions of liberty and culture and his commitment to the criticism which is an outgrowth of both.

The great problem of thought, LeSueur claimed, was to achieve a "harmony with what is already known or assumed to be known."[41] But how could any lasting contribution to social progress be made if one's conclusions can at any moment be discarded as erroneous? The answer, he concluded, lay in the fact that the best thought is never pursued for individual ends: "it springs, instead, almost wholly from the social nature of man." Successful thought will fundamentally be that which is pursued for social ends:

> What a man thinks—if he thinks sincerely—holds good, or should hold good, not for himself alone, but for all men. . . . But as we all err more or less in the conceptions we form, it is manifest that the most satisfactory progress will be made in thought where there is the freest possible social comparison of views, and where men most frequently remind themselves that thought is not destined to serve merely individual purposes. Thought will make its best advance when men consciously or unconsciously try to think together. . . . The man who has a strong impulse to think, desires to think with others, or at least desires others to think with him; for he knows that whatever is true is true for all, and whatever is important is important for all. He does not therefore seek to fence himself off from the rest of mankind, but takes up his work as a continuation of what others have done before him. . . . Better [by] far, in a social point of view, the most dogmatic and absolute spirit than the mere worship of *la petite culture* in matters intellectual. It has not been by standing apart from one another, each man with his private thought and purpose, that the greatest triumphs of humanity have been won, but by the effort of all to universalize truth and to merge individual differences in a common intellectual and spiritual life.[42]

This passage from "Free Thought and Responsible Thought" is especially important because it provides a crucial link between two seemingly disparate "isms" with which LeSueur was later to be linked: positivism and conservatism. When identified with the former in the 1870s and 1880s, he was seen as a dangerously heterodox social radical; yet in Mackenzie King's Canada he was to be portrayed as a Tory reactionary. In one sense, LeSueur *was* dangerously radical, for he openly advocated the use of positivistic assumptions in shaping social ethics. He had little use for the closed-minded dogmatism of traditional Christianity. Moreover, his writings in defence of modern thought were consistent with the generally accepted tenets of positivism, which basically asserts that "science is the only valid knowledge and facts the only objects of knowledge; that philosophy does not possess a method different from science; and that the task of philosophy is to find the general principles common to all the sciences and to use these principles as guides to human conduct and as the basis of social organization."[43] Because of his basic acceptance of its general principles, LeSueur's pronouncements—no matter how gracefully put—were seen to be challenges to Christian metaphysics (indeed, to the very idea of "metaphysics") and to the knowledge gained through faith as opposed to that gained from the scientific method.

In fact, as will become apparent, LeSueur was a radical only insofar as he challenged Christian dogma. His "positivism" owed far more to the spirit of Christianity than his opponents cared to admit. Furthermore, his understanding of social reality was profoundly not a radical one, for it was based upon the notion of society as an historically evolved social organism. Here was the point of union between the Comtean positivism of his youth and the almost Burkean conservatism of his later years: both stressed the organic nature of society and the necessity of subordinating individual to social ends, whether in the political process or in the process of thought.

LeSueur's essay "Free Thought and Responsible Thought" also illustrates the complexity of his thought. In it can be seen an articulation of aspects of the myths of freedom and concern which together constituted his particular brand of the nineteenth-century progressivist creed. Indeed, it is as a progressivist (positivism must be seen as one variant of "progressivism") that LeSueur must primarily be viewed, for only in so doing can one adequately understand his acceptance of some tenets of the liberal and positivist doctrines and his rejection of others. In an earlier article he had defended Mill's insistence upon intellectual tolerance and the free expression of opinion, and had severely criticized Fitzjames Stephen for putting forward the claim that in certain circumstances such tolerance should end.[44] Yet while, like Mill, LeSueur was committed to free inquiry, he took issue with the conception of liberty put forward by Mill in 1859. "Let men but be allowed to think freely, and give free play to their several individualities," went LeSueur's version of Mill's creed, "and a new and better order of things would speedily arise."[45] The weakness of such a view was, not that freedom of thought was not a good thing, but that it could be abused because it does not follow that free thought is necessarily responsible thought. Again LeSueur turned to the positivist variation of progressivism.

If the course of thought consists of "progressively wider interpretation of the universe in which man's lot is cast," it becomes apparent, said LeSueur, "that individual thought cannot properly, or with any advantage, separate itself from the thought of the race.... When, therefore, a demand is made for freedom, it becomes a question of much importance whether the freedom claimed is freedom to pursue truth in a social spirit for social ends, or mere freedom to think what one chooses without regard to ends and without any sense of responsibility." LeSueur insisted that both views be permitted; it was sufficient to point out the fallacies contained in the latter:

> The great lesson which "free-thinkers" have to learn is that all true thought is universal in character, not individual; and that nobody can be said to be thinking in the right sense of the word unless he is thinking for all, and endeavouring to promote the general harmony of human thought. It is unfortunately too common to find "free-thinkers" look upon the privilege of free thought as a mere private possession, something for the use of which they owe no account to any one, not even to themselves. They only realize their intellectual freedom in differing from others not in agreeing with them. This is, no doubt, a not unnatural reaction from the intellectual tyranny of the past; but none the less does it lead to a hurtful dissipation of mental energy as well as to a dangerous weakening of social bonds.[46]

We see put forward here one of the most critical relationships of the nineteenth century: "intellectual freedom" and the "social bonds," liberty and authority, freedom and concern. Positivism embodied both elements: it sought to be a force for liberation from entangling superstitions and institutions in its advocacy of the scientific method; yet its social theory lent itself to the establishment of a new orthodoxy which could subjugate individual freedoms for the social aggregate and replace one set of priests and prophets with another.

LeSueur's particular attempt to reconcile the demands of liberty and authority (in their various forms) was not simply a combination of the spirits of Mill and Comte, the fusion of an insistence upon the necessity for sustained individual inquiry into all matters with a refusal to elevate the individual above the social whole.[47] It was one which sought to wed Comte's concern for humanity with a conception of culture not unlike that of Matthew Arnold. LeSueur, like Arnold, read widely in the literatures of classical antiquity and his appreciation of the classics remained with him to the end of his life. Arnold, like LeSueur, viewed Sainte-Beuve as the literary critic who had most helped to shape, as he admitted to Cardinal Newman in 1872, his "habits, methods, and ruling ideas."[48] In that year LeSueur published his second article; its subject was the poetry of Matthew Arnold.

It was the combination of universalism with a "warmth of moral emotion" that LeSueur admired in Arnold's poetry. In commenting upon the last two stanzas of Arnold's "Lines Written in Kensington Gardens," he contrasted the moral stance of Marcus Aurelius (no less an influence upon LeSueur than upon Arnold), whose stoicism called for man to find peace of mind by "bringing his own nature into subjection," with that of Arnold, which "finds a support for his good resolutions in the very constitution of the universe." Arnold's stance, like the stoic's, offered justice and dignity; yet it did so with a humility that the latter sometimes lacked. Moreover, it offered modern man "the power of sympathy, the power of feeling not merely *for* others but *with* them," a power which could potentially "become a distinct object of desire with even the best of men."[49]

This potential was in perfect harmony with LeSueur's positivistic commitment to "humanity"—itself an extension of his own belief in the existence of a cosmic moral order. This belief found parallel expression in the petition of prayer expressed by Arnold in "A Wish," a poem which LeSueur viewed as "one of the best Mr. Arnold ever wrote." The poem, LeSueur stated, was "full of that noble faith which looks upon the universe as a divine work, and the destinies of man in the future as wholly beyond the power of any human agencies or artifices to control."[50] LeSueur's universalism found perfect poetic utterance in Arnold's desire to "let me gaze, till I become/In soul with what I gaze on wed!/To feel the universe my home." LeSueur's positivism offered him the belief that he was free to control his destiny in a way that Arnold felt impossible. In "A Wish," Arnold asked only "that my death may find/The freedom to my life denied."

Lionel Trilling once wrote that Empedocles' misery in Arnold's poem "Empedocles on Etna" was that "he cannot endure the social world, not only has he lost community with Nature, he has lost community with his fellow-men." Trilling added that Arnold chose Empedocles "to embody his own social feelings," emotions which saw "the very social organism . . . [to be] fatal to the best of human values."[51] Arnold's Empedocles, faced with the death of imagination and the loss of self through the force of his own rationalistic and materialistic knowledge, committed suicide.

LeSueur's would instead have found a life fulfilled: *his* Empedocles would have been a nineteenth-century Frazier presiding confidently and optimistically over the positivist's Walden. "From one point of view," he said of "Empedocles on Etna," "it may be regarded as a poetical rendering of the Positive Philosophy: there are verses in it which breathe the Positivist spirit in its purest and most essential form."[52]

LeSueur also shared many of the imperatives of Arnold's moral imagination, and this was not inconsistent with his own commitment to the positivist spirit. Indeed, it says something about the nature of that positivism. His essay on Arnold's poetry concluded with the declaration that while one may find faults and deficiencies in Arnold's work, "it is beyond dispute that his influence as a writer, whether in prose or verse, tends constantly to the refining of our taste, and the ennobling of our moral sense."[53] LeSueur, like Arnold, found philosophical and religious creeds negative and incapable of affirming life. Like Arnold, he was concerned less with formulas for morality than with the force of moral vision. He warned against such a restrictive view of morality in his essay on criticism. "In some cases," he wrote, "an undue preoccupation with moral interests destroys, or at least impairs, the sense of art."[54]

The thrust of moral vision, unlike the concern for enforcing one's own moral lessons, leaves this essential connection between morality and art intact. It is essential because it is the quintessence of Culture. Arnold's declaration in *Culture and Anarchy* that Culture is "the best that is known and thought in the world" is well known; less so is his statement of its aims, which he expressed in the words of Bishop Wilson: "to make reason and the will of God prevail." By "the will of God" Arnold meant "the universal order which seems to be intended and aimed at in the world, and which it is man's happiness to go along with or his misery to go counter to."[55] Arnold's Culture was a quest for inward perfection, life lived as art. This was no less true for LeSueur. LeSueur's commitment to the scientific spirit meant that there were natural laws in the physical world which were inviolable, and his commitment to the cause of Culture equally meant the operation of moral laws for the spiritual world. Life in the natural world meant that man was bound to the face of the earth by the law of gravity; the ideal life meant that he must be equally governed by "the law that binds him to the true and beautiful." The ideal life, the life of Culture, is a life of humility, disinterestedness, and patience. The man who attempts to live this ideal life recognizes the existence of "a moral order of the universe" and is willing voluntarily to subject himself to "law"—"not to an outward code of observance, but to that inward voice which bids a man ever to seek and practice the best." It is life conceived as "something whose rules were not to be sought in the customs of the marketplace, but deep down in the most secret and intimate convictions of the individual soul, as something whose standard was nothing short of the eternal beauty of holiness."[56]

The first and most fundamental stage in William Dawson LeSueur's life was thus the story of his attempt to construct a workable philosophy, one which harmonized with the laws—natural and spiritual—which many men of his day conceived to be in conflict.[57] While abundantly eclectic in the sources of its inspiration, it nevertheless achieved a high degree of consistency and integration by a basic commitment to a progressive view of man and history, an organic conception of social reality, and a universalistic conception of life in general which was the product of both progressivism and organicism.

Civilized life rested, for W. D. LeSueur, upon an almost sacred connection between the critical spirit and the spirit of Culture. The invocation of moral sanctions which hindered the critical process—whether by dogmatists of religion, science, politics, or history—had necessarily to be combated. "Perpetual fussiness in morals is not the great preservative of moral order," he wrote, ". . . the world lives, and is likely to live, by such laws as conduce to its well-being, and can do without the leading strings of even the best-intentioned nurses. To know this is culture, and is one foundation at least for a true criticism of life and whatever claims to represent life."[58] LeSueur's search for these laws of social life in an age when science was making great and obvious advances resulted in his articulation of a scientific spirit which owed much to Auguste Comte; yet this positivistic commitment to the cause of humanity, it may now be seen, was derived just as much from classical culture and the spirit of the Christian tradition. In a word, LeSueur's positivism owed much to the Pauline dictum "Finally be of one mind, united in feeling." Whether derived from Comte or St. Paul, this message, LeSueur claimed, led to a widening of experience, knowledge, and sensibility. It disturbed the pre-critical state of mind; it led to a wider culture; it created a temperament in which a man would "become a critic in spite of himself."

Science, Ethics, and Evolution

A second major stage in LeSueur's intellectual life began when he and his Canadian critics engaged in polite, yet utterly serious, debate from the mid-1870s through the 1880s. The opposing battlements were those of modern scientific thought and Christian orthodoxy; the battlegrounds were the newspapers, periodical press, and pamphlets. At stake was the nature of the ethical systems by which men governed their lives. As an editorial writer for the Toronto *Mail* wrote when responding critically to LeSueur's article "The Future of Morality": "one of the questions which our age is debating somewhat anxiously is the connection between the ethics of a nation and its faith."[59]

Basically, the charges made by LeSueur's accusers fell into a few general areas. First, they claimed that—extended into the realm of ethics—science led to materialism, agnosticism, and scepticism. Second, as such, science was devoid of any real spiritual substance; hence, it could put forward no adequate guide for human conduct. Third, it was guilty of the very sin with which it charged Christianity: dogmatism. These were the charges which LeSueur sought to dispel in his various writings on science and modern thought.

That science fostered a materialistic and sceptical outlook on life was the most frequent charge made against it in the 1870s and 1880s. Indeed, some critics claimed that by its very nature it was materialistic and sceptical.[60] Defenders of Christianity could provide evidence for these propositions by pointing out the influence of both Epicureanism and sensationalism upon scientists; they could note the way in which the Scottish philosopher Alexander Bain took the empirical tradition into the realm of psychology by tracing both thoughts and "moral apprehensions" to the bodily system. They could illustrate the agnostic "materialism" in Herbert Spencer's social evolutionism by quoting him, often without due regard to the corpus of his thought. Similarly, they could support their arguments by drawing evidence from T. H. Huxley's article on protoplasm as the physical basis of life. They could also allow such "materialists" to ridicule themselves by quoting, equally without adequate regard for context, such snippets as: "The brain secretes thought just as the liver secretes bile"; "The soul is the product of a peculiar combination of matter"; or "Mental activity is a function of the cerebral substance."[61]

Charges that modern science was materialistic reached their peak, however, after the delivery and publication of John Tyndall's "Belfast Address," given to the British Association for the

Advancement of Science in 1874. Tyndall, professor of natural philosophy in the Royal Institution, enjoyed a widespread reputation in the 1860s and 1870s, owing mainly to the many lectures he gave for laymen. The opinions expressed in his 1874 presidential address to the association were all the more horrifying because they came from one of the most eminent and respected British scientific authorities.

Tyndall infuriated his listeners, and later his readers, because he sought to unite the findings of the science of his day—in biology, physics, chemistry, and psychology—with the philosophical atomism of the ancients, especially Democritus. Tyndall's own religious convictions led him to advocate a vague sort of pantheism and to put forward his belief that religious feelings could not aid man in arriving at an objective understanding of his place in nature. Only science could do this. Science, he concluded, had by 1874 reached an "impregnable position" which he claimed could be described in a few words: "We claim, and we shall wrest, from theology the entire domain of cosmological theory. All schemes and systems which thus infringe upon the domain of science must *in so far as they do this*, submit to its control, and relinquish all thought of controlling it."[62] Here, it seemed, was excellent evidence of the materialistic nature of an agnostic, dogmatic, and arrogant science.

Within hours of the delivery of the "Belfast Address," its author was under attack in England. The next day, a London merchant suggested to the Home Secretary that Tyndall be brought to trial under a British statute that dealt with the expression of blasphemous opinions. *Punch* satirized him in poems and cartoons. So did the Scottish physicist James Clerk Maxwell in the following light verse: "From nothing comes nothing they told us/naught happens by chance but by fate;/There is nothing but atoms and void, all else/is mere whims out of date."[63] The debate between Tyndall, his defenders, and his opponents continued into the late 1870s. The very phrase "Belfast Address" became synonymous with the cluster of words such as "materialism" which were seen to pose dire threats to orthodox religious belief.

This was no less the case in the new Canadian nation than it was in the more serene atmosphere of the English parsonage. In 1876 the professor of mathematics and natural philosophy at McGill University, Alexander Johnson (also vice-dean of the Faculty of Arts), was called upon to convince the university's students in engineering and theoretical physics that in entering their new professions they were not enlisting in the ranks of the materialists. "My subject is one that has been agitating the minds of many during nearly two years past," he said.

> A wave of disturbance originating in the address of the President of the British Association for the Advancement of Science in 1874 has rolled over the mother country, and crossing the Atlantic, diffused itself here far and wide. The disturbance then excited, the agitation of men's minds, and the discussions that followed, are still in full vigour, not only in Great Britain, but here in Canada. . . .
>
> The discussions are carried on or noticed, not only in books, reviews and pamphlets, but in newspapers and in the social circle. When the newspapers teem with quotations from Tyndall, Huxley, Darwin and Herbert Spencer (no later than this morning I saw one from the last mentioned), and the mind of the nation in general is agitated, it is not to be supposed that the student's mind will escape that apprehension which lays hold of many when they are told that Science and Religion are irreconcilably at variance. When after this, the student hears, as he must do, in his lectures, of "molecules," "atoms," "vibrations," and other terms which are bandied about so freely in these discussions, he may have some fears that he is entering on dangerous ground, and a feeling of uneasiness may seize hold of him though he can see no precise cause of it.

Professor Johnson judged from the questions asked in the classroom that just such an uneasiness was present in the minds of his students. The remainder of his address was therefore an attempt to persuade them that, in his own words, "there are no good grounds for the impression that what are called the Atheistic or Materialistic conclusions, so loudly proclaimed by certain scientific men and among them, by Dr. Tyndall, have any support in Physical Science."[64]

The spectre of Tyndall and his "Belfast Address" was thus part of the intellectual context within which the debate over science and religion was conducted in Canada. Both Graeme Mercer Adam, the energetic editor of the *Canadian Monthly*, and Goldwin Smith, mentor of the Canadian periodical press for the last quarter of the nineteenth century, were well read in much of the "heterodox" thought of the day; and not a little of it found its way onto the pages of their various journalistic enterprises. John Tyndall's reply to the critics of the "Belfast Address" appeared in the

Canadian Monthly in February 1875, thus launching the "materialism debate" in its pages. Tyndall's heresies were kept in the reader's mind by the republication of such items as his address "'Materialism' and Its Opponents."[65]

A second area of controversy, that over the domain of physical laws, took a recent book by George J. Romanes, *Christian Prayer and Natural Laws*, as its starting point. Here began the "prayer debate." A Canadian by birth (he was born in Kingston in 1848, the son of a Queen's College professor of Greek), G. J. Romanes was raised in England to which his family returned when the father came into an inheritance. Although his many biological writings gave him a reputation as one of the leading scientific naturalists of his day (the *Times* stated in 1886 that "Mr. George Romanes appears to be the biological investigator upon whom in England the mantle of Mr. Darwin has most conspicuously descended"), he may perhaps be described more accurately as one of those men whose views on life hovered "between science and religion." *Christian Prayer and Natural Laws* (1873), written while Romanes was still a student at Cambridge, was an essay which sought such a middle way.[66]

Yet it was precisely Romanes's moderation on the question of the extent to which the physical laws governing the natural world also exerted control over the world of the spirit that exercised defenders of science and religion in Canada. In seeking a middle way he satisfied no one in Canada, whether, on the one side, LeSueur, or, on the other, Agnes Maule Machar.[67] Each recognized that at the centre of this argument over prayer and natural laws lay the foundations of religious belief. The modern observer will agree, but add that the debate was a superb illustration of the process of secularization, for at stake was the idea of the miraculous. As Owen Chadwick has recently observed, "If miracles, which had been thought to be supernatural interruptions of the course of nature, ceased to be regarded as possible, or began to be regarded as so improbable that rational men would assume them (despite any evidence) not to have happened, was that only a change in Christian doctrine ... or was it touching some vital root-canal of religious power over men's minds and hearts?"[68] One cannot suggest a more succinct or accurate description than this of why LeSueur and Machar spent so many evenings examining each other's thought on the nature of prayer.

Another area of debate, over evolutionary ethics, was in large measure an extension of that over natural laws. The prayer question had begun with the query: Given the fact that we live in a

158 Chapter Five

world which science shows is governed by natural laws, to what extent can we petition God to have our prayers answered? (To what extent, that is, can we expect God to "violate" those natural laws?) The debate over evolutionary ethics began essentially with the question: Given the fact that we live in a world which science shows to be governed by natural laws, to what extent can those laws serve as the basis for our systems of belief and conduct? The debate thus included discussions of the validity of evolutionary theory, the evidences for the truth of the Christian doctrine of the immortality of the soul (as well as the question of the very existence of such an entity), and the possibility of establishing an evolutionary or natural system of morality. It began with considerations of the scientific work of Darwin and the speculations of Goldwin Smith, continued with attacks upon and defences of *The Data of Ethics*, and came to a conclusion (as an ongoing debate, though of course the issue itself remained) with the Canadian reactions to Goldwin Smith's pessimistic essay "The Prospect of a Moral Interregnum."[69]

W. D. LeSueur found himself in the midst of each of these controversies. With few exceptions, his contributions to the debates were the only ones which took seriously the framework of scientific assumptions. With the exception of certain articles by John Watson, the British Hegelian philosopher at Queen's University, Kingston,[70] his were also the only pieces which sought to move beyond special pleading to a larger synthesis that could reconcile the two warring camps by setting forward a coherent philosophy of life. It cannot be said that his viewpoint was without significant areas of weakness, or even that he managed at all times to measure up to the standards of criticism he set for himself.[71] Yet LeSueur's writings in defence of science were above all an extension of his plea for a critical spirit into all areas of inquiry. The scientific spirit was, in essence, simply the critical spirit in a special form, and whether LeSueur addressed himself to such American eminences as John Fiske, the evolutionist, Lyman Abbott, the evangelical preacher, and Noah Porter, the ex-president of Yale University, or to their Canadian counterparts such as G. M. Grant, the Presbyterian divine, or John Travers Lewis, the Anglican archbishop of Ontario, this spirit permeated all his arguments.[72]

A Defence of Modern Thought
It was entirely appropriate that W. D. LeSueur's essays on science, ethics, and modern thought began to appear at about the

same time as his essays on the critical spirit, for his conception of the nature of science was derived from the same premises as his theory of criticism. In its essence, he claimed, the purpose of science is not to determine inviolable truths. It is a simple matter of inquiry. From the time of Bacon, science had "kept to the true path," because it had been Bacon who first conceived of science as "a progressive interrogation of nature." Its prime function is "to interpret to man the world in which he lives." Since at the level of the mind it is the intellect that renders the randomness of experience into an intelligible order, thus making such an interpretation possible, the intellect itself—in a very real sense—*is* science. "Science," LeSueur wrote, "... is the minister of man's thinking faculty"; it "is simply the intellect of man, exercising itself in a certain direction."[73]

Once again LeSueur's insistence that "truth" is not an objective body of data is to be noted. Just as he conceived the critical spirit to be a continual and open process of affirmation and rejection by which judgements are made, so he saw the scientific spirit as simply the critical process extended into the observation of the natural world. "Science," he wrote in 1889, "is nothing else than knowledge of the facts and laws of the universe." But these "facts and laws" do not constitute an absolute truth any more than do religious creeds. Science does not advance the interests of an Absolute Truth. Those engaged in modern science, LeSueur concluded, have a far more humble task: they "are simply gathering facts and deducing laws, subject to rectification when further facts shall have been gathered."[74]

This commitment to a scientific spirit conceived largely as the process of continual critical inquiry was most evident in LeSueur's response to the charge that the science of his day was as dogmatic as the institutional Christianity which was then under attack. No article published in Canada set this charge forward more clearly, or with more force, than "The Marvels of Scientific Logic" by G of Toronto. The triumphs of physical science since the time of Bacon, said G, were both magnificent and indisputable. Science had liberated itself from the "fetters" of theological "slavery" and the "tyranny of mind" that such a restriction imposed. Still, it had liberated men from one form of mental slavery only to subject them to another, "a dogmatism which makes man the foolish sport of undesigning chance." With its emphasis on the reality of the "seen" as opposed to the "unseen" and its commitment to sensory experience as the datum of consciousness and belief, it declares triumphantly that Haeckel and Huxley have a better *a priori* claim on "truth" than St. Paul. Science insists on positive "proof" for the verification of all laws, yet though it cannot disprove the existence of an intelligent Creator of the universe or the existence of a universal moral order derived from laws of the world of the spirit, it rejects these as patently false mainly on the basis of their inconsistency with scientific postulates. "If she cannot fully explain the mystery that lies all around her," concluded G, "let her confess that for her at least the *super*natural exists, and let her learn humility."[75]

LeSueur was scarcely one to take the problems of dogmatism lightly. "The great intellectual issue of the present day," he wrote in 1886, "however some may try to disguise it, is that between dogma on the one hand and the free spirit of scientific enquiry on the other." He made no attempt to conceal the fact, as his article "Morality and Religion" shows, that to his mind specific religious "systems"—theologies—constituted "dogmatism" as he elsewhere defined it: "a traditional opinion held and defended on account of its truth."[76] The scientific spirit stood in direct opposition to dogmatism; yet LeSueur admitted that science was not always undogmatic. Its very success in enlarging men's understanding of their world had led it to this dangerous trap. "Dogmatism," he warned when discussing the scientific spirit, "is nothing but the temper of command unreasonably exercised. Science in the present day wields command, and it only too easily falls into the snare of dogmatism."[77]

The remedy for this situation was for scientists to remind themselves constantly that all scientific theories are essentially provisional, and any theory framed by them is "a working hypothesis and no more." Hence the scientific spirit, like the critical spirit in general, must also be characterized by humility. Again like the critical spirit, it must have as its ultimate end the pursuit of culture, the quest for individual, social, and moral perfection. If the scientist is to assume the momentous task of aiding man "to interpret [to other men] . . . the world in which he lives," he has assumed a burden which he must not take lightly: "It . . . is, therefore, of vast importance that the leaders in scientific investigation should set clearly before the world where the chief interest and glory of science lies, that they should visibly make it the instructor of humanity to all noble ends, that they should put it forward as the great liberaliser of thought, the enemy of superstition and confusion, the beautifier of life, and that in which man's highest faculties can find unfailing exercise and satisfaction."[78]

This assertion of the cultural aims of science would have been severely undermined if LeSueur had been unable to counter the charge that science was materialistic. His conception of social progress was, it seemed, that of an evolutionary and positivistic naturalist. How, then, could he separate himself and his philosophical outlook from this charge? One writer in *Rose-Belford's Canadian Monthly* had asked, rhetorically, what materialism was and had then defined it: "It is the supposition that all the changes of the universe, all the phenomena of the natural and of what *we* may call the spiritual world, are due to the combination of primordial atoms whose 'essential properties are extension and solidarity.'"[79] Was this not a more or less accurate description of LeSueur's philosophy, and was his talk of science as the "beautifier of life" and the minister of "man's highest faculties" not simply a gratuitous addendum to what was really a materialistic view of life?

The answer to this question lies, not in LeSueur's social philosophy, but in his psychology. His thinking about the mind was shaped by the "scheme of scientific ideas" which, as Alfred North Whitehead claimed, has dominated thought since the seventeenth century. This thought, Whitehead stated, "involves a fundamental duality, with *material* on the one hand and on the other hand *mind*."[80] This was one of the costs of the scientific revolution of that century, for it resulted, as an historian of psychology has observed, in "the isolation of mind from nature and the study of purposive behavior from the advance of the scientific method. The fragmentation of the world into primary and secondary qualities, outer and inner, body and mind, and the exclusion of final causes from science have plagued the study of mind and behavior at least since Descartes."[81]

LeSueur was a dualist within this tradition, an observer whose belief in the inviolable distinctions between mind and matter was strengthened by the authority of science. Yet his dualism, perhaps reinforced by his original training at the University of Toronto in the tenets of Common Sense, was articulated at a time when scientists such as Karl Vogt and his followers, working in the area of physiology, were uncovering the mysteries of the central nervous system and making the distinction between mind and brain increasingly murky.[82] The fragmentation of the old mind-body dichotomy introduced immense problems for many individuals, especially those who dealt professionally with the mentally ill. In Canada, for example, both Dr. Daniel Clark, in charge of the Toronto Asylum for the Insane, and Dr. Richard Maurice Bucke, superintendent of the provincial asylum at London, Ontario, went through much intellectual agony to reconcile the new findings in physiology with their own moral and emotional constitutions.[83]

The extent to which LeSueur knew of the work of psychologists such as Franz Joseph Gall is not known. It is certain, however, that he did not relinquish his belief in the dualism of mind and body. For him, as for R. M. Bucke in the 1870s, the mind and the body were essentially distinct: the processes of thought and of biology operated at different, yet parallel, planes. LeSueur therefore rejected flatly the findings of the typical physiologist of his day, "whose passion was to show that the various modes of social action were nothing more or higher than the processes of secretion, digestion, nutrition &c., with which his peculiar studies had rendered him familiar." Even more reprehensible to LeSueur than the materialistic physiologist, who extended the principles of biology into the study of social action, was the materialist who "loves to dwell on the physical basis of mind, and to ignore the utter impossibility of expressing any of the phenomena of mind in terms of matter."[84]

Here LeSueur agreed with Tyndall: matter cannot be transformed into thought. To accept such an unthinkable notion would undermine the basis of moral judgement and render statements of value—words like "wise or foolish, just or unjust, brave or cowardly"—meaningless. Furthermore, it would degrade the very idea of thought. The "true scientist," whose aim, like the philosopher's, is the pursuit of Culture, will not accept such a false view of the scientific spirit. "No one knows better than a true man of science," LeSueur wrote, "that nerve vibrations and molecular movements in the brain are no more the equivalent of thought than the pen with which Tennyson wrote, was the equivalent of 'In Memoriam.'"[85]

Here is an excellent example of the way certain scientific findings can be drawn upon and others ignored to support an individual's moral and intellectual point of view. LeSueur clearly recognized that an acceptance of the findings of certain of the physiologists and psychologists of his day would have aided his cause by calling severely into question the whole superstructure upon which Christian metaphysics rested; yet such an acceptance would thereby have also challenged the reality of any spiritual world, independent of both matter and Christianity. He was unwilling, perhaps unable, to give that world up.

An examination of LeSueur's essay "Materialism and Positivism" shows his fundamental belief in two inviolable orders of phenomena, one of mind or spirit and another of matter. Comtean positivism appealed to LeSueur not only because it was progressivist, organic, and universalistic, but also because it did not essentially challenge the existence of a universal moral order. It was a "positive philosophy" because it did not seek to invoke spiritual authorities; it was content to deal with "facts"—that is, with "whatever produced a complete and definite impression upon the mind." But it was *not* materialistic, for it did not necessarily limit "facts," positive knowledge, to the world of material substance. "Now, the difference between the materialist and the positivist lies in just this," he wrote, "that the former is embarrassed at the decided effects which he sees produced by impalpable things, while the latter escapes such embarrassment entirely simply by not having set up any arbitrary standard of what constitutes reality. The materialist does not want to recognize anything as real that does not more or less resemble his piece of granite, that does not affect the tactual sense; while the positivist is content to recognize all things as real that reveal their existence to the mind by affecting it in a definite manner."[86] Here LeSueur's dualism came in very handy. Just as there was a mental faculty which operated on a separate plane from the bodily organs, so there was also a distinct emotional and moral nature which functioned in relationship to a "reality" different from that involved in man's physical relationship with nature. The hold upon the Victorian mind of the school of Reid and Stewart was a tenacious one indeed.

In 1879 LeSueur reviewed R. M. Bucke's new book, *Man's Moral Nature*, and admitted that he was "struck" by it. By 1879 Bucke had begun to acquire a reputation in North America as one of the most innovative medical men engaged in psychological research and practice. One passage in particular from the book engaged LeSueur's interest:

> The activity and efficiency of the intellectual nature is largely dependent upon the degree of development of the moral nature, which last is undoubtedly the driving-power of our mental mechanism, as the great sympathetic is the driving-

power of our bodily organization. What I mean is, and I think everyone will agree with me here, that, with the same intellectual power, the outcome of that power will be vastly greater with a high moral nature behind it than it will be with a low moral nature behind it. In other words, that, with a given brain, a man who has strong and high desires will arrive at more and truer results of reflection than if, with the same brain, his desires are comparatively mean and low.[87]

Bucke, like LeSueur, assumed that the "moral nature" had a distinct and autonomous existence within the human constitution. Like LeSueur (and Comte), he also believed that this moral nature existed in different men at different levels.

LeSueur was convinced that Bucke was right: the lessons of everyday experience told him so. Some men, even though intelligent, failed to make a mark on society because they had a poorly developed moral nature. They had no distinct "moral aims," did not "aspire to moral influence," were not "compelled to any enterprises of moral conquest, and [did] not appeal to the emotional side of any one's nature." On the other hand, men of "culture and humanity" did not lead such narrow lives. Theirs was an intellectual power energized and given direction by a highly developed moral nature. They saw what others failed to see. "*They see into themselves*, and, seeing into themselves, they see into others. They are at home, so to speak, in the region of the soul." The ultimate lesson of Bucke's book was thus also the lesson of Arnold's *Culture and Anarchy*: Bucke showed "in a very striking manner how natural is the connection between 'Sweetness' and 'light.'"[88]

The operation of these universalistic assumptions within LeSueur's mind made Herbert Spencer a likely authority upon whom to draw for ideas. In the 1870s and 1880s Spencer's reputation as the greatest man of his age reached its peak in the Anglo-American community. His "synthetic philosophy" was both comprehensive and scientific and made him, in the words of Richard Hofstadter, "the metaphysician of the homemade intellectual, and the prophet of the cracker-barrel agnostic." His was a philosophy that—because of its comprehensiveness—was all things to all men, and scarcely an intellectual in the transatlantic community remained unaware of "Spencerism."[89]

The dominant view of Spencer's social philosophy that emerges from Richard Hofstadter's influential book *Social Darwinism in American Thought* (1944) is that of a grand "scientific" justification for an economic enterprise unimpeded by government regulation or control, a philosophy which in the hands of Spencerian disciples, such as the American social theorist William Graham Sumner, could give sanction to such claims as that which said: "The millionaires are a product of natural selection, acting on the whole body of men to pick out those who can meet the requirements of certain work to be done."[90]

W. D. LeSueur drew no such conclusions from his own reading of either Spencer or Darwin. He objected strenuously in 1885 to John Fiske's claim that "in the desperate struggle for existence no peculiarity has been too insignificant for natural selection to seize and enhance," for such a view seemed to suggest that natural selection was "some vigilant intelligence watching for opportunities to advance its designs." Natural selection, he insisted, carried with it no differentiation into "good" or "bad." "Darwin has discovered no law in nature by which good qualities (as such) are produced; he has simply discovered a law by which all kinds of qualities (differentiations), good, bad, and indifferent, are produced, and by which the bad ones (bad, i.e., in relation to the environment) are knocked off, like so many projecting angles, by the destruction of the individuals manifesting them. . . . If, therefore, we believe in natural selection, let us believe in it as it is, and be content to speak of it as it is. *Let us not make a god of what is, in its essence, the very negation of intelligent action.*"[91]

LeSueur's insistence upon a radical separation of ethics from the mechanism by which evolution took place did not presume, however, a divorce of ethics from the evolutionary process itself. It was precisely because Spencer's "synthetic philosophy" was also fundamentally an ethical one that he was attracted to it. Furthermore, while Spencer's comprehensive system treated all things as subject to natural laws, it did not deny the possibility of a divinity and the existence of universal moral laws or obliterate the spiritual-material dualism which was so basic to LeSueur's discussions of the "moral nature" of man. To the charge that a "natural" system of morality is impossible since morality is derived from theology, LeSueur replied: "The broad fact that, everywhere, we see traces, however rude, of moral feeling is precisely the foundation upon which my whole argument is built; men cannot live together unless they are partially moral; unless, in other words, some general good results from their association."[92] He also denied emphatically that the evolutionism of Darwin and Spencer "materialized" the human spirit and involved "caprice in morality, tyranny in government, uncertainty in science," along with "a denial of immortality and a disbelief in the personality of man and of God." He did so on the grounds that Spencer in no way challenged the existence of the world of spirit or mind:

> Evolution, as taught by Herbert Spencer, does nothing to weaken the fundamental distinction between subject and object, between mind and matter. If Spencer teaches that both these aspects of existence may, or rather must, find their union and identification in the Knowable Cause, he does no more than the Christian, who believes that God is the author both of the visible world and of the human spirit. Evolution gives material laws for human thought, only in so far as it shows the dependence of each higher plane of life on those below it.

Nor, he added, did evolutionism *ipso facto* seek to subvert belief in immortality or in a personal God:

> The doctrine of evolution is simply a mode of conceiving and accounting for the succession of events on the earth. It is in no sense a metaphysical or ontological doctrine, and lays no claim to the absoluteness with which metaphysical and ontological doctrines are invested. It does not pretend to penetrate to essences or to unveil final causes. If it is regarded by some as solving all mysteries, that is simply because they do not adequately understand it. Mr. Spencer certainly has never given countenance to such an idea. It does, however, as Darwin said of his philosophy, call constant attention to the need for proving all things. It strikes at the idea of authority, always excepting the constitutional authority, as we may term it, of demonstrated truth.

The doctrine of immortality and the idea of God, LeSueur concluded, were undermined only insofar as modern science had discredited the theological system which served as the authority upon which such doctrines were taught. Science, he added, does not doubt that such notions may be true; it simply asks that they be given "more conclusive demonstration" by defending them "in the open field of philosophy."[93]

This second major stage in W. D. LeSueur's intellectual life was in general an optimistic one. It saw him reject theological systems of morals in favour of the spirits of positivism and of Herbert Spencer's attempt to show "the evolution of morality as an objective process." History, for Spencer and for LeSueur, was primarily the study of human conduct, and morality was one aspect of that conduct—"developed conduct." History seemed to show that human conduct, if looked at objectively (that is, from a social point of view rather than from the perspective of one's own consciousness), was in a state of constant ascendance from lower to higher, simplicity to complexity. In the long course of human evolution a point beyond the struggle for subsistence had been reached in certain societies, a stage at which the power of ethical choice in human action had become possible. Spencer's view was that the best interests of the individual were generally realized by obeying the dictates of his "higher" (later developed) faculties through the voluntary subordination of the "lower." This required self-control, but subordination of self in this way placed man in a greater harmony not only with society but also with himself.[94]

LeSueur thus drew upon evolutionary science in a way decidedly different from that of American Social Darwinists such as William Graham Sumner. He used Spencer's naturalism, his organicism, and his universalism as a means of consolidating the social bond, not as a rationalization for the existence or hegemony of an individualistic ethic. In part, this response was due to the dictates of LeSueur's own intellectual and moral premises. But if his life can be seen as one manifestation of the Anglo-Canadian moral imperative—if, that is, it represents part of a continuing tradition in Canadian thought—then perhaps LeSueur's particular use of Spencer's ideas is a small but not insignificant commentary on the nature of the Canadian cultural experience itself. Late nineteenth-century America can perhaps generally be characterized as a country overwhelmingly dominated by Frye's myth of freedom; and the individualistic element in Sumnerian Social Darwinism gave reign to freedom in the sphere of economic action. The myth of freedom in Victorian Canada was compromised significantly by a stronger presence of its myth of concern. Physically in the New World but culturally of the Old, those such as LeSueur drew naturally upon the historical ties with Europe and the organic evolution of Canadian society.

Herbert Spencer, as LeSueur understood him, had much to contribute to an understanding of such a culture and society. The organic analogy which was the basis of Spencer's thought could be used to criticize a *laissez-faire* society, for it stressed interrelationships and mutual dependence. While Spencer's methodological individualism allowed him to elevate the role of the individual within society ("society existed for the benefit of its members," not the other way round), his rejection of a mechanistic model of society in favour of the idea of "The Social Organism" (as he often called his basic metaphor) equally insisted upon the symbiotic relationship of individual and society:

> The individual citizen [is] embedded in the social organism as one of its units, moulded by its influence and aiding reciprocally to remould it.
>
> The cardinal truth, difficult adequately to appreciate, is that while the forms and laws of each society are the consolidated products of the emotions and ideas of those who lived through the past, they are made operative by the subordination of existing emotions and ideas to them.

Such ideas could have much meaning for English Canada, which drew seriously from both the liberal and conservative philosophical traditions and from the political culture which was something of a fusion of the two.[95]

While not ignoring the individualistic strand in Spencer's philosophy, LeSueur drew upon the organic aspect of his thought to show the way in which Spencer could provide a naturalistic social ethic for the modern age. "Let me not hesitate to say," he wrote, "that many in this generation are willing to take their stand, and live their lives, upon such basis of truth as they can discover in nature and in human relations.... Human ties are not less tender or precious for the knowledge that we hold our treasures in earthen vessels." Here were signs that W. D. LeSueur, Canada's philosophical radical of the nineteenth century, was "radical" for a fundamentally "conservative" purpose. As in his writings on criticism, so, too, in his writings on the scientific spirit was the tension present between the modern myths of freedom and concern and the corresponding polarity of liberty and order. LeSueur sought to reconcile the spirit of science with the spirit of Christianity, the concern for inquiry into all things with the concern for the preservation of human community. "What we want," said the exponent of the critical path, the opponent of Christian doctrine, "is a 'natural piety' that shall link our days together in continuous effort for the advancement of purely human objects, and link us in thought and sympathy with both the past and the future of mankind."[96]

There was, in the end, a fundamental contradiction in W. D. LeSueur's philosophy. Quite apart from the fact that he was associated in the eyes of the orthodox with the Children of Darkness, his progressive, organic, and universalistic philosophy was significantly compromised by the nature of his psychology. The essential expression of the humanity of man, he had claimed, is the expression of man's own self-consciousness. Here LeSueur had taken his lead from Hegel, whose philosophy was based upon the rejection of subject-object dualism. Had LeSueur been able to divorce himself from the faculty psychology which controlled his thinking more than he may have been aware, the logic of his own thought would have led him towards another philosophical stance which was based upon a denial of dualism and which, in the last quarter of the nineteenth century, was given articulate and sustained expression.

The irony of LeSueur's thought was that his "positivism" came within a hair's breadth of philosophical idealism. In 1886 he quoted a passage from one of the sermons of John Caird, the Hegelian idealist, who was the greatest Scottish preacher of his age. "We grow in elevation and nobleness of nature," Caird had said, "just in proportion as we merge our individual life and happiness in the happiness and life of others." "These words of Dr. Caird's," added LeSueur, "contain, as we think, the whole philosophy of religion. Even those ... who through fear of being misunderstood might refrain from using these precise words, would still be prepared to understand in them the substantial and essentially religious truth of man's dependence on and affinity with a higher unity than that of his individual organism."[97]

Here was the point of union between Comte and Hegel. Here, too, was another means by which evolutionary science, Christianity, and Culture could be synthesized. Philosophical idealism, not positivism, was to become a dominant current in Anglo-Canadian intellectual life for the half century that began when LeSueur's essay on Sainte-Beuve appeared in print in 1871. Indeed, just when that article first met Canadian eyes, a young Scottish philosopher, twenty-five years old, first saw the sights of Canada. The philosopher was John Watson, a student of Edward Caird and his brother, John, at the University of Glasgow. A new form of accommodation had reached Canadian shores, and a new episode in its intellectual life was about to begin.

6
The Secret of Hegel

Kant and Hegel have no object but to restore Faith—Faith in God, Faith in the Immortality of the Soul and the Freedom of the Will—nay Faith in Christianity as the revealed religion.
  J. Hutchison Stirling, *The Secret of Hegel* (1865)

The need for philosophy arises out of the broken harmony of a spiritual life, in which the different elements or factors seem to be set in irreconcilable opposition to each other.
  Edward Caird, "The Problem of Philosophy at the Present Time" (1881)

In Victorian England and America, it had been the literary imagination which first took notice of philosophical movements on the Continent, particularly in Germany. It is impossible, for example, to understand the thought of Coleridge, Carlyle, or Emerson without some knowledge of German philosophy of the late eighteenth and early nineteenth centuries.[1] In the 1840s and 1850s Sir William Hamilton became the first philosopher to make the British intelligentsia aware of the relevance of the Kantian categories and the "categorical imperative" to the Common Sense tradition. Later, J. Hutchison Stirling's provocatively titled book, *The Secret of Hegel* (1865), had sought to make Hegel's thought intelligible to the British public, and it is generally concluded that it did so.[2] Hegel also found an attentive audience in St. Louis, Missouri, the middle of the American frontier west, in the 1860s and 1870s. There, William Torrey Harris, William Conrad Brokmeyer, and others who collectively became known as the "St. Louis School" proclaimed that they, too, had discovered the secret of Hegel, and over the next half century they helped to suffuse Hegelian idealism into almost every aspect of American intellectual life.[3] In Scotland, there were also signs by the 1860s that the sway of

Common Sense was about to be ended by the intrusion of idealism. By 1870 two of the most popular and influential thinkers were men heavily indebted to the German tradition. The brothers Caird, John the preacher and Edward the philosopher, became the two centres of Scottish religious life and thought in the last quarter of the nineteenth century. Their mark upon the intellectual landscape of Canada was not to be light.

In the early 1870s that landscape was still dominated by the twofold orthodoxy of natural theology—shattered abroad and weakened at home by the work of Darwin and his followers—and the Common Sense philosophy. The hold of Common Sense was a strong one, as has been seen in the thought of William Dawson LeSueur; but by the 1870s it had been subjected to criticism by men who now found it inadequate to meet the needs of the age. Two such individuals were George Paxton Young and John Clark Murray. In the summer of 1872 Young prepared to assume the chair of metaphysics and ethics in Daniel Wilson's University College, thereby ending his four-year tenure as professor of mental and moral philosophy at Knox College. Clark Murray was also on the move, from Queen's University to McGill, where he was to occupy the chair of mental and moral philosophy for the next thirty-one years. By 1872 both Young and Murray were in a state of transition in their intellectual, as well as professional, lives. Neither had yet found an adequate philosophical alternative to Common Sense; this was to be the contribution of young John Watson, the brilliant student of Edward Caird. Watson had accepted the chair in philosophy just vacated by Murray.

"It was John Watson's conception of a University that dominated us," two of his distinguished friends later recalled, "a society whose function was 'to break up men's dogmatism and set them at a universal point of view.'"[4] The full measure of British idealism crossed the Atlantic with Watson in the summer of 1872 when, scarcely older than the students he was shortly to teach, he sat aboard ship, contemplated his prospects in North America, and put together in his mind the inaugural address he knew he would be called upon to give. The force and clarity of his ideas were to give him a strong influence on Canadian public life in the years to come, but the pathway to that influence had been partly cleared already by the gradual rejection of the Common Sense school by teachers such as Murray and Young. When Watson arrived in Canada, the doctrines of Reid and Hamilton were under strong attack by earnest seekers after the truth which Watson believed had been imparted by Edward Caird.

The Rejection of Common Sense

Paxton Young's few philosophical publications before 1870 reveal a scholar who could accept neither Common Sense nor idealism. He found J. F. Ferrier's idealistic philosophy, set forth in his *Institutes of Metaphysics* (1854), fraught with difficulties. Ferrier had sought to construct a system of "necessary truths" that would show that "knowing" consists of neither pure subject nor pure object but a "subject-knowing-an-object." In doing so, he had challenged the subject-object dualism upon which Common Sense was based. Although a Scot himself, Ferrier had had little encouraging to say about Thomas Reid, whom he had described as a man "with vastly good intentions, and very excellent abilities for everything except philosophy, [who] had no speculative genius whatever—positively an anti-speculative turn of mind, which, with a mixture of shrewdness and naiveté altogether incomparable, he was pleased to term 'common sense.'"[5]

Young found it impossible to accept Ferrier's attempt to "reduce all intelligence, whether divine or human, under the dominion of necessary laws" because it failed to distinguish God's knowledge from that of man. He regarded Ferrier's attempted synthesis of subject and object (Ego and Non-Ego) unproved, his definition of knowledge inadequate, and his effort to extend this epistemology into the area of ontology disastrous. He was willing to concede that Ferrier's idea of a subject-object synthesis was not wrong in itself; he objected mainly to the implications of Ferrier's system of "necessary truths" for Christian cosmology. "Even . . . if . . . what exists is a synthesis of the Ego and Non-Ego," Young concluded, "it would be gratuitous and, I have no hesitations in adding, false, to affirm that the synthesis thus recognized as existing, had the principle of its Being in itself, or, in other words, *is*, independently of a continued exercise of sustaining power on the part of the infinite Creator." He continued:

> There is nothing in philosophy opposed to, but on the contrary all its conclusions are in beautiful harmony with, what revelation teaches, that God is not far from every one of us, for in him we live and move and have our being. The universe was not created once for all, and then left in some inconceivable condition of independent and abiding existence; but it is at every instant upheld by God; it is a continued product of the continued exercise of his power.[6]

The exact relationship between subject and object, ego and non-ego, mind and matter (terms of the dualism changed according to the context of the discussion), clearly preoccupied Young during his formative years as a philosopher. As well as attacking Ferrier, he challenged the validity of Sir David Brewster's recently discovered law of visible direction, which dealt with how light strikes the retina of the eye in creating monocular vision. Here, discussed at the level of a particular scientific experiment, was the nature of the relationship between subject and object and the role of sensory perception. Here also was a nineteenth-century meeting place of physiology and metaphysics. There was more at stake in discussing Brewster's new law than, so to speak, met the eye.

Young's criticisms of Brewster need not be dwelt upon except to note that he challenged the British scientist's conclusions with an assertion that indicates the start of his gradual shift to idealism. He claimed that the image formed on the retina, the "'phenomenon' of an object, has no existence in absolute space, apart from the mind." He refused to state that such images were "*purely* subjective states . . . out of all relation to matter," but repeated with certainty "that it is subjective in such a sense that it has no existence in absolute space, apart from the mind."[7]

If these words sound vaguely Berkeleyan, it is because they probably were. When at the peak of his powers and influence thirty years later, Young was known as an idealist who gave great weight to Bishop Berkeley's thought. (On the day of Young's death, Daniel Wilson wrote in his diary of "the Berkeleyan tendencies of his metaphysical speculation.")[8] The first signs of that Berkeleyan influence could be seen in Young's critique of Ferrier, in which he compared the thought of Ferrier and Berkeley at some length.[9] At this point in his career, Young was not an idealist, but Berkeley seems to have caused him to question his own philosophical tradition. In the 1850s and 1860s this meant challenging the views of the prevailing leader of the Scottish philosophy, Sir William Hamilton.

Young's criticisms of Hamilton's philosophy were contained in two articles that were nominally book reviews, one of O. W. Wight's edition of the *Philosophy of Sir William Hamilton* (1853), the other Hamilton's own edition of *Reid's Works* (1854). Here Young fixed upon Hamilton's statements about the trustworthiness of consciousness. Hamilton's conception of consciousness—the relation between a knowing subject and an object of knowledge, a relation which is the condition of the existence of knowledge, feeling, and desire—had been built upon a dualistic epistemology. It had also been based on the belief, fundamental to the Common Sense school, that certain cognitions were "immediate," that they were (in Hamilton's words) "the essential conditions of our knowledge" and, hence, "*must* be accepted as true."[10] Hamilton was willing to admit that if primary data could be shown to contradict each other directly, "the veracity of consciousness" would be "disproved." One could then no longer trust his own root convictions. Hamilton had added, however, that no philosopher had yet been able to establish such a contradiction.

Even so, he had, in Young's view, "open[ed] the door to scepticism" and rendered it "obligatory upon us to hear the pleadings of counsel against consciousness." Young would not allow even the remotest possibility that the truth of primary cognitions might be challenged. Here the assumptions of Common Sense still dominated. "Now," he asked, "is it not palpable that, underlying this whole course of thought, is the silent implied concession, that the truth of our primary cognitions is not . . . certain; but that there is only a vast and incalculable probability, amounting to moral certainty, in favor? Philosophy, however, is impossible, unless we can vindicate for our primary cognitions, real and absolute, and not merely moral, certainty."[11] Young would have no part of Hamilton's conception of the relativity of knowledge and was not about to give metaphysics over to the sensationalists.

Despite his reservations about various aspects of Hamilton's philosophy, Young nevertheless had not entirely abandoned the Common Sense school. He was willing to admit that on certain matters of sense perception Thomas Reid had held views which "will no longer find a single intelligent defender,"[12] and had hardly mentioned the philosopher in his review of Hamilton's edition of *Reid's Works*, but he gave studious attention to Hamilton's thought, which he believed to be "the only consistent and plausible system of natural realism which is before the world."[13]

For the most part, Young was an advocate of the established pattern of orthodox thought in British North America during the 1850s and 1860s, even if the direction of his own thinking was changing. In 1856 he reviewed James McCosh's book, *Typical Forms and Special Ends in Creation*, a treatise on natural theology by the scholar who had assumed the mantle handed down by Hamilton. Young agreed wholeheartedly with the book's argument and aims and found little to criticize; for the most part he was content simply to detail its arguments. But his review also indicated that he now found both the school of Paley and that of Reid intellectually insufficient. "Pantheism is now making its influence more decidedly felt than ever," he warned, "and against its deadly errors, we must have other aid than a continuation of Paley."[14] Elsewhere in the review he placed a similar judgement on the views of Reid and Hamilton as they applied to the argument for design in nature. At the time, however, Young had no alternate philosophical system adequate to meet the needs of the day. For that matter, neither did Clark Murray, who had also grappled with Sir William Hamilton's thought in his first decade as a scholar and teacher.

As John Irving has pointed out, Clark Murray was the first "professional" philosopher in Canada.[15] Although an ordained Presbyterian clergyman, he was the first professor of philosophy in Canada who accepted the notion that his discipline above all required a critical intelligence. From his earliest experiences as an undergraduate, the nature of the education he received seems to have forced this conclusion upon him, perhaps because he was introduced to competing philosophical systems. (In the same year that he attended Sir William Hamilton's metaphysics class, he was introduced to Ferrier's recently published *Institutes of Metaphysics*, on which he took detailed notes and wrote a term essay.) Having discovered German philosophy under Hamilton, he spent the academic year 1856-7 in Germany, attending classes at Heidelberg and Gottingen universities.[16]

Whatever the circumstances by which Clark Murray came to question the Scottish Common Sense tradition, the fact is that by the 1860s, his years at Queen's, he did. In 1867 Murray wrote a series of four articles for the *Canadian Journal*, entitled "Sir William Hamilton's Philosophy: An Exposition and Criticism." The articles were more broadly significant than their title implied, for they placed Hamilton within the context of Scottish philosophical thought going back to the seventeenth century. It was the significance and usefulness of the Scottish Common Sense tradition, not merely the thought of one of its exponents, which were in fact under consideration. "Whatever value one may ascribe to the work which Sir William has performed in the world," he began, "it cannot be doubted that he is the representative of a very extensive philosophical school at the present day, and that for some time it will be required by friends and foes alike, that that school shall be estimated as it is represented in his writings." Hamilton's thought, Murray insisted, could not be studied except "in its relation to the national philosophy" of which it was "ostensibly an exposition and defence."[17]

Like that of Paxton Young, Murray's critique of Hamilton and the school of Reid invoked the thought of Bishop Berkeley. Murray was far more taken, however, with Berkeley's idealism during the 1860s than Young had been. Berkeley, he claimed, was a philosopher "who appears to have at once displayed keener philosophical insight, and attained more nearly the true theory of knowledge, as well as the true theory of existence," than had Locke. In one sentence Murray had established not only his idealistic mentor but his philosophical enemy. Much of the remainder of his introductory discussion of Scottish philosophy was devoted to illustrating the indebtedness of the school of Reid to Berkeley and to pointing out that Reid's thought was not as significant for its attack upon Berkeley's idealism as it was for its criticism of the empiricism of Locke and Hume.[18]

Murray pointed out that Reid had always asserted that the philosophical importance of his work was that it questioned the idealist assertion that the only objects of thought were ideas or images in the mind; yet in order to disprove the "ideal theory," Murray added, Reid had been "obliged to adduce beliefs which he regard[ed] as originated by the very constitution of our minds, and as therefore having an origin prior to experience." Thus, he concluded, "a correct historical estimate of Reid's philosophy seems forced to raise into special prominence his assertion, for some of the elements which constitute human knowledge, of an existence independent [of] experience."[19] Thomas Reid, in Murray's view, had been something of an idealist.

Reid had not been a very good one. He had had a "very slender grasp" of the antiempirical quality of his own thought, and therefore had applied it in a highly "unskilful manner," possibly because he had not fully been aware of this aspect of his system. Even so, he had been the philosopher in whose thought, concluded Murray, "is included all that is distinctive of Scottish metaphysical philosophy previous to Hamilton."[20] But if Reid, the master, could be so criticized, what of Hamilton?

The remaining three articles in Murray's series on Hamilton were highly technical and lengthy. One systematically summarized the corpus of Hamilton's thought—no easy task; the second criticized his conception of the nature of consciousness; the third examined his doctrine of external perception.[21] Hamilton's theory of consciousness, said Murray, was inadequate because while Hamilton declared consciousness to be "the fundamental norm" of mental activity, not (as Reid had maintained) simply a special faculty of knowledge, he had also stated that it was "only a small circle in the centre of a far wider sphere of action and passion."

Here was an apparent contradiction which in Murray's eyes raised one of the key questions of the age: "If there be states of mind without consciousness, what is the quality that forms the difference between a mental fact and a physical?"[22] What, in short, was the relationship between mental philosophy and the new science of physiological psychology?

Hamilton had refused absolutely to countenance the idea that consciousness bore any relationship to human physiology. The work of the German scientist Franz Joseph Gall, and the phrenological "science" that had been inspired by it, had proved to Hamilton "that no assistance is afforded to Mental Philosophy by an examination of the Nervous System." The science of mind could be advanced only by a study of consciousness; no aid could come from studying the brain. Murray rejected this view. To criticize phrenological quackery was one thing, but to dismiss physiological science in its entirety was quite another:

> We should be far from his [Hamilton's] conclusion that the study of the nervous system cannot supersede reflection in the science of mind, still farther from the position, that that science cannot even be aided by such a study. For the general theory, which makes mental science altogether dependent on the physiology of the nervous system, is not involved in the truth or falsity of particular theories on the special functions of different parts of that system. It is therefore incumbent on the psychologist to adduce some grounds, apart from any properly physiological doctrines, to prove that consciousness, if not the only competent informer, is certainly an independent source of reliable information, with regard to mental phenomena. Yet this is exactly what Sir William Hamilton has failed to do.

Each day, he added, the philosophy of mind and the physiology of the nervous system drew nearer each other in their common quest for the datum of consciousness. Each day Hamilton's assertion of a consciousness unperturbed by human physiology grew increasingly untenable. "It is altogether impossible," Murray concluded, ". . . to analyse so complex a phenomenon as any one act of sense-perception into its constituent elements so as to extricate the purely mental without ascertaining the nervous processes by which they have been conditioned; and the determination of many still unsolved problems regarding sensation is to be sought as much from physiology as from psychology."[23]

On the surface, Murray thus appears to have been moving intellectually in two directions at once in his gradual rejection of the Common Sense school. On one hand, he looked towards idealism, invoking Berkeley as an authority whose philosophy was superior to that of Hamilton (as he did at length in his essay on Hamilton's doctrine of sense perception);[24] on the other, he supported the view that physiological psychology could enable one to understand the nature of consciousness. It was as if he had stepped mentally towards both Plato and Pavlov. In fact, two courses of intellectual transition were then taking shape in Murray's mind, which together help resolve this apparent contradiction. First, he was coming to reject the intuitionism of the Common Sense school. Second, he was also beginning to reject any dualistic conception of physical or human nature.

The rejection of Common Sense constitutes a minor but important milestone in the course of critical intellectual inquiry and philosophical enterprise in Canada. Hamilton's basic problem, Murray concluded, had been that he was too much under the sway of Reid, particularly Reid's constant references to the "ordinary convictions of mankind" as the highest form of scientific inquiry into the nature of external perceptions. This, Murray insisted, was not scientific but unscientific, not inquiry but the *absence* of inquiry. "To refer to these convictions," he wrote, "as if they superseded all the recognized processes of science, was to foreclose the very inquiries, which constitute the science of mind, into the nature and the origin of mental phenomena." For the first time in the Canadian experience, the philosophic endeavour had been recognized as necessarily a matter of critical intellectual inquiry. Murray was not about to allow his audience to miss this essential point. He continued:

> If the argument from common sense be, as is maintained by Hamilton, merely a reference to the ultimate and simple facts of human consciousness, then the Common Sense school is indistinguishable from other schools of speculation; for there is no philosophy which does not professedly seek to discover by what smallest number of ultimate and inexplicable facts the phenomena of the universe may be explained, or which dreams of denying these facts after they have been discovered. But when any circle of inquirers distinguish themselves by their habit of appealing to common sense, it is difficult to understand for what purpose such an appeal can be habitually made, unless it be to array the unscientific

opinions that are universally current among men against speculative conclusions which cannot be rebutted by the recognized methods of science.[25]

A decade later Murray put these views—now honed to razor-sharpness—before the British public in an article entitled "The Scottish Philosophy" in *Macmillan's Magazine*. "The truth is," he wrote, "Reid's thinking never represents the speculative toil of a philosophic intellect, but merely the refined opinions of ordinary intelligence." And of Hamilton, the student of Reid, he concluded: "He never succeeds in establishing any *real* distinction, between a philosophical appeal to Common Sense and the unphilosophical citation of vulgar opinion against unpalatable conclusions of science."[26] By 1878 Murray's break with Common Sense was complete. There were, in his mind, only two other ways of accounting for "the Common Necessities of Thought": empiricism and idealism.

This willingness to countenance what many regard as antithetical modes of thought points towards the second major shift in Murray's thought. Both physiological research and philosophical idealism resolved the problem of the nature of consciousness by refusing to acknowledge any rigid subject-object dualism. It was the idea of a unified conception of nature that allowed him, despite his idealistic inclinations, to pay careful attention to the work of Alexander Bain, whose book *The Emotions and the Will* (1850) was a pioneering attempt to show the relationship of the nervous system and human consciousness. Such consideration did not imply acceptance, for Murray rejected Bain's ascription of consciousness "to all the nerve-centres distributed throughout the nervous system." Bain had not, in Murray's view, confronted the fact that man is self-conscious as well as conscious. Nerve-force alone was not a sufficient explanation. "What then is this consciousness, which is neither consciousness, as usually understood, nor yet a purely physical state? It is not enough to say, that it is something, but that what it is, cannot be defined."[27]

In his quest, Murray's thought gradually turned during the 1860s and 1870s towards idealism.[28] Perhaps *it* held the key to the problem of the nature of consciousness. By 1878 he had reached the conclusion that it did. He pointed out in that year that there had been idealistic elements within the Common Sense tradition from its inception—Hamilton, for example, had acknowledged that on the matter of perception there was a close approximation between his own "Realism" and an Absolute Idealism. The most recent Scottish philosophers, such as Ferrier and Stirling, seemed to have built upon this implicit connection. Finally, Murray noted, "Professor Caird's recent work on Kant is an evidence that the teaching which issues from the chair of Reid goes to a length which he could never have surmised, in protesting against the illusion which reduces human knowledge to a mere complexus of sensations."[29]

Murray, like Young, continued throughout the 1870s to work his way towards a philosophical position that could mediate the claims of empirical science and the needs of the spirit. At the same time, in Kingston, Edward Caird's most brilliant pupil sought to propagate the answer.

John Watson and the Secret of Hegel

John Watson brought to Canada a commodity that was significantly lacking in the 1870s: a certainty of conviction derived from a philosophy of life that appeared to contain the solutions to the major intellectual problems of his day. Elsewhere in the country, men were engaged in personal searches for solutions to their intellectual and spiritual troubles. Those of Clark Murray and Paxton Young continued. William Lyall remained within the orbit of Common Sense, but he found no solutions to problems imposed by a materialistic science except to warn against its inroads. Increasingly his attention turned to the study of literature.[30] W. D. LeSueur continued to establish a middle path between the positivistic inclinations of modern science and the intuitionism of the Common Sense school. Goldwin Smith surveyed the course of the various debates of the 1870s and came to find no prospect better than a "moral interregnum." Even at the end of the century he could offer only "guesses at the riddle of existence."[31] In 1873, having taught chemistry and natural history at Victoria College for seven years, the Reverend Nathanael Burwash at last found an appointment at his college in the area of his major interest, systematic theology. But the conflict between science and religion had not left him unaffected, and for the next quarter century Burwash would attempt to establish a systematic theology that was based on the inductive, scientific method.[32]

There were others who engaged in a similar search. The Reverend D. J. Macdonnell, a student of James George at Queen's, left Canada for study in Scotland and Germany in the mid-1860s, only to return with a mind that was intellectually more alive but forever incapable of dogmatic commitment to the fundamental tenets of his creed.[33] John Beattie Crozier, a student of James Bovell and graduate of the University of Toronto Medical School in 1871, found the intellectual atmosphere in Ontario stifling. He left the country, never to return. By 1871 he had discovered social evolutionism by reading Herbert Spencer, and although he later rejected Spencer's views, his goal came to be nothing less than to write the definitive history of the evolution of the human intellect. By the time of his death, shortly after the First World War, he had established a substantial reputation in London intellectual circles.[34] Dr. Richard Maurice Bucke, superintendent of the Ontario Asylum for the Insane, found himself on an intellectual journey that took him from the articulation of *Man's Moral Nature* in 1879, in a book which did not significantly violate the assumptions of the Common Sense school, to the discovery of *Cosmic Consciousness* by the turn of the century.[35]

By the time of his arrival in Canada, Watson's search had already ended. He was, as he later admitted, "a somewhat self-satisfied young man," having just completed a brilliant career at Glasgow University.[36] But it was a satisfaction derived from confidence rather than pride, for he knew that he held within his head the essential elements, each already in its place, of a complete philosophical system. It could, he was convinced, resolve the problems faced by the Common Sense school without denying the fundamental moral nature of man. It constituted a new conception of design and purpose operating in the universe, one that could encompass, rather than capitulate to, evolutionary science. It offered a critique of empiricism, and put empiricists on the defensive by revealing the limitations of scientific enterprise without attacking science irrationally. It cultivated a pious disposition in the minds of students without belittling intellectual inquiry. It showed the essential rationality of the universe and placed everything within the perspective of a new and modern interpretation of the Christian experience, even while defending the essentials of the faith. Not surprisingly, then, the twenty-five-year-old Watson was "self-satisfied" when in August of 1872, he arrived at Summerhill, the stone building that constituted one of the two structures on the Queen's campus and met the six professors who made up its entire faculty.

John Watson had just spent six years at the University of Glasgow, where his life had been transformed. He arrived there in 1866, after having been at Edinburgh University only a month or two. He was drawn to Glasgow by the reputations of John Caird, professor of divinity, and his younger brother, Edward, who had just been appointed to the chair of moral philosophy. Watson had been raised an orthodox Presbyterian, but by his late teens was uncomfortable within the tradition as he had come to know it—as a faith that somehow had drawn apart from the larger world to which it should have given meaning.[37] Nor did the words and writings of the Common Sense philosophers, still dominant in Scotland, inspire him. Scottish philosophy, he later wrote, "was at the low-water mark," for the tradition of Reid and Stewart did little more than allow men "to jog along contentedly, with no very strong faith and no very disquieting disbelief."[38] At this stage in his life, according to his daughter, Watson was "impatient . . . of anything approaching the conventional in the intellectual and spiritual world," and so "gravitated towards those who were untrammelled by tradition."[39]

In the person of Edward Caird he found a mentor who had an equal disregard for continuity of tradition for its own sake, and his attendance at Caird's inaugural address was perhaps the most seminal event in his life. More than forty years later, Watson would recall "being forcibly struck by what then seemed to me the curious way in which he spoke in the same breath of Socrates and Christianity, Aristotle and St. Paul. I had been accustomed to regard Christianity as a thing apart, and I imagine that to others also this was the first glimpse into the kinship of Greek Philosophy and the Christian Religion, and in general the first vague apprehension of the principle of organic development." He did not enter Caird's moral philosophy class until his senior year, three years later, but when he did a new world had been born to him:

> Day by day, week by week, [I] saw unrolled before me the ideas by which Caird exhibited before his pupils the process by which Greek Philosophy gave rise to the categories by means of which Christian experience was gradually developed into a theology that enabled it to conquer the world, though not without loss, and by which in modern times the spirit thus generated has formed the all-pervasive leaven, which has been transforming the whole mass of humanity into its own image. All this was nothing less than the disclosure of a new world to a Scottish youth, who from his early years had been accustomed to roll like a sweet morsel under his tongue such abstract themes as the relations of faith and works, predestination and foreknowledge. The close shell of Calvinism was burst.[40]

One cannot, then, overemphasize the extent to which Watson was influenced, both personally and intellectually, by Edward Caird. He accepted Caird's philosophical views from the first, and his own philosophical system, articulated over the span of the next half century, was virtually identical with that of his master. It would in fact do injustice to neither philosopher to say that Watson's many writings elaborated much of Caird's thought but never transcended it. This is an important point because it means that Watson's observations on the primary principles of Caird's philosophy are equally a commentary on his own. Thus, when he wrote in Caird's obituary for the *Philosophical Review* that "the central idea of his philosophy was the principle that the various stages in the history of man, and especially in the history of philosophy, exhibit the progressive evolution of reason,"[41] he had set forward his own central idea as well as Caird's. At the same time, he had indicated that Edward Caird was above all indebted to Hegel for his major philosophical insight.

Caird had discovered German philosophy through his love of literature, not by studying philosophy. It was Carlyle, not Hamilton, who had led him to examine German thought and, inspired by Carlyle's idealistic vision, he was thoroughly familiar with the works of Schiller and Goethe by the time he left Glasgow to study under Benjamin Jowett at Oxford.[42] There Jowett introduced him to Hegel's thought, although he had already imbibed the spirit of Hegel from his literary reading and from a year's sojourn in Germany. At Oxford his closest friend had been T. H. Green. Together, in the early 1860s, they mastered the thought of Kant and Hegel and worked at constructing an idealistic critique of empiricism, then the dominant philosophical school in England.[43]

Kant's "critical philosophy" taught Caird that empiricism could be transcended because experience, as Watson expressed it, "is inexplicable from a mere series of feelings without the cooperation of thought." But Kant had not carried the idealistic implications of his philosophy to their logical conclusions. This had been done by Hegel. Kant had contended that the existence of the universal principle of reason within man lifts him above the seeming limitations of the senses. Confined within the limitations of space and time, man, Kant had claimed, is a self-determining subject and is conscious of subordination only to the law of duty—the "categorical imperative"—which is the law of his own reason. Hegel had built upon Kant's philosophy by dissolving the dualism of Kant—man as natural and spiritual—by means of his notions of organic unity and organic development. Hence, dualisms such as "materialism and spiritualism, sensationalism and idealism, empiricism and *a priori* speculation, individualism and idealism," were relative, not absolute. Hegel's philosophy provided Caird above all with a principle of reconciliation suitable to an age dominated by the notion of evolutionary, progressive change, for he had claimed that the historical process consisted of "a regular ascent from inorganic things, through organic things, to the self-conscious life of mind."[44]

The universe was an organic whole; all change was part of the self-evolution of that whole; all observations were comprehensible only when it was recognized that the objects of observation were only partial manifestations of a single principle. Here, for Caird and for Watson, was the heart of the secret of Hegel: the historical process was but the unfolding of a single principle, *and that principle was spiritual.* Hence, noted Watson, it "manifests itself fully only in the life of man, with his self-conscious intelligence. Hegel's doctrine thus seemed ... to be the philosophic rendering of the essential principle of Christianity, the union or identity of the human and divine." By means of this Hegelian influence, religion, for both Caird and Watson, became, in Watson's words, "the process by which man comprehends, and comprehends ever more clearly and fully, the spiritual unity which combines all existence and manifests its power in that process, while the salvation of society and the influence of great men he [Caird] ascribed to the free play of reason in converting all that seems foreign to it into a means of its own realization."[45]

By the time Watson left Scotland for Canada, he had learned the all-encompassing secret of Hegel. Caird's idealism had taken full hold upon him, and there seemed to be no problem with which it was inadequate to deal. That this was the case may be seen in Watson's own description of what he took away from Caird's class. The passage which follows is lengthy, but it is also extremely important, for it constitutes a succinct anatomy of the thought of a lifetime:

> We gradually learned to seek for truth in the interpretation of experience, conceived in the widest way as the experience of the race, and as comprehending the vast, slow, never hastening, never resting, movement of humanity. Thus philosophy ceased to be a mere academic theory, or even a special investigation into a particular section of human life, and expanded into the nobler discipline of an interpretation of social and political life and institutions, of art and religion, as these

developed into ever higher and more perfect forms in the great secular process of history. And philosophy itself, as Caird explained it, was in no sense to be divorced from the concrete life of man. It had a law of its own, no doubt; but this was the law by which human reason gradually unfolded itself, when aroused by the conflicts and oppositions which on a less self-conscious plane never ceased to emerge. For reason as it is in man—so we were taught—was not something peculiar to him, something which was inflected by his finitude; on the contrary, it was that in him which connects him with the Divine. Hence, it was true, in a literal sense, that man is "made in the image of God," and therefore is able to comprehend the nature of God. How else, indeed, should one obtain any knowledge? and how otherwise should he act morally? If the true principle of the universe lies beyond our reach—beyond both our theoretical and our practical consciousness—what sense can there be in speaking either of knowledge or of morality? If we have no glimpse of what really is—if we cannot penetrate to the heart of things and see God there—we must obviously live for ever in a vain show, from which no efforts of ours shall ever deliver us; nay, if it were so, how should we even know that we were living in a vain show? As Caird often put it: How can we know that we are limited unless we are in some sense beyond the limit? A being living in a world of mere appearance would never know it.[46]

The system of philosophy articulated by Watson for the rest of his life was largely elaborative, rather than evolved. He expanded at length each of the tenets set forward in this passage, but he repudiated none. Subjective idealism, pragmatism, and logical positivism, each in its turn failed to alter the coordinates of his mind.

Science and the Idealist Alternative
Among the few possessions that Watson brought with him to Canada was his scrapbook, and in August of 1872—possibly aboard ship—he pasted into it an item which may have given him the subject of his inaugural address at Queen's. The scrapbook clipping, from an unidentified Scottish newspaper, was the text of W. B. Carpenter's presidential address to the British Association for the Advancement of Science, given in Brighton earlier that summer. Its title was "Man as the Interpreter of Nature." Its pur-

pose was to remind the best British scientists that even the most empirical and exact of the sciences were highly interpretative when examined closely. All science, Carpenter said, tended towards convergence; this was testimony both to the universality of the scientific method and to the unity of nature. It was this tendency towards agreement by scientists, he added, which gave rise "to the general belief—in many, to the confident assurance—that the scientific interpretation of nature represents her not merely as she seems, but as she really is. When, however, we carefully examine the foundation of that assurance, we find reason to distrust its security."[47]

Carpenter's address to the British association was an unusual one for, unlike most earlier presidential speeches to the group, it was speculative. It sought to outline the limitations of British empiricism without doing so in a fashion that would place its author in the camp of the philosophical idealists. Carpenter was a philosophical "mugwump," and his lecture struck a middle ground between John Stuart Mill's severely empirical *System of Logic* (1843) and William Whewell's Kantian antidote to Mill, *Philosophy of the Inductive Sciences* (1840). Nevertheless, the fact was that the president of the British association for 1872 had openly declared that the interpretation of nature was rightfully a matter of philosophical inquiry.

This was precisely Watson's major point in his inaugural lecture, delivered in October at Queen's. Entitled *The Relation of Philosophy to Science*, it declared at the outset that "truth, from its very nature, is a complete unity" and that there could therefore be no branch of knowledge that directly contradicted any other. There could not, then, be an absolute opposition between philosophical and scientific knowledge. All men of science were in error, Watson declared, who claimed that philosophy and science were at odds. This included T. H. Huxley, the prime exponent of that point of view, who insisted flatly that philosophy led as inevitably to idealism as science did to materialism. In one case, claimed Huxley, matter was shown to depend upon mind; in the other, mind upon matter.[48]

Watson quickly revealed what he thought to be the source of this problem. "There is nothing new," he stated, "in the assertion of an absolute opposition between Philosophy and Science, Thought and Nature, Reason and Experience: it is, as Mr. Huxley candidly admits, simply the philosophy of David Hume, adjusted to the advances of modern science; and transformed, we may add, from a Scepticism into a Dogmatism." What Carpenter had only suggested, Watson stated outright. The empirical tradition was the culprit that had helped to create the division between philosophy and science, for it had mistaken the limited, phenomenal truths it examined for Truth itself. Starting from the world of the ordinary consciousness, empirical science had mistakenly assumed the passivity of mind, mind as receiver of sensations; and from this had come the implicit but unwarranted assumption of its materiality. In so doing, it had failed to come to grips with the active nature of the self-conscious mind.[49]

Here, philosophy had the advantage over science. Science and its method depended upon a dualism that assumed the independent existence of the external or phenomenal world. It could not tell what nature is "in itself"; only that nature exhibits certain laws. It could not provide explanations of ultimate reality. Philosophy could. Unlike the special sciences, Watson claimed, it "does not deal with a particular section of knowledge, but with the essential nature of all knowledge; hence it aims at revealing ultimate or necessary truth." The "special business of philosophy," he went on, was nothing less than "to transcend the world of phenomena and to disclose the world of real being, by a discovery of the true bond of connection between thought and nature." True philosophy broke down the false dualism of subject and object, recognized the limitations of scientific claims, and placed those claims within the universal frame of reference that alone could give them true meaning. Not that all so-called philosophical systems were as meritorious as that, of course. Herbert Spencer's philosophy, for example, reduced space, time, and even consciousness to expressions of mere "Force." What a difference there was when such an outlook was contrasted with one that was truly philosophic in the idealist's sense:

> The world, to the eye of Science, is . . . a vast level plain; to Philosophy, on the other hand, it is, like the celestial orbs in Dante's "Paradiso," an ascending series of realms, of which the first rests on earth and the last terminates in heaven. Beginning with physical forces, Philosophy ascends gradually upwards, through chemical energy and vital action; till it attains to the sphere of man, regarded as a spirit, from which the ascent to God, the first and last, upon whom all the lower spheres are dependent, and whose nature alone supplies the key that unlocks the whole universe, is easily and necessarily made.[50]

An idealistic philosophy, Watson had just proclaimed, provided the ultimate means of raising for all time the final veil of Isis.

If there was a sceptic in Professor Watson's audience on that October day, he might well have found the speaker's intellectual presumptions very great indeed. The speaker was, after all, only twenty-five years old; yet he had condemned the whole empirical tradition from Locke, through Hume, to Mill. Each empiricist philosopher had made the mistake of denying the active role of consciousness. "Starting with the absolute independence of nature, and therefore virtually with the assumption that consciousness is entirely dependent upon the material world," empiricism had tried "to build up the external world and the world of thought out of sensation." The inevitable result, Watson concluded, was "Absolute Nihilism."[51] But what alternatives do you offer? the sceptic might have asked silently. These Watson now proceeded to provide.

The key, he claimed, lay in the nature of thought. Man's self-consciousness, overlooked by the empiricist, meant that in the act of apprehending Self, one also apprehended that which was not Self. The two were inseparably united, for, in so thinking, the object was brought "under the dominion of thought" and "the universality or permanence that belongs to thought. Spirit, therefore, in virtue of Thought, destroys the assumed independence of Nature and assimilates it to itself." Far from being *passively* implanted upon the mind, the external world was really the product of the *activity* of "the universalising power of reason."[52] This synthesizing power of self-consciousness led Watson into a discussion of Kant, who had revolutionized philosophy by insisting upon the active powers of mind. But Kant had not shown how a true metaphysic, based on the active mind, could be brought about. Watson did not mention Hegel's name at all in his address, but he was about to reveal to his audience the solution Hegel provided for this thorny philosophical problem.

The problem of "Metaphysic," Watson declared, was to show, not simply that there was unity in nature and in thought, but that the former could be resolved into the latter; for "only in this way can an ultimate unity that embraces both be obtained." Hegel's developmental philosophy showed how this could come about, for it showed that the course of thought, as seen in the history of the human race, passed through a series of stages which culminated in ultimate truth. The dialectical nature of thought dictated this historical necessity, for "an examination of the universal consciousness of mankind" would show that thought was "impelled on from one stage to another by the inner necessity of its own nature."[53] Watson could thus offer an alternative to the appeal to the new consciousness of historical evolution by the positivist and his law of three stages. The Hegelian idealist could also proffer stages in the growth of mankind, and Watson did.

His particular stages in the history of thought ranged from that of Sensuous Consciousness (which corresponded to "the infancy of the race"), through that of Observation, to that of "the Observing Consciousness." At this highest stage the world was no longer observed simply as a series of objects. Here, "the phenomena of nature are now transmuted by the action of thought into exemplifications of necessary laws, and thus half-subjective generalizations are raised to objective truths." Science exists at this level, but so does philosophy; and philosophy is the higher form of thought because only it truly can claim universality. The philosophic mind will view man, his history, and his thought as part of a larger organic reality. This alone, Watson believed, was what defined the rational and therefore the real. "We must exclude our *individual* fancies or opinions," he insisted, "and hold only that to be a law of nature which all intelligences or universal thought would recognise to be true; for law in its true sense means an inseparable unity, an indissoluble connection, of distinct relations. The Understanding, therefore, has penetrated into the inner soul of Nature and found it to be rational."[54]

Watson's address had come full circle. He had returned to the essential limitation of scientific inquiry, which was that it universalized the phenomenal. "And thus," he concluded,

> the special sciences are not fully conscious of the truth they reveal, because of the dualism they assume between nature and intelligence. Viewed from the higher platform of philosophy, the lesson taught us by the progress of science is the continuous discovery of a greater and greater unity between Thought and Nature; and, although Science does not perceive that in mastering nature it is at the same time revealing the thought latent in it, its unchecked progress is a prophecy of ultimate triumph—the reduction of the whole external world to a system of laws—the revelation of the absolute rationality of the universe. The progress of thought has been, as it still is, an ever greater assimilation of nature into itself, and thus to philosophy Thought and Nature are found to be but obverse sides of the same shield.[55]

A freshman attending Watson's address as his first university lecture, hearing the outlines of philosophy for the first time, might possibly have wondered why the famous war between science and religion had arisen in the first place. If he had been able to accept Watson's major premise—that all truth was a complete whole and, following from this, that any aspect of thought reflected only part of that great organic whole—everything Watson said made perfect sense and seemed to coincide with the major tendencies of the age. The nineteenth century marked the greatest triumphs in human thought in the history of mankind, whether in science or in society in general (or so the mid-Victorian often believed).[56] It *was* the age of intellectual inquiry. What, then, was wrong in declaring the supremacy of mind and proclaiming that man *can* know ultimate reality by exerting its powers? The age was one of obvious progress in almost every way. Societies and civilizations, no less than species, evolved. Watson's stages in the progressive evolution of thought offered an alternative to the materialistic social evolutionism of Herbert Spencer and his disciples. Moreover, and most important of all, the philosophy Watson espoused did not seem to undermine the Christian experience. Did it not see Christianity as the ultimate expression of human thought? Had Watson not declared, near the end of his address, "that Logic and Metaphysics and Ethics were incomplete if they did not, as their final result, lead us up to the Infinite and God"? And his peroration had proclaimed that "the human Spirit, made in the image of God, Nature, 'the visible garment of God,' and Duty, the voice of God speaking in the innermost depths of our moral nature, agree in pointing upwards to the Great Being whose essence they unfold. And thus the assurance which Religion gives to the individual man of the existence of a Supreme Being whom he must reverence and love, Philosophy endorses and supports."[57]

The confident philosophy of John Watson offered a great deal. It rendered Common Sense superfluous by maintaining its own insistence on the "moral nature" of man while asserting the active powers of mind. It made defences of a Paleyite natural theology in the face of materialistic, "anarchic" evolutionism unnecessary because it spoke of a purposive evolution of the race, which was also the evolution of mind or spirit and within which scientific theories of organic evolution must fall. Finally, it marked a new variation of the pious disposition. Man *could*, Watson asserted, come to know Ultimate Reality, although he could not know it in its totality because reality itself was progressively unfolding. But thought expressed in universal terms would ultimately "lose itself in the all-embracing glory of God." In the end Watson's idealism offered what traditional Christianity never had, for in its final formulation, he declared, universalized thought would achieve a "unity with the divine nature."[58] This was the ultimate expression of piety.

It was once said of the American idealist philosopher Josiah Royce that "his was a mind of depth and fertility, yet it is not unfair to say that he reproduced his whole thought in every chapter and in every article."[59] This was also very true of Watson. In his inaugural address he had stated briefly almost every major point that he was to develop at length over the next two decades. He had spoken about science and materialism, Darwinism and morality, empiricism and the "critical philosophy," and the philosophy of Herbert Spencer. Each was to be the subject of books and articles published by Watson between 1872 and 1890. Similarly, Watson's very popular textbook, *An Outline of Philosophy* (1898), originally published three years earlier as *Comte, Mill, and Spencer*, followed the structure of his 1872 address and systematically developed the major assertions contained in it.[60] It is not necessary, then, to examine in detail the bulk of Watson's many nineteenth-century writings in order to capture the essence of them. It is sufficient to note his active part in the several international controversies—and their Canadian manifestations—to which other Canadians, notably William Dawson LeSueur, also paid sustained and interested attention.

Watson's first entry into public controversy was his rebuttal in 1876 of the materialism of John Tyndall's "Belfast Address." He had not been the first person in Canada to do so. It is instructive to note the difference between his critique of Tyndall and that of Clark Murray. In 1875 Murray had offered a criticism of Tyndall's address in a *Canadian Monthly* article attacking the atomism that underlay Tyndall's philosophy. Atomism, Murray had said, was a mere hypothesis which, although valuable as a means of rendering physical phenomena intelligible, failed to explain "the simplest act of consciousness" or to invalidate the basis of theism.[61] Murray's argument, however, was of limited force. He could point out the contradictions inherent in the "school of recent philosophical physicists," of which Professor Tyndall was "the mouthpiece" (such as the fact that though Tyndall was a phenomenalist he nevertheless admitted the existence of something beyond mental impressions).[62] But he could offer no systematic alternative to Tyndall's philosophy. His argument had concluded with the claim that "modern physicism, therefore, has adduced nothing to interfere with the ancient faith of man, that the Lord of all 'by wisdom hath founded the earth, by understanding hath established the heavens.'"[63] In England, the Reverend James Martineau had also published a criticism of Tyndall's address as it related to Christian theology. Tyndall had replied to it. This reply and Martineau's rebuttal found their way into the pages of the *Canadian Monthly*.[64] It was at this point that Watson entered the fray. Unlike Murray, he offered not only a critique but an alternate philosophical vision.

Queen's University students would have found Watson's argument familiar. "A restless spirit of inquiry," it went, has marked the present age, one result of which has been the assault on theology by science. Science has made undeniable progress, but, in doing so, it has become "intolerant of rival methods" of arriving at truth. It has forgotten its proper boundaries. "And thus it has come about that some of the most distinguished of living physicists claim for their own department of truth undisputed possession of the domain of real knowledge, reserving for religion the nebulous realm of untested belief and unverifiable conjecture."[65] In Watson's view, this was a major error. But there were errors which Tyndall shared with scientists as illustrious as Herbert Spencer. These, too, were familiar to those of Watson's students who read the *Canadian Monthly* article.

Both Tyndall and Spencer denied, in their common scepticism, that man was capable of truly knowing reality. Both were dualists who held a "rigid antithesis of mind and matter." Both also contradicted themselves by asserting that there existed a "Power" or "Force" which was "unknowable" or "inscrutable"—yet to make the assertion was to acknowledge the existence of such a force or power. Finally, both denied the supremacy of thought. "What we claim," Watson replied, "is that, if it were possible for *all intelligence* to be removed, the natural world would at the same time fade away for ever, leaving not a wrack behind. Try to conceive of anything that is entirely dissociated from consciousness, and the utter futility of the attempt will at once become manifest." The natural and mental worlds, he insisted, were alike governed by the laws of thought which render those worlds intelligible and coherent, and "that which is comprehensible by an intelligent being, such as man, must itself be the product of an Intelligence." But man was a moral as well as an intelligent being, a creature of conscience and intellect. Hence the Supreme Power, manifested in nature and in the mind of man, must also be an intelligent and moral Being.[66] Like Clark Murray, Watson had ended his reply to Tyndall with a vindication of theism, but his was an affirmation which contained within it a radical reconstruction of reality.

Watson's entry into the world of intellectual controversy was at two levels of debate, both of which helped to build his reputation at home and abroad. One was that of his Canadian audience. He continued during the 1870s to contribute to the *Canadian Monthly*. In October 1876 he responded, for example, to Goldwin Smith's claim that the doctrine of evolution made necessary the rewriting of manuals of moral philosophy. Watson denied that Darwinian evolutionism could be taken legitimately into the realm of social and moral phenomena and could therefore have no bearing on "moral conceptions."[67] Social Darwinism having found a Canadian defender in J. A. Allen, Watson was still in the midst of debate eight months later.[68] But Allen had invoked the authority and theories of Herbert Spencer, "that man of profound thought and colossal intellect,"[69] and Watson's reply, while addressed to Allen, was largely part of a critique of Spencer upon which he had already embarked elsewhere.

Watson's criticisms of Herbert Spencer were set forward at the international level and in a more technical form than his Canadian articles. The first of these, "The Relativity of Knowledge," appeared in the January 1877 issue of the *Journal of Speculative Philosophy*. There he attacked the empirical basis of Spencer's philosophy, the dualism of his epistemology, and the denial by the British social philosopher that human intelligence was capable of absolute knowledge. "If with Mr. Spencer," he concluded, "we throw in our lot with immediate knowledge, we must be content to see all real knowledge overthrown, and scepticism in undisputed possession of the field. One after another, nature and mind, object and subject, body and soul, and lastly consciousness itself, go down in a vain contest with unsubstantial phantoms invulnerable to the most skillful strokes."[70] Over the next three years, Watson published substantial criticisms of Spencer's conception of "Force" and offered in the place of Spencer's fundamental categories those of Kant.[71]

In the 1880s Watson led the "Kantian Revival" in the English-speaking world. His study "The Method of Kant" appeared in the influential British philosophical journal, *Mind*, in 1880. In 1881 *Kant and his English Critics* was published, marked by four editions in its first year. The same year saw him invited to speak to the Concord School of Philosophy. His address was entitled "The Critical Philosophy in its Relations to Realism and Sensationalism."[72] "I wish you would look at some of the neo-Kantians, who are becoming dominant," Herbert Spencer wrote to a friend in 1883, "and who, as for example, Watson, think they have made unanswerable attacks upon Evolutionary Empiricism."[73] Shortly thereafter, in another letter, he acknowledged Watson as the leader of the "neo-Kantians."[74]

Further commentaries on the philosophy of Kant followed from Watson's pen,[75] but the culmination of his contribution to Kantian scholarship came in 1888 when *The Philosophy of Kant as Contained in Extracts from his own Writings* appeared. Watson's translations from Kant, the revision of a more modest collection published in 1882 for the use of his students, met with critical success; was regularly reprinted; and found use in Canadian, British, and American universities well into the twentieth century.[76] Yet in the decades when Spencerian social evolutionism was in vogue and the spectre of doubt at large, it was nevertheless also very much a tract suitable for its times. As the Kingston *News* put it: "Although intended primarily for university students, the work ought to be in the hands of all who, having long been tossed on the sea of modern scepticism, are longing to heal the mental cleft and once more feel themselves in harmony with themselves. Kant's philosophy is not an affair of merely academic interest. It must interest every thinking man."[77] The "critical philosophy," set within the developmental, progressivist Hegelian framework, provided a moral philosophy suitable for an age dominated by the idea of evolution.

Conscience and Community
The achievement of Watson in establishing a reputation which made him, with Edward Caird, T. H. Green, and Josiah Royce, one of the top exponents of Absolute Idealism in the world, constitutes in itself an important chapter in the history of Anglo-Canadian thought. There can be no doubt that his rise to eminence in the 1870s and 1880s helped keep mental and moral philosophy *primus inter pares* within liberal arts curricula in Anglo-Canadian colleges. But there can be equally little doubt that this golden age of philosophy in Canada—between the 1880s and the second or third decade of the twentieth century—was not his achievement alone.[78] During those years Canadian philosophers enjoyed remarkable, sometimes legendary, reputations within their universities. In this respect Watson's nineteenth-century career was

simply part of a larger reorientation of the Canadian academic community towards idealism as the philosophical creed most acceptable as an antidote for scepticism and as a social ethic adequate to suit the needs of the late nineteenth century. An indication of this reorientation will be given later in the chapter. For the moment it is necessary to consider the nature of the social philosophy provided by Watson, the best-known proponent of idealism in Canada.

The major tenets of that social philosophy had first been put forward in Watson's 1872 inaugural address. The purpose of ethics, he stated, was to resolve the contradiction of freedom and necessity. The key to the resolution of this difficulty, he claimed, lay in conceiving of freedom, not, as the empiricist said, as "the exemption from all external influences and restraints," but rather as an action which "is regulated by the highest laws of our nature." Here, of course, Watson invoked the Kantian "categorical imperative." "He ... who regulates all his actions by eternal principles of duty, may seem to be bound by the chains of necessity, but he really enjoys the highest liberty. For he is not subject to any external necessity, but only to the inner necessity of his own nature, in obeying which he purifies and strengthens his will and becomes a master where others are slaves."[79] Hence, by the seemingly contradictory process of "working out one's freedom through seeming necessity," one was brought to a universal point of view.

It is difficult, if not impossible, to establish a causal connection between the growth of idealism and the rise of imperial sentiment in Canada. It can at least be stated that those of a political frame of mind who listened to Watson throughout his career on the subject of the relationship between freedom and moral responsibility heard much that could serve to give the argument for an increased imperial connection much philosophical substance. "It is true that he must render implicit obedience to those of authority over him," Watson conceded,

> ... but in so doing he learns to free himself from an undue accentuation of his own individual desires, and to seek his freedom where alone it can be found—in the subordination of his own will to the good of others. By and by he is liberated from the restrictions of the family, but he finds himself another and a heavier burden; he is now a citizen—a member of the State—and as such he not only enjoys the rights of a citizen, but is also bound down by the duties of his new rela-

tion, which hold him as by adamantine chains. . . . He cannot, further, be a member of the State without being more than this; for a state is but one of the community of nations, and he who is a member of the one is a member of the other also. He alone, therefore, is free who recognises in every man of whatever country or position that humanity which unites the race by the bonds of a common brotherhood, and who freely discharges the duties he owes to all.[80]

By "the race," it is important to note, Watson meant nothing less than the human race. But others, less concerned with the intricacies of philosophical idealism and with a tendency to extend the perceived attributes and interests of the British "race," applied this idealistic vision to the Anglo-Saxon. A Canadian imperialist, George Parkin, whose debt to philosophical idealism has recently been noted, once proclaimed "that there is a reason for the maintenance of a united British Empire more profound in its appeal to our highest instincts, more inspiring to the idealism of many minds, than any considerations of material success, commercial security, or even of social and political welfare. . . . It has its foundations in our sense of Christian responsibility."[81] How different, one might ask, was Parkin's conception of "Christian responsibility" from that of Watson?

The idea of Christian responsibility was what Watson, in any event, sought to instil into the minds of his students and his reading public. His textbook, *An Outline of Philosophy*, the product of twenty years of lectures to students of Queen's University, illustrates this. After criticizing the relativity of knowledge in the positivism of Auguste Comte, the experiential basis of John Stuart Mill's theory of mathematics, and the sceptical agnosticism of Herbert Spencer's idea of social evolution, Watson turned to the moral philosophy of Kant and of Hegel. Despite the fact that more than two decades separated his first address and his *Outline*, Watson's social philosophy had not changed. Several generations of students had learned from him that the ideas of duty and freedom lay at the basis of all moral conceptions; that doing one's duty meant, not becoming an ascetic, but the subordination of the natural desires "to the realization of the complete nature of the self." His students had been taught that duty was to be defined as "the realization of the universal through the particular . . . , at once the willing of the universal or law, and the willing of the particular."[82] They had learned that Kant's view of duty, while erroneous in some particulars (for example, Kant's absolute opposition of desire and reason), was fundamentally correct.[83] Kant, Watson insisted, had pointed out rightly that morality consisted ultimately in acting "as if we belonged to a 'kingdom of ends'; in other words, each individual must conceive of himself as a member in a social organism."[84]

Here Watson neared the centre of his ethical ideal, for in his view "the true good of the individual" was inseparable from "the consciousness of a social good."[85] "What holds human beings together in society," he said, "is this idea of a good higher than merely individual good. Every form of social organization rests upon this tacit recognition of a higher good that is realized in the union of oneself with others." The dialectical framework of Watson's thought, allowing him to reconcile seemingly opposite notions, thus enabled him to construct the social ethic W. D. LeSueur had sought but never fully found. LeSueur had never overcome the problems imposed by the dualism of his conception of mind. Watson had dissolved the dualism. LeSueur's was an ethic in which the older conception of social responsibility and the new ideas of political and social freedom had reached an uneasy truce. Watson offered a new ethic of concern that so defined the idea of freedom that it became the ultimate expression of duty.[86] In an increasingly complex commercial and industrial society, it was a rearticulation of the idea of a moral community that could help combat disintegrative forces. The individual could take as his sole authority only "the law of his own reason"; but the social embodiments of that reason lay in "custom and law."[87] The ultimate form of community, of course, was that of humanity; hence, it would seem that men could never achieve it. But this was not to say that a moral state could not be attained, for just as men could conceive of the moral ideal, so they could seek to reach it.

The core of Watson's social philosophy consisted of the desire to create a moral community based on the universalizing capacity of human reason. Just as the individual could not realize his potentialities in isolation from the social whole, the moral community itself had to be conceived in universal, organic terms:

> Morality must no longer be identified with the customs and laws of the narrow civic community, but it must rest upon the wider basis of humanity. This is the principle which is tacitly recognized in all forms of the community, however inadequately it may be realized. It is still true that only in

identifying himself with a social good can the individual realize himself. And the reason is that in the community the idea of humanity of organic unity is in process of realization. That the community has not reached its final form only shows that the moral life is the gradual realization of the ideal life. It is not true, therefore, that the ideal of humanity is a *mere* ideal: it is an ideal that is continually in process of realization. Hence the individual man can find himself, can become moral, only by contributing his share to its realization. He must learn that, to set aside his individual inclinations and make himself an organ of the community is to be moral, and the only way to be moral. He may criticize, and seek to improve the community, but his criticism must rest upon a recognition of the principle that the individual has no right to oppose himself to the community on the ground of inclination, but only on the ground that the community as it actually is in some ways contradicts the principle of the community, the principle that it is the medium in which the complete realization of man is to be found. No criticism can be of any value that denies the principle of a social good, and seeks to substitute the mere individualism of caprice.[88]

This is the most revealing and suggestive statement made by a Canadian philosopher in the nineteenth century. It sets forward not only a certain conception of the social good, but also the form of criticism that must follow from it. Much of the social philosophy and criticism put forward by Anglo-Canadians in the twentieth century can be seen as a continuation of this particular form of the moral imperative.[89]

These were convictions that saw publication in 1895, and in his later publications much of Watson's attention was paid to placing the capstones on his philosophical system.[90] But Watson had put forward the same views to students of Queen's, both in lectures and in "lay sermons," for fifty years, from the time of his appointment in 1872 until his retirement in 1922. As early as 1873, he had insisted that the only ethic suitable for an industrial civilization was one that repudiated that of individualism. "It is only by mutual dependence upon each other," he said at the opening of the university session in October of that year, "that the best powers of men are called forth into exercise. Wide-spread industry tends to eliminate purely self-referent interests; by bringing men into intimate relations with each other, it generates that mutual trust and confidence which result in a healthy tone of public morality.... The seeming sacrifice of independence is really the condition of the only independence that is worth having."[91] The ideal of the university, he emphasized year after year, should be to create the frame of mind necessary to realize such a conception of freedom. "The aim of the university," he proclaimed in 1888, "is to produce noble, intelligent, unselfish men, and if it fails in that, it has failed of its highest vocation. The true ideal is to lift men to an attitude where they shall be able to contemplate human life as an organic whole, ruled by the idea of order and law, and where they shall be moved as by a divine constraint to consecrate their life to the common weal."[92]

Other philosophers in Canada began to profess variations of the idealist creed during the 1880s. At the University of Toronto, Paxton Young's conversion was by then complete, and even before his death he had become a legendary figure. As an undergraduate, the literary critic Archibald MacMechan first saw Young just as he, MacMechan, was about to write a final examination. "He was an old gentleman with a bald head, a white beard and a rasping voice," MacMechan later wrote, "and I wondered with all the wonder of a Freshman why the others cheered. My dignified senior told me that it was 'Young,' but the name meant nothing to me. Later I was one of those who cheered the casual mention of his name on a programme, much more his bodily presence."[93] Other worshippers of Young were no less reverential; some later revealed what had inspired that reverence. It was not until he was aged that Young became acquainted with the idealism of T. H. Green, noted one student; yet for years he had taught views identical with those of the British idealist.[94] Others recalled the extent to which his criticisms of the materialism and agnosticism of the 1870s and 1880s had "placed more than one sinking and wavering belief on the solid rock of scientific truth," and all claimed to have been inspired by the way Young seemed to exude the spirit of "the ideal life."[95]

After Young's death in 1889, his two successors both professed to cultivate the moral ideal embodied in his life and teachings. James Mark Baldwin, the new professor of logic and metaphysics from the United States, was not in a technical sense a philosophical idealist; he was, at this early stage in his career, an exponent of experimental psychology and urged in his inaugural address in 1890 the development of laboratory facilities at the University of Toronto. But he was also in search of his own version of a moral community rooted in the social good and found it necessary to repudiate any form of philosophy that denied the existence of a universal moral law. "If morality is custom," he asked, "why may I not deviate from custom? ... If law is convention, and convention convenience, why not my convenience? A doctrine which runs to the brink of the French Revolution—a social disintegration due to individualism in philosophy."[96]

A year later, in 1891, the new professor of ethics and the history of philosophy gave his inaugural lecture. James Gibson Hume, a native son of Toronto, had been an admiring student of Young. His address was an acknowledgement of debt to Young and to Kant, as well as public proclamation of his own idealism. Central to his idealist ethics was the notion of will. This, for Hume, was the psychological entity without which the universal moral community would cease to exist. "Will," he proclaimed,

> desires to effect a union and reconciliation, so that what appears to the individual consciousness as universal or existing for others may become private also ... and, on the other hand, that what appears as existing for the individual consciousness alone may exist for others also as well as for the individual, that is, become actualized, realized. We thus see that the Will is the active, conciliating, unifying, living, organizing, constitutive principle in the conscious process. It is, in fact, the consciousness expressing itself. It is the vital element ... in consciousness. It is the fundamental principle in personality.[97]

Hume's declaration lacked the crispness and clarity of Watson's writing, but it shared the conviction that education clearly was a matter of training the will as well as the intellect.

In the Maritimes, idealism also found a major exponent during the 1880s. There, Jacob Gould Schurman, a native Nova Scotian fresh from studies in Germany, published *Kantian Ethics and the Ethics of Evolution* in 1881, while professor of logic and metaphysics in Acadia College.[98] Schurman's book examined the ethical systems of both Kant and Spencer, and while its author was by no means uncritical of Kant, he found Spencer's views far less acceptable. The book, John Watson claimed in a review for the *Journal of Speculative Philosophy*, "seems to be the best contribution to the critical study of the Ethics of Kant which has so far appeared in English."[99] (He was perhaps too modest, since his own *Kant and his English Critics* had also been published in 1881.)

Schurman moved to Dalhousie University in 1882, taught there for four years, and made considerable impact upon students both through his popular philosophy courses and through various public lectures.[100] In 1886 he received an appointment, turned down by Watson, as Sage Professor of Philosophy at Cornell University and was its president within a decade. His second book, *The Ethical Import of Darwinism*, appeared in 1888; its object was to distinguish—as Watson's inaugural address had done sixteen years earlier—"between science and speculation in the application of Darwinism to morals."[101] Schurman was instrumental in founding the *Philosophical Review* in 1892. His choice for the honour of contributing the first article to its premier number was John Watson, who proceeded to pen "The Critical Philosophy and Idealism," a lengthy article showing how idealism had reached new heights in the combination of Kant and Hegel in the mind of Edward Caird.[102]

Clark Murray was the most popular professor at McGill University in the 1880s. By 1888 his course in Honours philosophy had nearly one-third more students than that of his nearest competitor, Sir William Dawson, who came to regard Murray as "unsafe."[103] By the 1880s Murray, too, had committed himself to the idealist vision. In 1881 he reviewed Watson's *Kant and his English Critics*, and not only—with Watson—repudiated empiricist ethics but also enthusiastically embraced those of Kant.[104] Henceforth, like Watson, he insisted that his students read their Kant at first hand rather than through commentators.[105] Yet Murray was no blind follower of the philosophical systems of others. In 1885 he published *A Handbook of Psychology*, which attempted to reconcile the idealist and empiricist views of psychology. Six years later appeared *An Introduction to Ethics*, which applied this psychology to notions of "the moral consciousness," "the supreme Law of Duty," and "Habit."[106]

As with J. G. Hume at the University of Toronto, Murray saw the process of education as essentially a training of the will. "All education," began an essay he wrote for Nicholas Murray Butler's *Educational Review* in 1891, "is, in a sense, educational of will." The will, he went on to say, could be defined as "active intelligence stimulated by emotion: or, as it may equally well be described, it is active emotion directed by intelligence." The will directed intelligence towards the ends of life and pointed towards the means of achieving those ends. "Here, therefore, lies the value of a general culture of intelligence for the education of the will, because a disciplined intelligence can of course discover more clearly the rational ends of life, and can master more rapidly the most effective methods by which they may be achieved."[107] Once again the moral imperative had been given an articulated presence in Anglo-Canadian thought.

7
The Sadness and Joy of Knowledge

> In much wisdom is much grief: and He that Increaseth knowledge Increaseth sorrow.
> Eccles. 1:18

> The school discipline that educates in self-command and self-restraint, by its very success makes itself no longer necessary. Its rules and restraints have not achieved their purpose, unless they have fitted us for that mental and moral freedom which makes them useless.
> John Caird, "Things New and Old," in *University Sermons* (1898)

By the 1890s the old orthodoxy of ideas, founded on constraint and dominated by a myth of concern that was largely closed, had been shattered. Common Sense had been dismissed as faulty in its psychology and inadequate in its conception of mind; it was incapable of meeting the needs and challenges of an age of inquiry and analysis. The Paleyite natural theology had in large measure been replaced by an equally teleological, but dynamic, Hegelian conception of social evolution. The Baconian ideal in science had also proved inadequate under the onslaught of the Darwinian method. A new era of scientific inquiry at the universities in Canada had in fact been presaged as early as 1877 when James Loudon, recently appointed to the University of Toronto, suggested at convocation that scientists should be concerned more with laboratory results than with metaphysical disputes.[1]

The hegemony of idealism had begun, but only the first signs of its ultimate influence could then have been discerned. In the nineties, idealism was a force for intellectual change that came to dominance at a time when change was everywhere. Every epoch is a time of transformation, but the 1890s marked a clear departure from the past in the nature and quality of Canadian life. John Watson's *Outline of Philosophy* was put before a Canadian reading public that witnessed in the decades to come a social and industrial upheaval for which there was no precedent in the history of the nation. His *Christianity and Idealism* (1897), a series of lectures given before the Philosophical Union of the University of California at Berkeley, appeared in the first flush of the Laurier boom; published in 1912 as *The Interpretation of Religious Experience*, the lectures were given when the rate of social and industrial change had reached its height.

Above all, Canada experienced a social transformation during these years, and the idealist preached what was fundamentally a social ethic. Even at the level of intellectual speculation, the social good was necessarily to prevail. And as with thought, so lives and careers were also seen to be meaningful only when regarded from a universal perspective. Society, it was argued, must be conceived as an organism. The individual must subordinate private interests to serve the greater whole. Watson had spoken from the first of "the various spheres of the universe," each forming "an ascending series, in which each higher realm includes while it transcends the lower."[2] Each "sphere" could become a focus of attention for Canadians whose thought was informed by the new moral imperative, articulated in a different form for a new age. One could perform one's social duties in ascending forms of service to an ever-greater good, whether at the level of the church, the civil service, or the empire. During the thirty years that followed 1890, Canadian intellectual life was thus suffused with the idealist variant of the Anglo-Canadian moral imperative.[3]

Idealism exerted its greatest influence, however, on Canadian Protestant thought and practice. The full nature and extent of this influence will be determined only with more substantial historical investigation, yet a brief examination of the thought of certain key figures in early twentieth-century Protestant circles may serve to suggest the general nature of the intrusion of idealist assumptions upon Protestant thought in Canada.

Faith through Reason

The late nineteenth-century idealist delighted in using his creed to resolve seemingly irresolvable problems, and in Canada he took great pleasure in being simultaneously a force upholding the essentials of the Christian experience, while inaugurating a profound transformation in religious life. The result, however, was a reorientation of Canadian Protestantism that by the 1920s scarcely resembled that desired by the nineteenth-century clerical advocates of a reconciliation of science and religion through idealism.

Idealists inspired by Watson taught that reality consisted of the secular process of history infused with a spiritual principle that was at once the heart of knowledge and synonymous with the mind of God. "In God we 'live and move and have our being,'" Watson told a Kingston meeting of the Y.M.C.A. in 1901; "we are spirits capable of communion with the Spirit of all things; the meanest as well as the highest object within our reach witnesses of this universal spirit; and, living in it, we may become worthy members of the family, the community, the state, the race. To realize this spirit in all its forms is our true life work."[4] So it was, but it was also a quest with a profoundly ambiguous legacy.

Watson's address was entitled "The Sadness and Joy of Knowledge," its text taken from Ecclesiastes 1:18, which said "In much wisdom is much grief: and He that Increaseth knowledge Increaseth sorrow." This was a paradox such as Watson delighted in resolving, for the idealist's universal vision and dialectical mode of argument could show how the "perils and storms of the intellectual life"—the sorrow—would be quelled by the simple recognition that in this very sadness lay the source of joy. Strenuous effort in the search for universal truth by means of intellectual inquiry would gradually result in a deeper consciousness of reality, one in which "at each step we feel we are penetrating a little deeper into the nature of things, and learning to re-think the embodied thoughts of God."[5] A generation earlier, such a statement would have been roundly condemned in Canadian Protestant circles, for it would have been seen as the height of intellectual arrogance. Watson's large claim was an expression of a piety shorn of the Christian's awareness that because of the sinfulness of man, he could never fully achieve identity with the mind of God, however much he might strive for it. But by the twentieth century this was a notion which found increasing acceptance in Canadian churches and Protestant denominational colleges.

The pervasiveness of idealist assumptions in Canadian university circles is suggested by even the most cursory of examinations of student newspapers such as *Queen's Journal* or Victoria College's *Acta Victoriana*. This is likewise the case with the fledgling academic journals *University of Toronto Quarterly*, which began in 1895, and *Queen's Quarterly*, first published two years earlier. The editors of the latter proclaimed solemnly in an opening statement that the quarterly sought to keep its readers aware of "what Queen's is doing and thinking" and "to try to throw some rays of light on the questions that men's minds must always be most concerned about."[6]

Not surprisingly, the honour of making the first statement about such weighty questions fell to John Watson, who provided a piece entitled "The Middle Ages and the Reformation." Luther's reformation of the Christian church, Watson stated, was based upon the simple principle that reconciliation with God was possible only through "a spiritual act, an act of faith." Luther, Watson argued, had accomplished this by stressing the "duty of private judgment" and the "principle of justification of faith." Yet he had not gone far enough in assessing the application of his own principle. Watson insisted that by retreating to the Augustinian notion of the "alienation of man from God in his immediate or natural state, the impossibility of getting rid of the consciousness of sin by conformity to an external law," Luther had not taken into account the fact that "the individual's consciousness of God" transcends individuality and "is conditioned by the past history of the consciousness of the race." Luther, that is to say, had not taken into account the principle of development, since he had not recognized that religious consciousness evolved "with the growing intelligence and will of humanity." Once wedded to the idea of the progressive development of consciousness, however, Protestantism would "purify the state by making it an embodiment of reason." This was the "logical consequence of the Protestant idea," one in which "the ideal is the real, and what contradicts the ideal must ultimately be annulled."[7]

Watson's essay appeared in July 1893. In February of that year occurred a very important event in the history of university extension in Canada. Initiated by Principal G. M. Grant, the first Theological Alumni Conference took place on the campus of Queen's University. Lasting for ten days, it was attended by Presbyterian ministers across the Dominion. Others, not graduates of Queen's but attracted by the intellectual vitality of the place, also attended. There they heard the principal speak on a variety of doctrinal and practical subjects, and they were also exposed—as the alumni had been as undergraduates—to John Watson's confident and hermetic philosophy. A sign of their appreciation of his views came in their closing resolutions, for they recommended the inauguration of a permanent lectureship and stipulated that it first be held by a professor from Queen's and that he "should treat some subject bearing on the relations of Philosophy and

Theology." Any doubt as to whom they wished to hold the first lectureship is dispelled by the fact that when Chancellor Fleming announced later in the year his intention to sponsor the desired lecture series, he stipulated that "no one could better fill the position than Dr. Watson, who did so much to make the first conference a success."[8]

Yet even as idealism gained adherents in theological circles in the early twentieth century, voices of protest could be heard. For some, the idealist's version of the heart of the Christian experience led, not to its enrichment, but to its destruction. In February 1906, for example, Albert Carman, general superintendent of the Methodist church in Canada, received a letter from the pastor of Douglas Methodist Church, Montreal. It was marked "Personal and Private," and for good reason. The Reverend C. T. Scott had learned from a profoundly agitated correspondent in London, Ontario, that dangerous doctrines were being taught in the Bible Institute there, which was sponsored and run by the Methodists.[9] Those in attendance at institute meetings had been told that on certain matters Jesus had clearly been mistaken; that the Bible was only one of a number of inspired religious messages, including the writings of Buddha and Socrates; that Mrs. Mary Baker Eddy could be considered a Christian prophet; and that the Bible was not the only standard of truth because "every man's standard of truth is that which he cognizes of it." To the question "What was the final test for action, the Bible or our own reason?" the answer had been, "Where our reason coincides with the Bible, the Bible; where our reason does not coincide with the Bible, our Reason." Such teachings, and earlier those of Dr. George Workman (whose notions of biblical prophecy had been the subject of much controversy when he had been a member of the Theology Department of Victoria College in the late 1880s), resulted in a significant drift away from the Methodist church in London towards Unitarianism. Indeed, said Reverend Scott's correspondent, "almost every man who is taking any active part in the new Unitarian Church" had been one of Workman's "adherents" when he had lectured regularly in London.[10]

Scott understood clearly what constituted the main source of the problem. "It has been evident to me for some time," he told Carman, "that there is a decided drift in the ministry of our church which plainly augurs a split in Methodism. When or how it will come to a focus I know not, but to some of us who hold to the old faith, we think the issue cannot be raised too soon." He continued:

> I find many in this Conference saturated with what they call "The new ideas," and it has become a sort of fad—a pretence of scholarship—to parade radical ideas. I have raised a few conflicts thus far, and expect to have more as I come in contact with these men. When the strife comes I find it is not so much the Higher Criticism . . . that I am forced to combat, but the Hegelian philosophy. It is abstruse and difficult to combat, but so far I have been able to maintain my positions by simply denying their first postulates, and when the onus of proof is put on them they fail to "make good." I find that nearly every man who passed through "Queen's University," and a coterie who follow this set, are preaching Hegelianism. It is a sad plight.[11]

So it was, indeed, for Methodists or Presbyterians in Canada who wished, in the early twentieth century, to retain the fundamentals of their faith as handed down by earlier generations.

Queen's University was not alone, however, in disseminating the heresies observed in London by Scott. In Victoria College itself, George Workman, for example, continued to find a following even after his dismissal from its faculty in 1890 for holding heterodox views on messianic prophecy. For years thereafter he could frequently be seen in its halls, and when he died, the funeral took place in the college chapel. Nathanael Burwash, for many years the chancellor of "Vic," was a defender of the Higher Criticism, and, in his attempt to reconcile science and religion, he had come to set forth a conception of Christian theism in which man's knowledge of God and his knowledge of self were vitally related. His view that one might know God "from that which we find within ourselves" could be seen as one similar to Watson's idea of self-consciousness to those disposed towards idealism.[12]

But idealism was given its most sustained expression at Victoria College by a far younger graduate of that institution, George John Blewett. In 1897 Blewett had won the Governor-General's Gold Medal, placing first in his philosophy class, and aided by the George Paxton Young Memorial Fellowship he did graduate work at Harvard, in Germany, and finally at Oxford under Edward Caird (the Master of Balliol). After a stint at Wesley College in Winnipeg, he returned to Victoria College where he taught and wrote until his untimely death in 1912. By then, like Young before him, he had gained disciples—both through his brilliant and inspiring lectures and through his two books, *The Study of Nature and the Vision of God* (1907) and *The Christian View of the*

World (1910). In the preface to the former, Blewett noted that he had first been introduced to philosophy through T. H. Green's *Prolegomena to Ethics*. Yet the book was stamped with the mark of Caird. Blewett had not been exaggerating when, also in his preface, he had written of his "reverence and gratitude" to Caird, "whose venerable primacy in philosophy among English-speaking men makes him 'our father Parmenides.'" [13]

The combination of the views of Blewett (who could write that "the nature of God ... may be expressed by putting together the three words, reason, righteousness, love") with the more abrasive and less spiritualistic rationalism of the Higher Criticism was a powerful force for change in Canadian religious thought. However much idealists such as Blewett and Watson attempted to infuse reason with a Christian spirituality, the fact was that in stressing the way early Christianity "had inherited the intellectual spirit of the Greeks," they helped clear the path towards the application of an essentially secular rationalism to the Christian revelation. What difference would the average interested layman have perceived between Blewett's claim that once imbued with the spirit of the Greeks, Christianity was "certain to come more and more to intellectual possession of its implicit faith," [14] and the "intellectual possession" that characterized the answers to questions posed by troubled Christians at meetings of the London institute?

> Q. What is the ultimate authority in religion? Reason? or the Holy Scriptures?
> A. In asking that question, what do you appeal to in me? Is it not to my reason? Well, that is the answer. We test every Scripture by reason.
> Q. If every man's reason is the ultimate authority in religion, we have nothing infallible.
> A. No, we have not.
> Q. If everything must submit to reason, you must reject the entire miraculous element of Scripture.
> A. Well, probably. Though perhaps some of these would be rational.
> Q. Are the virgin birth and the resurrection of Jesus rational?
> A. Well no. . . .
> Q. I see no ground upon which to stand without the Scriptures.
> A. Because I do not believe in many of the Bible stories, except as legends, that does not affect my faith.

Q. The ordinary man will reject the entire Bible, if he believed any part of it was not true.

A. Well, perhaps for a time, but ultimately he would come out all right.[15]

To the philosophically astute, Blewett's conception of a reason that transcended, but did not challenge, faith was distinctly different from one that simply equated faith with irrationality and therefore dismissed faith as a mode of thought. But to someone less initiated into the subtleties and the rhetoric of idealist philosophy, someone who found the argument persuasive but the logic and the jargon difficult at times to follow, such distinctions were perhaps never fully clear. For such a person it may have been sufficient simply to remember that Caird, Watson, and Blewett had said that Christianity was evolving through the secular process of history; that this religious progress was essentially a spiritual one, which nevertheless was everywhere manifested in concrete terms; that in this (admittedly vague) unfolding of the consciousness of the race, religious faith could be better comprehended through rational—even intellectual—understanding; that piety and intellectual activity were not at odds since faith could not be faith if it defied intellectual inquiry; and that, finally, somehow in this ongoing cosmic process the old divisions between the spiritual and the material, the sacred and the secular, God and man, were obliterated.

Pastoral Epistles
Such a union of seeming opposites can be a power that inspires men and gives great clarity and direction to the social vision. But it can also be a philosophical achievement that exacerbates religious uncertainty. Consider, for example, the case of Mr. J. M. Grant, an otherwise anonymous Presbyterian from Toronto who corresponded with Watson a number of times between 1911 and 1918. The Grant-Watson correspondence shows the essence of Watson's philosophy as it applied to Christianity, and it does so in concrete terms. Watson's 1897 book, *Christianity and Idealism*, had, to be sure, laid out his views on the matter in detail and on a more abstract plane, but the philosopher of religion's correspondence with Grant, a very troubled soul, shows precisely the way those views could appeal to, yet puzzle, an earnest seeker after religious truth.

Grant's first letter to Watson provided the merest hint at his religious difficulties. He had been reading with much interest

Watson's *Philosophical Basis of Religion*, seeking answers to certain problems the nature of which were intimated in several questions for which he sought the philosopher's answers. "The doctrine of the Trinity puzzles me much. Is the orthodox view tenable? What is the bearing of the inviolability of natural law on the doctrine of the resurrection of Jesus Christ?" Watson replied at some length: Trinitarian doctrine must be viewed in terms of the idea of the Self-Manifestation of God. He was an immanent deity, especially manifested in man, "of whom Christ is the perfect type." Christ must be seen "as the manifestation of the inner essence of God as love," and the Holy Spirit is simply the Spirit "involved in the identification of man with God." Hence, the notion of the Trinity comprised as separate Beings must be done away with, and in its place the idea that "Father Son and Spirit" were "aspects of the one God" must be substituted. As to the domain of natural law, the answer was simply that although its inviolability could not be doubted, it must be seen as applicable "in strictness only to that phase of reality which is dealt with by the special sciences." Finally, Christ's Resurrection could not be viewed in terms of any literal interpretation of the New Testament.[16]

Perhaps encouraged by such lengthy answers, Grant continued to pose ever more complex questions for Watson. What is perfection? If the idea of the absolute involves an expression of God's perfect love, how is sin to be accounted for? How can this immanent God allow suffering? "If every finite self-conscious reason became unconscious or non-existent what would the self-conscious reason of the Infinite be? In or with the mind of the finite is there another *mind* of the Infinite? What would the mind of the Infinite be if expressed only in material nature?" So the questions continued. Again Watson replied fully, and for some time Grant's doubts seemed to have been allayed. "You make your position clearly as to the distinction between the consciousness or mind and the infinite mind . . . ," he wrote. "What remains for me is to make less misty to myself the immanence of God." He turned, for a possible clarification of the problem, to Watson's *Outline of Philosophy*.[17]

He did not find one. By May of the next year, 1914, he had reached a state of spiritual crisis. "I sincerely hope that I am not boring you or drawing too much upon your time," he wrote. "Difficulties are pressing upon me heavily. My position as Superintendent of a Presbyterian Sunday School compels me to substantial clearness of thought on what is essentially true and helpful in the moral and spiritual life.... It may be, ... but I hope not, that I may have to leave the Presbyterian body and join the Unitarians, and if so my opportunity of good practical work would be all uncertain." Then, once again, came the questions. But they no longer dealt with aspects of the idealist interpretation of Christianity. They now involved the doctrinal foundations of the faith. "What place does your philosophy leave or allow," he asked in a scrawling, panic-laden hand, "to Jesus as (1) the forgiver of sin, (2) the Saviour, (3) atoning for sin, (4) giving eternal life, and as (5) the Judge of all mankind? What, in the light of your teaching, is or should be his gospel, that is, how should it be interpreted and used?" Other questions followed, but the challenge—for it had become a challenge—had by then been put.[18]

Watson's reply, marked "confidential," was as measured in tone and penmanship as Grant's had been frenetic. "I hope before joining the Unitarian Church you will consider carefully whether you can find in it a type of faith of a fundamentally satisfactory kind." Watson clearly felt the force of Grant's challenge, for he was now prepared to talk starkly about essentials. "Do you think it really matters," he wrote with barely controlled impatience, "from the point of view of the essence of religion, whether one accepts what is called the divinity of Christ? What, to begin with, are we to understand by it? Does it mean that a man existed from all eternity, who yet was not a man but God? That, of course, is a thoroughly unthinkable thing. And St. Paul evidently felt it to be so; for what he seems to have believed in was a 'man from heaven,' who was finally to give up all things to God, who was then to be 'all in all.' Of course this figurate mode of expression does not really convey the deeper spiritual truth which St. Paul was anxious to express, which, I take it, was at bottom the fundamental identity of the nature of man with the nature of God." As for the specific questions Grant had asked, the answer to each followed easily from the premises just stated:

> You will understand that I cannot accept any of the doctrines of any Church literally. (1) The forgiveness of Sin is bound up with the nature of man as potentially and in his deepest nature divine. Man can be forgiven only by a "change of mind," as the New Testament calls it: and the forgiveness of sin is the same thing as this change of mind. It is no external act of kindness, but a thing that cannot be made one thing or another by any individual, Jesus or another. Man's life is in one way a perpetual experiment. . . . (2) The atonement for

sin is exemplified in a striking way in Jesus, who reached the highest height of self-abnegation, but of course he is only one of millennia who follow in the same path. (3) "Eternal life" is not something arbitrarily bestowed upon men: it is his higher and real nature. (4) Of course it is only a figure of speech when Jesus is called the "judge of all mankind." He is judge in the sense that he has, as I believe, expressed the eternal nature of God, the infinite Love. (5) The immortality of Jesus is based on the same ground as the immortality of man in general. Of course one can't accept the mystical account of his resurrection. (6) Granting . . . any individual man . . . eternal damnation . . . assumes that Man will never discover his own God-like nature.[19]

It was, as Watson admitted, "a hasty and crude indication of the general way" he looked at things. But it was also a supremely accurate one. Like his mentor, Edward Caird, Watson desired above all to reassert the moral and religious dimension of life which had been undermined by modern scepticism. Yet his method of doing so—Objective Idealism—resulted ultimately in a form of belief that bore a distinct resemblance to the declared enemy, evolutionary naturalism. Both accepted the principle of evolutionary change; both asserted the fundamental unity of nature. This convergence between Hegelian idealism and the new naturalism, John Passmore has argued, was one of the most important and distinctive results of Darwin's impact on British metaphysics. "It has been said," Passmore concludes, "that pantheism is a polite form of atheism: to assert that everything is God is certainly to deny that there is a God, as that word is ordinarily understood. And similarly one cannot but be struck by the resemblances between naturalism and the Absolute Idealism of philosophers like Caird and Bosanquet: so concerned are they to insist that there is nowhere a gap between the spiritual and the material, between the human and the natural, that one is often inclined to say—Absolute Idealism is the polite form of naturalism."[20]

Judged by any general understanding of the fundamentals of Christianity, Watson was willing, in effect, to scrap much in order to "preserve the essence of the Christian consciousness—the unity of man & God." The Trinity, the divinity of Christ, Original Sin, the Atonement, Eternal Life, the Resurrection—each in its generally accepted meaning was an impediment to an understanding of the union of man, God, and reason. Even Watson's correspondent, Grant, was taken aback at such liberality, for no letter was received from him for a couple of weeks. When the reply came, its author was still largely without words. "It is not improbable that the desire to reach and say something satisfactory was at least one reason for not acknowledging your very kind letter of May 17th. It is a letter so radical that it demands my most careful thought." Accordingly, he began to re-read Watson's *Interpretation of Religious Experience*, found it "fascinating," and noted that "the meaning is gradually clearing up by repeated study." A few exchanges of letters took place between 1914 and 1918, mainly over difficulties of Grant and his friends with the nature of the Absolute ("It baffles us entirely to think how the finite mind can, at one and the same time, be the individual's mind and also be a part of the Divine mind"), but they now came with less frequency. By 1918 Grant had come to believe that the main outlines of Christian Science were perhaps the closest he would arrive at an Answer.[21]

One can only speculate upon the extent to which others, Presbyterians and Methodists alike, were similarly affected by the idealist's perception of the essence of Christianity. "No creed of any church can be accepted," Watson had written to Grant at the height of the latter's spiritual crisis, "and I don't think the Church be based upon any belief except that it is an organization for making men better."[22] How many of the divinity students trained under Watson in the fifty years from 1872 to 1922 came to accept Watson's simple definition of the Church? For a half century, in his writings, in his sermons, in his addresses at convocation, in his Sunday afternoon addresses to the Kingston community, but above all in his compulsory honours seminar to generations of senior arts and divinity students, Watson had taught that the Christian message was best understood and acted upon, not by depending on traditional creeds or doctrines—which he viewed as impedimenta hindering the growth of consciousness—but by the application of idealist social thought to life in the secular world. In so doing, the secular world would be spiritualized and the Kingdom of Heaven would arrive.

The Sacred, the Secular, and the Social Gospel
For some, it is clear, the idealist philosophy was a revelation equal to that imparted to Watson by the Caird brothers in the 1860s. The social gospel in Canada was a movement diverse both in its membership and in its origins; men and women drew their ideas on the social teachings of the gospel from sources as differ-

ent as Ralph Waldo Emerson and Albrecht Ritschl. But they also drew, and perhaps in a more sustained and direct fashion, from the messages of men such as George M. Grant, John Watson, George Blewett, and S. D. Chown (who was general superintendent of the Methodist church from 1910 until Church Union in 1925). These intellectual and institutional leaders of Canadian Methodism and Presbyterianism helped provide the intellectual foundations upon which the social gospel movement in Canada was constructed between 1890 and 1914.

The full extent of this idealist influence upon a movement more often associated with democratic socialism will not be appreciated until a full-scale study is done on these and other men in similar positions, and a complete examination is made of the relationship between moral philosophy and Protestant theology in the early twentieth century. Yet even in outline can be seen the deeply ironic legacy of the idealists upon Protestantism in Canada.

In one of the thousands of lectures he must have given to divinity students at Queen's, Principal Grant once stated that "practical preaching" consisted of "preaching which deals with actual life, inspires to action, and aims at establishing the Kingdom of God on earth." Here was the idea of a social gospel given voice by an idealist who was as much a man of action as his colleague Watson was a man of reflection. This view was communicated to congregations, too, for Grant was an eminently practical preacher, and he preached what he taught. "The Lord calls us to preach the Gospel to the living," went one of his sermons, "& to deal with its application to living issues, instead of concerning ourselves with the controversies of the past & other dead issues." As with Watson, Grant's commitment to a progressive evolutionism, both spiritual and material, gave him little patience with obstructions from the past, and this obtained for religious, as well as for political, institutions. "We must fight the battles of today," he went on, "instead of recalling the wars of our forefathers. We are to study the past, that we may understand the principles that were at stake, that we may be warned to avoid the errors of the combatants, & that we may reach the common ground that is generally to be found at the basis of all controversy. Preaching the Gospel does not mean the repetition of doctrinal formulas; but the proclamation of the ever-living message of the love of God to all men, & the application of that message and the spirit which it implies to the ever-changing conditions of society."[23]

Above all, Grant preached a gospel of active social service, but one directed towards a spiritual end. In the name of the spiritual life, he advocated throughout his life the Christian's total commitment to the obliteration of the secularism of society. "Material things," he told Ontario's teachers towards the end of his career, "... are as nothing to the spiritual mind. They are dissolved in the vision of the Eternal." To reach this state, he advocated nothing more than the life of moral elevation, the building of personal "character." The nation's teachers, like its mothers and fathers, must be moral exemplars. "I say, then," he concluded, "magnify your office. We Canadians have an inspiring work to do, for just now we are presiding at the birth of our nation. We are getting the larger outlook which is indispensable to full national and imperial life." Grant's commitment to the "essentials" of Christianity—active service to society and the life of moral elevation—made him probably the most influential clergyman in Canada in the second half of the Victorian era. The philosophy Watson and Blewett taught and wrote about, he lived.[24]

By Watson's standards, Grant was by no means a man of reflection; but, to do him credit, neither was he a man without a consistent philosophy. While not one to follow Watson's philosophical position to the letter, he nevertheless accepted it in essence (for he too had been influenced by John Caird when at Glasgow), especially the evolutionary, organic vision and the rejection of dualisms. And just as Watson refused to divorce religion from the secular life—for that, too, created a dualism—so Grant held firmly to a similar view. "The relation of religion to the secular," he told an international congress of Presbyterians in 1880, "... is the relation of a law of life to all the work of life. This law of life is not a catechism, not a dogma, but a spiritual power or influence. Its relation to the secular is not arbitrary, but natural; not statical, but dynamical; not mechanical, but spiritual. Freedom is the condition of its healthful action."[25] The twentieth-century successors to Grant within the Protestant community in Canada also preached a message much like this one—a message which tended, as often as not, to undermine the distinction between the sacred and the secular, the spiritual and the material, and to make a radical separation of theological creeds and ethical conduct.

Principal Grant and the "Queen's spirit" of the 1890s inspired numerous individuals to engage in different forms of social service. Some, such as Adam Shortt (a gold medallist in philosophy under Watson) and O. D. Skelton, became prominent federal civil servants; others, a far greater proportion than the population

The Sadness and Joy of Knowledge 219

of Queen's warranted, became teachers throughout the country and sought to live up to the moral example set them by Grant and Watson.[26] Still others sought to be instrumental in the achievement of the Kingdom of Heaven on earth. No one more exemplified this ambitious spirit than the Methodist preacher Salem Bland, who was to become the most radical of the social gospellers in Canada.[27]

Born in 1859, Bland, the son of a British Wesleyan Methodist preacher, had been present in Kingston from 1884 through the 1890s, and in every respect he was a "Queen's man," proud to call himself a student of Watson and a disciple of Grant. Though never formally enrolled as a student at Queen's, he nevertheless read Kant and Hegel with Watson, attended political meetings and Sunday afternoon addresses with Grant, and thoroughly imbibed the new social and critical spirit of the nineties. The novelist Robert E. Knowles, himself a graduate of Queen's in the 1890s, noted at the time of Bland's retirement from public life that he had "enlisted and enmeshed and engaged in all her life and ferment. Few faces were more familiar about her halls."[28] There, instructed by Watson (and through him Hegel and Caird) and Grant, Bland's life and mind took a new direction. Signs of this could be seen in his yearly participation in the Queen's Theological Alumni conferences, especially those of 1898 and 1899. By then, much of his voluminous reading in Kingston was beginning to give definite shape to his thought, and he was nearly ready to give it practical application. "In Canada as in all English-speaking countries," he told the 1898 conference, "social questions are engaging increasing attention. Christianity is becoming primarily sociological, which is a good deal better than if it should be regarded as primarily ecclesiastical or even theological."[29]

The stamp of Grant, Watson, and Queen's remained on Salem Bland, and no doubt he prized the influence as much as he did the honourary doctorate awarded him (along with William Dawson LeSueur) by the university in 1900. In the twentieth century the reputations of Bland and Queen's would diverge radically, for by the 1920s Bland was best known as a radical socialist, whereas Queen's, under the successors to Grant, was gradually to assume an air of academic and humanistic detachment from fundamental social issues, even from Protestantism. Nevertheless, the connection between Bland and the Queen's spirit of the nineties existed and continued to give a philosophical basis for his evolving social views. In 1925 he jotted down some notes on a philosophy of life, and they consisted of three propositions: that man is fundamentally good; that there must be fullness of life for everyone; and that there must be a stronger social consciousness. In itself this philosophy was consistent with the social gospel in almost any of its derivations, but in the specific ways Bland sought to construct such a philosophy, the legacy of his years in Kingston can distinctly be seen.[30]

It would be inaccurate to assume that Bland came away from Kingston with the social gospel he was later to preach in full blossom. When in Smiths Falls, Ontario, in 1899, for example, he still taught that the Kingdom of God could be realized only through individual salvation. At this stage in his career, the traditional conception of a transcendent Kingdom held sway, if uneasily. Matters such as minimum wages, municipal ownership of natural monopolies, and more equitable taxation were, in Bland's mind, clearly "within the range of the gospel, to be manifestly implied in the Kingdom of Heaven which it came to establish." "*But these*," he added emphatically, "*do not make the Kingdom of God.*" At this point in his life, at the age of forty, the essential distinction between sacred and secular still held some meaning for him. "K[nowledge] of God is not . . . minimum wage of $1.50 a day, not free schools & free rides . . . not meat & drink, but *righteousness* & peace & joy in the Holy Ghost."[31] Yet if these remarks portray a Methodist committed to a traditional conception of righteousness as the main element in the Kingdom of God, they also suggest one who could not see the coming about of such a Kingdom without radical measures of social reform. What he had learned in Kingston suggested that righteousness and an earthly Kingdom were far from being incompatible, just as reason and faith were entwined. But for his first twenty years and more, those before his Queen's experience, his conception of the essence of Christianity, particularly on the question of eschatology, had been that of orthodox Methodism.

It took the Kingston experience and its disturbing intellectual adjustments before Bland was able to confront the unexamined convictions he had held during his first twenty years. Late in his life he noted that his career seemed to have fallen neatly into such stages. Of the second of these he wrote: "Those twenty years to me were the first twenty years of my ministry begun in the devout and untroubled acceptance of traditional orthodoxy in regard to the message and methods of the Evangelical Churches and the slow creeping in in spite of honest and resolute opposition of what at the first were unwelcome and even sinful doubts."[32] Could it be that by the late 1890s Bland had come to believe deep within that he was putting forward from the pulpit a conception of the Kingdom he had once accepted, still thought he ought to believe, but no longer did? Could it be that he had not yet quite summoned the courage to give full voice to the range of radical social reforms necessary to bring about the earthly Kingdom of Watson and of Grant, a spiritual domain manifested in the secular and material reforms brought about by Christians intent upon a better life for all?

No definitive answer can yet be given for these questions, but it is likely that Bland's admission of spiritual turmoil in the 1890s was, if anything, understated. The fact is that his insistence in 1899 on individual regeneration and a transcendent Kingdom was antithetical to his experience at Queen's. Second, within a very few years Bland was to do a complete about face on these very theological issues. In 1903 he moved to Wesley College, Winnipeg, as professor of church history and New Testament exegesis, thereby becoming for a few years a colleague of George Blewett. The complete change of environment, his reading of the works of British and American social reformers, his talks with Blewett, and the fact that life in the boom city of the West involved daily confrontation with the "social crisis" in its numerous aspects—poverty, inequality, crime, alcoholism, prostitution—each undoubtedly contributed to his complete "conversion" within a few years of his arrival. "The idea emphasized by Jesus," he told an overflow interdenominational audience in the City Hall in 1906, "was that of the kingdom, not of heaven but the kingdom of God on earth. Christianity was not a sort of immigration society to assist us from the hurly burly of this world to heaven; it was to bring the spirit of heaven to earth." "Christianity," he went on, "meant the triumph of public ownership. He believed in public ownership because it is an essential part of the kingdom of God on earth. It meant the substitution of co-operation for competition."[33]

The radicalization of Salem Bland's social views is well known. What must be noted is simply that the way had been cleared for him on the road to his Damascus. By the time he received his honourary degree from Queen's, he had been introduced to the idealist's conception of the essence of Christianity—a religion largely shorn of traditional doctrine and based on an organic and progressive evolution of society. These assumptions pervaded Bland's writings in the new century. Second, it was a religion which necessarily had to meet the test of reason, and reason was seen as the manifestation of the religious consciousness in thought. This notion, too, found its way deep into Bland's thinking. In the third place, it was a faith that separated the concerns of theology from those of ethics, and in so doing clearly subordinated the former to the latter. "Theology," Bland told the 1914 Methodist Conference, "is a very secondary consideration in the Christian life, and it has had too high a place in the Christian church from the beginning."[34] Finally, there could be no real opposition of the spiritual and the material life.

Like Watson and Grant, Bland delighted in using dialectical methods to establish dazzling argumentative advantage, and complaints about the alleged materialistic society of the Laurier years furnished one such opportunity. We are told this is a materialistic age, he declared in his column in the 1918 *Grain Growers Guide*; but it is in fact not materialistic enough. In words that directly echoed those of Principal Grant in the 1880s on the relation of religion to secular life, Bland insisted that Christianity could no longer "be treated as a distinct realm or department of life. . . . It has no independent existence. . . . It is life itself." Christianity must always, to be vital, be manifested in concrete experience. "One hears sometimes," he went on, "the phrase Applied Christianity. It is only as it is materialized that it reveals itself." Hence, neither doctrines nor sacred ceremonies constitute part of true religious fellowship. That fellowship is "to be found in the processes of industry and commerce. Co-operation in commerce and industry is the real Holy Communion."[35]

Thus was the Hegelian dialectic used to a degree and with a confidence that could have been equalled in Canada only by Watson himself. "Let us not be afraid of materialism," Bland concluded in triumph. "We are safe if we materialize everything including our religion. Then the long continued and deadly divorce between the spiritual and the material will be brought to an end. Spirituality will be nowhere because it will be everywhere."[36]

As it came to be given expression in Canada, British idealism made an important contribution to the rise of liberal Protestantism in two general ways, and both have been observed in the thought of Salem Bland. The first was that it made doctrinal or denominational differences seem essentially unimportant, if not simply irrelevant or even harmful, especially in an age of rapid social and industrial change. This view was especially appealing since many Methodists and Presbyterians in Canada had spoken favourably of constructing a national church transcending denominational barriers since the 1870s.[37] The second was that it provided the organic and evolutionary assumptions which led towards a social vision that stressed cooperation rather than competition. The example of Bland is the most obvious, direct, and extreme one; but others no less important than he also shared a social gospel that derived in part from idealist influences.

The social thought of J. S. Woodsworth, like that of Bland, was shaped by influences as diverse as his reading lists; yet he too came under the influence of British idealism. Unsettled after an intellectually disturbing year at Victoria College in 1898, he was persuaded to study at Oxford. His faith already shaken by the "modernism" taught at Victoria and at the Reverend George Jackson's Sherbourne Street Church, Woodsworth concentrated upon Christian ethics in his Oxford studies. He found himself even more disturbed with Canadian Methodism in its traditional form, however, after he had read philosophy with Edward Caird and religion with Andrew Fairbairn. While there, he was in contact with George Blewett to whom he was distantly related. At one point he puzzled over the fact that philosophers appeared to be forging a radical separation of ethics from Christianity, and, in a letter home, noted that "Blewett, one day speaking of this phase of the work, laughingly described himself as a pagan." Indeed, Woodsworth added, "It is true we take no account of the Christian revelation." By 1911, upon the publication of *My Neighbour*, he had largely come to grips with the seemingly pagan implications of Blewett's message, and Blewett could write to him: "You and Fred Stephenson and men like you and he, are the true light and heart of our church in its work for the country."[38]

In fact there were good reasons why Blewett should have congratulated Woodsworth, for Woodsworth's new book fully accorded with the social teachings of Blewett. Blewett's *Study of Nature and the Vision of God*, published four years before *My Neighbour*, had stressed philosophically what Woodsworth's work stated in practical terms. "And the truth of the world," Blewett had concluded, "the truth both of ourselves and of the world, is God; God, and that 'far-off divine event' which is the purpose of God, are the meaning of the world. And this means that the citizenship to which we are called is a heavenly citizenship; but it also means that that heavenly citizenship must first be fulfilled upon the earth, in the life in which our duties are those of the good neighbour, the honest citizen, the devoted churchman. The perfection of human life lies in being at one with God; but to that oneness with God men can come, not by departure from the world into eternal quietude, but only by flinging themselves into the labours and causes of the history in which

God is realizing His eternal purpose.... The man to whom the love of God is the central impulse of life must take his place in the world, must share in its labours and duties and affections and losses, must undergo the fate which it has for all its citizens. And that fate is seldom a light one."[39] These final passages of Blewett's study might well have been taken as an epitaph to the rest of Woodsworth's life.

Religion through Sociology
While the idealist influence on Canadian Protestant thought was a profound one in the early twentieth century, by no means did the leadership of the major denominations entirely accept its assumptions or fail to give voice to criticisms of its ultimate implications. Chancellor Burwash, as we have seen, was able to accept the idealist's preoccupation with self-consciousness, for he saw it consistent with his own, more traditional, conception of an inner, intuitive apprehension of the will of God. Similarly, he found the critical, yet constructive, approach of philosophers of religion such as George Blewett on the whole a desirable one in an age dominated by critical analysis. Yet he was also keenly aware of the dangers of taking the philosopher's approach to religion too far, and he once stated so in a long review of *The Study of Nature and the Vision of God*.

After first declaring that Blewett's attempt to harmonize philosophy and religion was an admirable one from which much "pleasure and profit" could be derived (for such a harmony was both desirable and possible), Burwash went on to assert essentially the same criticism of philosophers as that levelled at scientists by Watson almost thirty-five years earlier: they had gone too far, and had "laid claim to the last word in regard to all truth." Philosophers had forgotten that theirs, like those of the historian and the theologian, was simply one approach towards the apprehension of reality. Blewett's book epitomized this tendency:

> The work before us very naturally fixes our attention upon the relations of philosophy to theology and the more so as in our day these relations are of the most serious importance. A generation ago we heard much of the conflict of science with religion. The really serious conflict lay between a materialistic philosophy dominated by science and our current theology. The materialistic philosophy has largely disappeared and theology is slowly learning to permit science to explore the scientific field by scientific methods, and thus

> the conflict is rapidly disappearing. But the spiritual philosophy which has so largely displaced materialism brings a new form of conflict more subtle and not less dangerous than the cruder materialism which it has displaced. There are comparatively few who will cast away their religious faith and accept a bald materialism & spiritual philosophy does not require us to abjure religious faith. On the other hand it seems to place it upon a new and firm rational foundation. But in doing this it silently assumes that this is the one and only foundation upon which religious faith can be built and that all religious truth must be received by mind tested by the methods of philosophy.

Burwash then singled out both Edward and John Caird as the main individuals whose views, like those of Blewett, tended in this direction. He insisted that the foundations of religious belief must not be committed to purely philosophical reconstruction, however "spiritual" that philosophy might claim to be. Philosophy, he concluded, "reveals to us a power rather than a person, an optimism rather than a heart of love ... an evolution rather than a salvation, and a human rather than a Divine Christ." It would thus be nothing less than an irreparable misfortune if Christians ever attempted "to substitute the imperfect vision of philosophy" for the "wider, richer and more perfect vision of God which has come to humanity by the process of history."[40]

Burwash was no old-line Methodist pleading for a recovery of the revivalism of the mid-nineteenth century. He had long come to grips with scientific thought and had even constructed an intricate systematic theology along the principles of the scientific (inductive) method. He sought in his review of Blewett's book simply to make Canadian Methodists aware of the fact that in this new, "liberal" era, which sought a synthesis between Christianity and the new sciences in order to bring about the reforms necessary in an urban and industrial society, much was in danger of being jettisoned. By 1912, however, Burwash, then over seventy years of age, no longer held views shared by the majority of the members of Victoria College even on the minor matter of the manners of students, much less on more weighty questions. His resignation as chancellor was accepted in that year.

More representative of the rank and file of Canadian Protestants was the man who later led Canadian Methodists into Church Union in 1925, S. D. Chown. Elected general superintendent in 1910, a position he held with Albert Carman until

Carman's retirement in 1914, Chown exuded the new liberal and forward-looking spirit. What most strikes one about Chown's views by the second decade of the twentieth century is the complete substitution of sociological concerns for theological ones. His thought suggests in what peculiar terrains of Christian social thought a man could arrive who began his journey working from the inspiration of idealists. In 1914 Chown gave a lecture entitled "Socialism and the Social Teachings of Jesus," and commenced it by acknowledging his indebtedness to "Dr. Watson." "The Sermon on the Mount," he went on to say, "which is the very charter of Christianity and the constitution of the Kingdom Christianity came to realize, contemplates society as reorganized, inspired, and upheld by sacrificial brotherly love. The sayings of Christ therein contained are a picture in outline, and a prophecy of the perfect social state which is to be when Christianity comes into its own."[41]

For Chown, only the establishment of what he described as a "systematic sociology" would usher in the perfect social state. Only "a perfect sociology perfectly applied will result in the establishment of the Kingdom of God," he once stated in the lecture "The Relation of Sociology to the Kingdom of Heaven." His was the eschatology of a man uncertain as to whether he should be a clergyman or a social scientist (but who saw no reason why one could not be both simultaneously). His lectures on sociology are excellent illustrations of a certain stage in the transmutation of Christian moral philosophy of the nineteenth-century variety into a moralistic, yet essentially secular, study of social relationships. The law upon which this sociology must be based, he insisted, was "moral law," and the culture which arises "from a well directed study of sociology is not simply intellectual" but "partakes also of moral discipline."[42]

The code of conduct that was to give substance to this moral rigour was one centred in the conduct of Christ, not in his divinity or in the meaning of his blood sacrifice. "One of the most extraordinary signs of the times," noted Chown with obvious approval, "is that, while many of the doctrines which center about Christ have to great multitudes almost lost their meaning, his personality and his social teaching have acquired an interest never before felt. This trend of events gives direction to the development of the science of theology to-day, and is giving immense impetus to the coming of the Kingdom." So it was, and Chown's own views helped channel Canadian Protestantism along this direction. Lacking a systematic program either in theology or in sociology (in fact Chown's sociology was anything but "systematic" in any meaningful sense), he had been left with a Christ who was, at least in part, "Hellenized"—a Christ who embodied in his conduct not only traditional Christian morality but also the standards informing the "sweetness and light" of Matthew Arnold's conception of culture. Why should the student of the ministry study sociology? asked Chown. "I should say, firstly, for the sake of culture.... A sociologist who is true to the ideals of his science is particularly inclined to resist the utilitarian and commercial spirit of the times. This is so because he stands for justice; for sweetness and light amongst men rather than for imposing material achievement."[43]

Just as the British idealists had seen Kant through evolutionary and progressive Hegelian spectacles, so their vision of Christ was filtered through Hellenistic ones—for, after all, did Greek evolution not mark a later and therefore a higher stage in the evolution of spiritual consciousness than did the Judaic? While Chown's conceptions of Christ and of culture were similar to those of Arnold, they were also a direct legacy of an important element in British idealism: the classical ideal. Having helped strip essential doctrines of much of their traditional import and, hence, metaphysical authority, they substituted a code of right conduct (sometimes drawn from sources as diverse as Emerson's transcendentalism and Comte's positivism) which presumed to be Christian but which—at least as Chown gave voice to it—could be reduced to the proposition that "The Golden Rule" was "the sum and substance of the sociology of Jesus."[44]

But was that quite enough to satisfy the spiritual needs and the social consciences of Christians adrift in a twentieth-century world that largely accepted evolution as fact and increasingly viewed religious truth as relative to time and place? Those who in 1925 formed the United Church of Canada—Methodists, Congregationalists, and most Presbyterians—apparently thought so, for no church leader more embodied the new ecumenical and forward-looking spirit than did S. D. Chown. It is commonplace in Canadian religious historiography to observe that there was a singular absence of theological discussion during the debates on Church Union. Pressing problems in the West, it is said, created powerful forces for Protestant union that made churchmen set aside their theological and doctrinal differences. Doubtless this was so, but if the influence of philosophical idealism upon

Protestant thought in Canada resembled that suggested here, there may not have been many theological questions the advocates of union would have deemed important enough to debate.

In 1925, as one of the consequences of the creation of the United Church of Canada, the venerable Methodist magazine, the *Christian Guardian*, passed out of existence. Its place was taken by another journal whose very title reflected the profound reorientation of Anglo-Canadian social thought in the century just ended. The new magazine was called the *New Outlook*. Whereas the *Guardian* had been a kind of sentry in its protection of inherited tradition, accepted wisdom, and a closed Anglo-Canadian community, the *New Outlook* was more an advance scout in its orientation towards the contingencies made necessary by social change, shifts in thought, and communities in flux. A critical balance had been tipped. It remained now to be seen whether Anglo-Canadians could reap the benefits of the new forms of liberality without losing in the process the sense of moral concern and, with it, a sense of community that had become such a central element in their social inheritance.

Epilogue

By the twentieth century, the moral imperative in Anglo-Canadian thought was much more complex than its equivalent in the 1850s. At the beginning of university life in Canada, the force of moral authority had almost exclusively been one of constraint, a force bent on preventing "intellectual anarchy" of different varieties. By the advent of the 1920s, the word "intellectual" no longer was defined in terms of an eighteenth-century faculty psychology; by then, inquiry of an intellectual sort was seen as synonymous with the objective pursuit of knowledge. By then, too, the principle of critical inquiry had largely—at least in theory, for the idea of "academic freedom" had by no means been fully accepted by society—become one of the foundations upon which the modern university was being built. The English-Canadian university of the first quarter of the twentieth century, like the society itself, was one in a state of precarious balance between the weight of tradition and the currents of change. Hence, the academic could no longer be certain whether his role was to safeguard social stability or to facilitate social improvement. The first quarter of the twentieth century was not generally a happy time to be in Canadian academic life.[1]

The idealism that so dominated the intellectual life of the pre-War years in Canada was very largely an attempt to maintain the universal moral authority of traditional Christianity in the face of the massive challenge posed by the empirical sciences to the pre-Darwinian monistic world view. Moreover, the idealist had attempted to do so by conscripting critical analysis for his own purposes. Whereas in Great Britain and in the United States philosophical idealism had fallen into disrepute by the end of the Great War, in Canada its hegemony was still intact. To be sure, the formal edifice of idealism was crumbling by the sheer momentum of its own logic, yet its central core was to remain an important contribution to Anglo-Canadian thought.

230 Epilogue

By the onset of the First World War, the idealists were on the defensive. Already could be read the intellectual jeremiads of the contributors to Andrew Macphail's *University Magazine*; already could be seen the emergence of Canadian thinkers who had little use for the sentimental and idealistic musings of the generation of the 1890s; already could be noticed the increase in numbers of academics sympathetic to the new social sciences. The place of Watson was soon to be taken by George Sidney Brett, that of Parkin by J. S. Ewart, that of Macphail by Frank Underhill. Yet if, as the thought of Brett, Ewart, and Underhill suggests, the dominant notes of the interwar period in Canadian intellectual life were to be liberal, secular, empirical, and realistic ones, there nevertheless persisted the broad strain of cultural moralism that had always constituted an important element in Anglo-Canadian thought. "A moralist," said a successor of Watson at Queen's University, "is someone who seeks to draw a moral lesson either from an edifying story, from some event that has taken place, or from his observations on human behaviour."[2] The development of critical inquiry in Anglo-Canadian thought occurred within such a tradition—a tradition of broad moral observation which sought to reconcile inquiry with affirmation and which was brought face to face with the conundrums of the twentieth century by the idealists.

From the Conquest on, the moral imperative threaded its way through the fabric of Anglo-Canadian thought. It was perhaps first seen in John Graves Simcoe's concern for the creation in British North America of a society which was to be the "image and transcript" of the England he had left. It was given parallel expression in education and in letters by Thomas McCulloch, who, both at Pictou Academy and in *The Stepsure Letters*, had placed emphasis "not on raising the standard of living, but on making sure that it is a standard."[3] It was also present in Judge Haliburton's ambivalent mind and in the defensive gentility of Susanna Moodie. It comprised the dynamic behind the structure and aims of Anglo-Canadian higher education throughout the nineteenth century and was to be seen in the country's universities well into the twentieth. Politically, it was given expression in the articulation of a mythology of loyalism to a once-united British Empire and later in the development of an imperial ideal, which was similarly meant to serve as the basis of a form of desired cultural identification. One sees it in a less political form as part of the debate in the nineteenth century over the cultural implications of modern modes of thought. Here, too, it took a

Epilogue 231

variety of intellectual forms—from the "positivism" of W. D. LeSueur to the British Hegelianism of John Watson.

The moral imperative is doubtless a universal aspect of the human condition, for all men draw lessons from experience. What is most distinctive about this phenomenon in Anglo-Canadian thought is that despite its inevitable twists and turns, its different intellectual shapes and emotional shadings, the basic lesson has nevertheless remained constant from generation to generation, and it has also been given a sustained voice. The Anglo-Canadian intellectual elite, whether living in a God-centred British province or in a state-centred North American nation, has consistently urged that it is necessary to reach a *modus vivendi* between intellectual inquiry and conventional wisdom, between individual autonomy and the social good, between the myth of freedom and the myth of concern.

The continuity of this tradition into the twentieth century can be seen not only in the thought of religious and philosophical figures, but also in the writings of numerous other intellectuals who reflect the modern temper in Canada. Much of Stephen Leacock's serious criticism and many of the essays in Andrew Macphail's *University Magazine* attempted to give voice to a social ethic that reconciled traditional religious and humanistic values with science, material improvement, and social change. The publication of similar concerns by no means disappeared after 1920, as a careful reading of the *Canadian Forum* and *Queen's Quarterly* indicates. English-Canadian historians in the twentieth century have consistently been moral critics as concerned with telling Canadians how the Canadian past ought to have been or in what direction the future ought to go as with dispassionate historical analysis. Nor has the modern intellectual and imaginative landscape of the country been without those who have chosen to delineate its moral dimensions. The writings of Harold Innis on the nature and implications of communications, the novels and short stories of writers such as Hugh MacLennan, Margaret Laurence, and Hugh Hood, the moral philosophy and social criticism of George Parkin Grant, and the literary criticism and cultural analysis of Northrop Frye all bear the direct marks of their nineteenth-century cultural inheritance.[4]

In 1920 President Robert Falconer of the University of Toronto published a book that marked the apotheosis of nineteenth-century idealism in Canada. The volume was entitled *Idealism in National Character*, and in it Falconer set forward what for him and his generation constituted the essence of the Anglo-Canadian character. "What we are," he said, "is the long process of education of the will rather than the intellect; a few simple convictions have laid hold upon the people." A few pages later, he added: "A well educated community, that is one with a disciplined intelligence, will be ready to take part in the new forum without serious disturbance."[5] This was a statement that could equally have served as the motto of one of the Protestant colleges in the 1850s or of the Massey Commission a century later—a sign that the tension between criticism and control was not to be resolved.

At its worst, this desire for discipline could result in—and at times did—a narrow, conformist, and intolerant moralism, and it could thereby create an intellectual atmosphere that was both stifling and oppressive. It could nurture a cultural life that utterly failed to distinguish between the cosmopolitan and the colonial, and it could repress political and ideological dissent in the name of "peace, order, and good government." But at its best there could also be nurtured the largeness of vision that results from an honest acceptance of the burdens of both the past and the future, an open-mindedness that could weigh tradition and change, stasis and flux, and do so with a clear sense of the social good.

In one of the most sensitive essays written out of enthusiasm for Canada's centennial, the writer Hugh Hood attempted to remind Canadians of the essential integrity and continuity of their cultural inheritance. Despite the evidence of puritanical moralism and narrow provincialism, he reflected, at the core of the Canadian experience lay a "real integrity of conscience" that when united with imagination and reason, could result in a unique national life, "the first modern state, the country of the moral imagination, where what happened from 1775 to 1917, and everything that went before, are united, where compromise and squareness, far from being dirty words, are recognized as what they are, the vital and necessary complement of commitment."[6] Those were sentiments with which Robert Falconer, or, for that matter, John Watson, Egerton Ryerson, and numerous other ancestral arbiters of the moral imperative, would certainly have concurred.

Abbreviations

ChG   *Christian Guardian*
CJ   *Canadian Journal*
CMNR *Canadian Monthly and National Review*
PSM   *Popular Science Monthly*
RBCM *Rose-Belford's Canadian Monthly and National Review*

Notes

Chapter 1

1. Quoted in Lionel Trilling, *Matthew Arnold* (New York, 1955), 28. Emphasis in original.
2. Ibid., 27.
3. Mrs. Holiwell, "Holiday Musings of a Worker. I. The Poetry of Every-Day Life," *British American Magazine* I (May 1863), 42–3.
4. Ibid., 43–4.
5. Rev. Alexander Mathieson [minister of St. Andrew's Church, Montreal, and chaplain of the St. Andrew's Society], *A Sermon, preached ... on the Thirteenth Day of November, 1836 (St. Andrew's Day)* (Montreal, 1837), 26–7, 37.
6. Northrop Frye, *The Critical Path: An Essay on the Social Context of Literary Criticism* (Bloomington, 1973), 36.
7. Ibid., 36–7.
8. Mrs. Moodie, "Education the True Wealth of the World," *The Victoria Magazine* I, no. 4 (1847), 89, rpt. in *The Victoria Magazine, 1847–1848*, ed. Susanna and J. W. D. Moodie, introd. William H. New (Vancouver, 1968).
9. Mrs. Holiwell, "Holiday Musings of a Worker. II. The Love of Reading," *British American Magazine* II (Jan. 1864), 268. For a contrary viewpoint, see also P. B. Waite, "The Edge of the Forest," Presidential Address to the Canadian Historical Association, in *Canadian Historical Association Annual Report* (1969), 1–13.
10. Moodie, "Education," 91.
11. Ibid., 90, 91–2.
12. Nelles's speech paraphrased by C. B. Sissons, *A History of Victoria College* (Toronto, 1952), 95.
13. Nathanael Burwash, *The History of Victoria College* (Toronto, 1927), 466–7; see also Egerton Ryerson, "The Obligations of Educated Men," Address before Students of Victoria College, May 1848, in *ChG*, 10 May 1848. Also paraphrased in part in Sissons, *Victoria College*, 79–80.
14. A. J. O'Loughlin, *Man, a Material, Mental and Spiritual Being: A Lecture delivered in the City Hall, Kingston, C.W., January 6th, 1860* (Kingston, 1860), 5–6. Reported in Kingston *Daily News*,

9 Jan. 1860, p. 20. See also *Kingston Directory* (1857), 140, for information on O'Loughlin.
15. Isaac Fraser to John Macaulay, 9 Sept. 1851, Macaulay Papers, Public Archives of Ontario. I am grateful to Dr. Peter Baskerville for this reference.
16. O'Loughlin, *Man*, 6.
17. William Leitch, *Introductory Address at the Opening of Queen's College, November 8, 1860* (Montreal, 1860), 8.
18. Ibid., 9.
19. John S. Moir, ed., *Church and State in Canada, 1627–1867* (Toronto, 1967), ix–xx; H. H. Walsh, *The Christian Church in Canada* (Toronto, 1968), 102–27; William H. Elgee, *The Social Teachings of the Canadian Churches* (Toronto, 1964), 194–223; John S. Moir, "Sectarian Tradition in Canada," in John Webster Grant, ed., *The Churches and the Canadian Experience* (Toronto, 1963), 131–2.
20. D. C. Masters, *Protestant Church Colleges in Canada* (Toronto, 1966), 131–2.
21. Ibid., 23; Walsh, *Christian Church*, 190–2.
22. Masters, *Church Colleges*, 50–1, 54, 56–7; R. T. Appleyard, "The Origins of Huron College in Relation to the Religious Questions of the Period," M.A. thesis, University of Western Ontario, 1937, pp. 50–123.
23. Masters, *Church Colleges*, 5–44.
24. As cited by Major-General Robinson, *Life of Sir John Beverley Robinson*, quoted by T. C. S. Macklem, "Trinity College," in *The University of Toronto and Its Colleges, 1827–1906*, ed. W. J. Alexander (Toronto, 1906), 138–9.
25. Masters, *Church Colleges*, 25–6.
26. J. George Hodgins, ed., *Documentary History of Education in Upper Canada* II (Toronto, 1894), 9–10.
27. Ryerson quoted in Masters, *Church Colleges*, 32. R. D. Gidney, in "Centralization and Education: The Origins of an Ontario Tradition," *Journal of Canadian Studies* VII, no. 4 (1972), 33–48, notes: "Ryerson and Strachan had their differences; but on the aims of education and the means to achieve those aims, their views were remarkably similar" (p. 38). See also Strachan to Ryerson, shortly before the former's death, quoted by Ryerson in "The Religious Element in our Schools," Report for 1872 of the Superintendent of Education, in Hodgins, *Education* XXIII (1908), 273.

Strachan's debt to the Scottish educational tradition is traced in J. D. Purdy, "John Strachan's Educational Policies, 1815–1841," *Ontario History* LXIV (1972), 45–64. For further evidence of the extent to which educational ideals transcended denominational boundaries, compare Strachan's 1807 address to his Cornwall Grammar School (in ibid., 49) with the views of a prominent Maritime Baptist educator, John Mockett Cramp, on the need for "in-

culcating ... those principles of our common Christianity" (in T. A. Higgins, *The Life of John Mockett Cramp* [Montreal, 1887], 417). See also Masters, *Church Colleges*, 32–4.
28. J. W. Dunbar Moodie, "Religion and Loyalty," *The Victoria Magazine* I (1848), 104, 107.
29. The universities were largely successful in their attempts to train the nation's institutional and cultural leaders, and this continued to be the case well into the twentieth century. One example from a smaller university may suffice: "Of the 81 graduates [of Acadia University] from 1853 to 1869 thirty-two were ministers, many of whom became denominational leaders, sixteen were lawyers, fifteen became teachers, eleven were physicians, and seven entered business. At least five held the office of Inspector of Schools. T. H. Rand was Superintendent of Schools in two provinces, twelve were professors in the colleges of British America and the United States. Two of the graduates ... received the honor of knighthood" (R. S. Longley, *Acadia University, 1838–1938* [Wolfville, 1939], 80n.). For a statistical table of the occupations of arts graduates of the University of Toronto, 1845–99, see *University of Toronto*, ed. Alexander, 99. For a sociological profile of the "Clerisy of the Higher Learning," see John Porter, *The Vertical Mosaic* (Toronto, 1966), 491–519.
30. Cf. the diary of S. S. Nelles, appointed to teach at Victoria College in 1850, noted in Sissons, *Victoria College*, 88.
31. "The Object of Collegiate Life," *Dalhousie Gazette* III (23 Nov. 1870), 1. It is exceedingly difficult to obtain student opinion before the 1870s, since the first student newspaper (*Dalhousie Gazette*) was founded only in 1869.
32. J. W. Dawson, *The Duties of Educated Young Men in British North America: Being the annual University lecture of McGill University, Montreal, Session of 1863–64* (Montreal, 1863), 23.
33. Higgins, *Cramp*, 417.
34. Jasper H. Nicholls, *The End and Object of Education, lecture delivered before the Quebec Young Men's Protestant Education Union* (Montreal, 1857), 6–7.
35. Leitch, *Introductory Address*, 7.
36. Higgins, *Cramp*, 417.
37. *Report of the Resolutions adopted at a great Public Meeting of the Inhabitants of Kingston, Wednesday Evening, 6th March, 1861* (1861), 43; quoted in Sissons, *Victoria College*, 118.
38. Sissons, *Victoria College*, 44.
39. Rev. Egerton Ryerson, *Inaugural Address on the Nature and Advantages of an English and Liberal Education ... June 21, 1842 ...* (Toronto, 1842), 9.
40. Sissons, *Victoria College*, 17.
41. Ryerson, *Liberal Education*, 17.

42. Ibid. Emphases in original.
43. Ibid., 23.
44. Ibid., 23–4. The quotation is from Watson's *Discourses on the Qualifications for the Ministry*. As late as 1863, Watson's *Theological Institutes* (1823–9) were prescribed reading for Wesleyan Methodist theology students in Canada West during their first three years of training. Congregational church theologues were also required to read Watson as part of their courses in systematic theology and in evidences classes. See J. G. Hodgins, "Historical Sketch of Education in Upper Canada," in H. Y. Hind, ed., *Eighty Years' Progress of British North America* ... (Toronto, 1863), 442–3. For biographical material on Watson (1781–1833), see *Dictionary of National Biography* (London, 1899), LX, 27–9.
45. Ryerson, *Liberal Education*, 22–3, 19.

Chapter 2

1. W. J. Rattray, *The Scot in British North America* (Toronto, 1880–94).
2. T. W. Acheson, "The Social Origins of the Canadian Industrial Elite, 1880–1885," in *Canadian Business History, 1497–1971*, ed. David S. Macmillan (Toronto, 1972), 144–74; Sir Robert Falconer, "Scottish Influence in the Higher Education of Canada," *Transactions of the Royal Society of Canada*, sec. II (1927), 7–20, for a review of this influence; see also D. Campbell and R. A. Maclean, *Beyond the Atlantic Roar: A Study of the Nova Scotia Scots* (Toronto, 1974).
3. George Elder Davie, *The Democratic Intellect: Scotland and Her Universities in the Nineteenth Century* (Edinburgh, 1961), xiv, 4.
4. Ibid., 27–8, 10–24.
5. Herbert W. Schneider, *A History of American Philosophy* (New York, 1946), 238.
6. S. E. Ahlstrom, "The Scottish Philosophy and American Theology," *Church History* XXIV (1955), 267.
7. See Schneider, *American Philosophy*, 233–45; Gladys Bryson, "The Emergence of the Social Sciences from Moral Philosophy," *International Journal of Ethics* XLII (Apr. 1932), 304–23. The most comprehensive study of the influence of both the Common Sense philosophy and William Paley's natural theology (particularly his "theological utilitarianism") in antebellum America is Wilson Smith, *Professors and Public Ethics: Studies of Northern Moral Philosophers before the Civil War* (Ithaca, 1956).
8. Ahlstrom, "Scottish Philosophy," 260.
9. S. A. Grave, "Common Sense," in Paul Edwards, ed., *The Encyclopedia of Philosophy* (New York, 1967), II, 156–7. See also Ahlstrom, "Scottish Philosophy," 260–1.
10. For Reid and Hamilton, respectively, see Gladys Bryson, *Man and Society: The Scottish Inquiry of the Eighteenth Century* (New

York, 1966), 135; Timothy J. Duggan, "Hamilton, William," in Edwards, *Encyclopedia* III, 409.
11. The claim is made both by Schneider, *American Philosophy*, 237, who adds that "this mental approach to 'mental philosophy' dominated at least two generations of philosophers [from the 1820s on], created a new 'science,' and profoundly affected the course of academic studies in philosophy," and by Ahlstrom, who states: "This inward view and the systematic description of the landscape there beheld is his [Hutcheson's] great legacy to the Scottish philosophers" ("Scottish Philosophy," 260).
12. Bryson, *Man and Society*, 132–3.
13. Schneider, *American Philosophy*, 249.
14. Ahlstrom, "Scottish Philosophy," 268. It should be noted that Ahlstrom rejects the "old [Schneider] view" that the movement of Common Sense in America "was essentially a reactionary effort to shore up the ruins of orthodox theology." He claims that it may more accurately be viewed "as a liberal vanguard, even as theological revolutionaries" (259). Yet Ahlstrom's own argument runs counter to this claim. Scottish Common Sense was "revolutionary" only insofar as it sapped the vitality of orthodox Christianity and made necessary a shift to other philosophical sources by religious thinkers. He concludes that "the profound commitment of orthodox theology to the apologetical keeping of the Scottish Philosophy made traditional doctrines so lifeless and static that a new theological turn was virtually inevitable" (269). To say the least, this is a very peculiar "liberal vanguard."
15. S. A. Grave, *The Scottish Philosophy* (Oxford, 1960), 3.
16. Ahlstrom, "Scottish Philosophy," 267–8.
17. Peter Ross, *The Scot in America* (1896).
18. For a sample of the evidence of the teaching of moral philosophy and the use of textbooks which were part of the Common Sense school (works by Reid, Stewart, or Hamilton) or which were influenced by it (for example, Francis Wayland's *Ethics or Elements of Moral Science*) see the following. For Acadia, see D. C. Masters, *Protestant Church Colleges in Canada* (Toronto, 1966), 77; R. S. Longley, *Acadia University, 1838–1938* (Wolfville, 1939), 7, 41; for Bishop's, see Masters, *Church Colleges*, 67; for King's (York), see *The University of Toronto and Its Colleges, 1827–1906*, ed. W. J. Alexander (Toronto, 1906), 79; for Queen's, see Masters, *Church Colleges*, 41–2; *Queen's College Calendar, 1845–47*, 42–3; for the University of Toronto, see *University of Toronto*, ed. Alexander, 83, 88–9; for Victoria, see Masters, *Church Colleges*, 34, 36; C. B. Sissons, *A History of Victoria College* (Toronto, 1952), 62–3, 126–7; *University of Victoria College Calendar, 1861–62*, 9, 31–2; ibid., *1862–63*, 29–32.
19. Rev. Robert Campbell, "The Mental Hospitality of the Scot," *RBCM* VIII (Jan. 1882), 79–81.

20. Nathanael Burwash, *The History of Victoria College* (Toronto, 1927), 188–9. Victoria College calendar descriptions of the arts course verify the accuracy of this generalist approach. "The Curriculum is constructed on the principle of encouraging a well-balanced and varied culture, and not with the view of stimulating extraordinary proficiency in particular departments" (calendar for 1862–63; quoted in Sissons, *Victoria College*, 126).
21. Quoted in A. R. C. Duncan, *Moral Philosophy* (Toronto, 1965), 1.
22. "Lectures in Moral Philosophy Copied by George M. Grant, and given to Dan M. Gordon, July 1861," pp. 1–2, D. M. Gordon Papers, box 8, Queen's University Archives. Gordon, it appears, inherited not only the principalship of Queen's University from G. M. Grant; he also inherited his notes in philosophy. Gordon, ten years younger than Grant, also from Pictou County, Nova Scotia, also studied philosophy under William Fleming.
23. D. H. Meyer, *The Instructed Conscience: The Shaping of the American National Ethic* (Philadelphia, 1972), xii. The historian quoted was George P. Schmidt, from his study *The Old-Time College President* (New York, 1930), 143–5.
24. Masters, *Church Colleges*, 42–3.
25. *McGill University Calendar and Exam Papers, 1872–73* (Montreal, 1872), 31, 36.
26. Both Masters, *Church Colleges*, 77, and Longley, *Acadia University*, 41 (Masters's source), cite "Wayland's Ethics." Wayland wrote no such book, and it would appear that reference is made to a section of Wayland's *Elements of Moral Science*.
27. Candidus, writing in *ChG*, 22 May 1844; quoted in Sissons, *Victoria College*, 62–3.
28. *University of Victoria College Calendar, 1861–62* (Toronto, 1862), 31–2. See also the calendar for 1862–63, pp. 29–32, 126.
29. See J. A. Irving, "The Development of Philosophy in Central Canada from 1850 to 1900," *Canadian Historical Review* XXXI (Sept. 1950), 254–9. As Irving points out in this seminal article, Beaven holds the distinction of being the first academic philosopher in Central Canada: in 1850 he was appointed professor of metaphysics and ethics. He was, however, more a theologian than an "academic philosopher," and it will be as the author of a textbook in natural theology that he will merit attention in this study (see chapter 3).
30. Rev. Robert Campbell, in *Memorial of the Rev. James George, D.D.* (Toronto, 1897), 33. All biographical information on George, unless otherwise noted, is from this fifty-three-page sketch, only part of which is by Campbell.
31. Ibid., 38.
32. Quoted by Campbell, *George*, 39.
33. Irving, "Philosophy in Central Canada," 266, 267.

34. Ibid., 267.
35. James George, *What Is Civilization?—A Lecture delivered in the City Hall, with the view of aiding to raise the bursary fund* (Kingston, 1859), 13.
36. Ibid., 13–14. Emphasis in original.
37. Meyer, *Instructed Conscience*, 87–120ff. See also Claude Welch, *Protestant Thought in the Nineteenth Century, 1799–1870* (New Haven and London, 1972), 127–37.
38. Meyer, *Instructed Conscience*, 90, 93.
39. James George, *Thoughts on High Themes* (Toronto, 1874), 5–6, 110. See also idem, *Christ Crucified* (n.p., 1837).
40. James George, *An Address delivered at the Opening of Queen's College, 1853* (Kingston, 1853), 13, 22.
41. James George, *The Relation Between Piety and Intellectual Labor. An Address Delivered at the Opening of the Fourteenth Session of Queen's College* (Kingston, 1855), 9.
42. Ibid., 3.
43. George, *Address, 1853*, 4.
44. Ibid., 10–11. Emphasis in original.
45. Ibid., 14–15. Emphases in original.
46. Ibid., 18–19.
47. George, *Christ Crucified*, 22–3.
48. Biographical information on Lyall is drawn from George Maclean Rose, ed., *A Cyclopedia of Canadian Biography*, Rose's National Biographical Series, II (Toronto, 1888), 813; *Dalhousie Gazette* XXII (30 Jan. 1890), 93–4. See also J. Audrey Lippincott, "Dalhousie College in 'The Sixties,'" *Dalhousie Review* XVI (1936–7), 285–90.
49. *Dalhousie Gazette* XXII (30 Jan. 1890), 94. Emphasis in original.
50. *Encyclopaedia Britannica*, 11th ed., IV, 662; ibid., 1973, IV, 286–7.
51. William Lyall, *Strictures on the Idea of Power, with Special Reference to the Views of Dr. Brown, in his Inquiry into the Relation of Cause and Effect* (Edinburgh, 1842), 52.
52. Quoted in ibid., 12.
53. Ibid., 51–2.
54. Ibid., 13. See also p. 10.
55. Ibid., 21, 14, 7–9, 34–5.
56. John Beattie Crozier, *My Inner Life: Being a Chapter in Personal Evolution and Autobiography* (New York, 1908), I, 139–48.
57. Lyall, *Strictures*, 7–9.
58. William Lyall, *Intellect, the Emotions, and Man's Moral Nature* (Edinburgh, 1855), 3.
59. Ibid., 252, 252–3 passim. Emphasis in original.
60. Ibid., 4.
61. Ibid., 385.
62. Ibid., 280.
63. Ibid., 282, 279, 283.

64. George, *Piety and Intellectual Labor*, 17.
65. Lyall, *Intellect*, 341–6.
66. William Lyall, *The Philosophy of Thought. A Lecture delivered at the Opening of the Free Church College, Halifax, Nova Scotia, Session 1852–53* (Halifax, 1853), 8.
67. George, *Piety and Intellectual Labor*, 12, 8.
68. Lyall, *Philosophy of Thought*, 12. Emphasis in original.
69. *University of Manitoba Calendar, 1890*, gave separate three-hour examinations for Stewart, Kant, Paley, Reid, Mill, Hamilton, Locke, and others. The examiners were Roman Catholic, Methodist, and Anglican.
70. George, *What Is Civilization?* 19, 37.
71. Henry Gates Townshend, *Philosophical Ideas in the United States* (New York, 1934), 103.
72. Materials by or on McCosh, in the order that they appeared in the *Christian Guardian*, are as follows: review of *The Intuitions of the Mind* . . . , 1860, by McCosh, xxxvi (12 Sept. 1866), 146; McCosh, "Religious Crisis Predicted," xli (12 Jan. 1870), 5; idem, "Free Thought in Boston," xl (18 May 1870), 75; idem, "Human Understanding Limited," xli (2 Nov. 1870), 171; review of *Christianity and Positivism* (1871) by McCosh, xlii (1 Nov. 1871), 174; McCosh, "Modern Infidelity," xliii (10 Apr. 1872), 113; notice of *Christianity and Positivism*, "Literary Notices," xliii (11 Dec. 1872), 397; idem, "Order in Creation," xliv (12 Mar. 1873), 86; idem, "The Association of Ideas," xlv (18 Feb. 1874), 49; review of *Ideas in Nature Overlooked by Dr. Tyndall* (1875) by McCosh, xlvi (3 Nov. 1875), 349; review of *The Development Hypothesis: Is It Sufficient?* by McCosh, xlvii (27 Dec. 1876), 413; "Dr. McCosh on Development Hypothesis," xlviii (3 Jan. 1877), 1.
73. Adam Andras, "Sir William Hamilton," *Canadian Methodist Magazine* xii (Oct. 1880), 327. On Hamilton's reputation, see John Passmore, *A Hundred Years of Philosophy* (Harmondsworth, Middlesex, 1970), 29–30.
74. Sir William Hamilton, "The Existence of God, the Immortality of the Soul, and Materialistic Science," *Canadian Methodist Magazine* viii (Aug. 1878), 179–81.
75. Mrs. Holiwell, "Holiday Musings of a Worker," *British American Magazine* i (May 1863), 49. Passmore, *Hundred Years*, 32. See also Timothy J. Duggan, "Hamilton, William," in Edwards, *Encyclopedia* ii, 409–10, for a short modern description and assessment of Hamilton's philosophy and contribution.
76. "Literary Notices," *ChG* xli (27 Apr. 1870), 66.
77. Quoted in Townshend, *Philosophical Ideas*, 103. For another example of the gradual intrusion of continental European thought into Scottish philosophy, see Professor William Clark, "Answers to Hume," *The Week* iii (12 Aug. 1886), 590–1. Clark's article re-

veals as much of the problems faced by the Scottish philosophy as it does the answers provided by it.
78. A. W. M., "Original Poetry," *Dalhousie Gazette*, n.s. v (17 Jan. 1880), 50.
79. Nicholas Flood Davin, "John Stuart Mill," *CMNR* III (June 1873), 1–15.
80. F. Tracy, "The Scottish Philosophy," *University of Toronto Quarterly* II (Nov. 1895), 1–15.
81. George, *What Is Civilization?* 48–50.
82. Meyer, *Instructed Conscience*, 49.

Chapter 3

1. C. C. Gillispie, *Genesis and Geology* (New York, 1959), 29–30 passim.
2. Sir Robert Falconer, "Scottish Influence in the Higher Education of Canada," *Transactions of the Royal Society of Canada*, sec. II (1927), 7–20; idem, "English Influence on the Higher Education of Canada," ibid. (1928), 33–48; *The Royal Institute Centennial Volume*, ed. W. Stewart Wallace (Toronto, 1949), 171–232.
3. Quoted in Falconer, "English Influence," 33–4.
4. J. H. Nicholls, *An Address delivered before the Convocation of Bishop's College, Lennoxville, June 27, 1860* (Sherbrooke, n.d.), 12. Emphasis in original. See also Nathanael Burwash, *The History of Victoria College* (Toronto, 1927), 188–9.
5. Gillispie, *Genesis and Geology*; George H. Daniels, *Science in American Society* (New York, 1971), 206–23; Charles F. O'Brien, *Sir William Dawson: A Life in Science and Religion* (Philadelphia, 1971), 1–5.
6. James George, *The Relation Between Piety and Intellectual Labor. An Address Delivered at the Opening of the Fourteenth Session of Queen's College* (Kingston, 1855), i, 10. Emphasis in original.
7. Rev. Egerton Ryerson, *Inaugural Address on the Nature and Advantages of an English and Liberal Education . . . June 21, 1842 . . .* (Toronto, 1842), 22.
8. Ryerson did not himself give the Christian names of these men. Of the identities of the latter two there can be no doubt: he was referring to Joseph Butler and William Paley. The name "Campbell" could have referred to any one of the following three Scottish divines: Archibald Campbell (1691–1756), who wrote *Enquiry into the Original of Moral Virtue* (1733); Colin Campbell (1644–1726), the author of *A Brief Demonstration of the Existence of God against the Atheists, and of the Immortality of Man's Soul* (n.d.); or George Campbell (1719–96), a friend of Reid, Beattie, and others of the Common Sense school, whose *Dissertation on Miracles* (1760) was seen as a welcome rebuff to David Hume's earlier essay

on the same subject. It is most likely that Ryerson was referring to George Campbell.
9. See Elie Halévy, *The Growth of Philosophic Radicalism* (Boston, 1966), 22–5; Gillispie, *Genesis and Geology*. Russel B. Nye notes, in *Society and Culture in America, 1830–1860* (New York, 1974), that in America Paley's *Natural Theology* "was such standard reading for educated Americans that references to him need never be explained" (237).
10. Gillispie, *Genesis and Geology*, 37. See also William Paley, *Natural Theology—Selections*, ed. and introd. Frederick Ferré (New York, 1963), xi–xxxii.
11. From Paley's *Moral and Political Philosophy*; quoted in Gillispie, *Genesis and Geology*, 36.
12. Ibid., 39.
13. C. B. Sissons, *A History of Victoria College* (Toronto, 1952), 57, 59. See D. C. Masters, *Protestant Church Colleges in Canada* (Toronto, 1966), 34; Burwash, *Victoria College*, 463; *University of Victoria College Calendar, 1861–62* (1862), 31–2.
14. *The University of Toronto and Its Colleges, 1827–1906*, ed. W. J. Alexander (Toronto, 1906), 83. Paley's *Moral Philosophy* was also required during the 1850s and 1860s in the course of civil polity given within the Department of Philosophy.
15. R. T. Appleyard, "The Origins of Huron College in Relation to the Religious Questions of the Period," M.A. thesis, University of Western Ontario, 1937, pp. 162–4. C. P. McIlvain was bishop of Ohio. The full title of his book was *The Evidences of Christianity in their External Form*, originally published in New York in 1832 and with subsequent editions in the British Isles. In 1863 he was invited by Bishop Cronyn to give the inaugural address at Huron College. See C. P. McIlvain, *The Inaugural Address delivered at the Opening of Huron College, London, Canada West, On the 2nd of December, A.D. 1863 . . .* (London, 1864).
16. For King's (1843), see Masters, *Church Colleges*, 48 and 79; for Trinity (1864–5) and Bishop's (1857), see ibid., 56 and 67 respectively; for Knox (1863), see J. G. Hodgins, "Historical Sketch of Education in Upper Canada," in H. Y. Hind, ed., *Eighty Years' Progress of British North America . . .* (Toronto, 1863), 438; for Queen's, see *Calendar of Queen's University College, 1866–67* (Kingston, 1867), 27.
17. See the *University of Manitoba Calendar* for these years. Examinations are appended to the general calendar, but are unpaginated in all cases. The examinations in Paley were formulated by a committee of three examiners of different denominations.
18. Such military metaphors were used by clergymen with respect to the defence of religious orthodoxy against the challenges of science throughout the nineteenth century. The Most Reverend Cornelius

O'Brien, (Roman Catholic) archbishop of Halifax, when condemning the prevalence of "unbelief" and "agnosticism," urged the necessity of defending the "Citadel of truth" by "put[ting] on the 'armour of faith' and the 'helmet of Justice'" (*Pastoral Letter Addressed to the Clergy and Laity of the Diocese of Halifax* [Halifax, 1891], 8).

19. For further biographical information on Beaven, see *Dictionary of Canadian Biography*, vol. x, *1871 to 1880* (Toronto, 1972), 39–40; J. A. Irving, "The Development of Philosophy in Central Canada from 1850 to 1900," *Canadian Historical Review* XXXI (Sept. 1950), 254–9; John Campbell, "The Reverend Professor James Beaven, D.D., M.A.," *University of Toronto Monthly* III (Dec. 1902), 69–72.
20. James Beaven, *Elements of Natural Theology* (London, 1850), 1–2.
21. George, *Piety and Intellectual Labor*, 6.
22. Beaven, *Elements*, 3.
23. Ibid., 4–6. Emphasis in original. It should be noted here that both epigraphs beginning this chapter are taken from Beaven's *Elements*. The passage from Paley's *Natural Theology* is quoted on p. 146.
24. James Beaven, *Doctrine of the Holy Scripture, and of the Primitive Church on the Subject of Religious Celibacy; with a vindication of the Early Church from the Mistakes of the Author of "Ancient Christianity"* (London, 1841), 5–6, 12–14, 239–40. Emphasis in original.
25. James Beaven, *'That they all may be one.' A Sermon preached before the Synod of the Diocese of Toronto ... 7th June, 1859* (Toronto, 1859), 5, 6–15. This sermon is bound within a volume entitled "Pamphlets—Bishop Strachan" in the Trinity University Archives, University of Toronto.
26. Beaven, *Elements*, 6. Emphasis in original.
27. Ibid., 7.
28. George, *Piety and Intellectual Labor*, 9.
29. Beaven, *Elements*, 8.
30. Ibid., 9.
31. Ibid., 50–1. Titles in the series included *The Adaptation of External Nature to the Moral and Intellectual Constitution of Man*, by John Kidd, Regius Professor of Medicine at Oxford; *Astronomy and General Physics, considered with reference to Natural Theology*, by Rev. William Whewell, Fellow of Trinity College, Cambridge; *The Hand: Its Mechanism and Vital Endowments as Evincing Design*, by Sir Charles Bell; *Animal and Vegetable Physiology*, by Peter Mark Roget; *Geology and Mineralogy*, by Rev. William Buckland, Canon of Christ Church and Professor of Geology at Oxford; *The History, Habits, and Instincts of Animals*, by Rev. William Kirby; and *Chemistry, Meteorology, and the Function of Digestion*, by William Prout. One commentator has said that prob-

ably Paley himself may be called "in a real sense ... the author of The Bridgewater Treatises" (D. W. Gundry, "The Bridgewater Treatises and their Authors," *History* XXXI [1946], 141).
32. Beaven, *Elements*, 94. His use of Butler can be seen in chapter 13, "On a Future State," 181–90, and chapter 14, "On The Immortality of the Soul," 190–202.
33. Ibid., 66–7, 79. Buckland, Prout, and Whewell are quoted at length on pp. 66–93.
34. Ibid., 80–92, 93. See also p. 117.
35. Daniel F. Rice, "Natural Theology and the Scottish Philosophy in the Thought of Thomas Chalmers," *Scottish Journal of Theology* XXIV (1971), 23.
36. Irving, "Philosophy in Central Canada," 256.
37. Beaven, *Elements*, 148, 177–8, 208–9, 235.
38. Ibid., 148–9. Emphasis in original.
39. Ibid., 149–50.
40. Ibid., 235, 146–7. See also Irving, "Philosophy in Central Canada," 258–9, for more information on Beaven's extension of natural theology into the realm of social ethics.
41. Beaven, *Elements*, 237–9.
42. *Circular of the Medical Faculty of Trinity College, Toronto* (Toronto, 1853), 8. On the subject of the Trinity Medical Faculty and Bovell's connection with it, it is interesting to note the following words from the preamble of the statement which constituted the body: "Whereas it is admitted by all Christian men, that, without assuming Religion as the basis, no sound educational principles can be instilled into youth; and whereas the art of Medicine, more than any other, is influential in its practice in proportion as more or less of sound religious views pervades the minds of those who practise it. ..." The preamble then declared that the discipline and instruction of "the United Church of England and Ireland shall form the fundamental principles of its organization" (4–5).
43. More bibliographical material on Bovell may be found in the *Dictionary of Canadian Biography*, vol. X, *1871 to 1880* (Toronto, 1972), 83–5; C. E. Dalman, "The Reverend James Bovell, M.D., 1817–1880," in *Pioneers of Canadian Science*, ed. G. F. G. Stanley (Toronto, 1966), 81–100; *A Standard Dictionary of Canadian Biography: Canadian Who Was Who*, ed. Sir Charles G. D. Roberts and Arthur L. Tunnell (Toronto, 1938), II, 40–2; George W. Spragge, "The Trinity Medical College," *Ontario History* LVIII (June 1966), 63–98; A. J. Johnson, "The Founder of the Medical Faculty, Dr. James Bovell," *Trinity University Review* XV (1902), 104–6; W. B. Geikie, "An Historical Sketch of Canadian Medical Education," *Canadian Lancet* (Jan.–Feb. 1901), 8–9.
44. Published respectively in *Upper Canada Journal of Medical, Surgical, and Physical Science* I (1851–2), 59–60; *British American*

Journal of Medical and Physical Science v (1849–50), 1–5, 29–32; *CJ*, n.s. VIII (1863), 341–2; *British American Journal of Medical and Physical Science* II (1852–3), 48–50, 65–9, 128–37, 150–6, 182–9, 210–14. For a more extensive bibliography of Bovell's work in medicine, see appendix A in *Pioneers*, ed. Stanley.

45. Quoted in *Canadian Biography*, ed. Roberts and Tunnell, 41–2.
46. Gillispie, *Genesis and Geology*, 19.
47. James Bovell, *Outlines of Natural Theology, for the Use of the Canadian Student* (Toronto, 1859), i–ii.
48. Ibid.
49. Ibid., 9–10.
50. Ibid., 5–6.
51. Ibid., ii–iii.
52. George Boas, "Cousin, Victor," in Paul Edwards, ed., *The Encyclopedia of Philosophy* (New York, 1967), 247. My discussion of Cousin's three-faculty psychology draws heavily from this article.
53. Bovell, *Outlines*, 139. This quotation may in fact be from Alexander Crombie (probably from his *Natural Theology*, 1829). Crombie had been quoted at length on the previous page and Bovell (or his typesetter) frequently forgot to signify the end of his quotations. The point, however, is a minor one since, whatever the source, the quotation represents Bovell's own view.
54. Ibid., 108.
55. Ibid. My emphasis.
56. Ibid., 104.
57. Ibid., 23–4.
58. Ibid., 24–5.
59. Ibid., 643–4.
60. James Bovell, *The World at the Advent of the Lord Jesus* (Toronto, 1868), 4.
61. James Bovell, *Passing Thoughts on Man's Relation to God and on God's Relation to Man* (Toronto, 1862), xi, xii–xiii.
62. *An Exposition of the Creed. By John Pearson, D.D., Late Lord Bishop of Chester [1613–86]. With an Appendix, containing The Principal Greek and Latin Creeds*. Revised by the Reverend W. S. Dobson (New York, 1851). "Pearson on the Creed" was standard fare at Anglican divinity schools in the nineteenth century. The Dobson edition, which bore on its spine the phrase "Pearson on the Creed," was probably the most common edition used.
63. See S. F. Wise, "Sermon Literature and Canadian Intellectual History," *Bulletin* [of the United Church of Canada], no. 18 (1965), 16 passim.
64. See, for example, Hibbert, (Anglican) Lord Bishop of Nova Scotia, *A Charge Delivered to the Clergy at the Visitation held in The Cathedral Church of St. Luke, at Halifax, on the 1st Day of July, 1884* (Halifax, 1884), 26–47. The Roman Catholic clergy also used

the argument from design in a similar fashion: see the Most Reverend Cornelius O'Brien, *Pastoral Letter Addressed to the Clergy and Laity of the Diocese of Halifax* (Halifax, 1891), 1–10.

65. Provost George Whitaker, "'Questions and answers on the Catechism.' Notes on the lectures on the catechism taken by Edward Kaye Kendall," 2 pts. (unpaginated), Provost Whitaker Collection, no. 2, Trinity University Archives, University of Toronto. See also the extensive "Questions on Paley's Evidences of Christianity by the Provost of Trin. Coll.," in George Whitaker, "Notes of Lectures on the Catechism. Taken by Beverley Jones." 1 notebook (unpaginated), Provost Whitaker Collection, no. 2, Trinity University Archives, University of Toronto. For an assessment of Whitaker by a former student, see C. E. Thompson, "The Reverend Geo. Whitaker, M.A., First Provost, 1852–1881," *Trinity University Review* xv (June–July 1902), 100–1.
66. Walter F. Cannon, "The Normative Role of Science in Early Victorian Thought," *Journal of the History of Ideas* xxv (1964), 488.
67. Quoted in ibid., 496.
68. Peter J. Bowler, "Francis Palgrave on Natural Theology," *Journal of the History of Ideas* xxxv (Jan.–Mar. 1974), 144–7. Palgrave, Bowler points out, was an exception to this generalization.
69. Bishop Joseph Butler's *Analogy of Religion* was argued in this negative fashion.
70. For opinions of Beaven, see *University of Toronto*, ed. Alexander, 105; James Loudon, "The Memoirs of James Loudon," typescript, p. 9 (pagination irregular), University of Toronto Archives. For opinions of Bovell, see D. F. Bogert, "Student Life at Trinity. II. 1860 to 1865," *Trinity University Review* xv (Dec. 1902), 187; T. W. Patterson, "Student Life at Trinity. III. 1866 to 1869," ibid. xvi (Jan. 1903), 8. Bogert states that attendance at Bovell's lectures was "voluntary." This is at least partially inaccurate: the Trinity College calendar for 1859 notes that "attendance [was] required" for third-year students (19).
71. In a seminal article entitled "The Meaning of Romanticism for the Historian of Ideas," A. O. Lovejoy writes in a vein which supports this conception of "historical significance": "The things that a writer, given his premises, might be expected to say, but doesn't say—the consequences which legitimately and fairly evidently follow from his theses, but which he never sees, or persistently refuses to draw—these may be even more noteworthy than the things he does say or the consequences he does deduce. For they may throw light upon peculiarities of his mind, especially upon his biases and the non rational elements in his thinking—may disclose to the historian specific points at which intellectual processes have been checked, or diverted, or perverted, by emotive factors. Negative facts of this kind are thus often indicia of positive but inex-

plicit or subconscious facts. So, again, the determination of not-immediately-obvious incompatibilities between ideas may lead to the recognition of the historically instructive fact that one or another writer, or a whole age, has held together, in closed compartments of the mind, contradictory preconceptions or beliefs" (*Journal of the History of Ideas* II [June 1941], 264–5).

72. For an accusation that Bovell preached doctrines that more properly belonged in the "Church of Rome," see a letter by "A Protestant Clergyman" to the editor of the Toronto *Globe*. The letter, dated 12 Nov. 1860, is found in the original in the Trinity College Papers (see "Bovell"), Trinity University Archives, University of Toronto. Bovell's original reply, dated 16 Nov. 1860, is in the same collection. This controversy occurred in the midst of a dispute in which Bishop Cronyn of Huron accused Provost Whitaker of Trinity of teaching "Romish" doctrines (the catechism mentioned in the text was a prime piece of evidence used by Cronyn). See also Appleyard, "Huron College," for the full background of the dispute.

73. Nathanael Burwash, "God's Plan in Nature—For the Mechanic's [*sic*] Institute, Baltimore" (n.d.), pp. 25–7, in Nathanael Burwash Papers, now in the Archives of the United Church of Canada, Toronto, but at the time of examination in the Victoria University Archives, E. J. Pratt Library, University of Toronto. This manuscript may be fairly reliably dated by comparison (criteria: ink, type of paper, degree of ageing) with another manuscript in the then-unorganized Burwash papers. See "An Essay on the Coincidence of the Geological with the Mosaic Account of Creation, Jan. 1858." This latter address is also an excellent example of the degree to which William Paley's natural theology was still used on the eve of the publication of Darwin's *Origin*.

74. George Whitaker, *A Sermon; preached in the Church of Trinity College, Toronto, on Sunday, June 27, 1852. Published at the Request of the Students* (Toronto, 1852), 7, 9.

75. In scriptural terms, the dilemma of Anglo-Canadian natural theologians may be seen as a conflict between Rom. 1:19–20 (see epigraph) and Rom. 11:33: "O the depth of the riches of the wisdom, and the knowledge of God! how incomprehensible are his judgements, and how unsearchable are his ways." For examples of Canadians speaking from the pulpit and lectern on the relationship between authority, faith, and reason, in each case discussed in direct conjunction with natural theology (and in some cases science in general), see George Whitaker, *Soberness of Mind. A Sermon: preached in the Chapel of Trinity College, Toronto, on Sunday, June 25, 1865* (Toronto, 1865), 8–9; Rev. Prof. D. H. MacVicar, *Recent Aspects of Materialism: being a Lecture Delivered at the Opening of the Session of 1871–72, of the Presbyterian College, Mtl.* (Montreal, 1871), 9; Hibbert, *A Charge 1884*, 6; George Whit-

aker, *A Sermon Preached in the Chapel of Trinity College...
June 20, 1880* (Toronto, 1881), 11–12.
76. See Henry Mansel, *The Limits of Religious Thought* (1859; rpt. Boston, 1870), esp. p. 145.

Chapter 4

1. George Basalla, William Coleman, and Robert H. Kargon, eds., *Victorian Science: A Self-Portrait from the Presidential Addresses to the British Association for the Advancement of Science* (New York, 1970), 48.
2. "British Association for the Advancement of Science," *CJ*, ser. 2, v (Mar. 1860), 66–7.
3. Ibid., 67–8.
4. Basalla et al., *Victorian Science*, 19–20, 132, 400, 412–13, 415–16; George H. Daniels, *Science in American Society* (New York, 1971), 45–6; George H. Daniels, *American Science in the Age of Jackson* (New York, 1968).
5. Daniels, *American Science*, 71. For a short but apt description of the "Baconian method," see also p. 66.
6. Francis Bacon, *The Works of Francis Bacon*, ed. James Spedding et al. (London, 1883), IV, 32–3. I am indebted to Dr. Graham Reynolds for this reference.
7. Daniel Wilson, "The President's Address" (Read before the Canadian Institute, 7 Jan. 1860), *CJ*, ser. 2, v (Mar. 1860), 127.
8. Ibid., 119.
9. Daniel Wilson, "The President's Address," *CJ*, ser. 2, VI (Mar. 1861), 120.
10. Daniel Wilson, "Sonnet—from 'Spring Wild Flowers,'" *CMNR* VIII (July 1875), 8.
11. Quoted in a review (anonymous) of *Prehistoric Man: Researches into the Origin of Civilization in the Old and New Worlds*, in *British American Magazine* I (1863), 92. The fact that the reviewer chose this passage from the many other quotable ones in Wilson's book illustrates the hold of the metaphor of the veil upon at least one person other than Wilson and myself.
12. James Bovell, *Outlines of Natural Theology, for the Use of the Canadian Student* (Toronto, 1859), iii.
13. Basalla et al., *Victorian Science*, 48, 53.
14. Editorial, *Dalhousie Gazette* IV (27 Apr. 1872), 10–11.
15. John C. Greene, *Darwin and the Modern World View* (Baton Rouge, 1973), 4 passim. The historiography of nineteenth-century science is both brilliant and fascinating. See, for example, Loren Eiseley, *Darwin's Century* (New York, 1961); John C. Greene, *The Death of Adam* (Ames, Iowa, 1959); Cecil J. Schneer, *Mind and Matter* (New York, 1970).
16. Further information on Wilson may be obtained from these sources: H. H. Langton, *Sir Daniel Wilson: A Memoir* (Toronto,

1929); Jessie Aitken Wilson, *Memoir of George Wilson* (Edinburgh, 1860) (George Wilson was Daniel Wilson's young brother, who was Regius Professor of Technology at Edinburgh University and director of the Industrial Museum of Scotland until his death in 1859); G. M. Adam, "Daniel Wilson," *The Week* IV (6 Oct. 1887), 726–7; T. F. McIlwraith, "Sir Daniel Wilson: A Canadian Anthropologist of One Hundred Years Ago," *Transactions of the Royal Society of Canada*, sec. II, ser. 4 (1964), 129–36. Bruce G. Trigger, "Sir Daniel Wilson: Canada's First Anthropologist," *Anthropologica*, n.s. VIII (1966), 3–28.

On Dawson, see Rankine Dawson, ed., *Fifty Years' Work in Canada; Scientific and Educational; Being Autobiographical Notes by Sir William Dawson* (London, 1901); J. C. Sutherland, "Sir J. William Dawson," *The Week* V (1 Dec. 1887), 10–11; Frank Dawson Adams, "In Memoriam—Sir John William Dawson," *Transactions of the Royal Society of Canada*, sec. IV (1901), 3–14; Bruce G. Trigger, "Sir John William Dawson: A Faithful Anthropologist," *Anthropologica*, n.s. VIII (1966), 351–9; Charles F. O'Brien, *Sir William Dawson: A Life in Science and Religion* (Philadelphia, 1971).

17. He had also written pieces for *Tait's Magazine, Chambers' Information for the People,* and *The Scotsman,* among others. See Langton, *Wilson,* 36–9.
18. Daniel Wilson, *Prehistoric Annals of Scotland,* 2nd ed. (London, 1863), I, xvii.
19. J. W. Dawson, "On the Destruction and Partial Reproduction of the Forests in British North America," *Edinburgh New Philosophical Journal* XLII (1847), 259–71.
20. See Michael T. Ghiselin, *The Triumph of the Darwinian Method* (Berkeley, 1972). Ghiselin provides a remarkably brief but accurate description of the theory of natural selection as put forward by Darwin: "Organisms differ from one another. They produce more young than the available resources can sustain. Those best suited to survive pass on the expedient properties to their offspring, while inferior forms are eliminated. Subsequent generations therefore are more like the better adapted ancestors, and the result is a gradual modification, or evolution. Thus the cause of evolutionary adaptation is differential reproductive success" (46).
21. The very characteristics rejected by Dawson and Wilson constituted the essence of the Darwinian "revolution" in scientific method. See ibid., 63. It must be stressed that these reactions by Dawson and Wilson were by no means unique or uncommon. Similar objections were voiced by the most prominent British and American scientists of the day. See Sir William Armstrong's presidential address to the British Association for the Advancement of Science: "But when natural selection is adduced as a cause adequate to explain the production of a new organ not provided for in

original creation, the hypothesis must appear to common apprehensions, to be pushed beyond the limits of reasonable conjecture" (reproduced in *CJ*, ser. 2, IX [1864], 37). See also the presidential address several years later to the American Association for the Advancement of Science by J. Lawrence Smith. Darwin, said Smith, "is to be regarded more as a metaphysician with a highly wrought imagination than as a scientist. . . . He is not satisfied to leave the laws of life where he finds them, or to pursue their study by logical and inductive reasoning. His method of reasoning will not allow him to remain at rest; he must be moving onward in his unification of the universe" (reproduced in the *Canadian Naturalist and Quarterly Journal of Science*, n.s. VII [1875], 148–55).
22. J. W. Dawson, "Review of 'Darwin on the Origin of Species By Natural Selection,'" *Canadian Naturalist and Geologist* V (1860), 100.
23. Ibid., 101.
24. O'Brien, *Dawson*, 100.
25. Dawson, "Review of Darwin," 111–12.
26. O'Brien, *Dawson*.
27. Dawson, "Review of Darwin," 113.
28. Ibid., 112.
29. Ibid., 116.
30. Ibid., 116–17.
31. G. Mercer Adam, "Prominent Canadians. II. Daniel Wilson," *The Week* IV (6 Oct. 1887), 727.
32. William Nesbitt Ponton, "Lecture Notes—Professor Wilson's Lectures—1873—1st year," notebook, pp. 13, 15; "Rhetoric," 63–4, University of Toronto Archives, University of Toronto. Emphasis in original.
33. Wilson, "President's Address" (1860), 115–16.
34. Ghiselin, *Darwinian Method*, 63, 76–7.
35. Wilson, "President's Address" (1860), 116.
36. Ibid., 116, 117. Emphasis in original.
37. Ibid., 118. Emphasis in original.
38. Ibid., 120, 121.
39. Ibid., 119.
40. Dawson, "Review of Darwin," 119, also 117–18.
41. Wilson, "President's Address" (1860), 122.
42. Wilson, "President's Address" (1861), 114.
43. Bovell, *Outlines*, 486–500.
44. William Leitch, *God's Glory in the Heavens* (London, 1862), 274. For a very favourable reception of the book by a member of the Canadian scientific community, see *British American Magazine* I (July 1863), 308.
45. *CJ*, ser. 2, II (1857), 201–4ff.
46. *CJ*, ser. 2, V (1860), 60.
47. Ibid., 61.

48. *CJ*, ser. 2, VIII (1863), 389–90.
49. Ibid., 391, 393.
50. Ibid., 393.
51. Ibid., 393–4.
52. Ibid. See also Hincks's review of *Lectures on Elements of Comparative Anatomy* (1864) by Huxley, *CJ*, ser. 2, X (1865), 41.
53. Review of *Contributions to the Natural History of the United States* (1857) by Louis Agassiz, *CJ*, ser. 2, III (1858), 245.
54. Rev. W. Hincks, "Remarks on the Principles of Classification in the Animal Kingdom in Immediate Reference to a Recent Paper by J. W. Dawson . . . ," *CJ*, ser. 2, X (1865), 20, 23.
55. Rev. W. Hincks, "Some Thoughts on Classification in Relation to Organised Beings," *CJ*, ser. 2, XI (1866–7), 35.
56. Ibid., 44–5. For examples of Hincks's unwillingness to accept the Darwinian hypothesis, his commitment to natural theology, his suspicion of "ingenious speculation," unsupported by sufficient evidence, in science, and the fixity of species in accordance with a Divine plan, see his presidential addresses to the Canadian Institute (delivered on 16 Jan. 1869 and 14 Jan. 1870) in *CJ*, n.s. XII (1868–9), 97–107, 355–8. See also Rev. William Hincks, "An Attempt at an Improved Classification of Fruits," *CJ*, ser. 2, VI (1861), 495–7. A good example of the extent to which taxonomy was seen as a vital part of the scientific endeavour, but with a religious end, is provided in Henry Scadding, "On Museums and Other Classified Collections, Temporary or Permanent, as Instruments of Education in Natural Science," *CJ*, n.s. XIII (1871), 1–25. "It is discovered and is universally confessed, that throughout Nature laws reign," Scadding wrote. "These laws does not every sane man confess to be laws of God? It becomes then even a matter of religious obligation to inculcate a knowledge of those laws so far as is practicable and suitable in the education of the young" (23).
57. "The Effect of Essays and Reviews at Oxford" (letter to the editor), *ChG* XXXII, no. 18 (1 May 1861), 69–70. See also "Infidelity in the Anglican Church; The Essays and Reviews" (editorial), *ChG* XXXII, no. 17 (24 Apr. 1861), 66; "The Essays and Reviews" (from *Quebec Gazette*), *ChG* XXXIII, no. 8 (19 Feb. 1862), 29. The latter was highly critical of the work under review.
58. "Infidelity in the Anglican Church," 66. Emphasis in original.
59. "Infidelity in England" (editorial), *ChG* XXXIII (17 Sept. 1862), 152.
60. "Freethinking—Rationalism," *ChG* XXXV (28 Dec. 1864), 209.
61. "Hurst's History of Rationalism," *ChG* XXXVII (28 Feb. 1866), 34.
62. "German Infidels in America" (from the *New York Evangelist*), *ChG* XXXVII (25 Apr. 1866), 65. A year later the editor of the *Guardian* pointed out that rationalism in German schools and universities was on the decline, its place taken by an evangelical party. Even so, in the mass of the people, he warned, rationalism was still very strong (*ChG* XXXVIII [22 May 1867], 82). See also "Spurious

Liberality," *ChG* XLII (31 May 1871), 86, for the view that "genuine liberality can only exist in conjunction with settled principles."
63. "'Free Thought' and Freedom," *ChG* XXXVII (7 Feb. 1866), 22; "Religious Belief and Liberty of Conscience," *ChG* XL (8 Deç. 1869), 194.
64. "Modern Infidelity and German Mysticism" (from the *Edinburgh Review*), *ChG* XL (28 July 1869), 117; "What is Swedenborgianism?" *ChG* XXXVIII (16 Oct. 1867), 165; "Rationalism," *ChG* XLI (3 Aug. 1870), 119; Charles L. Thompson, "On Atheistic Philosophy" (from the *Independent*), *ChG* XLIII (7 Feb. 1872), 41.
65. "Science and Christianity" (from *Evangelical Christendom*), *ChG* XXXVII (14 Nov. 1866), 181; "Science and Scepticism" (editorial), *ChG* XXXIV (14 Oct. 1863), 165.
66. R. G. Ingersoll, "Reason and Faith," *ChG* XLII (13 Sept. 1871), 153.
67. W. F. Warren, "David Friedrich Strauss" (from *Zion's Herald*), *ChG* XXXVIII (10 July 1867), 110; "Westminster Review and Revealed Religion," *ChG* XLIII (11 Dec. 1872), 396; "Remarks on the Idea of Christianity Presented by the Author of 'Ecce Homo,'" *ChG* XXXVIII (17 Apr. 1867), 62.
68. "Unreasonableness of 'Rationalism,'" *ChG* XXXVIII (20 Feb. 1867), 30. Emphasis in original. See also "Experimental Knowledge" (from the *Christian Press*), *ChG* XLIV (2 Apr. 1873), 106. Emphasis in original.
69. "Experimental Knowledge," 106. See also "Modern Skepticism," *ChG* XLI (23 Mar. 1870), 45.
70. "Evils of Intellectual Pride," *ChG* XLIII (3 Apr. 1872), 108; "The Spirit of the Age," *ChG* XLIII (27 Mar. 1872), 100. See also "Be Not Wise in Your Own Conceits," *ChG* XLI (18 May 1870), 76; "Infidel Pretensions" (from *Sunday at Home*), *ChG* XL (28 Apr. 1869), 65; "Anti-Christian Literature," *ChG* XLIII (24 Jan. 1872), 28; "The Two Tyndalls" (from *The Advance*), *ChG* XLIII (23 Oct. 1872), 337.
71. "Evils of Intellectual Pride."
72. "How to Cure Skepticism," *ChG* XLIV (11 June 1873), 176; "Orthodoxy!" (unsigned letter to the editor), *ChG* XLI (23 Mar. 1870), 46; C. M. D., "The Innate Truths of the Holy Scriptures—The Teaching of Immortal Life," *ChG* XXXVIII (8 May 1867), 73; XXXVIII (29 May 1867), 85; see also his "The Innate Evidence of the Truth of Holy Scripture," *ChG* XXXIX (17 June 1868), 102. Other items in the same vein include "Revelation, The Antidote to Scientific Scepticism" (editorial), *ChG* XXXIV (9 Sept. 1863), 145; Prof. E. D. Sanborn, "The Internal Evidence of the Holy Scriptures," *ChG* XXXV (20 Jan. 1864), 13; Dr. Thomas Guthrie, "The Most Unfortunate Knowledge," *ChG* XLI (28 Nov. 1870), 187.
73. C. M. D., "What is Truth?" *ChG* XL (22 Dec. 1869), 201.
74. "Knowledge and Faith" (editorial), *ChG* XLI (28 Sept. 1870), 551.
75. "The Bible's Historical Accuracy" (editorial), *ChG* XL (29 Dec.

1869), 205; Henry Ward Beecher, "Conditions of Criticism," *ChG* XLIV (18 June 1873), 193.
76. Thomas Hurlburt, "Reply to Mr. Dutton's Friend," *ChG* XXXIII (12 Feb. 1862), 25; "Reply to Mr. Dutton," *ChG* XXXIII (26 Feb. 1862), 33; "Scripture and facts agree as to the Age of the World," *ChG* XXXIII (5 Mar. 1862), 37; "Indian Traditions and Mythology," *ChG* XXXIII (5 Mar. 1862), 40; "Remarks in Reply to Rev. T. Campbell," *ChG* XXXIII (19 Mar. 1862), 45; letter to the editor, *ChG* XXXIII (30 Apr. 1862), 69.
77. Joseph T. Dutton, "Reply to the Reverend T. Hurlburt," *ChG* XXXIII (5 Feb. 1862), 21.
78. Thomas Campbell, "The Emergence and Submergence Theory," pt. 1, *ChG* XXXIII (7 May 1862), 73; pt. 2, XXXIII (14 May 1862), 76. See also the following articles by Thomas Campbell: "The Reverend Thos. Hurlburt's Geology," *ChG* XXXIII (5 Mar. 1862), 37; "Remarks on Rev. Thos. Hurlburt's Difficulties Reconsidered," *ChG* XXXIII (16 Apr. 1862), 61; "The Emergence and Submergence Theory Tested by the Phenomena of the Local Measures," *ChG* XXXIII (28 May 1862), 85.
79. C. W. Goodwin, "A Review of the Essay No. 5 of *Essays and Reviews—On the Mosaic Cosmogony*" (letter 1), *ChG* XXXII (11 Sept. 1861), 142, and (letter 2) XXXII (18 Sept. 1861), 148; Philolithios, "Review of the Essay No. 5 ... Mr. Goodwin's Ignorance of Geology," *ChG* XXXII (25 Sept. 1861), 151; idem, "A Review of the Essay No. 5 ... On the Source and Character of Mr. Goodwin's Education," *ChG* XXXII (2 Oct. 1861), 157; idem, "A Review of the Essay No. 5 ... Mr. Goodwin's Creed," *ChG* XXXII (16 Oct. 1861), 163.
80. "Mosaic Cosmogony—Part I" (editorial), *ChG* XXXII (4 Dec. 1861), 191. See also part II, *ChG* XXXII (11 Dec. 1861), 195.
81. Ibid., pt. II.
82. Rev. Wm. Hincks, "The President's Address," *CJ*, n.s. XII (Aug. 1870), 355-8.
83. See for example W. H. W., "Darwinism and Christianity," *ChG* XLI (28 Dec. 1870), 204.
84. W. H. W., "Modern Science in its Relation to Christianity," *ChG* XXXVIII (16 Oct. 1867), 165.
85. "Sir Charles Lyell on the Glacial Period," *ChG* XXXV (12 Oct. 1864), 166; Lord Shaftesbury, "The Bible and Science," *ChG* XXXV (8 June 1864), 93; "Agassiz and Darwin's Theory," *ChG* XXXVII (18 July 1866), 113; "Geological Speculation," *ChG* XXXVII (19 Dec. 1866), 204; "The Miracles of Science: How They Illustrate the Truth of Religion," *ChG* XXXVII (12 Dec. 1866), 197; "The Bible and Modern Criticism," *ChG* XL (28 July 1869), 118; Mark Hopkins, "How Shall Modern Skepticism be Met?" *ChG* XLII (11 Oct. 1871), 173; C. M. D., "Astronomy Against Atheism," *ChG* XLIII (1 May 1872), 207; "Atheistic Science Rebuked," *ChG* XLIII (25 Sept. 1872), 308;

"Faraday, the Christian Philosopher," *ChG* XLIII (16 Oct. 1872), 329.
86. "Darwinism and Christianity."
87. "Darwin's Descent of Man," *ChG* XLII (5 Apr. 1871), 54.
88. Review of *Lay Sermons, Addresses, and Reviews, ChG* XLII (18 Jan. 1871), 10.
89. "Darwin and Huxley," *ChG* XLII (26 July 1871), 118.
90. C. M. D., "Different Phases of Modern Infidelity and Attacks on Christianity," *ChG* XLII (5 July 1871), 105.
91. "Religion and Science," *ChG* XLII (27 Sept. 1871), 154.
92. Review of *The Story of the Earth and Man, CMNR* III (May 1873), 454.
93. J. W. Dawson, "Annual Address, 1872," *Canadian Naturalist and Quarterly Journal of Science*, n.s. VII (1875), 1–2. Also published as "The Present Aspect of Inquiries as to the Introduction of Genera and Species in Geological Time," *CMNR* II (Aug. 1872), 154–6.
94. Quoted in Frank Dawson Adams, "In Memoriam—Sir John William Dawson," *Transactions of the Royal Society of Canada*, sec. IV (1901), 8.
95. Review of *Earth and Man*, 454. For similar comments a decade later, see J. G. Bourinot, "The Intellectual Development of the Canadian People. IV. Native Literature," *RBCM* VI (Mar. 1881), 225.
96. J. W. Dawson, *The Story of the Earth and Man*, new ed. with corrections and additions (New York, 1891), 167. See also J. W. Dawson, "The So-Called 'Conflict' of Science and Religion," *PSM* X (Nov. 1876), 72–4. This is perhaps the best short introduction to Dawson's views.
97. Dawson, *Earth and Man*, 156, 164–5, 175–7.
98. Ibid., 176.
99. G. Mercer Adam, "Daniel Wilson," *The Week* IV (6 Oct. 1887), 726.
100. Daniel Wilson, *Caliban: The Missing Link* (London, 1873), xi–xii.
101. Ibid., 2–4.
102. Ibid., 8, 11.
103. Ponton, "Lecture Notes," p. 26: "Literature," University of Toronto Archives.
104. Wilson, *Caliban*, 78.
105. Ibid., 20–1, 90–1.
106. Ibid., 93.
107. Ibid., 101, 113.
108. H. Alleyne Nicholson, "Man's Place in Nature," *CMNR* I (Jan. 1872), 35–7.

Chapter 5

1. Sara Jeannette Duncan, "Saunterings—The Age," *The Week* IV (3 Mar. 1887), 216–17.

2. Northrop Frye, *The Modern Century* (Toronto, 1967), 110ff.
3. Northrop Frye, *The Critical Path: An Essay on the Social Context of Literary Criticism* (Bloomington, 1973), 36.
4. Before 1872 Canadian periodicals were generally of a local nature and often experienced only a brief existence owing to publishing difficulties. The periodical press after the appearance of the *Canadian Monthly and National Review* (1872–8) was of a more national scope, and while these periodicals suffered no fewer publishing problems, throughout the rest of the nineteenth century one such journal or another was in existence: *Belford's Monthly Magazine* (1876–8), *Rose-Belford's Canadian Monthly and National Review* (1878–82), *The Bystander* (1880–intermittently to 1890), *The Week* (1883–96). See R. L. McDougall, "A Study of Canadian Periodical Literature of the Nineteenth Century," Ph.D. diss., University of Toronto, 1950, pp. 4–5.
5. W. J. R., "Man Here and Hereafter," *Belford's Monthly Magazine* III (May 1878), 757.
6. Fidelis, "The Seen and the Unseen," *CMNR* IX (June 1876), 495. Fidelis was the pseudonym used by Miss Machar (the daughter of a principal of Queen's University) throughout her life. See Norah Story, *The Oxford Companion to Canadian History and Literature* (Toronto, 1967), 488, for biographical information.
7. Goldwin Smith, "The Immortality of the Soul," *CMNR* IX (May 1876), 408.
8. James DeKoven, "The Gates of the Invisible," quoted in Paul A. Carter, *The Spiritual Crisis of the Gilded Age* (DeKalb, Illinois, 1971), 16.
9. H, "A Few Words About Nature," *Dalhousie Gazette* VII (19 Dec. 1874), 17.
10. Ibid., 18–19.
11. Ibid.
12. Carl Berger, "The Vision of Grandeur," Ph.D. diss., University of Toronto, 1966, p. 434. LeSueur believed that Fiske's attempts at such a reconciliation were wholly inadequate. See W. D. LeSueur, "Evolution and the Destiny of Man," *PSM* XXVI (Feb. 1885), 456–68.
13. L, "Science," *Dalhousie Gazette*, n.s. IV (Jan. 1879), 50–2.
14. Anon., "Is a Belief in Darwinism Consistent With a Teleological View of the Natural World?" *Dalhousie Gazette* XVIII (Apr. 1886), 141–3.
15. J. E. Creighton, "The Age and Its Tendencies," *Dalhousie Gazette* XVIII (Mar. 1886), 123.
16. See, for example, Dr. Luthardt, "Science and Christianity," *ChG* XLV (Feb. 1874), 57; "Is Materialism Atheistic?" (editorial), XLV (July 1874), 236; F. H. Hedge, "Science and Faith," XLVI (June 1875), 193; "Is Religion Opposed to Science?" (editorial), XLVII (May (1876), 156; "Science and Religion" (editorial), XLVIII (Dec. 1877),

388; "Indebtedness of Science to Christianity" (editorial), XL (Jan. 1879), 9. Such articles continued throughout the 1880s. Virtually all controversies outlined in this chapter were followed and commented upon at length in the *Christian Guardian*.
17. M. A. Jevons, "One Faith in Many Forms," *RBCM* (Oct. 1884), 344.
18. "Ste. Beuve," *Westminster Review* (Apr. 1871), 216, 213. The best short treatment of Sainte-Beuve's place in French letters is probably in Roger L. Williams, *The World of Napoleon III* (New York, 1957), 113–31. See also Irving Babbitt, *The Masters of Modern French Criticism* (New York, 1912), 97–188; and C. K. Trueblood, "Sainte-Beuve and the Psychology of Personality," *Character and Personality* VIII (1939–40), 120–43.
19. *Transactions of the Ottawa Literary and Scientific Society* (1897–8), 12.
20. For more extensive biographical treatment of LeSueur, see A. B. McKillop, ed., *A Critical Spirit: The Thought of William Dawson LeSueur* (Toronto, 1977).
21. W. D. LeSueur, "Teaching of History" (letter to the editor), Montreal *Gazette*, 9 Oct. 1912, p. 11.
22. For one such person, see the remarkable autobiography of John Beattie Crozier, *My Inner Life: Being a Chapter in Personal Evolution and Autobiography* (New York, 1908), I, 176–84ff. A contemporary of LeSueur, Crozier attended the University of Toronto where he was both University and Starr medallist in medicine in 1872. Finding the intellectual atmosphere of Canada stifling, he immigrated to England where, while practising medicine, he spent most of the rest of his life attempting to write a synthetic history of the evolution of the human intellect. Publications of Dr. Crozier, who achieved a considerable degree of eminence within British philosophical and literary circles, included *The Religion of the Future* (1880), *Civilization and Progress* (1885), *History of Intellectual Development* I (1897), II (1901), and *Last Words on Great Issues* (1917). For estimates of Crozier's career and philosophy, see Arnold Haultain, "A Search for an Ideal," *Canadian Magazine* XXII (Mar. 1904), 427–30; "Death of Dr. Beattie Crozier; Philosopher and Social Economist; Services to Speculative Thought," *Times* (London), 10 Jan. 1921, p. 15.
23. W. D. LeSueur, "Old and New in Canada," *CMNR* VII (Jan. 1875), 1–9.
24. W. D. LeSueur, "The Intellectual Life," *CMNR* VII (Apr. 1875), 321–2.
25. Ibid., 320.
26. W. D. LeSueur, "Idealism in Life," *CMNR* XIII (Apr. 1878), 414–15.
27. "Intellectual Life," 322.
28. W. D. LeSueur, "Free Thought and Responsible Thought," *RBCM* VIII (June 1882), 616.

29. For discussions of what might be termed the "morphology of piety," see Emile Durkheim, *The Elementary Forms of the Religious Life* (London, 1964), 36–42; Robert A. Nisbet, *The Sociological Tradition* (New York, 1966), 261–3; George Santayana, *The Life of Reason*, 1 vol. ed. (New York, 1955), 258 passim.
30. "Intellectual Life," 323–4.
31. Ibid.
32. Maurice Mandelbaum, *History, Man, and Reason: A Study in Nineteenth-Century Thought* (Baltimore, 1974), 199.
33. Edward Alexander, *Matthew Arnold and John Stuart Mill* (New York, 1965), 1. See also 12, 243.
34. "Free Thought and Responsible Thought," 615.
35. "Intellectual Life," 328.
36. "Free Thought and Responsible Thought," 615.
37. "Intellectual Life," 322–3. Emphasis in original.
38. Ibid., 320.
39. Hegel quoted in Mandelbaum, *History*, 175.
40. "Intellectual Life," 325.
41. Ibid., 323–4.
42. "Free Thought and Responsible Thought," 615–16.
43. Nicola Abbagnano, "Positivism," in Paul Edwards, ed., *The Encyclopedia of Philosophy* (New York, 1967), VI, 414. See also Abraham Kaplan, "Positivism," *International Encyclopedia of the Social Sciences* (New York, 1968), XII, 389; Stanislav Andreski, ed., *The Essential Comte* (New York, 1974), 7–18.
44. W. D. LeSueur, "Liberty of Thought and Discussion," *CMNR* X (Sept. 1876), 202–12. LeSueur's article was a critical review of Stephen's book *Liberty, Equality, Fraternity* (1872). The title of LeSueur's essay is essentially the same as those of the second chapter of both Mill's *On Liberty* and Stephen's *Liberty, Equality, Fraternity*. Fitzjames Stephen's argument for limiting the toleration of free discussion was based on the assumption (to use his own words) that "people should not talk about what they do not understand" and that "most people have no right to any opinions whatever ... except in so far as they are necessary for the regulation of their own affairs." It should be added that LeSueur doubtless took umbrage at Stephen's book because much of it (chaps. 4 to 6) was a devastating attack on the political manifestations of the positivist religion of humanity. For an excellent treatment of the premises from which Stephen worked in formulating his views, see introduction to R. J. White, ed., *Liberty, Equality, Fraternity* (Cambridge, 1967), 1–18.
45. "Free Thought and Responsible Thought," 614.
46. Ibid., 618–19.
47. See Auguste Comte, "Plan of the Scientific Operations Necessary for Reorganizing Society," in Philip Rieff, ed., *On Intellectuals*

(New York, 1969), 277ff.; Mandelbaum, *History*, 164–74; W. M. Simon, *European Positivism in the Nineteenth Century* (Ithaca, 1963), 4.
48. Cited in Alexander, *Arnold and Mill*, 6.
49. W. D. LeSueur, "The Poetry of Matthew Arnold," *CMNR* I, no. 3 (Mar. 1872), 222. See also Lionel Trilling, *Matthew Arnold* (New York, 1955), 175. Emphasis in original.
50. "Poetry of Arnold," 222.
51. Trilling, *Arnold*, 103; also 80–3.
52. "Poetry of Arnold," 229.
53. Ibid.
54. "A Few Words on Criticism," *RBCM* III (Sept. 1879), 325–6.
55. Trilling, *Arnold*, 241–2.
56. "Idealism in Life," 415, 417, 415–16.
57. Carter, *Spiritual Crisis*; Frank Miller Turner, *Between Science and Religion* (London, 1974), 1–37, 247–56; John Dillenberger, *Protestant Thought and Natural Science* (New York, 1960), 217–38ff.; Richard D. Altick, *Victorian People and Ideas* (New York, 1973), 226–37.
58. "A Few Words on Criticism," 325–6.
59. "Morality and Religion" (unsigned editorial), Toronto *Mail*, 10 Jan. 1880, p. 2.
60. See D. H. MacVicar, *Recent Aspects of Materialism: being a Lecture Delivered at the Opening of the Session of 1871–72, of the Presbyterian College, Montreal* (Montreal, 1871), 1–11; Rev. James Carmichael, *Design and Darwinism* (Toronto, 1880), 5; Surena, "Modern Scepticism," *CMNR* II (Aug. 1872), 173; "Round the Table," *CMNR* XI (May 1877), 547–8; G, "The Marvels of Scientific Logic," *RBCM* V (Oct. 1880), 361–71. For an indication of the plight in which men suspended between the worlds of religion and science could find themselves, see these articles on W. E. Mallock by R. W. Boodle: "Modern Pessimism," *RBCM* III (June 1879), 591–601; "Mr. Mallock's 'Romance of the 19th C'—A Review," *RBCM* VII (Sept. 1881), 322–7; "Mr. Mallock: A Retrospect," *RBCM* VI (Feb. 1881), 195–203.
61. Each of these examples is drawn from MacVicar, *Recent Aspects of Materialism*, 3–4. In a prefatory note to this pamphlet, MacVicar noted that "the arguments advanced against Materialism were delivered *in substance* in the Class-room three years ago, and in several respects more fully developed than in their present form."
62. For Tyndall's address and a discussion of the context in which it was delivered, see George Basalla, William Coleman, and Robert H. Kargon, eds., *Victorian Science: A Self-Portrait from the Presidential Addresses to the British Association for the Advancement of Science* (New York, 1970), 436–78. The quotation from Tyndall is drawn from pp. 474–5. Emphasis in original.

63. Ibid., 437.
64. Alexander Johnson, *Science and Religion: an Address Delivered at the Convocation of McGill University, May 1st, 1876, to the Bachelors of Applied Science* (Montreal, 1876), 6–7. The address was originally published in the Montreal press at the request of the students.
65. Articles which bear directly on the controversy include John Tyndall, "Reply to the Critics of the Belfast Address," *CMNR* VII (Feb. 1875), 183–95; "Current Literature" (editorial note), *CMNR* VIII (Dec. 1875), 549–51; John Tyndall, "'Materialism' and Its Opponents," *CMNR* IX (Jan. 1876), 56–68; Rev. James Martineau, "Modern Materialism: Its Attitude Towards Theology," *CMNR* IX (Mar. 1876), 223–37.
66. "The essay, though clearly favouring the possibility of answered prayer," wrote F. M. Turner, "revealed neither zeal for orthodoxy nor firm adherence to naturalistic opinion. Rather, it sought to fend off the dogmatic claims of both positions." The biographical information and quotations are drawn from "George John Romanes: From Faith to Faith," chap. 6 in Turner, *Between Science and Religion*, 134–63.
67. The debate was heralded by a detailed review of Romanes's book in *CMNR* VII (Mar. 1875), 284–6. It was launched, however, by an article by Agnes Maule Machar which reviewed the prayer question as it had evolved in England (and as set forth in an appendix to Romanes's book entitled, "The Physical Efficacy of Prayer"): see A. M. Machar, "Prayer for Daily Bread," *CMNR* VII (May 1875), 415–25. This was followed by LeSueur's rebuttal, "Prayer and Modern Thought," *CMNR* VIII (Aug. 1875), 145–55. After the publication of these two articles, the debate proceeded apace: Fidelis, "Prayer and Modern Doubt," *CMNR* VIII (Sept. 1875), 224–36; idem, "Prayer and Christian Belief," *CMNR* VIII (Oct. 1875), 328–34; S. E. Dawson, "Prayer and Modern Science," *CMNR* VIII (Dec. 1875), 512–22; George J. Romanes, "The Physical Efficacy of Prayer," *CMNR* IX (Mar. 1876), 211–21; Fidelis, "The Divine Law of Prayer," *CMNR* X (Aug. 1876), 144–5.
68. Owen Chadwick, *The Secularization of the European Mind in the Nineteenth Century* (Cambridge, 1977), 16.
69. See Goldwin Smith, "The Immortality of the Soul," *CMNR* IX (May 1876), 406–16; Fidelis, "The Seen and the Unseen," *CMNR* IX (June 1876), 495–508; Professor J. E. Wells, "Evolution and Immortality," *CMNR* X (Oct. 1876), 291–8; W. J. R. [W. J. Rattray], "Man Here and Hereafter," *Belford's Monthly Magazine* III (May 1878), 757–78; A. W. Gundry, "Spencer's 'Data of Ethics,'" *RBCM* III (Dec. 1879), 646–50; Goldwin Smith, "The Prospect of a Moral Interregnum" [a revised version of an article published slightly earlier in *Atlantic Monthly*], *RBCM* III (Dec. 1879), 651–63;

G. A. M., "Mr. Goldwin Smith's *Atlantic Monthly* Article," *RBCM* III (Dec. 1879), 663–5; W. D. LeSueur, "The Future of Morality," *RBCM* IV (Jan. 1880), 74–82; idem, "Morality and Religion," *RBCM* IV (Feb. 1880), 166–71; Rev. J. F. Stevenson, "Morality and the Gospel," *RBCM* IV (Apr. 1880), 335–42; Fidelis, "The Source of Moral Life," *RBCM* IV (Apr. 1880), 343–51; W. D. LeSueur, "Mr. Spencer and His Critics," *RBCM* IV (Apr. 1880), 413–22; idem, "Morality and Religion Again.—A Word With My Critics," *RBCM* IV (June 1880), 642–55; idem, "Mr. Goldwin Smith on 'The Data of Ethics,'" *PSM* XXII (Dec. 1882), 145–56.

70. See John Watson, "A Phase of Modern Thought," *RBCM*, n.s. III (Nov. 1879), 457–72.

71. See G. J. Romanes's critique of LeSueur's first article on the prayer question, in "The Physical Efficacy of Prayer."

72. LeSueur's essay criticizing Fiske was "Evolution and the Destiny of Man," *PSM* XXVI (Feb. 1885), 456–68; his essay on Lyman Abbott was "Evolution Bounded by Theology," *PSM* XXIX (June 1886), 145–53; on Porter, "Ex-President Porter on Evolution," *PSM* XXIX (Sept. 1886), 577–94. LeSueur's debate with G. M. Grant began with a discussion of the merits of the theological claims made by the American evangelists, Dwight L. Moody and Ira Sankey, but soon broadened to a full discussion of the place of Christianity itself in "modern culture." LeSueur wrote under the pseudonym "Laon," but by 1885 Laon had been identified in print: see William Cushing, ed., *Initials and Pseudonyms*, rev. ed., 1st ser. (New York, 1885), 165. The author is indebted to Ms. Marilyn G. Flitton for this last reference. The Laon-Grant debate consisted of the following pieces: Laon, "Messrs. Moody and Sankey and Revivalism,"*CMNR* VII (June 1875), 510–13; Rev. G. M. Grant, "Laon on 'Messrs. Moody and Sankey and Revivalism,'" *CMNR* VIII (Sept. 1875), 250–5; Laon, "Proofs and Disproofs," *CMNR* VIII (Nov. 1875), 437–41; Laon, "Modern Culture and Christianity," *CMNR* VIII (Dec. 1875), 523–33. For the debate with Bishop John Travers Lewis, see *Agnosticism—a lecture Delivered in St. George's Hall, Kingston, on the Occasion of the Meeting of the Synod of the Diocese, June 12, 1883, by the Lord Bishop of Ontario* (Kingston, 1883), 32; W. D. LeSueur, *A Defence of Modern Thought. In Reply to a Recent Pamphlet, by the Bishop of Ontario* (Toronto, 1884), 40 (a shorter version appeared as "A Defence of Modern Thought," *PSM* XXIV [Apr. 1884], 780–93); Vindex, *A Criticism of Mr. W. D. LeSueur's Pamphlet, entitled "Defence of Modern Thought"* (n.p., n.d.), 16; W. D. LeSueur, *Evolution and the Positive Aspects of Modern Thought. In Reply to the Bishop of Ontario's Second Lecture on "Agnosticism"* (Ottawa, 1884), 43. I have been unable to locate a copy of Lewis's second lecture.

73. LeSueur, "Science and Materialism," *CMNR* XI (Jan. 1877), 24–6.

74. W. D. LeSueur, "Science and Its Accusers," *PSM* xxxiv (Jan. 1889), 375, 379.
75. G, "The Marvels of Scientific Logic," *RBCM* v (Oct. 1880), 361, 371.
76. "Ex-President Porter on Evolution," 577.
77. "The Scientific Spirit," *RBCM* iii (Oct. 1879), 438.
78. Ibid., 439, 441.
79. C. W. Parkin, "Diderot and Materialism," *RBCM* vii (Dec. 1881), 642. Emphasis in original.
80. Alfred North Whitehead, *Science and the Modern World* (New York, 1967), 57. Emphasis in original.
81. Robert M. Young, *Mind, Brain and Adaptation in the Nineteenth Century* (Oxford, 1970), 2.
82. It was Vogt who had pronounced, in his *Physiological Epistles* (1847), that "the brain secretes thought just as the liver secretes bile." See chap. 2, "Materialism, Naturalism and Agnosticism," in John Passmore, *A Hundred Years of Philosophy* (Harmondsworth, Middlesex, 1970), 35–47, for background and context.
83. See Daniel Clark, "Physiology in Thought, Conduct and Belief," *RBCM* vi (Apr. 1881), 363–77; R. M. Bucke, "The Correlation of the Vital and Physical Forces," *British American Journal* iii (May, June, July 1862), 161–7, 225–38; idem, "The Moral Nature and the Great Sympathetic," *American Journal of Insanity* xxxv (Oct. 1878), 229–53; James Horne, "R. M. Bucke: Pioneer Psychiatrist, Practical Mystic," *Ontario History* lix (1967), 197–208.
84. "Science and Materialism," 41, 64.
85. Ibid., 25.
86. "Materialism and Positivism," *PSM* xx (Mar. 1882), 617–18, 619.
87. W. D. LeSueur, "The Moral Nature and Intellectual Power," *RBCM* iii (July 1879), 104–5.
88. Ibid., 105. LeSueur's emphasis.
89. Richard Hofstadter, *Social Darwinism in American Thought* (Boston, 1970), 32. See esp. chap. 2, "The Vogue of Spencer." For a more recent estimate of the rise and decline of Spencer's reputation, see J. D. Y. Peel, *Herbert Spencer: The Evolution of a Sociologist* (New York, 1971), chap. 1, "The Man and His Work," and chap. 9, "History's Revenge."
90. From William Graham Sumner, *The Challenge of Facts*, quoted in Hofstadter, *Social Darwinism*, 58. See Richard D. Altick, *Victorian People and Ideas* (New York, 1973), 232, for an equation of "Social Darwinism" (in this sense) with the philosophy of Herbert Spencer.
91. "Evolution and the Destiny of Man," 467–8. Emphasis in original.
92. "Morality and Religion," *RBCM* iv (Feb. 1880), 169.
93. "Ex-President Porter on Evolution," 589–90, 591.
94. "A Vindication of Scientific Ethics," *PSM* xvii (July 1880), 413,

414–15. This article was originally published under the title "Mr. Spencer and His Critics," *RBCM* IV (Apr. 1880), 413–22.
95. The substance of this paragraph is drawn from Peel, *Spencer*, chap. 7, "The Organic Analogy," 166–91.
96. "Morality and Religion," 171.
97. "Evolution Bounded by Theology," 148.

Chapter 6

1. See J. Robert Barth, *Coleridge and Christian Doctrine* (Cambridge, 1969); Sherman Paul, *Emerson's Angle of Vision* (Cambridge, (1969); M. H. Abrams, *Natural Supernaturalism: Tradition and Revolution in Romantic Literature* (New York, 1973).
2. J. Hutchison Stirling, *The Secret of Hegel* (Edinburgh, 1865). See also John Passmore, *A Hundred Years of Philosophy* (Harmondsworth, Middlesex, 1970), 51; Jerome Hamilton Buckley, *The Victorian Temper* (New York, 1951), 197.
3. See William H. Goetzmann, *The American Hegelians: An Intellectual Episode in the History of Western America* (New York, 1973), 3–20; Perry Miller, ed., *American Thought: Civil War to World War One* (New York, 1954), xiii–xvii.
4. T. R. Glover and D. D. Calvin, *A Corner of Empire: The Old Ontario Strand* (Toronto, 1937), 134.
5. Quoted in Passmore, *Hundred Years*, 52–3.
6. The Reverend George Paxton Young, "An Examination of Professor Ferrier's Theory of Knowing and Being," *CJ*, n.s. I (Feb. 1856), 110, 116, 123–4.
7. The Reverend George Paxton Young, "On Sir David Brewster's Supposed Law of Visible Direction," *CJ*, n.s. II (July 1857), 272–3.
8. Daniel Wilson, "Diary," pt. 2, 26 Feb. 1889. Copy in University of Toronto Archives. For other references to Young's esteem for Berkeley, see Daniel Wilson, *Convocation Address* (Toronto, 1889), 14; John Macdonald Duncan, "George Paxton Young, LL.D.," *University of Toronto Monthly* II (Dec. 1901), 62.
9. Young, "Examination of Ferrier's Theory," 117–19.
10. Paxton Young, review of *Philosophy of Sir William Hamilton* . . . (1853), *CJ*, ser. 2, I (1856), 380. Emphasis in original.
11. Ibid., 381, 383.
12. Young, "On Brewster's Supposed Law," 275.
13. George Paxton Young, review of *Reid's Works* . . . (1854), *CJ*, ser. 2, II (1857), 285.
14. George Paxton Young, review of *Typical Forms and Special Ends in Creation*, by James McCosh and George Dickie, *CJ*, ser. 2, I (1856), 539.
15. J. A. Irving, "The Development of Philosophy in Central Canada from 1850 to 1900," *Canadian Historical Review* XXXI (1950), 268.
16. On Murray's notes on Hamilton's lectures on metaphysics and Ferrier's *Institutes of Metaphysics*, see J. C. Murray Papers, micro-

film reel 1, items 12, 13, McGill University Archives. See also Murray's student essay, "On Ferrier's Institutes of Metaphysics," ibid., item 34.
17. J. Clark Murray, "Sir William Hamilton's Philosophy: An Exposition and Criticism. I. The Scottish Philosophy," *CJ*, n.s. XI (Jan. 1867), 207.
18. Ibid., 212, 221.
19. Ibid., 222.
20. Ibid., 224.
21. Murray, "Sir William Hamilton's Philosophy... II. Exposition of Hamilton's System," *CJ*, n.s. XI (Sept. 1867). Hamilton's prose was later described by Murray as "unintelligible to the ordinary English reader of the time," owing to his studies of medieval Latin and German literature. J. Clark Murray, "The Scottish Philosophy," *Macmillan's Magazine* XXXIX (Dec. 1876), 122–3. The second and third of these articles are "Sir William Hamilton's Philosophy... III...," *CJ*, n.s. XI (Dec. 1867), 367–88; "Sir William Hamilton's Philosophy... IV...," *CJ*, n.s. XI (Dec. 1868), 57–85.
22. Murray, "Sir William Hamilton's Philosophy. III," 370, 371.
23. Quoted in ibid., 379, 380, 382–3.
24. Murray, "Sir William Hamilton's Philosophy. IV," 58–9.
25. Ibid., 69.
26. Murray, "The Scottish Philosophy," 121, 123.
27. Murray, "Sir William Hamilton's Philosophy. IV," 79–83.
28. See J. Clark Murray, "The Dualistic Conception of Nature," *The Monist* VI (Apr. 1896), 382–95.
29. Murray, "The Scottish Philosophy," 125–6.
30. "Dr. Lyall's Inaugural," *Dalhousie Gazette* II (29 Nov. 1869), 2–5; "Professor Lyall's Address," ibid. VII (21 Nov. 1874), 1–3, 7–8; "Remarks on Metaphysics—Dr. Lyall," ibid., n.s. V (29 Apr. 1880), 139–40; William Lyall, "Wordsworth. A Criticism," *Belford's Monthly Magazine* III (Apr. 1878), 612–27.
31. Goldwin Smith, "The Prospect of a Moral Interregnum," *RBCM* III (Dec. 1879), 651–63; idem, *Guesses at the Riddle of Existence and Other Essays on Kindred Subjects* (New York, 1897).
32. See "Life and Labors of Nathanael Burwash," chap. 15, "Inductive Theology," typescript, Nathanael Burwash Papers, United Church Archives, Toronto. The fruit of Burwash's effort to construct an inductive theology was his *Manual of Christian Theology on the Inductive Method*, 2 vols. (London, 1900).
33. Probably the best source (because it contains much documentary material) remains Prof. J. E. McCurdy, ed., *Life and Work of D. J. Macdonnell* (Toronto, 1897). But see "The Case of the Reverend D. J. Macdonnell," Toronto *Globe*, 5 Nov. 1875, pp. 2–3; "Rev. D. J. Macdonnell's Case," ibid., 30 Apr. 1876, p. 2.
34. J. B. Crozier, *My Inner Life: Being a Chapter in Personal Evolution and Autobiography* (New York, 1908), 1; "Death of Dr. Beattie

Crozier; Philosopher and Social Economist; Services to Speculative Thought," *Times* (London), 10 Jan. 1921, p. 15.
35. R. M. Bucke, *Man's Moral Nature: An Essay* (New York, 1879); idem, *Cosmic Consciousness: A Study in the Evolution of the Human Mind* (Philadelphia, 1901). An edition of *Cosmic Consciousness* was published by E. P. Dutton & Co., in 1923; by 1964 it had reached its twenty-second edition.
36. *Queen's Journal* xxviii (9 Nov. 1900), 43. Among student awards he received were the prize for senior logic (1869); a prize for his essay "Scientific Induction" (1869); a Coulter Prize for the best essay on Kant's *Critique of Pure Reason* (1870); the class prize in senior philosophy, awarded by student vote, "for General Eminence in the Exercises and in Examinations...," as well as the first prize for excellence in written examinations on the lectures of the session (1870); the class prizes in junior divinity and in English literature (1872); the Rector's Prize of thirty-five pounds for the best essay on Hume's influence on literature and philosophy (1872); the Buchanan Gold Medal in English Literature (1872). Harriet Watson Sweezey, "John Watson of Queen's—As Teacher and Philosopher," manuscript (n.d.), pp. 10–19, R. O. Sweezey Papers, box 1, file 11, Queen's University Archives. This manuscript will henceforth be cited as Sweezey.
37. Sweezey, 6–8.
38. John Watson, "The Idealism of Edward Caird. i," *Philosophical Review* xviii (Mar. 1909), 150. See also John Henry Muirhead, "Glasgow University in the Seventies," in *Reflections of a Journeyman in Philosophy*, ed. John W. Harvey (London, 1942), 29.
39. Sweezey, 8.
40. John Watson, "Edward Caird as Teacher and Thinker," *Queen's Quarterly* xvi (April, May, June 1909), 304. For evidence of Caird's antitraditional views, see G. E. Davies, *The Democratic Intellect* (Edinburgh, 1961), 84–7.
41. John Watson, "Edward Caird," *Philosophical Review* xviii (Jan. 1909), 108.
42. On Carlyle's influence on Caird, see Edward Caird, "The Genius of Carlyle," *Essays on Literature* (Glasgow, 1909), 217–50; Sir Henry Jones and John Henry Muirhead, *The Life and Philosophy of Edward Caird* (Glasgow, 1921), 22–6; Watson, "The Idealism of Edward Caird. i," 151–2; Muirhead, "Glasgow University," 31–2.
43. Watson, "The Idealism of Edward Caird. i," 155–8 passim.
44. Ibid., 158–9.
45. Ibid., 160, 157. Compare with the passage in which J. Hutchison Stirling reveals Hegel's "secret": Stirling, *Secret of Hegel*, 96–7. Caird used Stirling's book in his class. See Muirhead, "Glasgow University," 34.
46. Watson, "Edward Caird as Teacher and Thinker," 304–5. For the testimony of another of Caird pupils to become of major philo-

sophical importance, see Muirhead, "Glasgow University," 35–6.
47. John Watson Papers, box 1, scrapbook 4–5, Queen's University Archives. The address is also reprinted, with variations in wording, in George Basalla et al., eds., *Victorian Science* (New York, 1970), 418–19 passim.
48. John Watson, *The Relation of Philosophy to Science. An Inaugural Lecture* ... (Kingston, 1872), 3–5. Put another way, the leading idea of Watson's system was "the internal relation of all entities." Clifford J. Williams, "The Political Philosophy of Two Canadians: John Watson and Wilfred Currier Keirstead," M.A. thesis, University of Western Ontario, 1952, p. 1.
49. Watson, *Relation of Philosophy to Science*, 6, 8–9.
50. Ibid., 9, 10, 13–14.
51. Ibid., 22.
52. Ibid., 23.
53. Ibid., 26–7.
54. Ibid., 28–32. Emphasis in original.
55. Ibid., 32.
56. Walter Houghton, *The Victorian Frame of Mind* (New Haven, 1967), 1–23; Asa Briggs, *The Age of Improvement* (London, 1969), 394–402; W. L. Burn, *The Age of Equipoise* (New York, 1965).
57. Watson, *Relation of Philosophy to Science*, 36–7.
58. Ibid.
59. Miller, *American Thought*, xiii.
60. John Watson, *An Outline of Philosophy: Comte, Mill and Spencer*, 3rd ed. (Glasgow, 1901), xi–xxi et seq.
61. J. Clark Murray, "Atomism and Theism," *CMNR* VII (Jan. 1875), 31–9.
62. Ibid., 36.
63. Ibid., 39.
64. John Tyndall, "'Materialism' and Its Opponents," *CMNR* IX (Jan. 1876), 56–68; Rev. James Martineau, "Modern Materialism: Its Attitude Towards Theology," *CMNR* IX (Mar. 1876), 223–37.
65. John Watson, "Science and Religion, A Reply to Prof. Tyndall on 'Materialism and Its Opponents,'" *CMNR* IX (May 1876), 384.
66. Ibid., 385, 395, 396–7. Emphasis in original. For a later critique of Tyndall, less respectful of the British physicist for having thrown in his lot with Herbert Spencer, see John Watson, "Professor Tyndall's 'Materialism,'" *RBCM* I (1878), 282–8.
67. John Watson, "Darwinism and Morality," *CMNR* X (Oct. 1876), 319–26; Goldwin Smith, "The Immortality of the Soul," *CMNR* IX (May 1876), 408–16. Compare Watson's reply with J. E. Wells's meandering attempt, "Evolution and Immortality," *CMNR* X (Oct. 1876), 291–8.
68. J. A. Allen, "The Evolution of Morality. A Reply," *CMNR* XI (May 1877), 490–501; John Watson, "The Ethical Aspects of Darwinism: A Rejoinder," *CMNR* XI (June 1877), 638–44.

69. Allen, "Evolution of Morality," 501n.
70. John Watson, "The Relativity of Knowledge. An Examination of the Doctrine as held by Mr. Herbert Spencer," *Journal of Speculative Philosophy* xi (Jan. 1877), 48. Watson had earlier criticized the British empirical tradition at the international level. See "Empiricism and Common Logic," ibid. x (Jan. 1876), 17–36; "Kant's Reply to Hume," ibid. x (Apr. 1876), 113–34.
71. John Watson, "The World as Force. With Especial Reference to the Philosophy of Mr. Herbert Spencer," *Journal of Speculative Philosophy* xii (Apr. 1878), 113–37; idem, "The World as Force... ii. Indestructibility of Matter," ibid. xiii (Apr. 1879), 151–79; idem, "Kant's Principles of Judgement," ibid. xiv (Oct. 1880), 376–98.
72. Later published in the *Journal of Speculative Philosophy* xv (Oct. 1881), 337–60.
73. Spencer to Richard Hodgson, 17 Jan. 1883, in David Duncan, *The Life and Letters of Herbert Spencer* (London, 1911), 228.
74. Spencer to G. Croom Robertson, 22 Jan. 1883, ibid., 229.
75. John Watson, "Kant on the Infinite Divisibility of Space," *Journal of Speculative Philosophy* xx (Apr. 1886), 219–21; "Mr. Spencer's Derivation of Space," *Mind* xv (Oct. 1890), 537–44.
76. John Watson, *The Philosophy of Kant as Contained in Extracts from his own Writings* (Glasgow, 1891, 1894, 1897, 1908, 1919, 1923). For an indication of the critical reception, see *Scottish Leader*, 16 Aug. 1888; *Athenaeum*, 22 Sept. 1888; *The Week*, 4 Oct. 1888; *RBCM* vii (Sept. 1881), 327–9. Watson's daughter, after checking with authorities at Harvard University, found it in use in 1936 (Sweezey, 56). Professor Ramsay Cook, of the Department of History, York University, has told me that he had used the book as an undergraduate at the University of Manitoba in the 1950s.
77. "Dr. Watson's Work," clipping, Kingston *News* (n.d.), Watson Review Scrapbook, Queen's University Archives.
78. See John A. Irving, "One Hundred Years of Canadian Philosophy," in *Philosophy in Canada: A Symposium* (Toronto, 1952), 6–26.
79. Watson, *Relation of Philosophy to Science*, 32, 34–5. It should be noted that the ideas of freedom and necessity had been the subjects of a controversial address by Paxton Young. See Paxton Young, *Freedom and Necessity: A Lecture* (Toronto, 1870), 19; Rev. A. Carman, *Prof. Young's Doctrine of "Freedom and Necessity" Reviewed* (Belleville, 1872), 26.
80. Watson, *Relation of Philosophy to Science*, 35–6.
81. Quoted in Terry Cook, "George R. Parkin and the Concept of Britannic Idealism," *Journal of Canadian Studies* x (Aug. 1975), 25.
82. Watson, *Outline of Philosophy*, 211, 212.
83. Ibid., 245.
84. Ibid., 227.
85. Ibid., 229.

86. Ibid., 235-48.
87. Ibid., 229-30.
88. Ibid., 232-3.
89. See Stephen Leacock, *The Social Criticism of Stephen Leacock,* ed. and introd. Alan Bowker (Toronto, 1973), esp. 41-50; Andrew Macphail, "Certain Varieties of the Apples of Sodom," *University Magazine* x (Feb. 1911); Pelham Edgar, "A Confession of Faith and a Protest," ibid. VIII (Apr. 1909); A. B. McKillop, "Science, Values, and *The Canadian Forum,* 1920-1927," ms. in the possession of the author; J. W. Carey, "Harold Adams Innis and Marshall McLuhan," *Antioch Review* XXVII (1967); H. A. Innis, *Empire and Communications,* rev. ed. (Toronto, 1972); George Woodcock, "A Nation's Odyssey: The Novels of Hugh MacLennan," in A. J. M. Smith, ed., *Masks of Fiction* (Toronto, 1961); P. A. Morley, *The Immoral Moralists* (Toronto, 1972); Donald Creighton, *Towards the Discovery of Canada* (Toronto, 1972); G. P. Grant, *Philosophy in the Mass Age* (Toronto, 1966); idem, *Lament for a Nation* (Toronto, 1970); idem, *Technology and Empire* (Toronto, 1969); Northrop Frye, "Culture and the National Will" (convocation address at Carleton University, 1957); idem, *The Modern Century* (Toronto, 1967); idem, *The Critical Path: An Essay on the Social Context of Literary Criticism* (Bloomington, 1973).
90. See John Watson, *Christianity and Idealism* (Glasgow, 1897); *The Philosophical Basis of Religion* (Glasgow, 1907); *The Interpretation of Religious Experience,* 2 vols. (Glasgow, 1912); *The State in Peace and War* (Glasgow, 1919).
91. John Watson, *Education and Life. An Address...* (Kingston, 1873), 8ff.
92. *Queen's Journal* (30 Oct. 1888), 183. See also ibid. (22 Nov. 1887), 10-12; "The Ideal Life," ibid. (26 Feb. 1888), 101-4; "The University and the State," ibid. (26 Nov. 1898), 23-8; "The Higher Life of the Scholar," ibid. (21 Dec. 1899), 88-92.
93. Prof. Archibald MacMechan, "Reminiscences of Toronto University" (n.p., n.d.), 7. See also idem, "George Paxton Young. An Acknowledgement of Debt," *University of Toronto Monthly* VIII (Mar. 1907), 110-15, VIII (Apr. 1907), 138-43; R. F. B., "Professor Young, LL.D. of University College, Toronto," *Dalhousie Gazette* XXI (14 Mar. 1889), 125-7.
94. John Macdonald Duncan, "George Paxton Young, LL.D.," *University of Toronto Monthly* II (Dec. 1901), 61; James Gibson Hume, *The Value of a Study of Ethics. An Inaugural Lecture* (Toronto, 1891), 23.
95. *Memorials of Chancellor W. H. Blake, Bishop John Strachan, Professor H. H. Croft, and Professor G. P. Young...* (Toronto, 1894), 13 (this testimonial was by W. J. Robertson); Duncan, "George Paxton Young," 61-2; W. H. Blake, "Professor Young in his Lec-

ture-Room," *University of Toronto Monthly* II (Dec. 1901), 63–5; J. G. Hume, "Professor George Paxton Young," ibid. xxviii (Oct. 1927), 21–2; Daniel Wilson, "Diary," pt. 2, 26 Feb. 1889.

96. James Mark Baldwin, *Philosophy: Its Relation to Life and Education* (Toronto, 1890), 6. Baldwin left Toronto in 1893 for Princeton, where he became one of the most eminent public moralists in America. See R. Jackson Wilson, *In Quest of Community: Social Philosophy in the United States, 1860–1920* (New York, 1970), 60–86, for an excellent portrait of Baldwin as "Conservator of Moral Community."

97. Hume, *Value of a Study of Ethics*, 15–16. For the writings of other idealists at the University of Toronto in the 1890s, see Albert H. Abbott, "Thoughts on Philosophy," *University of Toronto Quarterly* II (Jan. 1896), 133–47; A. W. Crawford, "Empiricism and Metaphysics," ibid., 148–54; A. M. Vicar, "The Relation of Philosophy to Religion," ibid. II (Mar. 1896), 196–205.

98. J. Gould Schurman, *Kantian Ethics and the Ethics of Evolution: A Critical Study* (London, 1881), 103.

99. *Journal of Speculative Philosophy* xvii (1883), 101–4.

100. For reports of Schurman's addresses and estimates of him in general, see *Dalhousie Gazette* xiv (7 Apr. 1882), 121–4; ibid. xv (11 Nov. 1882), 2–9; ibid. xv (9 Feb. 1883), 85; ibid. xviii (16 Jan. 1886), 67–9; ibid. xviii (27 Mar. 1886), 129–30; ibid. xx (17 Dec. 1887), 41–2.

101. Quoted in a review of *The Ethical Import of Darwinism* (London, 1888), in *Mind* xiii (1888), 127.

102. John Watson, "The Critical Philosophy and Idealism," *Philosophical Review* I (Jan. 1892), 9–23.

103. "Autocracy in McGill College," *The Week* (5 July 1888), 507. Murray's Honours course in 1888 drew thirty-one students; that of Dawson, twenty-two. W. H., "Professor J. Clark Murray," *University Magazine* xvii (1918), 565.

104. "Philosophy in Canada" (n.p., n.d.), Clark Murray Papers, microfilm reel no. 1, Clark Murray scrapbook 27, McGill University Archives. For evidence that Murray's idealism continued into the twentieth century, see his review of G. J. Blewett's *The Study of Nature and the Vision of God* (1907), in *University of Toronto Monthly* vii (June 1907), 202–5.

105. W. H., "Professor J. Clark Murray," 565.

106. *A Handbook of Psychology*, 2 vols., 2nd ed. (Paisley and London, 1885); *An Introduction to Ethics*, 2 vols. (Boston, 1891). For a criticism from Queen's that in the former Murray had not successfully overcome the dualism of his Common Sense days, see *Queen's Journal* xiii (9 Dec. 1885), 48–50. See Irving, "One Hundred Years of Canadian Philosophy," 6–7.

107. John Clark Murray, "The Education of the Will," *Educational Review* (June 1891), 57, 62.

Chapter 7

1. James Loudon, *Convocation Address* (Toronto, 1877).
2. John Watson, *The Relation of Philosophy to Science* (Kingston, 1872), 18. For the social and political context of the transformation of Canada, see R. C. Brown and Ramsay Cook, *Canada, 1896–1921: A Nation Transformed* (Toronto, 1974).
3. For the influence of idealism on, for example, a Canadian imperialist and a Canadian poet, see Terry Cook, "George R. Parkin and the Concept of Britannic Idealism," *Journal of Canadian Studies* x (1975); John Robert Sorfleet, "Transcendentalist, Mystic, Evolutionary Idealist: Bliss Carman, 1886–1894," in George Woodcock, ed., *Colony and Confederation* (Vancouver, 1974).
4. John Watson, "The Sadness and Joy of Knowledge," pt. II, *Queen's Journal* (29 Mar. 1901), 260.
5. John Watson, "The Sadness and Joy of Knowledge," pt. I, *Queen's Journal* (15 Mar. 1901), 233.
6. The Editors, "Salutatory," *Queen's Quarterly* I (July 1893), 1–2.
7. John Watson, "The Middle Ages and the Reformation," *Queen's Quarterly* I (July 1893), 6–11.
8. See editor's note, *Queen's Quarterly* I (July 1893), 88–91.
9. The institute in question was the District Institute for the Extension of University Teaching in Old Testament Literature and History and the History of the Christian Church, run under the auspices of the Educational Society of the Methodist Church and the General Sunday School and Epworth League Board. Its secretary-treasurer and main organizer was Rev. A. E. Lavell, who also instructed there. Other instructors were Rev. Eber Crummy and Rev. A. J. Irwin. The instructor quoted in the passages in the text is Crummy. See Albert Carman Papers, vol. 18, Archives of the United Church of Canada, Toronto, for more details about the institute.
10. Rev. C. T. Scott to Carman, 28 Feb. 1906, Carman Papers, vol. 18, no. 123.
11. Ibid.
12. On Workman's continued following, see C. B. Sissons, *A History of Victoria University* (Toronto, 1952), 192–3; on Burwash and idealism, see R. J. Taylor, "The Darwinian Revolution: The Responses of Four Canadian Scholars," Ph.D. diss., McMaster University, 1976, p. 236.
13. George John Blewett, *The Study of Nature and the Vision of God: With Other Essays in Philosophy* (Toronto, 1907), viii.
14. Ibid., 8, 265.
15. C. Keenleyside to Carman, 22 Feb. 1906, "Reported from the Crummy-Irwin-Lavell Meetings," Carman Papers, vol. 18, no. 123.
16. J. M. Grant to John Watson, 10 Nov. 1911; Watson to Grant, 16 Nov. 1911, John Watson Papers, Archives of Queen's University, Kingston.

17. Grant to Watson, 15 Sept. 1913; Watson to Grant, 18 Sept. 1913; Grant to Watson, 22 Sept. 1913, Watson Papers.
18. Grant to Watson, 13 May 1914. See also Grant to Watson, 15 Dec. 1913, Watson Papers.
19. Watson to Grant, 17 May 1914, Watson Papers.
20. John Passmore, "Darwin's Impact on British Metaphysics," *Victorian Studies* III (1959–60), 52–3.
21. Grant to Watson, 7 June 1914, Watson Papers. See also Watson to Grant, 13 Mar. 1917; Grant to Watson, 16 Mar. 1917; Grant to Watson, 16 Apr. 1916; Watson to Grant, 22 Apr. 1916; Grant to Watson, 7 Mar. 1917; Grant to Watson, 6 Apr. 1918; Watson to Grant, 10, 19 Apr. 1918. By 1918 Watson's patience had worn thin. His last letter to Grant was short. "Dear Mr. Grant ... I don't think I care to say any more about Christian Science, which to my mind is based upon indefinite thinking."
22. Watson to Grant, 17 May 1914, Watson Papers.
23. G. M. Grant, "Practical Preaching," typescript (n.d.), p. 1, G. M. Grant Papers, vol. 16, Public Archives of Canada, Ottawa; untitled manuscript sermon (n.d.), ibid., vol. 21, p. 3.
24. G. M. Grant, "An Old Teacher to his Young Canada," *Ontario Monthly* (May 1900), 84.
25. G. M. Grant, "The Relation of Religion to Secular Life," *RBCM* v (Dec. 1880), 619. For further evidence of Grant's organicism and of his rejection of dualisms, see his "Baccalaureate Sermon," *Queen's Journal* XXVI (29 Apr. 1899), 187.
26. The late Dr. Hilda Neatby once told me that as a young student on the prairies, she several times met enthusiastic teachers who had graduated from Queen's and expected respect by simple mention of the fact that they had been "students of Watson." For statistics that compare the percentage of Queen's graduates teaching in the collegiate institutes and high schools of Ontario with those of other Canadian universities, see Daniel Miner Gordon Papers, vol. 3, Archives of Queen's University, Kingston.
27. The scope of this chapter precludes treatment of a broad number of individuals. Yet another, very much infected by the "Queen's spirit" of the 1880s and 1890s, was Alfred Fitzpatrick, the founder of Frontier College. Fitzpatrick had taken his Bachelor of Arts degree there in 1889 and attended its Theological College from 1889 to 1892. During this time he became dedicated to the proposition that education and everyday life must not be separated, and he sought throughout his life to make the sacred and the secular meet. G. M. Grant was the greatest influence on his life, and when he wrote a book (never published) entitled "Schools and Other Penitentiaries," he dedicated it to "the memory of George Munro Grant, Canada's Greatest Force and Personality in Education and Statesmanship" (Frontier College Papers, vol. 194, Public Archives of Canada, Ottawa).

28. Toronto *Daily Star*, 24 June 1930. See also Salem Bland, "Memories of Old Kingston," ibid., 30 July, 2, 4 Aug. 1938. Bland's notes from Watson's courses are in the Salem Bland Papers, vol. 9, nos. 811, 812, Archives of the United Church of Canada, Toronto.
29. Quoted in Richard Allen, "Salem Bland and the Social Gospel in Canada," M.A. thesis, University of Saskatchewan, 1961, p. 52.
30. Salem Bland, "A Philosophy of Life," 26 Nov. 1925, Bland Papers, vol. 2, no. 158.
31. Salem Bland, "The Kingdom of God realized only in Individual Regeneration," 18 Jan. 1899, Bland Papers, vol. 4, no. 356. Emphasis in original. Bland's early years are treated in detail in Richard Allen, "Salem Bland: The Young Preacher," *The Bulletin* [of the Committee on Archives of the United Church of Canada], no. 26 (1977), 75–93.
32. Salem Bland, "A Contribution to a Possible Sketch of My Life" (n.d.), Bland Papers, vol. 9, no. 726.
33. Salem Bland, "The Place of the Kingdom of God in the Preaching of Today," unidentified newspaper clipping, 12 Feb. 1906, Bland Papers, vol. 3, no. 235. See also Richard Allen, "Children of Prophecy: Wesley College Students in an Age of Reform," *Red River Valley Historian* (1974), 15–20.
34. See Salem Bland, "A Faith Rational But Not Rationalistic," sermon, 22 Oct. 1921, Bland Papers, vol. 6, no. 544; "The Religiousness of Reason" (n.d.), vol. 9, no. 810; "Pre-eminence of Christ and Theology. Lecture III," 30 May 1914, vol. 3, no. 232.
35. Salem Bland, "The Deeper Life—Not Materialistic Enough," *Grain Growers Guide* (5 June 1918). Bland's statement echoed the 1913 comment of a Presbyterian clergyman, who began a Presbyterian assembly address entitled "The Messenger" by saying: "The task assigned to a Canadian preacher resembles nothing too much as the general managership of a big department store" (Rev. G. B. Wilson, in *Pre-Assembly Congress: Addresses delivered at the Presbyterian Pre-Assembly Congress, Held in Massey Hall...* [Toronto, 1913], 32).
36. Bland, "The Deeper Life."
37. See J. Warren Caldwell, "The Unification of Methodism in Canada, 1865–1884," *The Bulletin*, no. 19 (1967); William H. Magney, "The Methodist Church and the National Gospel," ibid., no. 20 (1968); Burkhard Kiesekamp, "Presbyterian and Methodist Divines: Their Case for a National Church in Canada, 1875–1900," *Studies in Religion* II (1973).
38. Quoted in K. W. McNaught, *A Prophet in Politics* (Toronto, 1963), 10, 14–16, 48n. See also William H. Brooks, "The Uniqueness of Western Canadian Methodism, 1840–1925," *The Bulletin*, no. 26 (1977), 68–9, 73n.
39. Blewett, *Study of Nature and the Vision of God*, 354. For a description of Woodsworth's view of the nature of religion by 1920, see

Richard Allen, *The Social Passion* (Toronto, 1971), 101–2. No attempt is made in this chapter to provide a comprehensive summary of the origins and course of the social gospel movement in Canada. For such treatment *The Social Passion* should be consulted. See also George N. Emery, "The Origins of Canadian Methodist Involvement in the Social Gospel Movement, 1890–1914," *The Bulletin*, no. 26 (1977), 104–19.

40. Nathanael Burwash, "The Study of Nature and the Vision of God," Nathanael Burwash Papers, United Church Archives, Toronto. (When I originally examined them, the Burwash Papers were completely unorganized and not placed in distinct volumes.) Precisely the kind of criticism given voice by Burwash here had been made in the late nineteenth century. See Donald Ross, "A Present Trend," *Queen's Quarterly* I (July 1893), 12–17.

41. S. D. Chown, "Socialism & The Social Teachings of Jesus, Vanc. Feb. 14, 1914," p. 6, S. D. Chown Papers, vol. 2, no. 58b, Archives of the United Church of Canada, Toronto.

42. S. D. Chown, "Sociology Course. Lecture II. The Relation of Sociology to the Kingdom of Heaven," pp. 1–2, Chown Papers, vol. 2, no. 51a; idem, "Sociological Course. Lecture I. Importance of the Study of Sociology," pp. 1–2, Chown Papers, vol. 2, no. 50b.

43. Chown, "Lecture I," p. 2. For other lectures by Chown which stressed the sociological concerns of Christianity, see "Sociological Course. Lecture III. Socialism and the Social Teachings of Jesus"; "Sociological Course. Lecture IV. The Problem of Political Purity," both in Chown Papers, vol. 2, nos. 52a and 52b; "The Preacher's Study of Sociology," Chown Papers, vol. 2, no. 60b.

44. "Sociological Course. Lecture II," p. 12. For an examination of the classical ideal and its relationship to philosophical idealism, see S. E. D. Shortt, *The Search for an Ideal* (Toronto, 1976), 59–76. See also H. Richard Niebuhr, *Christ and Culture* (New York, 1956), 1–115, for theological background and implications.

Epilogue

1. See S. E. D. Shortt, *The Search for an Ideal* (Toronto, 1976).
2. A. R. C. Duncan, *Moral Philosophy* (Toronto, 1965), 5–6.
3. Thomas McCulloch, *The Stepsure Letters*, introd. Northrop Frye (Toronto, 1960), viiff.
4. See chapter 6, n.90.
5. R. A. Falconer, *Idealism in National Character* (London, 1920), 12–13, 20.
6. Hugh Hood, "Moral Imagination: Canadian Thing," in Hood, *The Governor's Bridge Is Closed* (Toronto, 1973), 100–102.

A Bibliographical Note

This study is almost entirely based upon primary research, usually comprising materials that were published. The major journals consulted were *Belford's Monthly Magazine, Christian Guardian, Canadian Journal, Canadian Monthly and National Review, Dalhousie Gazette, Journal of Speculative Philosophy, Popular Science Monthly, Queen's Quarterly, Rose-Belford's Canadian Monthly and National Review, Transactions of the Royal Society of Canada, University of Toronto Monthly,* and *University of Toronto Quarterly*. Of these, the *Canadian Monthly* (in all three forms) is a veritable gold mine of information on Victorian beliefs and assumptions, and therefore constitutes the best way for the student to acquaint himself with the nineteenth-century Anglo-Canadian frame of mind. Valuable in making this acquaintance is Robert L. McDougall's dissertation, "A Study of Canadian Periodical Literature of the Nineteenth Century" (University of Toronto, 1950). More readily available are C. T. Bissell's short but perceptive essay "Literary Taste in Central Canada during the Nineteenth Century" (*Canadian Historical Review*, xxxi, Sept. 1950); A. G. Bailey's *Culture and Nationality* (Toronto: McClelland and Stewart, 1972); and A. B. McKillop's edited collection, *A Critical Spirit: The Thought of William Dawson LeSueur* (Toronto: McClelland and Stewart, 1977). Material from chapter 5 of *A Disciplined Intelligence* was originally published, in altered form, in *A Critical Spirit* and is reproduced here through the kind permission of Macmillan of Canada.

The major unpublished manuscript collections used, most of them the papers of religious figures or philosophers, are McGill University Archives: John William Dawson and John Clark Murray; Public Archives of Canada: G. M. Grant and William Dawson LeSueur; Queen's University Archives: Daniel Miner Gordon, R. O. Sweezey, John Watson; Trinity University Archives, Toronto: Provost Whitaker; United Church Archives, Toronto: Salem Bland, Nathanael Burwash, Albert Carman, S. D. Chown; University of Toronto Archives: James Loudon (memoirs), Daniel Wilson (diary); University of Western Ontario Archives, London: R. M. Bucke, W. C. Keirstead.

Secondary literature which treats the intellectual life of Canada, particularly as related to religion and education in the nineteenth century, touches only peripherally upon the questions which are central to this inquiry. Modern examinations of education, such as D. C. Masters's *Protestant Church Colleges in Canada* (Toronto: University of Toronto Press, 1966), are predominantly written from institutional perspectives. This is also the case with histories of Canadian churches. The life of the mind receives minor attention, for example, in John Webster Grant's *The Church in the Canadian Era* (Toronto: McGraw-Hill Ryerson, 1972). More fruitful for the historian of ideas are a number of contemporary biographies and autobiographies. For example, *Principal Grant* (Toronto: Morang, 1905), by W. L. Grant and C. F. Hamilton, contains many insights into the dynamics of a Presbyterian mind of major significance in the late nineteenth century; Salem Bland's biography of *James Henderson* (Toronto: McClelland and Stewart, 1926) pays warranted attention to the intellectual life and development of an important Methodist. Many articles and books, not themselves intellectual history, allow the historian to obtain glimpses of different facets of Anglo-Canadian thought, but few attempts at more general synthesis have thus far been made.

Certain important exceptions to this observation must be noted. A. G. Bailey's collection of essays, *Culture and Nationality* (1972), has already been mentioned; it is a book that is synthetic in nature and full of insights. While his studies of nineteenth-century Anglo-Canadian cultural life tend to focus upon the political culture of the emerging nation, they also examine the adjustment made by Canadians to such strands of thought as literary convention and evolutionary theory. A second work of synthesis is Carl Berger's study of the ideas of Canadian imperialists, *The Sense of Power* (Toronto: University of Toronto Press, 1970). Of pioneering importance, Berger's book established the fact that the ideas of its subjects had origins much earlier than the advent of the late nineteenth-century imperial adventure, and also made clear the fact that at times this thought approached a level of presentation sufficiently formal to move beyond the category of "informed opinion" to that of social philosophy.

That early twentieth-century Anglo-Canadian social critics who were not themselves philosophers held coherent and sometimes sophisticated —if also eclectic—philosophies of life is established in S. E. D. Shortt's book, *The Search for an Ideal: Six Canadian Intellectuals and Their Convictions in an Age of Transition* (Toronto: University of Toronto Press, 1976). Shortt's suggestive and original study looks at the social criticism and the "world views" of several Canadian men of letters prominent in the first third of the twentieth century. Although it fails to make the critical distinction between subjective idealism (which appealed to intuition and sentiment) and objective idealism (which relied solely on reason), Shortt's book shows clearly the legacy and burden of the nineteenth-century conflict between empiricism and its intellectual enemies—particularly idealism—set forward in *A Disciplined Intelli-*

gence. In this respect it marks an amplification of the story told in these pages.

Certain other studies also provide information and interpretations which complement the views set forward here. Alison Prentice's *The School Promoters* (Toronto: McClelland and Stewart, 1976) illustrates the extent to which the assumptions of faculty psychology held sway in the minds of public-school educators in the mid-nineteenth century. "The Primacy of the Will in Late Nineteenth-Century American Ideology of the Self," by Anita Clair Fellman and Michael Fellman (*Historical Reflections/Réflexions Historiques*, IV, Summer 1977), provides an important comparative perspective in which to assess Canadian assertions of the importance of "will." Robert Taylor's Ph.D. dissertation, "The Darwinian Revolution: The Responses of Four Canadian Scholars" (McMaster University, 1976), examines the thought of William Dawson, Daniel Wilson, John Watson, and Nathanael Burwash.

Several books in American and British history provide especially important cross-cultural bases of comparison for this study. Frank Miller Turner's *Between Science and Religion: The Reaction to Scientific Naturalism in Late Victorian England* (London and New Haven: Yale University Press, 1974) is a series of biographical essays on several British intellectuals of the middle rank who attempted to come to grips with evolution while preserving the fundamentals of Christian morality. Had William Dawson LeSueur, like fellow Canadian John Beattie Crozier, immigrated to England after an uninspiring education at the University of Toronto, he might well have become a candidate for inclusion in Turner's book. The Hegelian variant of this accommodation is treated in William H. Goetzmann's comprehensive collection of documents on the rise, influence, and thought of the "St. Louis School," *The American Hegelians: An Intellectual Episode in the History of Western America* (New York: Knopf, 1973). Goetzmann's volume, which includes an excellent introductory essay, is a salutary reminder to students of Canadian thought that significant intellectual movements need not necessarily emanate from centres of empire. Morton White's classic study, *Social Thought in America: The Revolt Against Formalism* (Boston: Beacon, 1957), examines the development of American pragmatism from C. S. Peirce to John Dewey, and traces the influence of pragmatic claims in social criticism, economic thought, jurisprudence, and education. It serves as a valuable counterpoint to some of the individuals who are the major subjects of the present study, many of whom stood for the very "formalism" of thought against which the American pragmatists rebelled. The Canadian equivalent of America's pragmatists, those who revolted against "formalism," were, of course, the idealists. Finally, there is R. Jackson Wilson's *In Quest of Community: Social Philosophy in the United States, 1860-1920* (New York: Oxford University Press, 1970), which shows that a number of American academics of the late nineteenth and early twentieth centuries, like their colleagues in Canada, rejected an individualistic social ethic in favour of an organic one.

Needless to say, the works mentioned in this brief bibliographical note are by no means the only scholarly studies of value in the writing of this book. Numerous articles and books, hopefully given adequate acknowledgement in the notes, have together helped to map out the largely uncharted historical topography *A Disciplined Intelligence* seeks to make more familiar.

A Bibliographical Note, 2001

The terrain of Canadian intellectual and religious history is not nearly as uncharted as it was in 1979. The best access to much of this scholarship is found in *Canadian History: A Reader's Guide*. 1 ed. M. Brook Taylor, *Beginnings to Confederation*, and 2 ed. Doug Owram, *Confederation to the Present* (Toronto: University of Toronto Press, 1994). Certain works, however, merit special notice in order to indicate the historiographical redirection that has taken place over the past two decades.

In 1983 Ronald P. Frye, citing the influence of *A Disciplined Intelligence*, initiated The Frye Library of Canadian Philosophy, intended to provide access to important primary sources. Its first volume was *Religion and Science in Early Canada*, ed. J. D. Rabb (Kingston: Ronald P. Frye & Company, 1988). Other notable works on nineteenth-century Canadian thought are Carl Berger, *Science, God, and Nature in Victorian Canada* (Toronto: University of Toronto Press, 1983); S. F. Wise, *God's Peculiar Peoples: Essays on Political Culture in Nineteenth-Century Canada*, eds. A. B. McKillop and Paul Romney (Ottawa: Carleton University Press, 1993); Susan Sheets-Pyenson, *John William Dawson: Faith, Hope, and Science* (Montreal and Kingston: McGill-Queen's University Press, 1996); Marinell Ash et al., *Thinking with Both Hands: Sir Daniel Wilson in the Old World and the New*, ed. Elizabeth Hulse (Toronto: University of Toronto Press, 1999); Clifford G. Holland, *William Dawson LeSueur (1840–1917): A Canadian Man of Letters* (San Francisco: Mellen Research University Press, 1993); Henry A. Hubert, *Harmonious Perfection: The Development of English Studies in Nineteenth-Century Anglo-Canadian Colleges* (East Lansing: Michigan State University Press, 1994); A. B. McKillop, *Contours of Canadian Thought* (Toronto: University of Toronto Press, 1987), and McKillop, *Matters of Mind: The University in Ontario, 1791–1951* (Toronto: University of Toronto Press, 1994). A comprehensive history of philosophy in Canada is found in Leslie Armour and Elizabeth Trott, *The Faces of Reason: An Essay on Philosophy and Culture in English Canada 1850–1950* (Waterloo: Wilfrid Laurier University Press, 1981). See also Leslie Armour, *The Idea of Canada and the Crisis of Community* (Ottawa: Steel Rail Publishing, 1981).

Works associated with the "secularization" thesis include: Richard Allen, *The Social Passion; Religion and Social Reform in Canada 1914–1928* (Toronto: University of Toronto Press, 1971); Ramsay Cook, *The Regenerators: Social Criticism in Late Victorian English Canada* (Toronto: University of Toronto Press, 1985); William Westfall, *Two Worlds: The Protestant Culture of Nineteenth-Century Ontario* (Montreal and Kingston: McGill-Queen's University Press, 1989); and David B. Marshall, *Secularizing the Faith: Canadian Protestant Clergy and the Crisis of Belief, 1850–1940* (Toronto: University of Toronto Press, 1992). Ramsay Cook's assessment of his most strident critics may be found in "Salvation, Sociology and Secularism," *The Literary Review of Canada* 6 (April 1997): 10–12.

For studies that argue, in contrast, a "continuity" thesis, see Marguerite Van Die, *An Evangelical Mind: Nathanael Burwash and the Methodist Tradition in Canada, 1839–1918* (Montreal and Kingston: McGill-Queen's University Press,1989); Michael Gauvreau, *The Evangelical Century: College and Creed in English Canada from the Great Rivival to the Great Depression* (Montreal and Kingston: McGill-Queen's University Press, 1991); and Phyllis D. Airhart, *Serving the Present Age: Revivalism, Progressivism, and the Methodist Tradition in Canada* (Montreal and Kingston: McGill-Queen's University Press, 1992). In *A Full-Orbed Christianity: The Protestant Churches and Social Welfare in Canada, 1900–1940* (Montreal and Kingston: McGill-Queen's University Press, 1996) Nancy Christie and Michael Gauvreau assail almost all Canadian scholars in the field for their alleged interpretive wrongheadedness, especially in footnotes that are needlessly dismissive and churlish. See also George A. Rawlyk, ed., *The Canadian Protestant Experience, 1760–1990* (Burlington, Ont.: Welch Publishing Company Inc., 1990) and Rawlyk, ed., *Aspects of the Canadian Evangelical Experience* (Montreal and Kingston: McGill-Queen's University Press, 1997).

Propelled by such fertile works, and often edited and written by those of an evangelical religious persuasion and subsidized by organizations such as The Jackman Foundation and the Pew Charitable Trusts, several substantial edited collections on the subject of Canadian evangelicalism appeared in the 1990s. They proved overwhelmingly critical of any "secularist" perspective on the religious traditions they examined. Most prominent among these are John G. Stackhouse Jr., *Canadian Evangelicalism in the Twentieth Century: The Introduction to Its Character* (Toronto: University of Toronto Press, 1993); Mark A. Noll, David W. Bebbington, and George A. Rawlyk, eds., *Evangelicalism: Comparative Studies of Popular Protestantism in North America, the British Isles, and Beyond, 1700–1900* (New York: Oxford University Press, 1994); and Rawlyk, ed., *Aspects of the Canadian Evangelical Experience* (Montreal and Kingston: McGill-Queen's University Press, 1997). The sociopolitical context of much of this scholarship, and the influence of the late George Rawlyk on it, is examined in Preston Jones, "Bible Bill's Children," *The Literary Review of Canada* 5 (Oct. 1996): 20–2.

Several review articles on the historiography of Canadian Protestantism appeared in the 1980s and 1990s. Among the better of these are William Westfall, "Order and Experience: Patterns of Religious Metaphor in Early Nineteenth Century Upper Canada," *Journal of Canadian Studies* 20 (Spring 1985): 5–24; Leslie Armour, "Philosophy and Denominationalism in Ontario," *Journal of Canadian Studies* 20 (Spring 1985): 25–38; Michael Gauvreau, "Beyond the Half-Way House: Evangelicalism and the Shaping of English Canadian Culture," *Acadiensis* 20 (Spring 1990): 158–77; Burkhardt Kiesekamp, "Christendom, Nationalism and the Fate of the Nineteenth-Century Evangelical Consensus," *Acadiensis* 25 (Autumn 1995): 125–44; James W. Opp, "Revivals and Religion: Recent Work on the History of Protestantism in Canada," *Journal of Canadian Studies* 32 (Summer 1997): 183–94.

Studies in the intellectual and ethical dimensions of twentieth-century Canadian social thought include Barry Ferguson, *Remaking Liberalism: The Intellectual Legacy of Adam Shortt, O. D. Skelton, W. C. Clark, and W. A. Mackintosh, 1890–1925* (Montreal and Kingston: McGill-Queen's University Press, 1994); Doug Owram, *The Government Generation: Canadian Intellectuals and the State 1900–1945* (Toronto: University of Toronto Press, 1986); Sara Z. Burke, *Seeking the Highest Good: Social Service and Gender at the University of Toronto, 1888–1937* (Toronto: University of Toronto Press, 1996); Marlene Shore, *The Science of Social Redemption: McGill, the Chicago School, and the Origins of Social Research in Canada* (Montreal and Kingston: McGill-Queen's University Press,1987); and Carl Berger, *Honour and the Search for Influence: a History of the Royal Society of Canada* (Toronto: University of Toronto Press, 1996).

Works emphasizing the continuity of a moral imperative in twentieth-century Canadian thought are Bruce Elder, *Image and Identity: Reflections on Canadian Film and Culture* (Waterloo: Wilfrid Laurier University Press,1989); Hubert Krygsman,"Freedom and Grace: Mainline Protestant Thought in Canada, 1900–1960" (Ph.D. dissertation, Department of History, Carleton University,1997); Donald Wright, "The Professionalization of History in English Canada to the 1950s" (Ph.D. dissertation, Department of History, University of Ottawa, 1999); Philip Massolin, "'What's Past Is Prologue': Canadian Intellectuals, the Tory Tradition and the Challenge of Modernity, 1939–1970" (Ph.D. dissertation, Department of History, York University, 1998); and Leonard Kuffert, "'A Secret Understanding': Critical Responses to 'Modern Life' and Mass Culture in English Canada, 1939–1963" (Ph.D. dissertation, Department of History, McMaster University, 2000).

Other significant studies of Canadian intellectuals after 1930 include Paul Litt, *The Muses, the Masses, and the Massey Commission* (Toronto: University of Toronto Press, 1992); Judith Stamps, *Unthinking Modernity: Innis, McLuhan, and the Frankfurt School* (Montreal and Kingston: McGill-Queen's University Press, 1995); Arthur Kroker, *Technology and the Canadian Mind: Innis/McLuhan/Grant* (Montreal: New World

Perspectives, 1984); Philip Marchand, *Marshall McLuhan: The Medium and the Messenger* (Toronto: Random House, 1989); Joan E. O'Donovan, *George Grant and the Twilight of Justice* (Toronto: University of Toronto Press, 1984); Arthur Davis, ed., *George Grant and the Subversion of Modernity: Art, Philosophy, Politics, Religion, and Education* (Toronto: University of Toronto Press, 1996); William Leiss, *C. B. Macpherson: Dilemmas of Liberalism and Socialism* (Montreal: New World Perspectives, 1988); John Ayre, *Northrop Frye: A Biography* (Toronto: Random House, 1989); David Cook, *Northrop Frye: A Vision of the New World* (Montreal: New World Perspectives, 1985); Graeme Patterson, *History and Communications: Harold Innis, Marshall McLuhan, the Interpretation of History* (Toronto: University of Toronto Press, 1990); and Robert E. Babe, *Canadian Communication Thought: Ten Foundational Writers* (Toronto: University of Toronto Press, 2000).

Index

Abbott, Lyman, 158
Acadia College, 11, 33
Acadian Geology (Dawson), 100
Acta Victoriana, 139, 207
Adam, G. Mercer, 129, 156; on Wilson, 104–5
Agassiz, **Louis**, 115, 125
Agnosticism, 154, **200**
Ahlstrom, **Sydney** E., 26, 28–9, 239 n14
Albert, **Prince** Consort, 97, 98; and Victorian science, 93–5
Allen, J. A., 194
Analogy of Religion, The (Butler), 64, 69
Anarchy, intellectual, 5–9, 34, 62, 229
Anglicans, 9, 86–7
Archaeology and Prehistoric Annals of Scotland, The (Wilson), 99
Archaia (Dawson), 100, 112
Aristotle, 183
Arminianism: of Methodists, 9
Arnold, Matthew, 137, 164; on critical intellect, 1–2, 3; as a progressivist, 146; and Culture, 150–2, 227
Arnold, Thomas, 35
Astronomy and General Physics (Whewell), 69
Atheism, 119, 126, 215; Beaven on, 68
Atomism, 192
Aurelius, Marcus, 151

Bacon, Francis, 94–5, 116, 159
Bain, Alexander, 45, 154, 180
Baldwin, James Mark, 200–1, 270 n96
Baptists, 9
Beaven, James, 29, 34, 64, 85, 95, 142; natural theology of, 65–73, 74, 76, 87–8; on critical thought, 67; on atheism, 68. Work: *Elements of Natural Theology*, 64–73
Beecher, Henry Ward, 122
"Belfast Address": of John Tyndall, 154–6, 192. *See also* Tyndall, John

Berger, Carl, 139
Berkeley, George, 57, 174, 177, 179
Bishop's College, 10–11, 60, 64
Bland, Salem: biographical sketch of, 219; idealism of, 220–3
Blewett, George John, 217, 218, 221; biographical sketch of, 210–11; idealism of, 211–12; and Woodsworth, 223–4; criticized by Burwash, 224–5. Works: *The Christian View of the World*, 210–11; *The Study of Nature and the Vision of God*, 210–11, 223–5
Bosanquet, Bernard, 215
Bovell, James, 29, 64–5, 87, 88, 95, 97–8, 105, 182; natural theology of, 73–85. Works: *Outlines of Natural Theology, for the Use of the Canadian Student*, 64, 73–4, 76–83, 84, 110, 111; *Passing Thoughts on Man's Relation to God and on God's Relation to Man*, 75, 83–5, 86; *Preparation for the Christian Sacrifice, or Holy Communion*, 75, 83; *The World at the Advent of the Lord Jesus*, 75, 83
Brampton Lectures, 90
Brett, George Sidney, 230
Brewster, David, 174
Bridgewater Treatises, 69, 74, 111, 245 n31. *See also* Natural theology
British American Magazine, 2
British Association for the Advancement of Science, 93, 98, 126, 154–5, 156, 186
Brokmeyer, William Conrad, 171
Brown, Thomas, 36, 57; Lyall on, 45–8
Browne, Thomas, 130
Browning, Robert, 132
Bucke, Richard Maurice, 162; LeSueur on, 163–4. Works: *Cosmic Consciousness*, 182; *Man's Moral Nature*, 163–4, 182

Buckland, William, 69
Buffon, Comte de, 98
Burke, Edmund, 106
Burwash, Nathanael, 31, 34, 181, 210; on intellect, 6–7; and "God's Plan in Nature," 88–9; criticism of Blewett, 224–5
Butler, Joseph, 62, 64, 69, 84, 120
Butler, Nicholas Murray, 202

Caird, Edward, 169, 171, 181, 195, 202, 225; influence on Watson, 172, 183–5; influence on Blewett, 210–12; and evolutionary naturalism, 215; and Woodsworth, 223
Caird, John, 169, 172, 182–3, 205, 218, 225
Caliban, 108, 129–32 passim
Caliban: The Missing Link (Wilson), 129–32
Calvin, John, 24
Calvinism, 104
Campbell, George, 62, 243 n8
Campbell, Robert, 30, 35, 36
Canadian Forum, The, 231
Canadian Institute, The, 95, 96, 100, 106, 110, 124
Canadian Journal, The, 93, 100, 112, 113, 176
Canadian Methodist Magazine, The, 140
Canadian Monthly and National Review, The, 128, 137–8, 143, 156–7, 192, 193, 194
Canadian Naturalist and Geologist, The, 100, 115
Carlyle, Thomas, 171, 184
Carman, Albert, 209, 225–6
Carpenter, Edward, 125
Carpenter, W. B., 186–7, 188
"Categorical imperative," 54, 184, 196. See also Duty; Kant, Immanuel
Central nervous system, 57–8
Chadwick, Owen, 157
Chambers' Journal, 99
Chapman, E. J., 112, 113
Chemistry, Meteorology, and the Function of Digestion (Prout), 69
Chown, S. D., 217, 225–7
Christ Crucified (George), 37
Christian Guardian, The, 55–6, 133, 228; and McCosh, 54, 57; on classes at Victoria College, 63; and science, 116–24; and *Descent of Man*, 125–7
Christianity and Idealism (Watson), 206, 212

Christian Prayer and Natural Laws (Romanes), 157
Christian View of the World, The (Blewett), 210–11
Church of England, 9; and natural theology, 86–7
Church Union (1925), 227–8
Clark, Daniel, 162
Clough, Arthur Hugh, 1
C. M. D., 126
Colenso, J. W., 143
Coleridge, Samuel Taylor, 57, 171
College of New Brunswick, 10
Common Sense school, 46, 49, 77, 172, 175, 191, 205; in Canada, 23–58 passim; in United States, 26–7, 28, 239 n14; dualism of, 28–9; and ideas, 70; and Beaven, 70–2; and Bovell, 79–82; and Watson, 182–3
Community, idea of, 198–9, 207, 228
Comte, Auguste, 57, 120, 137, 150, 153, 169, 197, 227
Comte, Mill, and Spencer (Watson), 192
Congregationalists, 227
Conscience, 38, 39
Conservatism, 86, 136, 138; LeSueur and, 148–9
Cosmic Consciousness (Bucke), 182
Cousin, Victor, 44, 57, 81–2, 83; and Common Sense, 79–80
Cramp, John Mockett: on education, 15–16
Crawley, E. A., 11, 33
Critique of Pure Reason (Kant), 90
Cronyn, Benjamin, 11, 67
Crozier, John Beattie, 182; biographical sketch of, 258 n22
Culture: LeSueur on, 150–3; Arnold on, 152; Chown on, 226–7
Culture and Anarchy (Arnold), 143, 164
Cuvier, Georges, 98

Dalhousie Gazette, 45, 98, 139
Dalhousie University, 32, 44, 49, 50, 100, 139, 202
Darwin, Charles, 45, 57, 76, 90, 120, 137, 156, 158, 172, 215; theories of, received in Canada, 100–10, 112–15, 165–6; and heterodoxy, 117, 123; on man, 128–9. Works: *The Descent of Man*, 124–34, 143; *The Origin of Species*, 60, 63, 73, 75, 83, 87, 99–110, 112, 117, 125–8 passim, 133, 137, 143
Darwin, Erasmus, 76
Darwinism. See Evolution, Darwinian

Index 285

Data of Ethics, The (Spencer), 158
Dawson, John William, 29, 56, 111–12, 115, 130, 202; on education, 14–15; biographical sketch of, 99–100, 101; on Darwin's *Origin*, 100–4, 113–14, 132–3; on science and piety, 101–2; on *Descent of Man*, 127–9, 132–3. Works: *Acadian Geology*, 100; *Archaia*, 100, 112; *The Story of the Earth and Man*, 127–9
Deists, 66
DeKoven, James, 138
Democracy, 119; Jacksonian, 2
Democritis, 155
Descent of Man, The (Darwin), 124–34, 143
Design, 63; 90, 111, 114–15, 136, 138–9, 140, 176, 182
Dialogues Concerning Natural Religion (Hume), 90
Disraeli, Benjamin, 137
Dualism, 133, 169, 188, 218; in Common Sense, 49, 173; Murray's rejection of, 180–1; Watson's rejection of, 184–5
Duncan, Sara Jeannette, 135, 137
Duty, 19, 54, 184, 191, 196, 197–8, 202
Du Vrai, du beau et du bien (Cousin), 80

Ecce Homo (anon.), 120
Eddy, Mary Baker, 209
Edinburgh New Philosophical Journal, 100
Edinburgh University, 44, 182
Education: aim of, 12–21; liberal, 16–21, 59; in Scotland, 24–5
Educational Review, 202
Elements of Moral Science (Wayland), 34
Elements of Natural Theology (Beaven), 64–73
Eliot, Charles, 6, 7
Emerson, Ralph Waldo, 171, 217, 227
Emotions and the Will, The (Bain), 180
Empiricism, 79, 112, 120, 182, 187; Watson on, 187–8, 189
Epicureanism, 154
Essays and Reviews, The, 117–18, 123, 143
Essays in Criticism (Arnold), 143
Ethical Import of Darwinism, The (Schurman), 202
Ethnology, 107–8
Evolution: Darwinian, 90, 99–110, 117, 124, 125–33, 140, 165–6; Hegelian, 183–6 passim, 189–91, 206, 217
Ewart, J. S., 230
Examination of Sir William Hamilton's Philosophy (Mill), 33, 57
Exposition of the Creed (Pearson), 88

Faculties. See Psychology, faculty
Fairbairn, Andrew, 223
Falconer, Robert, 231. Work: *Idealism in National Character*, 231–2
Faraday, Michael, 125
Ferrier, J. F., 173, 174, 176, 181
Field and the Men For It, The (George), 37
Fiske, John, 139, 158, 165
Fitzpatrick, Alfred, 272 n27
Fleming, Sandford, 209
Fleming, William, 31, 32
Fredericton Academy, 10
Free Church College (Halifax), 52
Freedom: LeSueur on, 146–50
Frye, Northrop, 3, 136, 167, 231

Gall, Franz Joseph, 162, 178
Geological Evidences of the Antiquity of Man, The (Lyell), 112
Geology: pre-Darwinian, 104; religion and, 123; and Baconian science, 124
Geology and Mineralogy (Buckland), 69
George, James, 32, 44, 56, 58, 181; biographical sketch of, 34–5; and Common Sense, 36–9; on moral government, 39–40; on piety and intellect, 40–3, 50–1, 52, 61–2, 66, 68; on civilization, 53. Works: *Christ Crucified*, 37; *The Field and the Men For It*, 37; *Moral Courage*, 37; *On Baptism*, 37; *The Relation Between Piety and Intellectual Labor*, 41, 43, 51; *Sabbath School of the Fireside*, 37; *Thoughts on High Themes*, 37, 39; *The Value of Earnestness*, 37; *What Is Civilization?* 37–8
Gillispie, C. C.: on Paley, 63
God's Glory in the Heavens (Leitch), 111
Goethe, 184
Grain Growers Guide, 222
Grant, George Munro, 158, 208; and moral philosophy, 31–2; and social gospel, 217–19, 221, 222
Grant, George Parkin, 231
Grant, J. M., 212–16
Great Instauration, The (Bacon), 95
Green, T. H., 184, 195, 200, 211
Greene, John C., 99

Haliburton, Thomas Chandler, 230
Hamilton, William, 24, 26, 33, 36, 44, 56, 57, 184; faculty psychology of, 27; and Kantian tradition, 54–5; Young and Murray on, 172, 174–81
Handbook of Psychology, A (Murray), 202
Harris, William Torrey, 171
Hegel, Georg Wilhelm Friedrich, 57, 137, 147, 169, 184, 189, 202, 219
Hegelianism, 171–228 passim; of Watson, 183–92, 196–9; and social gospel, 206–28 passim
Hellenism, 227
Herschel, William, 98
Hickock, Laurens P., 81
Higher Criticism, 117, 210, 211
Hincks, Francis, 113, 116
Hincks, William, 112, 124; and Darwinian science, 113–16, 253 n56
History of Oliver Cromwell (Wilson), 99
History of Rationalism (Hurst), 119
History of the Puritans (Wilson), 99
Hofstadter, Richard, 164
Holiwell, Mrs., 2, 3, 5, 55
Hood, Hugh, 231, 232
Hopkins, Mark, 125
Horae Paulinae, 63–4
Horton Academy, 11
Hume, David, 45, 46, 47, 82, 90, 177, 187, 189
Hume, James Gibson, 201, 202
Huron College, 11, 63
Hurst, J. F., 119
Hutcheson, Francis, 26, 27
Huxley, Thomas Henry, 57, 113–14, 124, 126, 127, 128, 143, 154, 156, 187

Idealism: influence of, in Canada, 171–230 passim; of Young, 174; of Murray, 180–1; of Watson, 183–92, 196–9; and social ethics, 196–203, 206 passim; and Protestant thought, 205–28
Idealism in National Character (Falconer), 231–2
Idea of a University, The (Newman), 87
Imperialism: and idealism, 196–7
Individualism, 199
Industry: and idealism, 199–200
Ingersoll, Robert G., 120
Inglis, Charles, 10, 85
In Memoriam (Tennyson), 90
Innis, Harold, 231

Inquiry into the Relation of Cause and Effect (Brown), 45
Institutes of Metaphysics (Ferrier), 173, 176
Intellect, the Emotions, and Man's Moral Nature (Lyall), 44–52
Interpretation of Religious Experience, The (Watson), 206, 216
Introduction to Ethics, An (Murray), 202
Intuition, 19, 46, 48, 70, 72, 79
Intuitions of the Mind, The (McCosh), 54
Irving, John, 37, 38, 176

Jackson, George, 223
Jameson, Robert, 100
Jeffrey, Francis, 25
Johnson, Alexander, 155–6
Journal of Speculative Philosophy, 194, 201
Jowett, Benjamin, 184

Kant, Immanuel, 54, 57, 90, 98, 171, 181, 219, 227; Watson on, 189, 202
Kant and his English Critics (Watson), 194, 202
Kantian Ethics and the Ethics of Evolution (Schurman), 201
"Kantian Revival," 194–5
King, William Lyon Mackenzie, 148
Kingdom of Heaven, 216, 219, 220–1, 226
King's College (New Brunswick), 10
King's College (Nova Scotia), 10
King's College (York), 11, 64
Kipling, Rudyard, 55
Knowles, Robert E., 219
Knox, John, 24
Knox, William, 111
Knox College (Toronto), 12, 44, 56, 64, 172

Lamarck, Chevalier de, 70
Laplace, Pierre Simon de, 98
Laurence, Margaret, 231
Lay Sermons (Huxley), 126, 143
Leacock, Stephen, 231
Lectures on the Philosophy of the Human Mind (Brown), 36
Leibniz, Gottfried Wilhelm von, 78
Leisure Hour, The, 127
Leitch, William, 8, 15. Work: *God's Glory in the Heavens*, 111
LeSueur, William Dawson, 135–7, 192; on critical intellect, 141–6; biograph-

ical sketch of, 142; on history, 142, 167; as a progressivist, 146–7; as a relativist, 146–7; on the social nature of man, 148; positivism of, 148–50, 151, 152, 231; on dogmatism, 149, 160; organicism of, 149, 168; on free thought, 149–50, 259 n44; on Culture, 152–3; and Darwinian science, 154, 158–69; psychology of, 161–3, 169, 198; and Social Darwinism, 165–7; and Common Sense, 172, 181
Lewis, John Travers, 158
Liberal education, 16–21, 59
Liberalism, 136, 168
Liberty, 119, 145
Liddell, Thomas, 29, 35
Life of Jesus (Strauss), 120
Locke, John, 78, 177, 189; conception of ideas, 70
Logan, William, 100
Loudon, James, 205
Lovejoy, A. O., 248–9 n71
Loyalism, 230
Luther, Martin, 208
Lyall, William, 32, 43, 58; biographical sketch of, 44–5; and Common Sense, 45–52, 56, 181; and the idea of power, 46–7; and faculty psychology, 47, 48, 49–50; fear of intellect, 50–2. Works: *Intellect, the Emotions, and Man's Moral Nature*, 44–52; *The Philosophy of Thought*, 51–2; *Strictures on the Idea of Power*, 47
Lyell, Charles, 98, 100, 112, 113, 123, 125

McCaul, John, 142
McCosh, James, 28, 53–4, 57. Works: *The Intuitions of the Mind*, 54; *The Scottish Philosophy*, 57; *Typical Forms and Special Ends in Creation*, 175
McCulloch, Thomas, 29, 32, 44. Work: *The Stepsure Letters*, 230
Macdonnell, D. J., 181
McGill University, 33, 45, 56, 100, 128, 155, 172, 202
Machar, Agnes Maule, 137, 157
McIlvain, Charles P., 64, 244 n15
MacLennan, Hugh, 231
Macleod, Norman, 35, 125
MacMechan, Archibald, 200
Macmillan's Magazine, 180
Macphail, Andrew, 230, 231
Mail, The (Toronto), 154
Malthus, Thomas, 100

Malthusianism, 103–4
Mandelbaum, Maurice, 146
Mansel, Henry, 90
Man's Moral Nature (Bucke), 163–4, 182
Martineau, James, 193
Massey Commission, 232
Materialism, 119, 121, 143, 154–5, 161, 181, 192, 200, 222, 224–5
Mathieson, Alexander, 2
Maxwell, James Clerk, 155
Memorials of Edinburgh in the Olden Time (Wilson), 99
Methodism, 10, 123, 209, 210, 216, 217, 220, 222, 223, 227
Meyer, D. H., 58
Mill, John Stuart, 45, 57, 137, 143, 150, 187, 189, 197; as a progressivist, 146; and free expression, 149
Miller, Hugh, 112
Mind, 194
Montreal High School, 142
Moodie, Dunbar, 13
Moodie, Susanna, 4, 5–6, 230
Moral Courage (George), 37
Moral government: doctrine of, 39–40, 42, 43; Beaven on, 69, 71–2
Moral imperative, 3, 5, 53, 137, 145, 167, 199, 229–32 passim
Moral law, 49, 52, 54, 58, 84, 96, 109, 226
Moral nature: of man, 77, 84, 98, 128–9, 164, 165, 182, 191
Moral philosophy: purpose of, in university, 18–19
Mountain, G. J., 10, 85
Murray, John Clark, 33, 56, 129, 172, 194; rejection of Hamilton and Common Sense, 176–81; and idealism, 180–1; on Tyndall's atomism, 192–3; on education of will, 202. Works: *A Handbook of Psychology*, 202; *An Introduction to Ethics*, 202; *Outline of Sir William Hamilton's Philosophy*, 33
My Neighbour (Woodsworth), 223
Myth: of concern, 3–4, 5, 136, 149, 167, 168, 205, 231; of freedom, 136, 149, 167, 168, 231

Natural History Society of Montreal, 127
Naturalism, evolutionary, 215
Natural philosophy, 60
Natural selection, 100–1, 110, 111; Dawson's rejection of, 103–4; Wil-

son's rejection of, 107–8; *Christian Guardian* on, 125, 126; LeSueur on, 165; definition of, 251 n20
Natural theology, 19, 30, 58, 172, 205, 249–50 n75; and education, 59–65, 89–91; and Beaven, 65–73, 88; and Bovell, 73–85, 88–9; and Anglicans, 85–7; and Dawson, 103; and Hincks, 114; and Young, 175; and Watson, 191
Natural Theology (Paley), 59, 63, 106, 126
Nelles, S. S., 6, 7, 34, 55–6
Nelson, Thomas, 99
Neo-Kantians, 194–5
Newman, John Henry, 87, 151
New Outlook, 228
Newton, Isaac, 87, 96, 98
Nicholls, J. H.: on education, 15, 60–1

O'Loughlin, A. J., 7–8
On Baptism (George), 37
On Liberty (Mill), 137
Ontario Law School, 142
Origin of Species, The (Darwin), 60, 63, 73, 75, 83, 87, 99–110, 112, 117, 125–8 passim, 133, 137, 143
Osler, William, 75–6, 105
Outline of Philosophy, An (Watson), 192, 197, 206, 213
Outline of Sir William Hamilton's Philosophy (Murray), 33
Outlines of Natural Theology, for the Use of the Canadian Student (Bovell), 64, 73–4, 76–83, 84, 110, 111
Owen, Richard, 110, 111
Oxford University, 90

Paley, William, 30, 58, 74, 84, 86, 98, 116, 120, 121, 127, 139, 175; natural theology of, 62–4, 87–8, 111, 114, 128. Works: *Natural Theology*, 59, 63, 106, 126; *The Principles of Moral and Political Philosophy*, 63; *A View of the Evidences of Christianity*, 63, 64. See also Natural theology
Pantheism, 118, 121, 155, 175–6, 215
Parkin, George, 197, 230
Passing Thoughts on Man's Relation to God and on God's Relation to Man (Bovell), 75, 83–5, 86
Passmore, John, 55, 215
Pearson, John, 85, 86, 88
Pentateuch ... Critically Examined, The (Colenso), 143
Periodicals, Canadian, 257 n4

Phenomenology of Mind, The (Hegel), 147
Philosophical Basis of Religion, The (Watson), 213
Philosophical Review, 184, 202
Philosophy of Kant as Contained in Extracts from his own Writings, The (Watson), 195
Philosophy of Sir William Hamilton (Wight), 174
Philosophy of the Active Powers and Moral Powers in Man (Stewart), 33
Philosophy of the Inductive Sciences (Whewell), 187
Philosophy of Thought, The (Lyall), 51–2
Phrenology, 178
Physiology of the Human Mind, The (Brown), 36, 49
Pictou Academy, 29, 44
Pictou County, 99
Piety: and intellect, 52, 61–2, 77, 145–6, 212; of LeSueur, 168; of Watson, 192, 207, 212; morphology of, 259 n29
Pine Hill Divinity School, 44
Plato, 31
Platonism, 78
Porter, Noah, 158
Positivism, 150; of LeSueur, 148–50, 151, 152, 231; definition of, 148–9; logical, 186
Pragmatism, 30, 186
Prehistoric Man (Wilson), 93, 97
Preparation for the Christian Sacrifice, or Holy Communion (Bovell), 75, 83
Presbyterianism, 9–10, 137, 210, 213–14, 216, 217, 218, 222, 227
Pride, intellectual, 121–2
Principles of Moral and Political Philosophy, The (Paley), 63
Progressivism, 146–9, 208
Prolegomena to Ethics (Green), 211
Protestantism: and idealism, 207–28. See also Methodism; Presbyterianism
Prout, William, 69
Providence, 12, 60ff, 76, 78, 86, 109, 146
Psychology, 128, 154, 202; faculty, 16–19, 29, 38, 39, 47–50, 57–8, 129, 228; physiological, 49, 161–2, 178, 179
Punch, 155
Purpose. *See* Teleology
Pusey, E. B., 60

Index 289

Queen's Journal, 139, 207
Queen's Quarterly, 207, 231
Queen's Theological Alumni Conference, 208–9, 219
Queen's University, 12, 29, 33, 35, 50, 56, 61, 66, 111, 129, 139, 158, 172, 197, 208, 210, 218–19, 221, 230

Rational Cosmology (Hickock), 81
Rationalism, 118–21 passim, 143, 211
Rattray, W. J., 24, 137
Reason, 82, 145–6, 211–12, 221–2
Reid, Thomas, 36, 44, 53, 54, 58, 70, 81, 163, 172, 173; and Common Sense school, 23–8; influence on Cousin, 79; and Hamilton, 175; Young on, 175; Murray on, 177, 179–80, 181; Watson on, 183
Relation Between Piety and Intellectual Labor, The (George), 41, 43, 51
Relation of Philosophy to Science, The (Watson), 187
Religio Medici (Browne), 130
Republicanism, 3
Rhodes, Cecil, 55
Ritschl, Albrecht, 217
Romanes, George J., 157. Work: *Christian Prayer and Natural Laws*, 157
Romanticism, 2
Rose-Belford's Canadian Monthly and National Review, 140, 161
Ross, James, 44
Ross, Peter, 29
Royce, Josiah, 192, 195
Rugby School, 118
Ryerson, Egerton, 12–13, 32, 34, 62, 232; on education, 17–20, 236 n27; and natural theology, 63

Sabbath School of the Fireside (George), 37
St. Andrew's University, 35, 99
Sainte-Beuve, Charles Augustin, 141, 143, 151, 169
"St. Louis School": of idealism, 171
Scepticism, 2, 78, 84, 112, 118, 122, 143, 154, 175, 188, 193, 195, 196
Schiller, Friedrich, 184
Schneider, Herbert, 28
Schurman, Jacob Gould, 201–2. Works: *The Ethical Import of Darwinism*, 202; *Kantian Ethics and the Ethics of Evolution*, 201
Science, 7, 20, 60ff, 94–5; Baconian, 77, 87, 94–5, 97, 100–1, 102, 104, 106, 110, 115–16, 124, 127, 130, 133, 205; Newtonian, 87; LeSueur on, 159–60 passim; and idealism, 186–95
Scot in America, The (Ross), 29
Scotland, 171; influences of, on Canadian thought, 24–32; and "democratic intellect," 24
Scott, C. T., 209–10
Scottish Antiquarian Society, 99
Scottish philosophy. *See* Common Sense school
Scottish Philosophy, The (McCosh), 57
Secret of Hegel, The (Stirling), 171
Secularism, 218, 222
Sexual selection, 126
Shaftesbury, Lord, 125
Shakespeare, William, 129–30, 132
Shortt, Adam, 218
Simcoe, John Graves, 11, 230
Skelton, O. D., 218
Skepticism. *See* Scepticism
Smith, Adam, 24, 26
Smith, Goldwin, 137, 156, 158, 181, 194
Social Darwinism, 165–7, 194
Social Darwinism in American Thought (Hofstadter), 164
Social gospel, 216–28
Sociology, 224, 226–7
Species, 100–15 passim
Spectator, The (London), 140
Spencer, Herbert, 45, 154, 156, 164–8, 182, 188, 191–5, 201
Spinoza, Baruch (*or* Benedict), 78
Spiritualism, 79
Stephen, James Fitzjames, 149, 259 n44
Stephenson, Fred, 223
Stepsure Letters, The (McCulloch), 230
Stewart, Dugald, 26, 163, 183; and Common Sense school, 23, 24, 34, 36, 44, 48, 53, 54
Stirling, J. Hutchison, 171, 181
Stoicism, 151
Story of the Earth and Man, The (Dawson), 127–9
Strachan, John, 29, 32, 67, 73; on education, 12, 236 n27; and natural theology, 85–6
Strauss, David Friedrich, 120
Strictures on the Idea of Power (Lyall), 47
Study of Nature and the Vision of God, The (Blewett), 210–11, 223–5
Sumner, William Graham, 165, 167
System of Logic (Mill), 187

Teleology, 46, 63, 76, 136, 138–9
Tempest, The (Shakespeare), 129, 130
Temple, Frederick, 118
Tennyson, Alfred, Lord, 90
Testimony of the Rocks, The (Miller), 112
Thompson, William, 126
Thoughts on High Themes (George), 37, 39
Tracy, Francis, 57
Trilling, Lionel, 1–2, 151
Trinity College (Toronto), 11, 29, 64, 73, 86
Turner, William, 99
Tyndall, John, 113, 124; "Belfast Address" of, 154–6; materialism of, 162; atomism of, 192–3
Typical Forms and Special Ends in Creation (McCosh), 175

Underhill, F. H., 230
Unitarians, 214
United Church of Canada, 227–8
United Presbyterian Church, 44
University College (Toronto), 56, 85, 100, 112, 113, 124, 129, 172
University Magazine, 230, 231
University of Edinburgh, 99
University of Glasgow, 31, 35, 44, 169, 182
University of Manitoba, 64
University of Toronto, 11, 63, 70, 100, 142, 200, 205
University of Toronto Quarterly, 57, 207
Upper Canada Academy (Cobourg), 11, 13
Upper Canada Journal of Medical, Surgical, and Physical Science, 73
Upper Canadian Assembly: on the idea of a university, 13

Value of Earnestness, The (George), 37
Vestiges of Creation (anon.), 123
Victoria College: at Cobourg, 11, 17–20, 31, 34, 62, 63, 139, 181, 209–10; at Toronto, 210, 223, 225
View of the Evidences of Christianity, A (Paley), 63, 64
Vogt, Karl, 49, 161

Watson, John, 158, 169; conception of a university, 172; as a student, 182–3, 266 n36; rejection of Common Sense school, 183; Caird's influence on, 183–6; Hegelianism of, 183–92; on empiricism, 188, 189; rejection of dualisms, 188, 198; organicism of, 190–1; on Tyndall, 193–4; social ethic of, 198–9, 206 passim; on Schurman, 201–2; and Protestant thought, 206–9, 212–16, 217, 218, 219, 221, 222–4, 226, 230–2. Works: *Christianity and Idealism*, 206, 212; *Comte, Mill, and Spencer*, 192; *The Interpretation of Religious Experience*, 206, 216; *Kant and his English Critics*, 194, 202; *An Outline of Philosophy*, 192, 197, 206, 213; *The Philosophical Basis of Religion*, 213; *The Philosophy of Kant as Contained in Extracts from his own Writings*, 195; *The Relation of Philosophy to Science*, 187
Watson, Richard, 20
Wayland, Francis, 34
Week, The, 129, 135
Wesley College (Winnipeg), 210, 221
Westminster Review, 141, 143
What Is Civilization? (George), 37–8
Whewell, William, 69, 187
Whitaker, George, 86, 89
Whitehead, Alfred North, 161
Wight, O. W., 174
Wilberforce, Samuel, 113
Will, 16, 201, 202–3, 232
Wilson, Daniel, 29, 111–12, 124, 142, 172; on science and piety, 95–6, 97–8, 106; biographical sketch of, 99–100; on Darwin's *Origin*, 100–1, 104–10, 113; on *Descent of Man*, 127, 129–33; on Young, 174. Works: *The Archaeology and Prehistoric Annals of Scotland*, 99; *Caliban: The Missing Link*, 129–32; *History of Oliver Cromwell*, 99; *History of the Puritans*, 99; *Memorials of Edinburgh in the Olden Time*, 99; *Prehistoric Man*, 93, 97
Withrow, W. H., 125
Woodsworth, J. S., 223–4. Work: *My Neighbour*, 223
Workman, George, 209, 210
World at the Advent of the Lord Jesus, The (Bovell), 75, 83

Young, George Paxton, 210; biographical sketch of, 56–7, 172; rejection of

Common Sense school, 173–6, 181;
on Ferrier, 173–4; on Hamilton,
174–5; on McCosh, 175; idealism of,
200, 201